THE JESUS FAMILY TOMB EXAMINED
DID JESUS RISE PHYSICALLY?

RENÉ A. LÓPEZ

FOREWORD BY DARRELL L. BOCK
AUTHOR OF THE *NEW YORK TIMES* BESTSELLER
BREAKING THE DA VINCI CODE

21stCENTURY PRESS
READING YOU LOUD AND CLEAR.

THE JESUS FAMILY TOMB *EXAMINED*

Copyright © 2008 by René A. López

Printed in the United States of America

Published by 21st Century Press
2131 W. Republic Rd. PMB 41
Springfield, MO 65807

Unless otherwise noted, Scripture citations are from The New King James Version, Copyright © 1979, 1980, 1982, by Thomas Nelson, Inc.

All rights reserved. No portion of this book may be reproduced in any form without the prior express written permission of the publisher, except in the case of brief quotations embodied in critical articles or reviews or as provided by USA copyright laws.

For more information about 21st Century Press visit our web site:
www.21stcenturypress.com

Book design: Michael D. Makidon and Zach Dyer
Cover design: Keith Locke

ISBN 978-0-9817769-0-3

To contact the author for comments and/or speaking engagements, please email René A. López at rema0612@verizon.net or see his website scriptureunlocked.com.

WHAT LEADERS ARE SAYING

Book editor

Have Jesus' bones actually been found? If so, then the biblical teaching that Jesus rose bodily from the grave is false. This in turn means that the Bible is unreliable because it states repeatedly that He rose from the dead. What's more, it means Jesus is a liar because He said He would rise from the dead after three days. Did He rise "spiritually" rather than bodily? This notion too runs counter to the testimony of Scripture.

López discusses these issues thoroughly and argues in detail for the authenticity of the biblical record that affirms Jesus' physical resurrection. López carefully and painstakingly debunks the foolish idea that some bones found outside Jerusalem are those of Jesus and His alleged family. This scholarly, thoroughly researched work, written in an easy-to-read style, stands as a strong defense of the physical resurrection of Jesus, a cornerstone truth of Christianity.

—Roy B. Zuck, Th.D.
Editor of Dallas Seminary's
theological journal *Bibliotheca Sacra*
and Senior Professor Emeritus of Bible Exposition
Dallas Theological Seminary

The sensational reporting of the alleged "Jesus tomb" at Talpiot in Israel has, in this work by René López, run up against the stubborn facts of careful research that seriously undermine both the premises and conclusions of the superficial journalism that has till now dominated the discussion. Point by point, López makes the case for the traditional view of the resurrection of Jesus Christ by citing the best of both ancient and modern scholarship. For believers and unbelievers alike, *The Jesus Family Tomb Examined* sets the issue in stark and clear terms that leave no doubt as to the historical legitimacy of the time-honored tradition.

—Eugene H. Merrill, PhD
Distinguished Professor of Old Testament Studies
Dallas Theological Seminary

Jesus gets Prime Time attention today, but unfortunately the Jesus presented is a no frills Jesus who demands neither adoration nor allegiance. Here is a book that sets the record straight by pointing out that the best scholarship leads us back to a Jesus who claimed to be God and had the evidence to prove it. In these pages we are shown why we can have confidence in the New Testament documents where we find a Jesus who can save us; a Jesus who is worthy of our worship and trust.

—Erwin W. Lutzer, LL.D.
Moody Church, Chicago Ill.

Sometimes the information which comes out of crypts can be, for lack of a better word—'cryptic.' But the supposed revelations that have come out of the Talpiot tomb in the past year have been trumpeted as proof positive that Jesus' bones have bee moldering in the grave for low these 2,000 years. With meticulous detective and scholarly work René López demonstrates in detail that the answer to the question Who is buried in the Talpiot tomb? is—NOT Jesus and his family. He shows at length that the location and the character of the tomb and also the evidence from inside the tomb itself positively rules out such a conclusion. This detailed scholarly book should put the final nail in the coffin of "the Talpiot tomb theory." This "cold case" has been solved, and it doesn't involve Jesus or his family. Highly recommended.

—Ben Witherington, III, Ph.D.
Amos Professor of NT
Asbury Theological Seminary
Doctoral faculty
St. Andrews University, Scotland

With the recent frontal attack upon the credibility of Christianity from both atheists and religionists, it is essential that the church have skilled and scholarly apologists who are able to make a defense for the hope that is in us. This book is a carefully crafted defense of the integrity of the Christian scriptures and the resurrection of Christ our Savior. For those who are troubled by the recent rash of books and television documentaries that have the "appearance of knowledge" as they deny the truth and trustworthiness of the biblical record, let not your heart be troubled. Read and be comforted & convinced.

—Fred Chay, Ph.D., Assistant
Professor of Theology &
Director of Doctoral Studies
Phoenix Seminary

This intriguing book investigates a range of sources (such as ancient languages, Gnostic texts and ossuary inscriptions) to soundly critique the artificial and tendentious approach of Cameron's Jesus Tomb. Those who enjoy reading mysteries will enjoy this book's exposure of the *real* conspiracy involved in Cameron's "documentary."

—Craig S. Keener, Ph.D.,
Author of countless books, and
Professor of New Testament
Palmer Seminary

When discussing our warfare with Satan and all his nefarious schemes to demean and defame the person and work of Jesus Christ, the Apostle Paul exhorts three times "Stand firm" (Ephesians 6:11-14).

Last year the obnoxious attack came via the movie *The Da Vinci Code* which 2003 book brought out dozens of books in previous years, both pro and con. But when the dust had settled and many millions of dollars wasted, it proved to be "much ado about nothing."

Now, this past year it is The Jesus Family Tomb and the denial of the physical resurrection of Jesus Christ—the very heart of the "good news" that is on the block.

At this juncture we can be very thankful for seasoned scholars, such as René López, who has carefully, thoroughly, and systematically answered the attack in the Spirit of Christ. I heartily commend his work to you. It will require some diligence but, I assure you, you will be better and stronger for it.

—Earl D. Radmacher, Th.D.
President Emeritus
Western Seminary

In *The Jesus Family Tomb Examined*, René López presents the most detailed treatment yet of the Talpiot Tomb discovery. For those who want to study the unabridged edition of the archaeological find itself, the subsequent sensational announcement that this was probably the burial tomb of Jesus' family, and the backlash of recent scholars, including their plethora of reasons for firmly rejecting this conclusion, I would strongly recommend López's fine volume.

—Gary R. Habermas
Distinguished Research Professor
Liberty University

Much discussion surrounding the person of Jesus in the media is fictional rather than factual. The Hollywood docudrama, "The Lost Tomb of Jesus," which aired last year around Easter kept the trend going. Many were flabbergasted by hearing that the alleged Jesus family tomb was discovered. Therefore, Jesus did not rise physically, because they now possessed the bone box and even some DNA residue where Jesus once rested. René López's work skillfully dismantles point by point the arguments made by these advocates and shows cogently how Jesus' tomb continues to remain empty, because He rose physically. I wholeheartedly recommend this work.

—Josh D. McDowell
International Author and Speaker

Too often around Easter evangelical Christians are confronted with presentations of Jesus' bodily resurrection that call into question the historical evidence on which one's Easter faith rests. René López has taken on one such challenge in response to the so-called *The Jesus Family Tomb*. His reasoned examination of this tomb along with his defense of Jesus bodily resurrection is a formidable apologetic in support of this indispensable foundation of Christianity.

—James F. Davis, Ph.D.
Associate Professor of New Testament
Capital Bible Seminary

Someone once said that there is no such thing as bad publicity. With all the fanfare for a major motion picture destined to be a "winner," the "facts" concerning this family tomb do not stand up to close scrutiny. In his usual diligent and clear style, López unearths and sheds light on what some have called "the incredible archaeological discovery in Israel that will change history as it shocks the world." He has delivered the goods to dismantle the hype while at the same time affirming the bodily resurrection of Jesus Christ. This is a must read for anyone interested in the facts surrounding the Family Tomb of Jesus and the bodily resurrection of Jesus Christ from the dead.

—Stephen R. Lewis, Ph.D.
President
Rocky Mountain Bible
College & Seminary

René López gives the Jesus family tomb theory the thorough debunking it so richly deserves. He points out countless errors and lapses in logic on the part Simcha Jacobovici and his associates, who have foisted on a naive public and gullible media a highly implausible scenario. Critical scholars and laity alike are appalled by this travesty. *The Jesus Family Tomb Examined* will go a long way toward setting the record straight.

—Craig A. Evans, Ph.D.
Payzant Distinguished Professor
of New Testament at Acadia Divinity College
and author of *Fabricating Jesus:
How Modern Scholars Distort the Gospels*

López painstakingly unearths the facts of the investigation in both *The Jesus Family Tomb* book and *The Lost Tomb of Jesus* documentary. He carefully contrasts conversations with scholars and what was actually reported to demonstrate hidden agendas and obvious assumptions in both the book and the documentary. Clearly and forcefully written, and with ample documentation, *The Jesus Family*

Tomb Examined provides much needed answers to the escalating attacks on the Christ of the Gospels.

—Roger Felipe, D.Min.
Director of the Master of Arts and Religion
and Florida Programs
Trinity Evangelical Divinity School

In 2007, Jacobovici and Pellegrino claimed that Jesus' family tomb had been found. One may have thought that the matter would have gone away after a nearly unanimous scholarly community agreed that the two were seriously mistaken. However, their proposal found new life when it became the subject of discussion at the *Princeton Symposium on Judaism and Christian Origins*. In this volume, René López provides an encyclopedic refutation of the Jesus Family Tomb hypothesis and gives it the dishonorable burial it deserves!

—Michael Licona
Author, *The Case for the Resurrection of Jesus*
and *Paul Meets Muhammad*
Director of Apologetics Evangelism,
North American Mission Board,
Southern Baptist Convention

This book is by far the most accurate and detailed response to the Talpiot Tomb I have read to date. A must read for anyone interested in the facts behind the hype!

—Dillon Burroughs,
Author, *What's the Big Deal about Jesus?*
and Staff Writer of Ankerberg
Theological Research Institute

Tired of the new docudramas attacking the historicity of Jesus and Christianity? René López's book, *The Jesus Family Tomb Examined*, is both fair and thorough. The light of truth and fact is shown into the darkness of doubts and unsubstantiated innuendoes. This book will help you navigate your way through the rapids of the multiple cultural

perceptions that keep arising against Christ and His cause.
—Mark L. Bailey, Ph.D.
President
Dallas Theological Seminary

René A. López has written a timely and thorough refutation of recent sensational theories that allege that the family tomb of Jesus has been found, with inscribed ossuaries which prove that Jesus was married to Mary Magdalene, had a son named Judas, and was not resurrected. His book also clearly and convincingly sets forth reasons for the historic Christian belief in Christ's resurrection.
—Edwin M. Yamauchi, Ph.D.
Professor of History Emeritus,
Miami University

René López, my dear friend and co-pastor in the work of God, has taken a complicated issue and accomplished two things simultaneously. He has satisfied the most erudite scholar who desires satisfactory proof as concerns the Jesus Tomb, and yet, he has also arranged and illustrated his material as to put it in reach of the person in the pew. René has "hit back-to-back home runs" with his masterpiece commentary on Romans (Romans Unlocked) and now with The Jesus Family Tomb Examined. May God use it greatly for His glory!
—Robert Vacendak
Senior Pastor
Ridge Pointe Fellowship
Dallas, TX

DEDICATION

I dedicate this book to the Lord (Jesus), for His grace in allowing me the time and health necessary to complete this project, to my loving wife (Marialis) for her continual sacrificial support, and to my son (Daniel Ariel) who is a gift from above.

FOREWORD

I have been involved in the Talpiot tomb controversy since very early on. The Discovery Channel asked me to preview the special on the tomb and give them my feedback before it went public. I did. I was very frank about the problems I saw. They graciously worked to put together the Ted Koppel Special that aired after the special to allow the discussion on the special's claims to begin. Few channels would have been as open as to allow such a critique of something they helped air. That special signaled that there were real and important issues tied to the history of Christianity that needed attention. It began the discussion and reaction to the claims that followed.

However, the controversy has not entirely died. This January Princeton Theological Seminary sponsored a symposium in Jerusalem on the issue of first century burials in Judaism. The tomb issue was a part of that discussion. Reports from magazines like *TIME* claimed that scholars were taking a fresh look at the Talpiot claims, reassessing the largely negative reception that initial claims received. Since then the scholars present at the Symposium, including its chairperson James Charlesworth, have challenged this take on the meeting. (For the discussion the Symposium generated, see the blog, http://www.primetimejesus.com, and search the many entries with the keyword, Jesus Tomb). The question is, what evidence is there for and against these claims?

This work by René A. López covers the issues these claims raise from every angle: archeological, historical, and theological. René has gone through the many discussions these claims have generated, giving them a close look. He is well equipped to guide one through the myriad of questions these claims have raised. This is the book to get on the Jesus Tomb claims. In it, you will be able to assess what the discussion is about. I commend the book with enthusiasm. I think you will "discover" a great deal in the process.

—Darrell L. Bock
Research Professor of New Testament Studies
Dallas Theological Seminary

Acknowledgment

Acknowledging the people that help an author of a book arrive at the finish line is like giving an acceptance speech at the Oscars—you do not want to leave out anyone. Many thanks go out to the reviewers of the manuscript. Especially I want to acknowledge those who gave me advice in making this book the best it could be: Eugene H. Merrill, Ben Witherington III, Craig S. Keener, Gary R. Habermas, Craig A. Evans, Roger Felipe, and Edwin M. Yamauchi. These scholars gave me valuable suggestions that saved me from errors. My publisher agent Lee Fredrickson, at 21stCentury Press, deserves recognition in seeing the importance and taking on to the task to publish this work. Working with Michael Makidon (typesetter) was also a delight since he is hardworking, professional and a friend. Finally, without the immense contribution of the following two scholars and friends, Darrell L. Bock and Roy B. Zuck (both of Dallas Theological Seminary), this book would have never reached its final form, and in the time that it was done. First, Dr. Bock served as the guide for the project. His suggestions for making this manuscript succinct and focus so that I may hit my target made me look like a professional marksman. Second, Dr. Zuck served as the editor whose advice and editing skills are worth gold and made this manuscript more polished. Whatever error may remain is totally my responsibility. Both, Dr. Bock and Dr. Zuck, made themselves available to me whenever I needed them, which words cannot express my appreciation and indebtedness to them. Of course, I cannot end without acknowledging my better half, Marialis, who sacrificed time with me in order for me to complete the book. She saw the importance of the work and was willing to sacrifice time with me for the greater good of others.

Abbreviations

Hebrew Bible		**Other Jewish and Writings**	
Gen.	Genesis	*Apocryphal/Deuterocanonical Books*	
Exod.	Exodus		
Lev.	Leviticus	Tob.	Tobit
Deut.	Deuteronomy	Jdt.	Judith
Josh.	Joshua	Add. Esth.	Additions Esther
Judg.	Judges	Wis.	Wisdom
Ruth	Ruth	Sir	Sirach
1 Sam.	1 Samuel		(Ecclesiasticus)
2 Sam.	2 Samuel	Bar.	Baruch
1 Kgs.	1 Kings	Let. Jer.	Letter of
2 Kgs.	2 Kings		Jeremiah
1 Chr.	1 Chronicles	Azar/Song Thr.	Prayer of Azariah
2 Chr.	2 Chronicles		and the Song of
Ezra	Ezra		the Three Jews
Neh.	Nehemiah	Sus.	Susanna
Esth.	Esther	Bel.	Bel and the
Job	Job		Dragon
Ps. (*pl.* Pss.)	Psalms	1 Macc.	1 Maccabees
Prov.	Proverbs	2 Macc.	2 Maccabees
Eccl. (*or* Qol)	Ecclesiastes	1 Esd.	1 Esdras
Song.	Song of Songs	Pr. Man.	Prayer of
Isa.	Isaiah		Manasseh
Jer.	Jeremiah	Add. Ps.	Psalm 151
Ezek.	Ezekiel	3 Macc.	1 Maccabees
Dan.	Daniel	2 Esd.	2 Esdras
Hos.	Hosea	4 Macc.	1 Maccabees
Joel	Joel		
Amos	Amos		
Obad.	Obadiah		
Jon.	Jonah		
Mic.	Micah		
Nah.	Nahum		
Hab.	Habakkuk		
Zeph.	Zephaniah		
Hag.	Haggai		
Zech.	Zechariah		
Mal.	Malachi		

For further Jewish writings see the *Pseudepigrapha* 2 vols. Also, for more Jewish writings see the Rabbinic Tractates (Babylonian Talmud, Palestinian or Jerusalem Talmud, Mishnah and Tosefta) and Josephus and Philo.

New Testament

Matt.	Matthew
Mark	Mark
Luke	Luke
John	John
Acts	Acts
Rom.	Romans
1 Cor.	1 Corinthians
2 Cor.	2 Corinthians
Gal.	Galatians
Eph.	Ephesians
Phil.	Philippians
1 Thess.	1 Thessalonians
2 Thess.	2 Thessalonians
1 Tim.	1 Timothy
2 Tim.	2 Timothy
Titus	Titus
Philem.	Philemon
Heb.	Hebrews
Jas.	James
1 Pet.	1 Peter
2 Pet.	2 Peter
1 John	1 John
2 John	2 John
3 John	3 John
Jude	Jude
Rev.	Revelation

Table of Contents

Endorsements 3
Dedication 11
Foreword 13
Acknowledgment 14
Abbreviations 15
Preface 19

Part I: The Jesus Family Tomb Examined
1. Introduction: Jesus' Bones Have Been Discovered! 23
2. What Do The Ossuary Inscriptions Really Mean? 39
3. Is Mary Magdalene's Name on the Ossuary? 53
4. Was Thomas the Undercover Judas Son of Jesus? 81
5. Multiple Languages in One Tomb 93
6. DNA Analysis and Other Possibilities 101
7. Statistical Combination of Names: Impressive or Inflated . 109
8. Conspiracy, Tenth Ossuary, and Patina Samples 119
9. Other Bizarre Theories and Allegations 131

Part II: Did Jesus Rise Physically?
10. The Physical Resurrection a Historical Fact 147
11. Physical Resurrection Nothing New 181
12. Old and New Testament Prophecies of the Resurrection 191
13. Death Before Resurrection 199
14. He Rose Physically 217
15. Transformation as Evidence of the Resurrection 231
16. Conclusion: Our Response 245

Appendix A: Efforts to Disprove the Biblical Jesus 253
Appendix B: The JFT One Year Later 269

Selected Bibliography .... .276
Endnotes 279
Scripture Index 361
Author Index .... .373
Subject Index .... .377

PREFACE

Has Jesus' family tomb been found? How do we respond to evidence showing that at least five or perhaps six out of ten ossuaries in a tomb discovered in 1980 have a cluster of names that belonged to Jesus' relatives? Why has there not been more news or discussion about the Talpiot[1] tomb discovery in Jerusalem since 1980? Could there be a cover-up plot since such a discovery may destroy Israel's tourist economy if the Christian community realizes that Jesus' family tomb emerged and that this disproves the Resurrection? Could one of the ossuaries discovered in the tomb be that of Mary Magdalene? If so, could recent DNA tests disprove motherly kinship between the *Jesus son of Joseph* ossuary and another containing the name of *Mariamne*—believed by some to be Mary Magdalene—prove that these two individuals were married? That is, since family tombs normally contain relatives' bones why would a woman appear in a family tomb not having the same mother as that of the *Jesus* ossuary if they were not married? Could the "missing" tenth ossuary be the controversial *James, son of Joseph, brother of Jesus* sarcophagus? Does the cluster of names in the same tomb mean that this is Jesus of Nazareth's family tomb? Can we really trust the Bible's account that Jesus rose from the dead? And if it can be trusted, should passages on Jesus' resurrection be understood as spiritual rather than physical? Does it make any difference if Jesus rose spiritually rather than physically?

While at my computer on February 27, 2007 I received an interesting and startling email. It read, "Good day, and look at this news. Tomb could be of Jesus, wife and son." Then the web address followed. Someone at my church wanted to know my reaction and explanation of the news that was all over the Internet, cable television, and in numerous newspapers. This email came only a day after (February 26, 2007) a major press release given by two well-known figures in the film industry claimed to have possibly discovered the lost family tomb of Jesus of Nazareth. This documentary of "The Lost Tomb of Jesus" produced by Oscar-winning James Cameron and directed by Emmy-winning Simcha Jacobovici was aired—not only nationally but worldwide—on the Discovery Channel on Sunday, March 4, 2007, at 9:00 pm ET/PT; and it drew millions of viewers. Also related to the documentary a (now best selling) book by Simcha Jacobovici and Charles Pellegrino entitled *The Jesus Family Tomb: The Discovery, the Investigation, and the Evidence That Could Change History* was published by HarperSanFrancisco on March 1, 2007.[2]

On that Sunday night I saw the documentary and the hour-long follow-up panel discussion of scholars that was hosted by Ted Koppel. I also read the book related to the documentary. At first blush the documentary appears to be very convincing, especially since it combines archaeological, theological, scientific, and mathematical analysis of the evidence. Coupled with cinematography effects that engage the emotions, this made an impressive, convincing, and entertaining presentation. All the questions above were directly or indirectly mentioned or alluded to at one point in the documentary or the book. However, as impressive as the documentary may seem, far too many issues remain unclear and unrevealed. Non-Christians should not believe the documentary and book too quickly, nor should Christians flippantly dismiss the claims either. Thus part of the task in the following pages is to examine if anything has been left out of their coverage of the tomb.

Unfortunately many people are too quickly dismissing the arguments made by the documentary and the book. Many do so because of lack of interest in studying. Others do so because they are trusting well-known scholars for their beliefs without themselves knowing how to answer questions about the subject. The position of being dependent on others is all too commonly found in religiously naïve people, some of whom tragically met their demise in Jim Jones's Guyana tragedy, David Koresh Branch Davidian tragedy, and other relig. movements. Of course, not everyone who refuses to be informed of biblical issues ends this way but some may in fact misunderstand the truth and miss discovering the greatest experience of life, and lose the chance to grow in knowledge, become mature, and attain freedom. The fact is that knowledge of the truth can bring about freedom and life. Hence whether one believes or disbelieves that the Scriptures are inspired of God, the Bible has prudent advice to the wise. As Hosea 4:6 records: "My people are destroyed for lack of knowledge." Though this was true for the Jewish people of old, this fact remains true today. Proverbs places a strong emphasis on gaining a detailed knowledge before deciding a matter:

> Every prudent man acts with knowledge,
> But a fool lays open his folly (13:16).
>
> A fool has no delight in understanding,
> But in expressing his own heart (18:2).
>
> He who answers a matter before he hears it,
> It is folly and shame to him (18:13).

James R. White correctly notes the impact the documentary and book have had: "This work is far more significant in its claims and its promoters far more savvy with the media."[3] Therefore we do a great disservice to ourselves to ignore the seriousness of these issues by not knowing all the facts and answers to questions posed by the documentary and book that seek to interpret the very foundation of Christianity, *the resurrection of Jesus Christ.*

While various scholars have spoken and written on websites to answer people's questions on this subject, along with various books that have already surfaced, a work is needed to treat in one volume all the issues in a balanced manner. I simplify many of the subjects discussed in this volume to help nonexperts understand without sacrificing content. Hence the motto used by Gary R. Habermas and Michael R. Licona is adopted here: "Everything should be as simple as possible, but not simpler."[4] Though this book is written to laypeople, is to attract the nonreligious, informed scholars by pro- (only when needed) in the body of the book technical but relegating most of this information to endnotes.

out the nature of Jesus' resurrection? Do extrabiblical and material validate a spiritual or a physical resurrection of Jesus? "People who believe in a physical Resurrection would not be affected by the discovery of Jesus bone box. In Gnostic Gospels, Jesus appears before the apostles as a sort of holy ghost—here again, gone again.... With respect to his Ascension to heaven, the New Testament also does not tell us that its chroniclers believed that Jesus, when he ascended, needed to take his entire body with him. So if you believe in a physical Ascension, the ossuary is a problem. But if you believe in a spiritual one, it becomes an object of veneration."[5] In this view the authors promote the possibility that the bulk of Christians could be wrong about their interpretation of a physical resurrection. But could that be correct? That is, could interpreting Jesus' resurrection as spiritual instead of physical be the correct way to understand Paul's statements in 1 Corinthians 15:44, 46: "It is sown a natural body, it is raised a spiritual body. There is a natural body, and there is a spiritual body.... However, the spiritual is not first, but the natural, and afterward the spiritual." Is spiritual instead of physical resurrection the normal and common Jewish and Judeo-Christian interpretation of the Resurrection, or have evangelicals and Roman Catholics gotten it wrong? Does the Jesus' family tomb make the spiritual resurrection of Jesus a viable and non-threatening interpretation?

It is unwise to opine conclusively on a matter before hearing all the evidence. My aim in writing this book is to examine the facts to see if what the documentary and the book claim is all there is to discover and to inspect what is the historic understanding of Jesus' resurrection (whether spiritual or physical) and thereby to surface data necessary for arriving at a sound conclusion on the issue.

— Chapter 1 —

INTRODUCTION: "JESUS' BONES HAVE BEEN DISCOVERED!"

The East Talpiot Tomb Discovery

> Does the Talpiot tomb discovery mean that Jesus did not rise from the dead? What does this mean for Christians who have believed that Jesus rose bodily from the dead? Is His resurrection a false rumor after all?

On March 1980 the entrance to a burial cave was exposed on Dov Gruner Street in the Jerusalem neighborhood of East Talpiot. A salvage excavation was undertaken by the late Yosef Gat of the Department of Antiquities and Museums.[1] A preconstruction site was being prepared that would soon be the home of apartments of a newly built suburb called Talpiot about three miles east of Jerusalem. About eleven o'clock on Friday, March 28, 1980, the Solel Boneh Construction Company, led by chief engineer Efraim Shochat, began clearing away the rubble with a bulldozer after having dynamited a section.[2] Suddenly after clearing the area the entire front south side of a door to a tomb lay bare for all to see (see Figures 1, 2, 3).[3]

Interestingly, "Many of Shochat's colleagues, striving to avoid expensive construction delays, were in the habit of averting their eyes from interesting new cavities in the ground and occasionally sacrificed

– 23 –

a tomb, especially if it happened to be small and appeared to consist of, say, only one or two ossuaries…. [But] what one of his bulldozers almost fell into was anything but small."[4] Yet bound by biblical law not to desecrate the burial place of the dead, Shochat, an Orthodox Jew, stopped the construction project until the Israel Department of Antiquities and Museums ([hereafter IDAM] that was later renamed Israel Antiquities Authority [hereafter IAA]) sent a team of archaeologists early Sunday.

On that very Friday a young eleven-year-old boy named Ouriel ran home and excitingly told his mother of the newly discovered find and begged her to come see it. Rivka Maoz, the boy's mother, was a newcomer to Israel and an emigrant from France, who was also an archaeological student. After inspecting the tomb's façade she called the IAA. Because it was Friday and the Sabbath was just hours away and many of the department's offices were closing, no excavation took place until Sunday in accord with the IAA's suggestion.

Unfortunately on Saturday morning before the archaeologists' arrival on Sunday, Rivka's son ran home again to alert his mother of the boys playing with skulls in front of the tomb. Immediately Rivka

Figure 1. The Tomb Facade

Introduction: Jesus' Bones Have Been Discovered!

and her husband arrived at the tomb shouting at the boys who were playing kickball with skulls. Some fractured skulls and broken jaws were then collected in a plastic bag by the Rivka Maoz's family and later given to the IAA.

Considering the evidence of the Talpiot tomb, this event becomes vitally important, since the remains within the tomb were disturbed. Hence no one knows for sure exactly how much of the evidence remained intact when the archaeologists arrived on Sunday.

On Sunday morning Eliot Braun drove the late Joseph (also spelled *Yosef*) Gat. Later Amos Kloner and Shimon Gibson, who was to sketch the tomb and map out the contents of its chambers, arrived at the tomb, whose façade is decorated as part of an inverted V carved

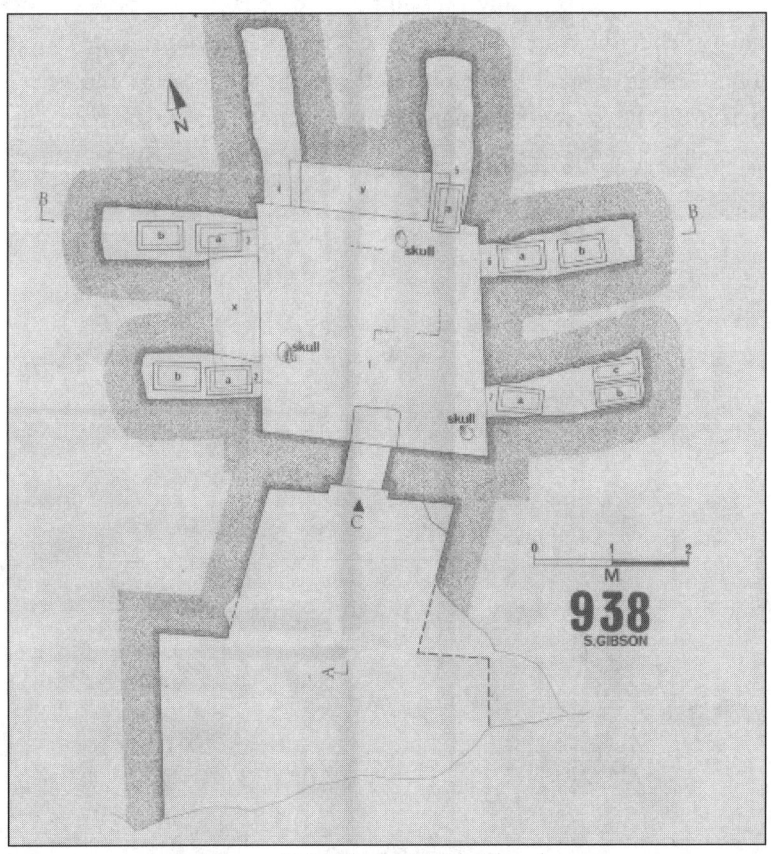

Figures 2. Inside the Tomb Chamber

above a door with a circle in the middle (see Figures 1 and 3). According to Gibson's drawing of the tomb there were about six *kokhim* (plural for *kokh* meaning "niche"), or narrow carved chambers in a tomb, that stored the ten bone boxes in question (see Figures 2).[5] Kloner wrote, "Entrances to six *kokhim* ... are located in the eastern, northern, and western walls, two in each wall. ... The interiors of the *kokhim* are roughly carved in comparison to the walls of the tomb. They have slightly inset facades, a common first century CE feature. ... Ten ossuaries were found within the *kokhim*, some of them broken. The bones within these ossuaries were in an advanced stage of disintegration. Two ossuary lids were recovered from the 0.5 m deep soil fill center of the room, where they had been discarded in antiquity.... Disturbed bones, probably swept off the arcosolia [resting places made of a bench with an arch over it], were found on the floor of the room. These included skull [three of them] and limb fragments and vertebrae. Only broken and powdered bones remained on the shelves of the arcosolia"[6] (see Figures 2 and 3).

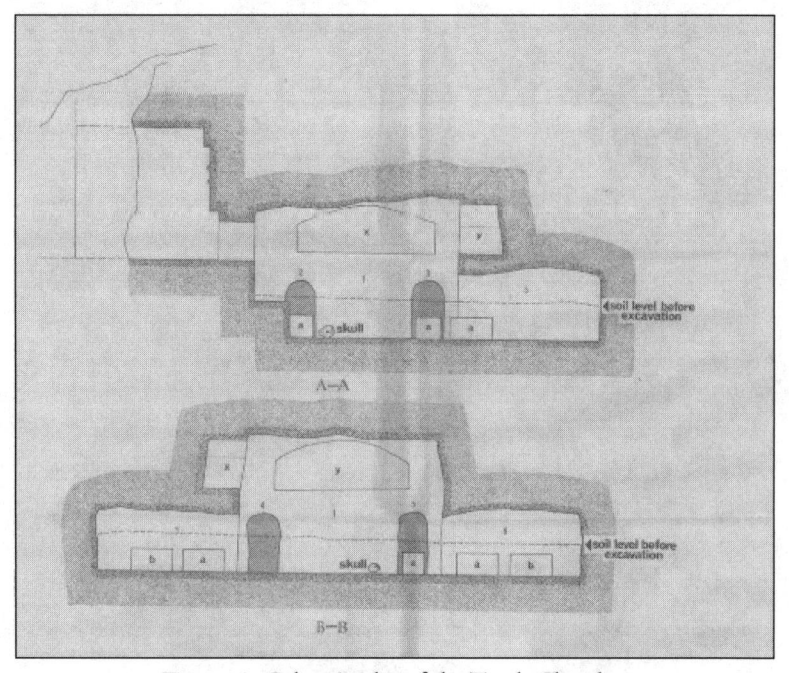

Figures 3. Other Angles of the Tomb Chamber

Many books, documentaries, and articles have recounted the discovery of the Talpiot tomb.[7] The facts of the discovery first appeared in 1981 in the journal *Hadashot Arkheologiyot*,[8] a publication of the IAA. In 1994, Levy Yitzhak Rahmani published a book by the IAA titled, *A Catalogue of Jewish Ossuaries in the Collections of the State of Israel*, which included findings of numerous ossuaries (ornamented and inscribed ones) along with nine of the ten ossuaries of the Talpiot tomb (80.500–508).[9] Kloner's article in 1996 refers to the 1981 article by Joseph Gat and also Rahmani's catalogue. Thus after Gat's article in 1981, two other publications and a documentary appeared in 1996. An article titled "The Tomb That Dare Not Speak Its Name" was published in the British newspaper, *The Sunday Times*, on March 31, 1996 (see Figure 4).[10]

A week later a BBC special documentary titled "The Body in Question" aired on a British television series *Heart of the Matter*. On April 1, 1996, headlines in *The Irish Times* read, "Holy Family Tomb Find Discounted," and on April 3, 1996, a caption in the *USA Today* newspaper read, "Coffin in Israel Is Not That of Jesus' Family, Experts Say."

In the same year (1996) James D. Tabor posted on a web-board named Orion Center at Hebrew University the discussion of the Jesus Family Tomb. Many scholars, including Dale M. Cannon, Kevin D. Johnson, and Niels Peter Lemche, said the tomb was not that of Jesus and His family.[11] The Talpiot ossuaries were again the subject of discussion in a section of John Dominic Crossan and Jonathan L. Reed's book, *Excavating Jesus*, published in

Figure 4. The Sunday Times 1996 Talpiot Tomb

2003. They concluded that finding Jesus' name along with other biblical names associated with Him is only "coincidental."[12] A paper titled "The Jesus Ossuary: A Critical Examination" was also presented in 2003 by Michael S. Heiser, professor at Grace College in Indiana, at the Near East Archaeological Society, where he dismissed any possibility that Jesus and His family were entombed in Talpiot.

Thus from the evidence it becomes difficult to imply or prove that Israeli authorities and Christians conspired to keep the Talpiot tomb a secret. Such a conspiracy is suggested in the book *The Jesus Family Tomb* (hereafter *JFT*) and *The Lost Tomb of Jesus* (hereafter *LTJ*) Discovery Channel documentary.[13] However, the onrush of publications soon after the discovery hardly supports the idea of an attempted cover-up.

The Allegations: Summary of the Arguments

Before summarizing the allegations made by the book and the documentary, we need to know the identity of the four people most responsible for this project. *Ad hominem*[14] attacks are not beneficial or appropriate. Instead, knowing parts of their resume can help disclose their worldview and allow the reader to recognize the predispositions that may influence the conclusions drawn by the book and the documentary.

James Cameron is one of the most successful Hollywood directors, producers, and screenwriters of all times. He has produced and directed such blockbusters as *The Terminator* (1984), *Aliens* (which he wrote and directed and for which he was nominated for seven academy awards in 1986), *The Abyss* (1989), *Terminator 2* (1991), *True Lies* (1984), and *Titanic* (being the highest grossing picture ever made, with $600 million domestically and $1 billion abroad and winning eleven Oscar awards in 1997).[15] Cameron financed the *LTJ* and coached Simcha Jacobovici and Charles Pellegrino in the making of the documentary.[16] Viewing the *LTJ* documentary one can easily spot Cameron's cinematographic talent that engages the emotions and lends a sort of realism to the story.

As a youngster Cameron went to church and as an adult he

accepted the theory of evolution.[17] In 2003 he released a documentary titled *Volcanoes of the Deep Sea* that suggested that life perhaps originated from the depths of the ocean. On April 16, 2006, he released another documentary titled *The Exodus Decoded*, which again betrayed his antisupernatural bias by suggesting in the film that the plagues of the Exodus resulted not from miracles but from natural phenomena.[18]

Simcha Jacobovici is an Emmy-award-winning documentary filmmaker who was involved with Cameron in the making of *The Exodus Decoded*. Jacobovici received a master's degree in international relations from the University of Toronto. He speaks four languages: English, Hebrew, French, and Romanian.[19] Along with Cameron, he was the director and major promoter behind the *LTJ* documentary and he and Charles Pellegrino wrote the *JFT* book. As an Orthodox Jew, he is not a biblicist nor does he subscribe to any major Christian tenets.

Charles R. Pellegrino is a writer and a documentary filmmaker. He wrote *Darwin's Universe: Origins and Crises in the History of Life* (1983) and *Return to Sodom and Gomorrah* (1995). The HarperCollins biographical sketch of him says this: "Pellegrino has been known to work simultaneously in entomology, forensic physics, paleo-genetics, preliminary design of advanced rocket systems, astrobiology, and marine archaeology. The author of eighteen books of fiction and nonfiction, including *Unearthing Atlantis*, *Dust*, *Ghosts of the Titanic*, and the New York Times bestseller *Her Name, Titanic*, he is the scientist whose dinosaur-cloning recipe inspired Michael Crichton's bestselling novel *Jurassic Park*."[20] He received a Ph.D. in paleobiology from Victoria University of Wellington, New Zealand. Pellegrino describes himself as an agnostic, and so he assumes an anti-supernatural bias.[21]

James D. Tabor is the only legitimate theologian of the team, has an interest in archaeology, and is a trained biblical scholar who received a Ph.D. from the University of Chicago. He serves on the faculty of the University of North Carolina at Charlotte. He is also well known as the author of the controversial book *The Jesus Dynasty*

(2006) and for his discovery (with renowned Jerusalem archaeologist Shimon Gibson) in 2005 of an ancient cave associated with the ministry of John the Baptist. Other books to his credit are *Things Unutterable* (1986) and *A Noble Death* (1992). He also holds an anti-supernatural view of miracles.[22]

Seeing the worldviews of these four men, it is not surprising that they deny Jesus' physical resurrection and ascension.[23]

Many efforts have been made by theologians throughout history and by contemporary writers to discredit Christianity similar to the arguments followed in the *JFT* book and *LTJ* documentary.[24] Here are the basic allegations being made that will be examined throughout the book.

Chapter 2 will investigate each of the six ossuaries inscriptions: Jesus son of Joseph, Mariame and Mara, Judah son of Jesus, Jose, Maria, and Matia (*Matya*). Since one of the ossuaries contains the inscription "Jesus son of Joseph" and since five ossuaries have inscriptions with biblical names associated with Jesus, each inscription needs to be evaluated to see whether there is more information than what the book and documentary disclosed. If the book and documentary are correct, it is surprising to find a tomb with such a cluster of names.

Chapter 3 will explain one of the key components to the book and the documentary by investigating the details surrounding the allegation that the Talpiot "Mariamne e Mara" inscription is that of Mary Magdalene. If it is, why does she appear in a tomb with an ossuary inscribed "Jesus son of Joseph" along with other names associated with the family of Jesus of Nazareth? What about other sources that seemingly suggest a marital relationship between Jesus and Mary Magdalene? This is one of the more forceful arguments in the book and the documentary. Are these sources referring to the biblical Mary Magdalene or not?

Chapter 4 will describe the possibilities that exist for Jesus having secretly given birth to a son. The JFT book alleges that Judas is

Thomas (known as Judas Thomas) who seems to be the "beloved disciple" mentioned in John's Gospel. Evidence for a possible son of Jesus will be examined.

Chapter 5 will briefly explain the reason various languages appear in one family tomb. Why is there more than one language in the Talpiot tomb?

Chapter 6 will investigate why the book and the documentary chose only to test one DNA from the "Mariamne e Mara" ossuary with that of the "Jesus son of Joseph" ossuary. Do other options better answer the DNA testing reported in the book and the documentary?

Chapter 7 will discuss how the allegation based on statistics is seemingly impressive, since it is difficult to find such a cluster of names associated with that of Jesus of Nazareth. But there is simply much more information to examine than what appeared in the book and the documentary.

Chapter 8 will briefly examine the validity of the allegation of equating the tenth ossuary at Talpiot with the famous James ossuary. What does the testimony of a respected scholar, Amos Kloner, say about such allegations since he was there and helped document the discovery? Could there be a conspiracy to hide some evidence?

Chapter 9 will conclude part one of the book by examining other significant details. For example, could Jesus' family tomb really be located in Talpiot? What about the x that is next to the "Jesus son of Joseph" inscription? Could that be the symbolic Christian cross? What about the secrecy of the Knights Templar concealing Jesus' death? Does not Dan Brown's book *The Da Vinci Code* already mention this in his novel? Is such a view historically credible? Could the chevron sign above the Talpiot tomb be a unique Christian symbol? What evidence do we possess that the Nazarene and Ebionite groups were the real Christians or did the early church condemn them as heretics?

Positive answers to most of these questions were given in the *JFT* book and the *LTJ* documentary as evidence that the Talpiot tomb was that of Jesus of Nazareth.

The book's second part will examine the evidence for Jesus' physical resurrection.

Chapter 10 will examine whether the Bible is an accurate historical document that can be trusted. Since Christians depend on the Bible as evidence that Jesus of Nazareth rose from the dead, can the Scriptures be trusted? And how does it compare to other historical documents? Is the "physical resurrection" historically accepted? What do the Hebrew Scriptures, Jewish sources, and Christian tradition believe about physical resurrection? Was physical resurrection the common belief, or a minority view of some?

Chapter 11 will examine the Bible to see if physical resurrections have occurred in the past. If they did, logically something occurring in the past could be expected to recur again in the future. But if not, the burden of proof lies on the one pointing to an empty tomb. Key Old Testament and New Testament passages referring possibly to physical resurrection (excluding those regarding Jesus' resurrection and 1 Corinthians 15) are discussed in this chapter.

Chapter 12 will show how incredible are the odds of some prophecies coming true, and will examine whether some of them advocating resurrection have come true. Another element to investigate is whether Jesus' resurrection was ever prophesied, or if it was an invention of the church.

Chapter 13 will investigate arguments made by some that suggest Jesus did not rise from the dead because He did not die. Various individuals claim the swoon theory that Jesus merely fainted on the cross and was revived. What is so important about the empty tomb and the Resurrection? This chapter will mention these arguments along with assessing the viability of whether Jesus rose bodily.

Chapter 14 investigates Jesus' resurrection appearances in the Gospels in order to see whether He rose spiritually or physically. The most debated passage, 1 Corinthians 15:35–49, regarding whether Paul and the disciples believed that Christians will receive a physical body at resurrection will also be examined.

Chapter 15 will examine various details that validate the Resurrection: Does science contradict the Resurrection? Logical arguments that validate the resurrection of Jesus are these: (1) enemies indirectly affirmed the Resurrection; (2) Rome and the seal of the tomb seem to argue for it; (3) who removed the stone and the body? (4) Saul went from being a Christian persecutor to Paul the Christian propagator; (5) and the existence of the church and changed lives indicate the Resurrection's affect on people throughout history.

Chapter 16 will briefly cover current news about the Talpiot Tomb and suggest how one should respond to the allegations of *The Jesus Family Tomb* book and *The Lost Tomb of Jesus* documentary.

First-Century Burial Practices

Jewish law demanded that after a person was executed, he was to be buried that day (Deut. 21:23). Some may wonder why Jesus' body was then placed in a tomb cut from a rock and not buried underground. First-century burial practice answers this. Jews practiced a "secondary" form of burial using ossuaries.

Since the book and documentary claim that the ossuary of Jesus of Nazareth has been found, a brief discussion is necessary to inform readers of the customary second-burial practice of gathering bones (known as *ossilegium*) in an ossuary after decomposition.

Because Jewish burial practices existed in the Greco-Roman culture, this does not mean they always adopted similar customs. Greeks and Romans commonly practiced cremation,[25] but the Jewish people first buried their dead in ditches and then after the flesh decayed they transferred the bones to ossuaries.[26] These ossuaries were then placed in a family tomb. "Jews practicing *ossilegium* endeavored to retain within the family tomb, the entire skeleton of each deceased separately once the flesh had completely decomposed."[27] Jews believed that decomposition of the body that usually lasted a year was necessary in order to achieve a "sinless state" of perfection before physical resurrection took place, which many deemed to be a "painful process."[28]

Though ossuary practice reflects Jewish belief in a future physical resurrection, one must be cautious in assuming that everyone employed this custom for the same reason. The Sadducees had ossuaries, but unlike the Pharisees they did not believe in the physical resurrection of the dead. Crossan and Reed point out that the Sadducees may have "adopted the common burial practice" of the day "among the wealthy Jerusalemites and did so in grand style." Thus they are correct in deducing, "We conclude that belief or theology alone cannot explain the phenomenon of ossuaries. Ossuaries *may* reflect a common belief in the resurrection, a heightened sense of individualism, or a subconscious desire to maintain identity and be protected in death, but their use was made possible by the Herodian-initiated Temple economy in Jerusalem and a well-trained stonemasons guild. And their distribution was not common but more upper class."[29]

Rahmani notes another important fact about the *ossilegium* practice of the Jews that should not be confused with that of their neighbors. The remains of non-Jewish family members buried in a tomb were moved aside to make room for other burials. In later practice remains were gathered into "depositories" under the floor chamber in tombs.[30] In the Hellenistic period a "communal charnel" (lit., "a common place for flesh") became the designated place to use for previous remains. Superstition seems the reason behind earlier *ossilegium* burial remains being left in the tomb, since it was thought this "assured the deceased of the benefit of food, drink, clothing and security, which the family clan was obligated to provide even to the most humble of its members."[31] Perhaps this type of spiritism practice may be what Jewish Law condemned (Lev. 19:26; 20:27; Deut. 18:11–14). On the other hand, Jews collected the bones of relatives and placed them in separate ossuaries. Apparently such a practice was based on the belief that the individual bones had to be kept ready for a future physical resurrection.[32] Thus the practice of *ossilegium* in Judaism argues for the common belief of physical resurrection, not a spiritual resurrection. While second burial practice was common in Jerusalem, often ossuaries contained the bones of more than one person.[33] Frequently many bones in burial chambers were pushed to the sides that were not stored in ossuaries,[34] perhaps because they could not afford bone boxes. Hence many Jewish families did not practice *ossilegium* because they could not afford it.

Significantly another issue to consider is whether Jesus and His family—being relatively poor—could afford to be buried in the rich Talpiot tomb. Wealthy families were the only ones able to afford elaborately ornamented ossuaries.[35] However, even plain nonornamented ossuaries, having only inscriptions or special protection formulas for the deceased, does not indicate poverty or a lack of care since many plain ossuaries have been found in rich tombs in Jerusalem. In fact Rahmani suggests, "Ethical and religious considerations may have dictated the choice of a simple ossuary."[36]

How did poor families like Jesus' family bury their own? Jodi Magness says normally the poorer classes of Jewish families buried their dead in simple individual trenches dug into the ground, much like today. The body would be buried in a "shroud" and then placed directly into the "rectangular" hole. Afterward the "trench" was filled with dirt and sometimes a small rough tombstone would be placed at one end.[37]

While Joseph of Arimathea was rich and buried Jesus in a wealthy tomb (Matt. 27:57–59; Isa. 53:9), no evidence exists to suggest that all of Jesus' family, including His father Joseph who died years earlier, were also buried in the same tomb. To support this notion one would have to posit the theory that Joseph of Arimathea donated a family tomb. If such a theory were true, surely the Bible or church tradition would have mentioned this charity. However, no such evidence exists.

Although *ossilegium* practice was thought to exist from about 40 B.C. to A.D. 70, this is debatable. Rahmani argues that ossuary practice—using hard limestone and chip-carved soft limestone materials—was introduced in Jerusalem around 20-15 B.C. to A.D. 70.[38]

Noting this, however, he sees ossuary practice continuing to at least until A.D. 135, but using more materials like clay, hard limestone, soft limestone, and the combination of hard and soft limestone on the same ossuary.[39] Others like Evans and Meyers believe that in a general sense *ossilegium* practice as a brand new custom did not appear abruptly around 40 B.C. and ended in A.D. 70, contrary to what the *JFT* book presents.[40] Evans points out that rabbinic tradition and archaeological evidence both attest to the continual use of ossuaries.[41] Also there is strong evidence that *ossilegium* practice was followed in Alexandria, Egypt; Carthage, Africa; and Spain.[42] Evans concludes by postulating the best reason for the increase in the use of specific kinds of ossuaries from 40 B.C. to A.D. 70:

> The most plausible explanation for the dramatic increase in the number of ossuaries put into use in the Herodian period is that it had to do with Herod's extensive building projects in and around Jerusalem, especially those concerned with the Temple Mount and the new Sanctuary.... It is in this chronological coincidence between Herod's massive building program, which employed thousands of stone-cutters and which ran from his reign, beginning in the 30s B.C.E., and extended to 64 C.E., and the appearance of thousands of ossuaries, carved from the same stone (limestone) from which almost all of the Temple Mount buildings were fashioned, that we find the answer to our question. The number of ossuaries, made of limestone, increased dramatically during the one century of temple-related building in Jerusalem, not because of a shift in the theology, or foreign influence, but because of the great number of stones-cutters, quarries, and rejected blocks of limestone. The increase of the city's population and its urban and suburban sprawl also encouraged greater density in burial sites. Simply put, more dead relatives can be interred in the family vault if they are placed in ossuaries than if they are left in niches or in full-sized sarcophagi.[43]

After thoroughly researching this topic Rahmani concludes. "There does not seem to be any direct link between these [later] Christian [burial] practices and the Jewish custom of *ossilegium*."[44] Hence to say that the Talpiot tomb was that of Jesus of Nazareth and His family, along with a cross on the bone-box that was supposedly a Christian symbol, as the *JFT* book claims, is anachronistic and misconstrues a customary belief system of one group and applies it to another. Perhaps Jewish Christians practiced *ossilegium* for different theological reasons than that of their unbelieving predecessors, similar to Paul's correct reason for offering sacrifices in Acts 21:26 contrary to the Judaizers' reasons for observing the Law (Galatians). That is, from the biblical evidence Jewish Christians believed that final *perfection* or a *sinless state* came through faith alone in Christ alone now (John 1:12; 2:23; 3:16; 5:24; 6:40, 47; 11:25–27; 20:30–31; Rom. 3:21–4:25; Eph. 2:8–9; Titus 3:5), which guaranteed a perfect physical body later (1 Cor. 15; 1 John 3:2; Rev. 22). Therefore decomposition of the body was not necessary to achieve this state before physical resurrection took place.

From the available evidence we cannot be sure why Jewish Christians practiced *ossilegium*, or if the custom was even copied. But if the practice was copied (and there is little reason to suspect otherwise since Jewish Christians often kept many of their Jewish practices), one thing is obvious from a cursory view of the evidence presented: Jews practiced *ossilegium* partly because they believed in a future *physical* resurrection, not a *spiritual* resurrection.

Furthermore, if the practice was in place longer than expected, then the pool of potential graves grows, and the likelihood that one can specify that a given tomb is from the first century (much less that of Jesus of Nazareth) becomes more difficult.

Conclusion

Looking at the history of the Talpiot tomb discovery, two things become clear. Since the tomb was disturbed before the IAA arrived, the evidence was compromised. This becomes important when postulating theories that in themselves are tenuous. Further evidence of a plethora of information documenting the tomb's history and contents must also put to rest any charge alleging conspiracy since from the beginning all the findings were public knowledge that surfaced throughout twenty-eight years.

Some facts about the men behind the allegations were also documented to help the reader identify predispositions that might influence conclusions drawn by the book and the documentary. An account of the arguments was summarized in order to point out the allegations that support the Jesus family tomb discovery.

By understanding some facts about second burial Jewish practice in the first century A.D., the reader can better determine whether some of the book's claims about the possibility of Jewish Christians believing in a spiritual instead of a physical resurrection is correct.

— Chapter 2 —

WHAT DO THE OSSUARY INSCRIPTIONS REALLY MEAN?

ONE THING WAS already certain: even though "Jesus," "Joseph," and "Mary" were common names in first-century Jerusalem, the *cluster* of those names now appeared very uncommon. Step by sequential step, the numbers were saying that this combination of names should *not* have occurred by chance even once during the entire lifetime of Jerusalem's ossuary culture.[1]

Finding a first-century A.D. tomb in Jerusalem with the inscriptions, "Jesus son of Joseph," "Mariamene and [or also known as] Mara," "Judas son of Jesus," "Jose," "Maria," "Matia/Matthew," and four other noninscriptive ossuaries is not unusual since all of these names were common at that time.[2] The argument centers, however, on whether this unique cluster of names refers to "Jesus of Nazareth" and His family.

One must not assume a conclusive understanding of inscriptions that are based on questionable interpretations. An engraving containing scratches, surface erosion, forgery markings, and physical damage can cause one to misread the inscription.[3] Thus before discussing whether this is the family tomb of Jesus of Nazareth, an analysis of

THE JESUS FAMILY TOMB EXAMINED

each ossuary inscription must be made including ossuaries that have no inscriptions.[4]

Yeshua [?] son of Yehosef

The inscription יֵשׁוּעַ בַּר יְהוֹסֵף (*Yeshua* [?] *son of Yehosef*) in Rahmani's catalogue appears as ossuary number 704/80.503. This is a nonornamented ossuary.[5] Here is how the inscription appears in Aramaic (a Hebrew related dialect):[6]

The *JFT* book notes that an estimated 80,000 male population existed in Jerusalem in the first century and calculates, "Out of these, 7,200 would have been called Jesus and 11,200 would have been called Joseph. Multiplying the percentages against each other (.09 x .14 x 80,000), we get 1,008 men who would have been called Jesus, son of Joseph during the century of ossuary use. In other words, approximately one in 79 males was called Jesus, son of Joseph."[7] Based on the common use of both of these names in Jerusalem we should not be surprised to find a number of tombs with the inscription "Jesus son Joseph."[8] In fact, the inscription "Jesus son of Joseph" already exists (see Figure 5).[9]

Yeshua son of Yehosef in left space–same side as *Yeshu*

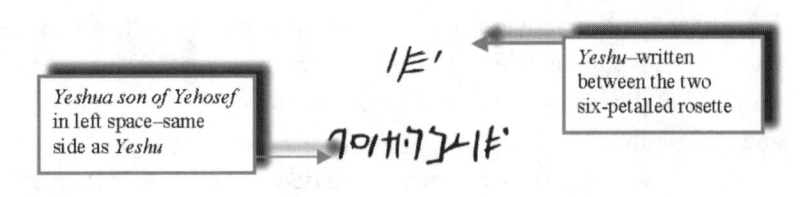

Yeshu–written between the two six-petalled rosette

Figures 5.

Eleazar Lippa Sukenik found the first ossuary "Jesus son of Joseph" in 1926, in the warehouse basement of the Israel Antiquities

– 40 –

What Do The Ossuary Inscriptions Really Mean?

Authority (IAA), and he published the find in 1931.[10] No reputable scholar has ever suggested this ossuary contained the bones of Jesus of Nazareth.[11] Furthermore the inscription of this ossuary appears clearly written.

Unfortunately this is not the case concerning the Talpiot tomb ossuary (704–80.503) inscribed "Jesus son of Joseph" (lit., *Yeshua bar Yehosef*; see Figure 6).[12]

A significant problem exists in how to read the inscription. The *JFT* book acknowledges this fact. "Of all the inscriptions found in the Talpiot tomb, the 'Jesus, son of Joseph' is the hardest to read. That's also a fact." Yet after admitting this they assert, "It's not that deciphering it is controversial; everyone, from the noted epigrapher L. Y. Rahmani to the legendary Frank Moore Cross of Harvard, agrees that the inscription on the ossuary must be read 'Jesus, son of Joseph' and no other way"[13] (see Figure 7).

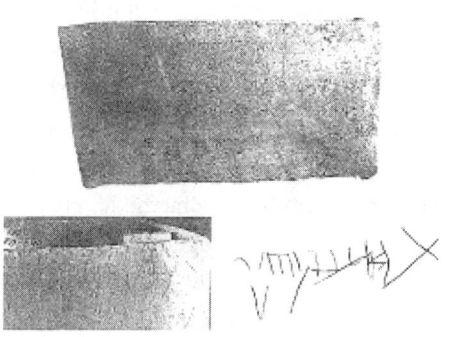

Figure 6. Ossuary of *Yeshua bar Yehosef*

Figure 7.[14]

– 41 –

Though almost all scholars have conceded that the ossuary reads "Jesus son of Joseph," it must be noted that they have done so with reasonable doubts.[15] Hence Amos Kloner (one of the archaeologists present in the 1980 discovery), who documented the find, places a question mark after Yeshua: "Yeshua (?) son of Yehosef." Because it is difficult to read, he had to corroborate the interpretation by looking at another ossuary (no. 2, 702) where the word appears in the inscription *Yehuda son of Yeshua*.[16] Similarly, two years before Kloner's article in 1996, Rahmani's *Catalogue of Jewish Ossuaries*, published in 1994, also questioned the certainty of the first name of the inscription "Yeshua (?), son of Yehosef" and concludes, "The first name, preceded by a large cross-mark, is difficult to read, as the incisions are clumsily carved and badly scratched." He also confirms the word *Yeshua* by looking at the unambiguous ossuary engraved *Yehuda son of Yeshua*.[17]

Other scholars have also voiced their doubts of the inscription. Stephen J. Pfann, Semitic language expert and president of the University of the Holy Land in Jerusalem, suggested that the inscription *Yeshua* may be *Hanun* (or someone else) that was reinscribed for another person having another name. This means that by writing over the name originally intended they assigned it to someone else.[18] Pfann believes that the name *Yeshua* was inscribed with an instrument different from that used in the rest of the inscription.[19] However, why would Jesus' followers bury such a respected person in an ossuary originally assigned to another person and then write His name over the other name in a sloppy manner? Rochelle I. S. Altman, a specialist in ancient phonetic-based writing systems, mentions Rahmani's doubt. "Rahmani put a question mark on the possible name. Further, Rahmani could not have made it [any] clearer that this was only a *possible* reading. And, as noted ... Pfann thinks [the correct reading] may be *Hanan*."[20]

In agreement with these scholars, Steve Caruso, noted Aramaic calligraphy expert, who also studied the inscription, admits that *Yeshua* may be one possible reading. He concludes, "It's possible to read it as 'Jesus son of Joseph,' but [it is] overall inconclusive. The handwriting is simply too messy and the carving too worn to make a definitive judgment."[21]

What Do The Ossuary Inscriptions Really Mean?

Other scholars take a more tentative approach. Émile Puech, a linguist professor of the French Biblical and Archaeological School in Jerusalem, wrote, "The 'Joseph' [word] is clear. The 'son of' is no problem. The 'Jesus?' It's certainly possible to read it that way." Joseph Naveh, an Israeli epigrapher, also concludes, "The 'Joseph' is unmistakable. The 'son of' is okay. And you can certainly read it as 'Jesus,' just not definitely. There are lots of additional lines here that don't belong." Ada Yardeni, a paleographic and script expert, similarly says, "'Son of Joseph,' for sure. The first name? Well, there are lots of markings here, but, yes, it could well be Jesus."[22]

Though most scholars have conceded that the inscription reads "Jesus son of Joseph" almost all scholars acknowledge that one cannot be absolutely sure of the reading of *Yeshua* in the inscription since this is the worst of all the six inscriptions.

Furthermore, since the name is written in a "graffiti-like"[23] manner, one needs to question how anyone would inscribe an ossuary so sloppily an honored figure like Jesus of Nazareth—whether risen or not. In fact, compared to Caiaphas's engraving (see Figure 8) the inscription of this honored person is crystal clear.[24]

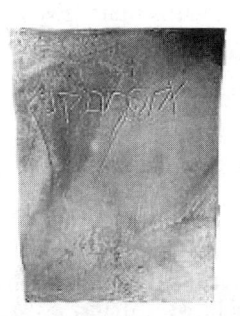

Figure 8. Yosef bar Caifa (Joseph son of Caiaphas)

Hence even if one grants the reading of "Jesus son of Joseph" (which interpretation is questionable at best and wrong at worst), it seems difficult to believe that any follower of Jesus of Nazareth would inscribe the name of such an honored person in such a scrappy way. Another question not addressed by the *JFT* book and the *LTJ* documentary is this: "If

Jesus is married, why do we not find the name of His wife and child on the same ossuary," which was a common practice?[25]

It also seems strange that Jesus' followers would not later build a shrine commemorating His burial place, if indeed this ossuary held the bones of Jesus of Nazareth.[26] In fact many who believe Jesus rose bodily from the grave commemorate such a shrine venerating Jesus' burial place known as the Holy Sepulcher, which is not in Talpiot, Jerusalem. In an email to me Harvard professor, François Bovon, said this is the strongest argument against the *LTJ* documentary. "The main argument against the hypothesis of the documentary is the strong tradition of the construction of the emperor Hadrian of a sculpture on the Golgotha in the second century. The emperor was probably fighting an early Christian worship tradition as the place of Jesus' burial place."[27]

Thus to assume this ossuary correctly reads "Jesus son of Joseph" without considering the problems surrounding the inscriptions and the highly unlikely possibilities of how devoted followers of Jesus of Nazareth would write such a messy inscription describing their honored leader, betrays the biased investigation of the *JFT* book and the *LTJ* documentary. Even if the inscription correctly reads "Jesus son of Joseph," the evidence suggests this cannot be Jesus of Nazareth but instead was one of many Jewish people of the day named Jesus.

Mariamene e Mara [?]

The inscription Μαρίαμηνου η Μάρα (Mariamene, who is [also called] Mara) appears in Rahmani's catalogue as ossuary number 701/80.500. This is an ornamented ossuary.[28] The inscription appears as follows:[29]

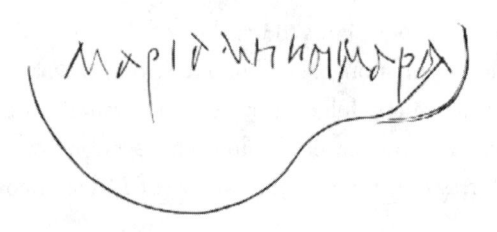

Out of all six inscriptions *Mariamene e* (?) *Mara* is the only one written in Greek. This inscription is key to the thesis of the *JFT* book and the *LTJ* documentary. They interpreted part of the inscription *Mariamene* as a Greek name meaning "Mary Magdalene" and the second part *Mara* as "a Greek rendering of an Aramaic word meaning 'Lord' or 'Master'" that was "preceded by a Greek symbol" *e* understood as "also known as."[30] According to *JFT* advocates the ossuary inscription would then read "Mary Magdalene, also known as Master."[31]

Since they believe this represents Mary Magdalene whose bones are in a family tomb, they say this may be the wife of Jesus and the mother of the boy of the ossuary inscribed "Judah son of Jesus." Yet if the *JFT* proponents misread the *Mariamene e Mara* ossuary, even if one grants the interpretation of the word *Yeshua* as that of the Jesus ossuary, the entire premise crumbles since this simply refers to another Mary, a common name of the time. Could this inscription really refer to Mary Magdalene?

The majority of scholars do not agree with the promoters of the film's interpretation of this inscription. Renowned experts, who questioned the interpretation of *Yeshua* of the Jesus bone-box, are also at odds with how the *JFT* book and *LTJ* documentary read this inscription. Both Rahmani and Kloner have cataloged the meaning of the first name simply as "Mariamene" (another form of Miriam), and the second word *Mara* as a contraction of the personal name "Martha," another very common name in Jerusalem. Both of these scholars read the inscription as *Mariamene of Mara*. Another way of saying this is, "Miriam, who is also called Martha."

On the other hand, Pfann believes the correct reading of the first word of the inscription is *Mariame*, the customary Hebrew name *Miriam*. Therefore the Greek inscription should not be read as *Mariamene e Mara* but instead as *Mariame kai Mara*, meaning, "Mary and Martha." Both of these Greek names are common forms of the Hebrew *Mariam* and *Mara*. Pfann, contrary to Rahmani and Kloner, understands this inscription as descriptive of two women whose bones are contained in one ossuary. Storing the bones of two individuals in one ossuary was a common practice in the first century A.D.

In addition, if this inscription refers to Mary Magdalene, who was married to Jesus of Nazareth, we need to ask, Why was Jesus' name excluded from her ossuary or her name excluded from His ossuary? Since it was a common practice to place the husband's name after a wife's name in an ossuary ("*X wife of Y*"),[32] why is that missing? Rahmani notes, "In eleven inscriptions referring to women, the names of husbands accompany their name and the relationship is explicitly stated."[33]

Thus to interpret this inscription as referring to Mary Magdalene becomes problematic on numerous levels. These will be examined in the next chapter.

Judah Son of Jesus

The inscription (יהודה בר ישו) (*Yehuda, son of Yeshua*) appears in Rahmani's catalogue as the number 702/80.501. This is an ornamented ossuary.[34] The inscription appears in Aramaic:[35]

יהודהברישוע

Yehuda (Judas or Judah) was the third most popular Jewish name during the period 330 B.C.–200 A.D. According to Tal Ilan's study, out of 2,509 males 179 people were found bearing this name.[36] *Yeshua* (Joshua or Jesus) was the sixth most common name of the same period. Out of the 2,509 males, 103 individuals bore this name.[37] Keep in mind, however, that if we had all of the names of the estimated 80,000 people who populated Jerusalem around 66 A.D. and the estimated four million population of the region, the numbers would increase exponentially.[38] Both of these names were among the most common names in Jerusalem. When describing this inscription the *JFT* advocates admit, "There is no written tradition that Jesus had a son. This small, child's ossuary may have held the mortal remains of the son of Jesus and Mary."[39] This, of course, could not be the son of Jesus of Nazareth for three good reasons. Biblical evidence, extrabiblical evidence, and church tradition do not state that Jesus fathered children.

Even if Jesus had a son, many scholars wonder if He would name him Judas? That Judas Iscariot would betray Jesus may not in itself have deterred Him from naming such a son Judas since this is the fourth most commonly used name among males of the first century, and belongs to a Jewish hero and patriot, Judas Maccabeus (166–160 B.C.; see 1 Macc. 2–10). Naming a son, however, is so personal that one wonders. It does make for a bizarre scenario, as Daniel B. Wallace paints:

> If Jesus knew early on that Judas Iscariot would betray him (as John 6.70 seems to affirm), is it really likely that he and Mary would name their son after his betrayer? I can see the conversation now. "Jesus, we have a son. Let's name him Judas." "Um, I don't think that's the best name.... You'll have to trust me on this one." The only alternative is to see Jesus and Mary as married *and* having a child *before* Jesus knew that Judas would betray him. And if that is the case, how likely is that the disciples would be unaware of Jesus' marriage of his son during his three-year ministry with them? Not a shred of evidence suggests any such awareness. Either this is an incredible cover-up of Titanic proportions or it's a figment. (And this is one reason why so many liberal scholars have rejected the premise of the film.) *The Lost Tomb of Jesus* is smelling more and more like *The Da Vinci Code*.[40]

Jose

The inscription יוסה (*Yose*) appears in Rahmani's catalogue as ossuary number 705/80.504. This is a plain ossuary.[41] The inscription is in Hebrew.[42]

יוסה

The *JFT* book and *LTJ* documentary claim the inscription of *Jose* (lit., *Yose*) is rare since only one ossuary out of 519 male ossuaries have been discovered with this inscription.[43] While granting Kloner's explanation that the name *Jose* functions as a contraction (or diminutive) of

Joseph, the second most common name in the Second Temple period,[44] Jacobovici changed *Jose* to *Joseph* and concludes, "I was going with 14 percent of males being called Joseph, that is, one out of every seven. If we multiply 365, 928 by 7, we get one in just over 2.5 million."[45] Such a calculation seems impressive and appears to present strong possibilities that this *Jose* was Jesus' brother mentioned in Mark 6:3.

Yet a number of details are undisclosed, and a number of assumptions must be made in order for this view to be accurate. First, Jacobovici formulates the number 365, 928 in this calculation on three highly questionable assumptions (that the majority of scholars deny). The inscription "Jesus son of Joseph" must be correct. As shown, problems exist in reading the name "Yeshua" in the inscription 80.503, which cause a number of scholars to have reasonable doubts. Jacobovici based his calculation on the observation that one out of 79 names contained the inscription "Jesus son of Joseph" in first-century ossuaries on the current 233 inscribed ossuaries cataloged by the IAA. His calculation, however, is based on a very limited amount of ossuaries unearthed from the first century, since out of the 233 ossuaries the name "Joseph" appears 14 percent of the time and Jesus 9 percent. Surely more than 233 inscribed ossuaries were used in a city containing an estimated population of 80,000 people. Hence his calculation would change if more digs were allowed in Jerusalem and more ossuaries were found since Jesus and Joseph were two of the most common names in the first century.

Similarly Jacobovici leaves out a number of details in the calculation of the name *Maria* (lit., *Marya*) in the inscription 80.505. He uses the *Acts of Philip*, a late apocryphal work (a spurious and non-accepted writing by the church), to claim that Mary of Nazareth appears there by the name Maria and "was differentitated from Mary Magdalene by the name Maria."[46] Thus Jacobovici also uses Professor Tal Ilan's calculation that out of 193 ossuaries 8 of them contain the name Maria; thereby, deducing that 1 out of 24 females was called Maria.[47] A huge problem exists with the former calculation of distinguishing between Maria and Miriam. In the New Testament the name *Maria* is a Greek translation of the Hebrew name *Miriam*, and in numerous places the name *Miriam* is transliterated from Hebrew to Greek and used interchangeably to

– 48 –

refer to the same person in the New Testament, either Mary Magdalene (cf. Matt. 27:56, 61; 28:1; Mark 15:40) or Mary, Jesus' mother (cf. Matt. 1:16, 18, 20; 2:11; 13:55; Luke 1:27, 30, 34, 38). This evidence must be factored into the equation, but if it is, Jacobovici's calculations will be greatly diminished.

Finally, why have the *JFT* and the *LTJ* people chosen not to include the Greek rendering of *Jose* of the Hebrew name *Yose* in their calculations? If they mention the spelling of the nickname *Jose* (a known contraction of *Iōsētos*)[48] in Mark 6:3 as Jesus' brother and link it to the Talpiot inscription, why not include in the calculation the Greek spelling of the name when it appears in other ossuaries? This reveals the prejudicial way of using and presenting the evidence to fit the desired conclusion. Numerous first-century ossuaries contain the Greek spelling of the inscription name *Jose* as documented by Rahmani (see Figure 4; 56–34.7753; 444–71.424; 576–75.674), P. B. Bagatti and J. T. Milik in the 1958 *Dominus Flevit* excavation, and others.[49] In fact the name *Jose* appears in three places in the Bible alone (Mark 6:3; 15:40; Luke 3:29).[50] If these details were taken into account, Jacobovici's calculation would have been different. His equation tries to connect too many dots at places where they simply do not match, and too many questionable assumptions must line up for his theory to work. Thus the contraction of the name *Jose* for *Joseph* is not as rare as the *JFT* and *LTJ* people suggest.

Maria

The inscription מריה (*Marya*) appears in Rahmani's catalogue as ossuary number 706/80.505. This is a plain ossuary.[51] The inscription literally appears "phonetically" in Hebrew letters but records the Latinized version "Maria" of the Hebrew name "Miriam" (Hebrew מִרְיָם)[52]

מריה

The ossuary inscription name *Marya*, or the Latin Maria, appears in Hebrew and is a very common name. Eight other ossuary inscriptions of the Latinized form of the name Maria written in Hebrew letters have been discovered.[5.] This is one of the most common Hebrew female names. It was so common that 21.3% of all women in the first century were named Maria (i.e., one out of five women).[54] Darrell L. Bock stresses this point in a comical manner by saying that every Jewish boy's dream was to grow up and marry a Mary. Actually the odds of that happening were very good. But to assume that this Mary refers to Jesus' mother is highly improbable, it is impossible to prove, and it is pure conjecture based on a number of erroneous assumptions. Since "Maria" or Mary was the most common name among women,[55] one would expect to find ossuaries all over the region with the name Mary. This proves absolutely nothing unless other assumptions are introduced into the calculation.

Matia (Matya)

The inscription מתיה (*Matya*) appears in Rahmani's catalogue as ossuary number 703/80.502. This is a plain ossuary.[56] The inscription appears in Hebrew as follow:[57]

מתיה

While the ossuary inscription name *Matya*, or the English form Matthew, cannot be linked to Jesus' immediate family, this name appears in Mary's genealogy in Luke 3:24–26. Based on this observation, the *JFT* advocates and James Tabor defend the appearance of an ossuary with Matthew's name as Jesus' relative, and the reason why it appears in a family tomb.[58] However, similar to the Maria inscription along with all other names of the Talpiot tomb, these names belong to the common limited pool of names of the first century.[59] Furthermore since there are no other genealogies from the first century, we cannot compare the repeated appearance of this name in other family lineages. In the New Testament Matthew is one of Jesus' disciples, and that is the sole connection made directly to Him. To say more than that is pure speculation.

Four Other Ossuaries:

The last four ossuaries are noninscribed. However, three of these are ornamented and are cataloged by Rahmani as 707/80.506, 708/80.507, and 709/80.508. Though all three of the ossuaries vary a bit in size and have small ornamented details, they all have a "six-petalled rosette inside a zigzag circle."[60]

Rahmani actually did not document the fourth ossuary that the *JFT* and *LTJ* advocates think belongs to Jesus' brother James because it was plain and nonornamented. Kloner, however, being one of the original excavators at the Talpiot site in 1980, does document the ossuary in his article and with the number at the IAA as "IAA 80.509 60 x 26 x 31.5 cm. Plain."[61] Kloner admitted in an interview with Bock that he saw and documented the tenth ossuary, and according to him it had no inscription. Thus to say otherwise is to imply Kloner and others present at Talpiot in 1980 lied.

Plain and nonornamented ossuaries do not make it into published catalogues since nothing appears on them. It would be cumbersome to handle a large volume that included plain ossuaries, costly to publish, and pointless to document plain and non-ornamented ossuaries since there is nothing to see or study about them. For years this has been the common way to handle noninscribed and nonornamented ossuaries. They usually end up in the IAA basement or courtyard with all the rest of plain and nonornamented ossuaries, which are the majority of ossuaries discovered.[62]

Conclusion

The inscriptions "Jesus son of Joseph," "Mariame and Mara," "Judas son of Jesus," "Jose," "Maria," "Matthew," in the Talpiot tomb are not that unusual. All these were common names of the day. Even less unusual is the other remaining four noninscribed ossuaries.

The argument does not necessarily need to center on whether the name "Jesus" in the inscription bearing "son of Joseph" is correct since a number of other issues initially raised in this chapter plague the *JFT* and *LTJ* advocates' theory. One of the intriguing assertions by the book and the film is whether the Mariame ossuary was that of Mary

Magdalene, which would truly help their case all the more. That is the fascinating topic of the next chapter.

— Chapter 3 —

IS MARY MAGDALENE'S NAME ON THE OSSUARY?

In June 2000, Bovon and Bouvier published the first complete translation—into French—of the Mount Athos version of the Acts of Philip, with its identification of Mary Magdalene as "Mariamne," the sister of the apostle Philip. The Acts of Philip provides us with a much more complete version of Mary Magdalene than the Gospels.[1]

If the alleged name *Mariamene e Mara* in L. Y Rahmani's catalogue refers to Mary Magdalene, then the *JFT* book and the *LTJ* documentary and others have a strong case.[2] "'*This* Mary Magdalene,' Bovon told Simcha, 'this Mary from the Acts of Philip, is clearly the equal of the other apostles—and, as depicted, is even more enlightened than Philip.'"[3] A few pages later, so that no confusion exists between two Marys mentioned in the Acts of Philip, are these words: "'To be clear,' said Bovon, 'in the Acts of Philip the first Mary—Magdalene—is called Mariamne. The second Mary is also mentioned, but only once, in speech about the birth of Jesus. And she is called—' 'Maria,' Simcha finished for him. '*Maria*,' Bovon repeated. 'And Mary Magdalene—' 'Is clearly Mariamne,' said Bovon. 'So there is no confusion here between the two persons.'"[4]

If the inscription *Mariamne* (or *Mariamene*) (*e*) *Mara* refers to Mary Magdalene, the *JFT* book and the *LTJ* documentary may have a strong case that the Jesus of Nazareth's family tomb has been discovered. But if not, the foundation crumbles.[5] Details related to the Mariamne inscription must be carefully examined, since this is the linchpin of the entire argument.[6]

How can Gnostic books help interpret whether the "Mariamne" ossuary inscription refers to Mary Magdalene of the New Testament (NT) Gospels, and if she was Jesus' spouse? What evidence are scholars using, and what exactly are they saying about it? Is François Bovon, a Harvard Divinity scholar, identifying the "Mariamne" in the Acts of Philip as Mary Magdalene? What exactly does Bovon mean? Since Rahmani is an expert on ossuaries, how does he read this inscription? Could there be more than one option in how to understand this inscription that better explains the evidence? What do the Gospels say about Mary Magdalene compared with the assessment of her by others? These questions are examined and answered in this chapter.

Gnostic Literature

Before assessing the texts that allegedly link the inscription *Mariamne* as Mary Magdalene of the NT Gospels in various Gnostic books, several things must be clarified briefly about these works.[7]

These books get their name "Gnostic" from the Greek word *ginōskiō*, "to know." Basically "*Gnostic* and *Gnosticism* refer to a belief that is rooted in special knowledge. Those in the know are called Gnostics."[8] Thus by its very nature Gnostic belief was condemned because it claimed to reveal new mysterious knowledge about the world, dichotomy between flesh and spirit, the person of Jesus, the role of women and other truths that were not in keeping with apostolic writings of the first century that its successors followed.[9] Though some today hold that "Gnostic beliefs"[10] were *not* deviant but were simply other forms of "Christianities,"[11] the evidence below shows otherwise.

Allegations of different forms of Christianities appear in Dan Brown's *The Da Vinci Code* novel, which mixes facts with fiction.

Brown's character, Leigh Teabing, charged the early church of conspiracy by suppressing "more than *eighty* gospels" and choosing the four NT Gospels (Matthew, Mark, Luke, and John).[12] This is wrong and misleads people to think that other late books ought to have been considered on an equal par with those in the NT as if there were "alternative" or competing "views of Christianity."[13] This appears to be the thought behind the *JFT* book and the *LJT* documentary since they are validating their arguments from three different Gnostic works (the Acts of Philip, the Gospel of Philip, and the Gospel of Mary).

First, *The Nag Hammadi Library*, third revised edition published in 1990, clearly shows that of the forty-five Gnostic books (discovered in 1945 by Muhammed Ali in a desert cave located in Nag Hammadi, Egypt) only five of them are named gospels: *Truth, Thomas, Philip, Egyptians*, and *Mary*, not sixty, seventy, or eighty.[14] In addition, though 1 Corinthians 15; 1 Timothy 1:3–7, 20; 2 Timothy 2:17–18, and 1 John may seem to argue for a fully developed form of Gnosticism, they do not. As Darrell L. Bock explains, "What these epistles describe as a different doctrine many regard as potentially similar to things that appear in even more detail in some of the newly discovered works that have been called Gnostic.... In other words, these remarks do not evidence the presence of Gnosticism, but the presence of elements that showed up later in Gnosticism. At best, they reflect what has been called *incipient Gnosticism*."[15] That is, these biblical passages contain traits in seed form of what later (mid to late A.D. second century) became full-blown Gnosticism. Thus the earliest "unambiguous" support of Gnosticism "by means of quotations by non-gnostic authors of the original documents begins, at the earliest, at the start of the second century CE [=Common Era or A.D.]."[16] This means there were no other forms of Christianities competing in the first century other than apostles correcting errors and misunderstandings arising within Christian churches.

Only until the late second, third, fourth, and fifth centuries did many church fathers' writings like these of Irenaeus (A.D. 130–200), Hippolytus (A.D. 170–236), Tertullian (A.D. 160–220), and Epiphanius (A.D. 310–403) describe and condemn the belief of this group[17] called "Gnostics."[18] Hence Bock concludes, "So elements of these doctrines taught in these writings, are not as 'secret' as some currently seeking to dramatize their nature have suggested. The views of such groups have been known for well over a millennium. They are 'ancient' history." Instead what is now "new" is that we no longer have to learn of the Gnostics from their critics, but they can now speak for themselves through their writings.[19]

Furthermore "almost all scholars" acknowledge that the Gnostic "gospels" were written in the second to fifth centuries A.D.[20] Besides Gnostic works being too late to classify as a credible firsthand account, they are also "pseudonymous" documents (falsely attributing a name to a document belonging to another in order to get wide acceptance).[21] Thus other than showing us what Gnostics themselves believed, how early Christians related to them, and their "value for us as historical documents," they are so far removed from the first century and so radically different from apostolic doctrines that they teach us nothing in regard to Christianity.[22] Nevertheless this has not stopped the *JFT* and *LTJ* advocates in espousing their views that Jesus and Mary Magdalene were married, based on three Gnostic books.

The Gospel of Philip's Reference to Mary

Did *The Gospel of Philip* teach that Mary Magdalene was Jesus' "spouse" as Brown (and others) claims, and did Jesus kiss her on the "mouth" as both Brown and the *JFT* advocates believe?[23] Perhaps the best of all passages suggesting Jesus was Mary Magdalene's husband appears in *The Gospel of Philip* 63:32–64:10:[24]

> As for the Wisdom who is called "the barren," she is the mother [of the] angels. And the companion of the [...] Mary Magdalene. [... loved] her more than [all] the disciples [and used to] kiss her [often] on her [...]. The rest of [the disciples ...]. They said to him, "Why do you love her more than all of us?" The savior answered and said to them, "Why do I not love you like her? When a blind man and one who sees are both together in darkness, they are

no different from one another. When the light comes, then he who sees will see the light, and he who is blind will remain in darkness."[25]

Does the text above prove that Mary Magdalene was Jesus' "spouse"? Did Jesus kiss Mary on the "mouth" or elsewhere? Even if Jesus kissed her on the mouth, does that imply sexual intimacy?

Unfortunately since there are breaks in the texts, specially where part of the debate focuses, we have to either supply words in the brackets, or where dots appear in the brackets the context and size of the break will determine the best suggested reading. Locating the words where breaks in the texts appear is not that difficult in most cases. For example, Daniel gr...ed his glove a.. .at and drove to the p..k to pl.. b... with .is fr....s.[26]

The transliterated Greek word *koinōnos* is a borrowed term employed by the Coptic language that translates "companion."[27] Though the term *koinōnos* can refer to a close relationship between two people (friends, cousins, spiritual sister, or even a wife), the usual Greek word for "wife" is *gynē*.[28] Hence Witherington correctly concludes, "The important thing is that it is not a technical term for 'spouse'; something else in the context would have to suggest marriage for it to mean such a thing in this text, and there is no such clue—not even in the larger context." In fact, "This text is in a highly ascetical document. It is hardly likely that the author would want to suggest or even hint that Jesus was married."[29]

Furthermore Harvard professor Karen King, in *The Gospel of Mary of Magdala*, favors the meaning of Mary being kissed on the mouth in the *Gospel of Philip* 63:32–33 because of the parallel context in sections 58–59, though she sees the latter as a spiritual fellowship kiss.[30] However, the mention of the word "mouth" appears three times in sections 58–59 without an explicit "locale of the kiss." Bock notes this but, unlike King, he links both passages in *The Gospel of Philip* 63:32-33 and 58–59 and says, "If the kiss of *Philip* 63 is similar to the kiss of *Philip* 58–59, then the reference likely is to a kiss of fellowship. If so, this kiss may be on the cheek and not on the mouth. King does suggest (correctly in my view) that the imagery is about Mary being associated with Wisdom and that this *spiritual* connection stands behind the reference. She probably does this because these kinds of texts often carry a symbolic or spiritual sense over a more literal one, as scholars often note. Even if the reference is to a kiss on the mouth, the basis for the text pointing to something primarily sexual does not exist. The reference merely pictures a tender, spiritual fellowship."[31] Hence King concludes, "The *Gospel of Philip* again offers literal images—kissing and jealousy—in order to interpret them spiritually. Kissing here apparently refers to the intimate reception of spiritual teaching, for ... the Lord suggests that the male disciples should seek to be loved by him in the same way."[32]

Similarly Witherington says, "Indeed the context suggests it was a spiritual relationship.... The so-called holy kiss referred to in Paul's own letters (see the end of 1 Corinthians 16) is in all likelihood meant here."[33] Furthermore, "The kissing referred to was a strange ritual that was believed to convey esoteric knowledge from one person to another. A form of holy kissing, it has nothing to do with romance."[34]

Like Bock, Craig A. Evans suggests the unlikelihood of such a kiss being on the mouth with sexual connotations. He denies that Mary was Jesus' spouse. "Some translations restore the text to read, 'he used to kiss her often on her mouth,' but that is pure conjecture. The author of this text may have imagined that Jesus kissed Mary often on the hand, forehead or cheek. We don't know what the original text said, and in any case there is no warrant for assuming from these passages in the *Gospel of Mary* and the *Gospel of Philip* that Jesus and Mary were lovers. The texts do *not* say this. There is no evidence from antiquity that anyone thought this."[35]

One should immediately be suspicious of an interpretation that promotes marital intercourse or a sexually motivated kiss from a book (or movement) that condemns sexual behavior of any form as defiling (81:34–82:19).[36] Wesley W. Isenberg, the translator of this late third-century A.D. Coptic text, makes this observation: "'Defiled women' are all women who participate in sexual intercourse, i.e., in 'the marriage of defilement,' which is fleshly and lustful."[37] Others have also seen this. Witherington says, "The Gnostics believed that, since creation is a fallen enterprise from the outset, normal human forms of relating, such as marriage and intercourse, are seen as inherently defiling, as the Gospel of Philip makes evident."[38] Bock observes, "If a kiss on the mouth is described, something unusual is indicated. The kiss does point to a level of intimacy between Jesus and Mary, but it probably represents a spiritual closeness as spiritual counterparts in the birth of creation that is associated with wisdom. It is far less likely that something sexual is in view or that their marital status is being addressed."[39]

We can safely deduce two things. The word "companion" is not the common word used for "spouse." Therefore it is highly improbable that this refers to Mary Magdalene being married to Jesus. Furthermore, according to *The Gospel of Philip* 63:32-33, Jesus kissed Mary Magdalene, but where He kissed her no one knows. His kiss, certainly, did not have any sexual connotation since the Gnostics saw any type of sexual expression as degrading. The reality is that *The Gospel of Philip* says nothing about Jesus kissing Mary Magdalene on the mouth or that she was Jesus' wife. Also there is not a shred of evidence from internal or external biblical sources that Jesus of Nazareth was ever married to anyone. On this issue, remarkably, almost all liberal and conservative scholars agree.[40]

The Acts of Philip's Reference to Mariamne

Jacobovici wrote, "From the beginning, we focused on this particular ossuary because it seemed to be the key to the whole story. Everything depended on this unique artifact." James Cameron confirms this on *The Today Show*, February 26, 2007, how interpreting the *Mariamne* inscription with the name found in *The Acts of Philip* became the discovered missing piece to the puzzle that allowed them to put it together.[41] Consequently they believe that "The Acts of Philip provides us with a much more complete version of Mary Magdalene than the Gospels."[42] To further strengthen their case they claim scholars believe that Mary Magdalene's real name was Mariamne.

What do we know about *The Acts of Philip* where the alleged name *Mariamne* appears? Who and what are the scholars claiming about the *Acts of Philip*, Mary Magdalene, and Mariamne? Does *The Acts of Philip* prove *Mariamne* refers to Mary Magdalene of the NT Gospels? Could there be better renderings of the inscription *Mariamne* other than that presented by the book and documentary?

The Acts of Philip. In 1974 François Bovon and Bertrand Bouvier were allowed to examine manuscripts of the library at the Xenophontos Monastery (founded in the tenth century) on Mount Athos in Greece. Incredibly Bovon discovered a pristine copy of a fourteenth-century nearly complete text of the "Acts of Philip" perhaps recorded from a fourth-century original. *The Acts of Philip* divides into fifteen acts much like *The Gospel of Thomas*.[43]

The *Harvard University Gazette* reports that Bovon, Bouvier, and Frédéric Amsler (a former Geneva doctoral student and assistant of Bovon) published in 1996 a French translation of *The Acts of Philip*. In 1999 the same three scholars published "a critical edition of the Greek text in the series *Corpus Christianorum*." In the same "collection," Amsler followed by publishing his dissertation that entailed a commentary on *The Acts of Philip*.[44]

Like all other Gnostic works shown above *The Acts of Philip* contains elements aberrant from traditional first-century Christianity. A number of bizarre things appear, such as talking leopards, goats, slaying of dragons (8:97), marital sex being condemned, water replacing wine for the Lord's Supper, and much more.[45]

Although we await an English translation of the complete *Acts of Philip*, critical portions in English already appear in numerous websites, specially the reference mentioned by the *JFT* book (8:94–95), which it is not *fully* cited by them.[46] Citing the entire reference in context would have avoided much confusion and identified the figure in question, which may not have been conducive to their argument.

The *JFT* book claims that "leading Mary Magdalene experts have concluded that the woman known in the Gospels as Mary Magdalene was actually called by the Greek version of her name: 'Mariamme,' [Mariamene, or Mariamne]."[47] James Tabor is one of the scholars who believe that Origen (185–254?) refers to Mary Magdalene by the name "Mariamme," as well as "the writer Epiphanus and noncanonical texts such as the *Pistis Sophia*. But the clincher is the Acts of Philip."[48]

Before looking at *The Acts of Philip* carefully, let us deviate for a moment (so as to leave no rocks unturned) to see whether these other references Tabor mentions identify *Mariamne* as the NT Mary Magdalene. As usually done by the *JFT* advocates, they cite no references or complete context to prove their point. The noted *Thesaurus Linguae Graece* containing almost the entire ancient and classical Greek works cites the Greek text in Origen's *Contra Celsum* 5.62.14–17, which is translated here:

> Celsus, on the one hand, certainly knows Marcellians also from Marcellinas, and Harpocratians from Salome, others whose names stems from **Mariammes**, and others from **Martha**. However, we are the ones according to our ability that not only love to learn the Word and know how to discern differences within them, but as much as was in our power we searched the truths of the philosophers but at any point did we associated with these groups.[49]

A careful reading of the Greek text shows how the transliterated *Mariammēs* (Μαριάμμης) does not read *Mariamnē* (Μαριάμνη),[50] allegedly the common Gnostic spelling of Mary Magdalene.[51] Exceptions do exist, however. Some manuscripts spell the common Gnostic name *Mariamnē* (Μαριάμνη) as *Mariammē* (Μαριάμμη).[52] Whether this is the case here is questionable since this is not even the exact same spelling, and this is an exception rather than the rule. Given that the name "Martha" immediately follows *Mariammes*, it makes more sense to identify these women as Lazarus's sisters (John 11:1).[53] Even if one sees the merging of Mary of Bethany, Martha's sister, with Mary Magdalene as a possible phenomenon occurring here as in *The Gospel of* Mary and *The Acts of Philip*, it shows nothing in regard to the historical Mary Magdalene who saw the risen Jesus, since Gnostic literature uses this figure to promote their view.[54] Furthermore it is impossible to determine whether Origen referred to Mary Magdalene. This is purely conjecture on the part of anyone making such a claim. It seems that if the entire context was cited, the reader would have obviously seen the weakness of their case, which may be the reason they neither referenced it nor cited it.[55]

Importantly, undisclosed by the *JFT* book is Tabor's position about Mary Magdalene's relationship to Jesus. "*The Jesus Dynasty* has no connection to recently popularized notions that Jesus married and fathered children through Mary Magdalene. While gripping fiction, this idea is long on speculation and short on evidence."[56] This is why no references are made by Tabor in the *JFT* book or *LTJ* documentary about Jesus' marriage to Mary Magdalene. It appears that he originally, like Bovon, as we will see below, makes a "literary" not a "historical" connection with Mary Magdalene and the Gnostics. Therefore the Gnostic connection to *Mariamnē* as Mary Magdalene functions as a literary reference and *not* a historical reference to Mary Magdalene of the NT Gospels.

Another search was conducted on the *Thesaurus Linguae Graece* to investigate the context where Epiphanius allegedly references Mary Magdalene by the name *Mariamnē*. But nothing appeared other than a loose connection similar to that in Origen's statement. Rather, the work various scholars reference is Epiphanius's *Against Heresies* (technically known as *Panarion*), dated around A.D. 375.[57] A closer look at that text also reveals inadequate connections. Even those linking it admit the ambiguity. "It is not altogether clear which Mary Epiphanius or the author of the *Questions of Mary* have in mind while writing the text. The fact that just a bit earlier Epiphanius had mentioned the mother of Jesus and called her the 'ever-virgin Mary'" (*Pan.* 26.7.5).[58] Nothing in this text points to the historical Mary Magdalene of the New Testament.

Tabor also mentions *Pistis Sophia*, but again he does not cite the text in the *JFT* book. Numerous texts could be cited but let us take that of 1.17-18:

> And Jesus, the compassionate, answered and said unto Mary: "Mary, thou blessed one, whom I will perfect in all

mysteries of those of the height, discourse in openness, thou, whose heart is raised to the kingdom of heaven more than all thy brethren." Then said Mary to the Saviour: "My Lord, the word which thou hast spoken unto us: 'Who hath ears to hear, let him hear,' thou sayest in order that we may understand the word thou hast spoken. Hearken, therefore, my Lord, that I may discourse in openness.'"[59]

Reading this quotation (and others within *Pistis Sophia*)[60] one can see how it has little to do with the historical Mary Magdalene and even less that she was Jesus' spouse. Besides, the identity of Mary Magdalene in this Gnostic book has not been conclusively established and continues to be a highly debatable topic. Here, as in other places, she argues with the apostles because she receives revelation from Jesus. The dialogue between Mary and Jesus focuses on validating her prominence in receiving revelation.[61] Consequently this validates esoteric revelation that promotes Gnosticism above traditional Christianity. Bock's comment on *The Gospel of Mary* and *The Gospel of Philip* clarifies the common stock genre used by the Gnostics to promote their agenda. "The claim is that she did receive revelation from God, even though Peter (read orthodoxy) could not believe it.... It confirms that the real fight was about who receives revelation from God and who can speak to what Christianity is."[62] Karen King also sees this common tension that existed between Gnosticism and traditional Christianity. Peter and Andrew, representative of the orthodox position, resist claims to receive revelation by Mary Magdalene, the patron saint of Gnosticism, who receives revelation and speaks for genuine Christianity.[63]

Most Gnostic scholars agree that Gnostic literature highly regards Mary Magdalene through which they channel much of their propaganda.[64] Yet their literature contains too many aberrant ideas from Judeo-Christian belief and this "Mary" appears one hundred to four hundred years too late to have any connection with the historical Mary Magdalene of the Gospels.[65]

Now we come to the reputable scholar, Harvard professor François Bovon. The *JFT* book and the *LTJ* documentary refer to him in validating the *Mariamne* inscription (80.500) as Mary Magdalene in *The Acts of Philip*. Bovon's dialogue with Jacobovici goes as follows: "'*This* Mary Magdalene,' Bovon told Simcha, 'this Mary from the Acts of Philip, is clearly the equal of the other apostles—and, as depicted, is even more enlightened.'… 'To be clear,' said Bovon, 'in the Acts of Philip the first Mary—Magdalene—is called Mariamne.'"[66] From Bovon's words Jacobovici extrapolates as follows. "It seems that the Acts of Philip are a window on early Christian belief, and on the meaning of the IAA 80/500–509 inscriptions." Elsewhere he said, "*And if this Mary of number 80/500 was supposed to be Magdalene, then what? Were 80/500 and 80/503—this Greek-inscribed 'Mary' and 'Jesus, son of Joseph'—married? And if these two were married, then was 'Judah' their son?*"[67] But is this Bovon's meaning, and does he refer to the Gnostic figure *Mariamne* as the historical first-century Mary Magdalene of the NT Gospels? After the *LTJ* documentary aired and Bovon saw how his comments were used, he immediately responded as follows:

> First, I have now seen the program and am not convinced of its main thesis. When I was questioned by Simcha Jacobovici and his team the questions were directed toward the Acts of Philip and the role of Mariamne in this text. I was not informed of the whole program and the orientation of the script.
>
> Second, having watched the film, in listening to it, I hear two voices, a kind of double discours [sic]. On one hand there is the wish to open a scholarly discussion; on the other there is the wish to push a personal agenda. I must say that the reconstruction of Jesus' marriage with Mary Magdalene and the birth of a child belong for me to science fiction.
>
> Third, to be more credible, the program should deal with the very ancient tradition of the Holy Sepulcher,

since the emperor Constantine in the fourth century C.E. built this monument on the spot at which the emperor Hadrian in the second century C.E. erected the forum of Aelia Capitolina and built on it a temple to Aphrodite at the place where Jesus' tomb was venerated.

Fourth, I do not believe that Mariamne is the real name of Mary Magdalene. Mariamne is, besides Maria or Mariam, a possible Greek equivalent, attested by Josephus, Origen, and the Acts of Philip, for the Semitic Myriam.

Fifth, the Mariamne of the Acts of Philip is part of the apostolic team with Philip and Bartholomew; she teaches and baptizes. In the beginning, her faith is stronger than Philip's faith. This portrayal of Mariamne fits very well with the portrayal of Mary of Magdala in the Manichean Psalms, the Gospel of Mary, and Pistis Sophia. My interest is not historical, but on the level of literary traditions. I have suggested this identification in 1984 already in an article of the NT Studies.[68]

Not wanting to be misunderstood, Bovon clarified that the fourth-century *Acts of Philip* might have represented Mary Magdalene by the name *Mariamne* as a *literary* rather than a *historical* real figure.

In a personal email to me, Bovon conveyed graciously how the documentary crew was "kind" to him and believed "they did not abuse" his "words." However, immediately he added, "but my presence as well as the presence of Frank Cross gave an air of serious scholarship to the documentary." Obviously the documentary wanted credibility but having "an *air* of serious scholarship" is not the same as "having serious scholarship." Though *JFT* advocates did not technically abuse the words of both of these scholars, they did misuse the *intent of the meaning of Bovon's words*. Since Bovon specifically said to them he "was interested in texts not in historical proofs,"[69] it is very deceptive to use Bovon's statements as if he was interested in connecting historically the *Mariamne* inscription with that of Mary

Magdalene of the New Testament.[70] Why did the *JFT* advocates not clarify Bovon's intended meaning that it was not "historical proofs" that caused him to study the *Mariamne* inscription but instead how it is used in Gnostic literature?

Not only has Bovon's letter exposed the *JFT* advocates' "wish to push a personal agenda," but interpreting Mariamne as Mary Magdalene in *The Acts of Philip* at any level, is highly debatable.[71]

> But what most people don't know is that there is debate about who Mariamne is in the Acts of Philip. Since Mariamne is simply another name for Mary, does it refer to Mary the mother of Jesus, Mary of Bethany, or Mary Magdalene? Most of the scholars who have studied this book don't believe Mariamne refers to Mary Magdalene because according to the gospel of John, Philip is from Bethsaida (John 1:43–46), a place east of the Jordan near where it empties into Lake Gennesaret. The Gospels never mention that Philip has a sister named Mariamne (let alone that this woman is to be identified with Mary Magdalene). The city of Magdala or, better, Migdal (the hometown of Mary Magdalene) is located on the shore of the Sea of Galilee to the north of Tiberias and is a few kilometers away from Bethsaida....
>
> Moreover, there is a serious question as to whether a fourth-century work, one of the later extrabiblical texts, can tell us anything about Mary and Jesus. This work is too far removed in time, in a loosely grounded appeal to events tied to Jesus, to be able to be trusted for information about Jesus. Interestingly, often the same people who raised questions about the first-century sources about Jesus are nonetheless open to accepting fourth-century sources about him.[72]

Hence the book had a good reason for not quoting the entire text of *The Acts of Philip* 8:94:

> It came to pass when the Saviour divided the apostles and each went forth according to his lot, that it fell to Philip to go to the country of the Greeks: and he thought it hard, and wept. And **Mariamne** his sister (it was she that made ready the bread and salt at the breaking of bread, but **Martha** was she that ministered to the multitudes and laboured much) seeing it, went to Jesus and said: Lord, seest thou not how my brother is vexed?[73]

A cursory reading of the text will clearly reveal that since Martha immediately appears in the same sentence as Mariamne, this Mary more likely refers more to Mary, Martha's sister, mentioned in John 11, than to Mary Magdalene.[74]

Even if one were to believe that Mary of Bethany and Mary Magdalene are the same person as a possible Gnostic phenomenon in *The Acts of Philip*, nothing here identifies *Mariamne* as the historical Mary Magdalene since Gnostic literature uses this figure to promote their agenda and not to refer to her as a real person.[75]

The Gospel of Mary

Does the *The Gospel of Mary* show evidence of sexual intimacy between Jesus and Mary Magdalene? The *JFT* advocates as well as Brown's *The Da Vinci Code* insinuate from *The Gospel of Mary* that Jesus and Mary Magdalene were perhaps lovers.[76] The text under consideration refers to Peter appearing jealous of Mary after receiving a revelation from the spiritually risen Jesus and questioning the genuineness of it. He then challenges her to tell the rest of the apostles, which dialogue ends by Peter being rebuked by Levi. Here is what the document says:

> Peter said to Mary, "Sister, we know that the Savior *loved you more than the rest of women*. Tell us the words of the Savior which you remember—which you know (but) we do not, nor have we heard them." [Mary tells them, but most of the leaves in the mss describing the revelation are missing]....

> When Mary had said this, she fell silent, since it was to this point that the Savior had spoken with her…. Peter answered and spoke concerning these same things. He questioned them about the Savior: "Did he really speak with a woman without our knowledge (and) not openly? Are we to turn about and all listen to her? *Did he prefer her to us?*"
>
> Then Mary wept and said to Peter, 'My brother Peter, what do you think? Do you think that I thought this up myself in my heart, or that I am lying about the Savior?" Levi answered and said to Peter, "Peter, you have always been hot-tempered. Now I see you contending against the woman like the adversaries. But if the Savior made her worthy, who are you indeed to reject her? Surely the Savior knows her very well. That is why he loved her more than us.[77]

While the italicized words above may seem to indicate a special sexual intimacy between Jesus and Mary Magdalene, nothing can be further from the truth. In fact three things must be noted before interpreting the text.

First, Harvard professor Karen King classifies the text above as belonging to a type of "genre of the gnostic dialogue" also found in *The Gospel of Thomas*, *Pistis Sophia*, and *The Gospel of the Egyptians*, where Peter and Mary Magdalene's confrontation appears. Thus this belongs to a common stock of propaganda literature that promotes Gnostic doctrine against traditional Christian views of the day.

Second, King correctly explains the tensions that existed between Gnosticism and traditional "second-century Christianity" and what Gnostics promoted. "Peter and Andrew represent orthodox positions that deny the validity of esoteric revelation and reject the authority of women to teach. The Gospel of Mary attacks both of these positions head-on through its portrayal of Mary Magdalene. She is the Savior's beloved, possessed of knowledge and teaching superior to that of the public apostolic tradition. Her superiority is based on vision and private revelation and is demonstrated in her capacity to strengthen the wavering disciples and turn them toward the Good."[78]

Third, as noted before by Bock, "these extrabiblical texts are more symbolic than historical."[79] Keeping this in mind helps the interpreter understand the point of the text. Since Gnosticism glorified the spirit against the flesh (body), sexual intimacy involving the body was very unpopular among them. Hence one should not assume this meaning in passages where Jesus appears favoring Mary Magdalene either by kissing her or revealing something to her.

> The conflict portrayed between Peter and Mary pictures the conflict in the early church. Peter, who represented the forces of orthodoxy, refused to accept that God could work with another group, apart from him (that is, believers who accepted secret knowledge). Mary in her role as the "underdog" female represented those who accepted secret knowledge. In fact, this description may well acknowledge that this Gnostic group was in the minority or that the group lacked persuasive power. The claim is that she did receive revelation from God, even though Peter (read orthodoxy) could not believe it. This gospel ends with Mary affirmed and Peter rebuked.
>
> What is important to understand about this reading of the *Gospel of Mary* is that the story is not about Peter and Mary at all or about gender roles. They symbolize the dispute over revelation…. It confirms that the real fight was about who receives revelation from God and who can speak to what Christianity is.[80]

Thus this gospel reflects nothing historical about Mary Magdalene or Jesus. Hence Evans concludes, "The *Gospel of Mary* may well reflect struggles over church polity, the role of women, the issue of legalism in one form or another, and the limits of apostolic authority. But this writing, however it is to be understood, reflects a setting no earlier than the middle of the second century. We find in it nothing that with confidence can be traced to the first century or traced back to the life and ministry of the historical Jesus and the historical Mary Magdalene."[81]

In conclusion, we have seen how *The Gospel of Philip*, *The Acts of Philip*, *The Gospel of Mary*, and other related texts do not prove that the *Mariamnē* inscription refers to Mary Magdalene of the New Testament. Furthermore, we have even assumed for the sake of argument that the *JFT* book and *LTJ* documentary of the Talpiot inscription correctly reads *Mariamnē*. But if it does not, the problems become even more insurmountable as the following shows.

The Talpiot Ossuary (80.500) Inscription

Rahmani documents all the details of the *Mariamenou (e) Mara* inscription (701–80.500) in his catalogue of the state of Israel (IAA).[82] We will discuss Rahmani's interpretation of this inscription in the next section, but here is the inscription as it appears.[83]

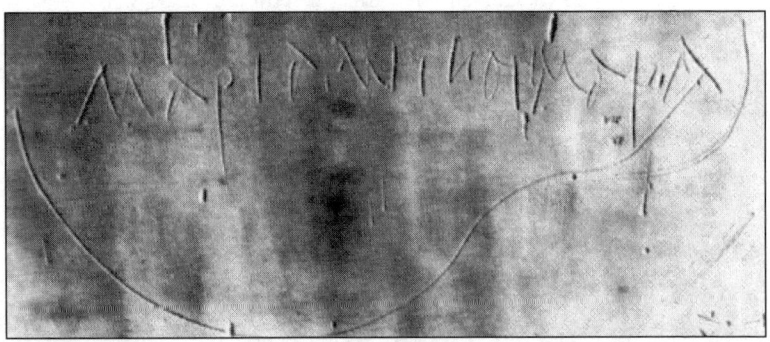

As noted earlier, the *JFT* and *LTJ* advocates interpreted part of the inscription *Mariamne* as a Greek name meaning "Mary Magdalene" (which meaning they defend from Gnostic literature) and the second part *Mara* as "a Greek rendering of an Aramaic word meaning 'Lord' or 'Master'" that was "preceded by a Greek symbol" "*e*" understood "also known as." They cite Tal Ilan, a "specialist" on Jewish names, who says *Mara* "means 'lord, master' in Aramaic…. This is one of the rare cases of a name serving for both males and females."[84] Thus they are reading the inscription as "Mariam or Mary (of Magdala) also known as Master or Lord." Tabor indicates that the inscription could read: "(This is the ossuary) of Mariamne, also known as the Master."[85] Thus Jacobovici concludes from the meaning of *Mara* in Aramaic (though written here using Greek letters) as "Master" and the evidence from how Gnostic literature uses *Mariamne* that this refers to Mary Magdalene.[86]

While the Hebrew inscription מרה (*mara*) meaning "Master" appears in two ossuaries (nos. 8 and 327), another ossuary appears inscribed in Hebrew on one side with a further description of the names of those interred in it along with a translation of the Hebrew word for Master in Greek κύριος (*kyrios*) as well.[87] However, what is not found is a single inscription containing a Hebrew and Greek transliteration of a Hebrew name, or a single inscription written half in Hebrew and the other half in Greek. In fact, Rahmani says, "Honorific titles and expressions [like that of 'elder' and 'master'] are very rare." This also applies to vocations like that of priests, or even teacher, as Rahmani also notes. "Professions are rarely mentioned."[88]

We have already seen that the *Mariamnē* inscription of Gnostic literature noted by the *JFT* and *LTJ* advocates has nothing to do with that of the NT Mary Magdalene. Yet what about the reading of this inscription? We know there are inscribed ossuaries with Greek or Hebrew names but not a single inscription with both a Greek and an Aramaic name? Could their rendering be correct, or could there be better options undisclosed by the book and documentary?

Other Renderings of the Inscription

The *JFT* and *LTJ* advocates render the inscription as "Mariamne also known as Mara [Lord/Master]." But it may be interpreted in two better ways.

ΜΑΡΙΑΜΕΝΟΥ ΜΑΡΑ (*Mariamenou Mara*). Documenting all of the details pertaining to ossuary 701–80.500, Rahmani reads the inscription as *Mariamenou (e) Mara*, which means "Mariamene, who is (also called) Mara" (i.e., Mariam who is also called Martha).[89] Two years later Amos Kloner in his 1996 *Atiquot* article on the Talpiot tomb also took the same reading.[90]

This view interprets *Mariamenou* as a grammatical genitive declension of the form *Mariamenon*, a diminutive of the name

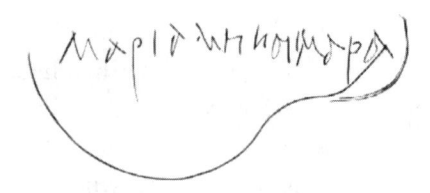

Mariamene, which is, one of many variant forms of the name *Mariam* or *Mariame*. This form was further contracted to *Mariamne*. Basically these are all different ways of saying the name "Maria" or "Mary."

Rahmani understands the second name *(e) Mara* as a contraction of Martha and a further description of the first name.[91] The "*e*" between the names *Mariamenou* and *Mara* also appears in the Bet She'arim inscriptions standing for the formula *os kai* (perhaps translated "who is also called") that was sometimes omitted.[92] A person can be referred to by another name or a title. For example, the Babylonian Talmud (TB) *Pesaḥim* (113b-114a) mentions a person named Judah, nicknamed "lion's whelp" (*gūr 'aryē* from Gen. 49:9), who is also known as *Aqavya*. In the same passage a person named *Aḥa* is also called *Pinḥas*. Similarly in a previous tractate TB *Gittin* (34b) mentions a women who had two names Miriam and Sarah, which may be similar to "Miriam Johanna."[93] This phenomenon also appears in a number of ossuaries documented by Rahmani (e.g., all of these refer to the same person "Sorra=Aristobola," "Alexa=Mara," and "Yehudan=Yason").[94]

Using two names or titles of the same person was not only fairly common in Talmudic materials and ossuaries but also in the Bible. Simon is called Peter (Matt. 4:18). Brothers James and John were also given the names Boanerges, which means "Sons of Thunder" (Mark 3:17). The disciple Thomas was also called "the Twin" (John 11:16). Therefore the evidence seems to favor Rahmani's reading of the inscription *Mariamenou (e) Mara* as "Maria who is also known as Martha."[95]

In a personal email to me, François Bovon appears to take a view similar to that of Rahmani and Kloner. "That the name Mariamne is present on one of the ossuaries is not surprising. I do not believe that one should read that she was a *mar* (a change from Greek to Aramaic in the same sentence would be strange, and the name *mar* means more Lord than teacher). I suspect the end of the inscription to offer an alternative name: *Mariamne* or *Mar* (or something similar)."[96] That is, he believes the inscription could perhaps read, "Mariam *could also be known as* Martha." On further investigation, however, he views another interpretive option. "I would add that another solution would be Mariamne and Martha (two names of the two different persons)."[97]

ΜΑΡΙΑΜΗ ΚΑΙ ΜΑΡΑ (*Mariame and Mara*). An even better reading of the inscription may indicate that perhaps there are two names belonging to two women buried in one ossuary with the inscription as "Mariam and Martha."

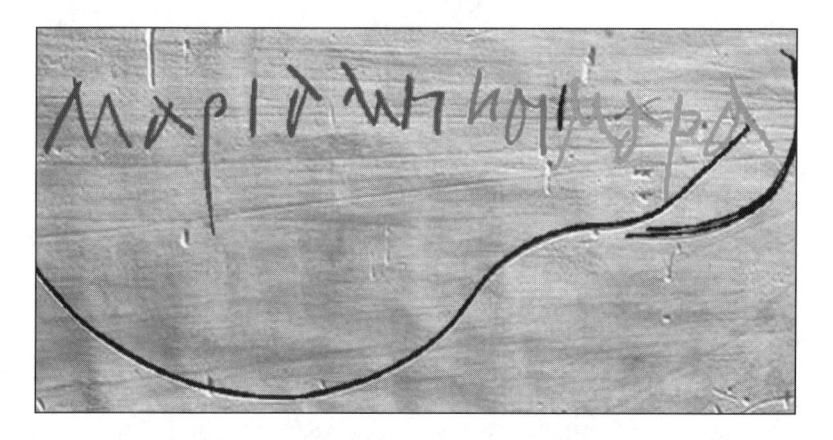

Stephen J. Pfann, president of the University of the Holy Land, in an article analyzes this inscription very carefully and notes word by word each nuance without a problem until the last words of the inscription beginning with the allegedly letter "N" (in middle gray above). Rahmani (and others) see the first letter as an "N." Yet the only way to read this letter as "N" is to read it backwards (or "retrograde") which raises doubts about its validity.[98] Of all "ossuaries inscribed in Greek listed in Rahmani's Catalogue and numerous ossuaries from Dominus Flevit (on the west slope of the Mt. of Olives), there are no cases in which it has been suggested that an 'N' has been written in this way. Furthermore, the following two letters (in middle gray above) do not resemble the combination 'OU,' as proposed in Rahmani's original publication."[99] The inscription shows, as Pfann also observed, that there is a gap between the last word in darkest gray and the first word in middle gray, indicating these are two separate words. Hence on closer inspection it is better to view the inscriber as having written in cursive form "KAI" (=and) instead of "NOU" (as in Mariame<u>nou</u>) which would strangely necessitate the writer changing his "handwriting style in mid-sentence."[100] Pfann provides various inscriptions where the KAI appears in cursive, similar to what he is suggesting:

We can also detect evidence of two different forms of handwritings. This may point to two different inscribers who perhaps wrote at different times. As Pfann explains, "The overall appearance of cursive writing is that there is a graceful sequence of looping strokes as can be seen in KAI MARA. This stands in contrast to the triangular, squared and rather jagged succession of strokes of the more formal script used by the first scribe while inscribing MARIAME." Each of the cursive "A's" in "KAI" is similar to that of "MARA" (in the lightest gray above).[101] Even the Greek letter "R" (pronounced *rho*) which resembles the letter "P" in the inscription MARA, was inscribed differently than the "P" in MARIA by having a longer stroke at the top end.

If two inscribers were in fact at work at different times, why would someone gather a person's bones and not complete the inscription until days, months, or years later? Most likely this family ossuary was later reopened to deposit the bones of another relative, which is when it was inscribed with KAI MARA (and Martha). As noted by Pfann, Rahmani, Ilan, and others, the name MARA "was a common form of the Aramaic name 'Martha.'"[102] Therefore it was customary to have two or more individuals with these common names in ossuaries.[103] Hence in the dig at *Dominus Flevit* one finds an ossuary containing both of these names (written three times in the same ossuary):[104]

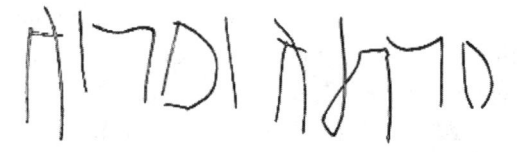

[Hebrew/Aramaic inscription]

Martha and Maria order reversed

Thus there is nothing unique about finding both of these names in one ossuary. Based on customary second burial practices of the period Kloner believes there were thirty-five to forty bodies buried in the Talpiot tomb. According to the average figure, ten ossuaries would contain the bones of seventeen individuals (i.e., 1.7 per ossuary), and eighteen individuals outside of the ossuaries.[105] Therefore assuming Kloner's calculation, one would expect to find ossuaries with even more than two individuals. For example, at the Dominus Flevit site an ossuary was found that contained at one time the bones of five individuals with their names inscribed outside: Zacharias, Mariame, El'azar, Simon, and Sheniit (?).

[Greek inscription: ΖΑΧΑΡΙΟΥ / ΜΑΡΙΑΜΗ / ΕΛΝΑΖΟΥ / ϹΙΜΩΝ / ΝΟϹ]

According to Pfann, an analysis of the inscription shows different people inscribed this ossuary using "distinct instruments." Thus "There may be the skeletal and DNA remains of at least five individuals in this

– 75 –

box (not accounting for others who went unnamed)."[106] All these details strongly indicate that the inscription on ossuary 80.500 refers to two women named "Mariam and Martha."

In conclusion, no spelling of the name *Mariamene* appears anywhere in the NT period, nor does this spelling along with that of *Mariamne* appear in the NT either. The names *Mariamne*, *Miriam* or the Latin form *Maria* are all different forms of the same name. Hence to spell the ossuary inscription 80.500 as *Mariamene* is erroneous.[107] However, whatever one's preference may be, one of these two options promotes a much better reading of the inscription 80.500 than that of the *JFT* book and *LTJ* documentary. The inscription on ossuary 80.500 rendered by Rahmani *Mariamenou (e) Mara* may read "Maria who is also known as Martha," or as Pfann suggests *Mariame and Mara* may refer to two women named "Mariam and Martha."

Mary Magdalene's Link to Jesus (Other places)

According to the NT and the church tradition, who is the real Mary Magdalene?

New Testament. We begin by noting that the name *Mariamnē* never appears in the NT.[108] Mary is the contemporary name for the Jewish form of the name Miriam.[109] This was the most popular name among ten common female names at that time.[110] In fact five individuals in the NT are named Mary: (1) Mary, the wife of Joseph and mother of Jesus (Matt. 1:18; 13:55; Luke 1:30–31); (2) Mary from Bethany (John 11:1); (3) Mary, Clopas' wife (John 19:25); (4) Mary the mother of James who was not Jesus' brother (Matt. 27:56); (5) Mary from Magdala (Luke 8:2).

Several facts may be noted about this list. In that culture females were identified by their city of origin, or the name of their families, or with males. The latter two are more dominant and it seems that when no males or families were in view the women were identified by their hometown. Thus if Mary Magdalene was married to Jesus, she most likely would have been called "Mary the wife of Jesus" somewhere in the NT or church tradition, since this was a male-dominated culture. But no such evidence exist.[111]

Mary Magdalene is mentioned in twelve passages in the NT (Matt. 27:56, 61; 28:1; Mark 15:40, 47; 16:1, 9; Luke 8:2; 24:10; John 19:25; 20:1, 18). Four facts may be noted about her.[112]

First, Jesus cast seven demons from Mary Magdalene. She appears to be one a number of ladies following Jesus who supported Him financially (Luke 8:1–3).

Second, she, along with a group of other women, was present at Jesus' crucifixion and agonized at the spectacle of such a horrific death (Matt. 27:55-56; Mark 15:40–41; John 19:25). "Mary was not singled out, but was part of a group of women, and many of the women at the cross were connected to known males. Had there been such a connection between Mary and Jesus, there was plenty of opportunity to make the point about Mary Magdalene in these earlier texts."[113]

Third, Mary Magdalene also appeared with the other women sitting "opposite the tomb," perhaps pondering the entire scenario just witnessed and waiting for the next day (after the Sabbath) so they could come and anoint the body with the other women (Mark 15:47).

Fourth, she is the first of the women to witness Jesus' resurrection (Matt. 28:1; Mark 16:1, 9; John 20:1).[114] She appeared again with a number of other women witnessing to the apostles about the risen Lord (Luke 24:10; John 20:18).

Nothing in the evidence suggests Mary was Jesus' spouse. Even the only text (John 20:11–18) that can be used to argue for intimacy between Mary and Jesus—when she tried clinging to Him—goes against the very argument made. For why would Christians mention a text detrimental to their argument, if they are trying to hide such a relationship? This makes no sense.

While it is true, however, that such a display of emotion between nonrelated individuals in public "were not culturally affirmed, except in the case of a greeting like a holy kiss (Rom. 16:16)," Mary's emotion of seeing Jesus caused her to "spontaneously" grab and perhaps hug Him.[115] Would we, if we were in her shoes? We grab and hug people in a moment of happiness when one's sports team scores. How much more would we not break into spontaneous joy on seeing the risen Jesus?

Church tradition. Apart from Gnostic literature, not much is said about Mary Magdalene, which may not be a bad thing. It seems bad things are always heralded rather than good things that go unmentioned. Church tradition does not say anything different about her from what is recorded in the Gospels.[116] Even if early church writer Hippolytus (A.D. 170–236) in his OT commentary on the book Song of Songs 24–26 mentions how women apostles saw the risen Jesus, there are no specific references to Mary Magdalene. Hippolytus referred to the group instead of singling out anyone.[117]

Throughout the years many have mistakenly believed Mary Magdalene was a prostitute. Pope Gregory the Great was the first to mention this in a sermon delivered in A.D. 591. Today almost all scholars agree that this was a mistake made by wrongly connecting Mary Magdalene mentioned in Luke 8:1–3 with the unnamed sinful woman who anointed Jesus' feet in Luke 7:36–50. However, Luke did not link the unnamed woman to Mary Magdalene, which he could have easily done if he so desired. Second, if one links the woman in Bethany who anointed Jesus by pouring an "alabaster vial of perfume" (Mark 14:3) on Him (recognized as Mary of Bethany in John 12:3) with the unnamed woman of Luke 7:36–50, one can mistakenly identify this as Mary Magdalene. However, enough time exists between both anointings that they should not be associated,[118] since one occurred in a Pharisee's house prior to Jesus' disassociation with them and the other occurred the last week of His crucifixion. Even determining whether the unnamed sinful woman of Luke 7:36–50 was a prostitute "is uncertain."[119]

Nothing, however, prevented medieval stories about Mary Magdalene from arising that have little to do with the NT. For example, eighth century *Golden Legend* (1.374–83) refers to Mary as "apostle to the apostles." Along with being lovely, having long hair, and having rich parents, she appears as the sister of Martha and Lazarus. Witherington further describes how bizarre this myth is, "Another story has her betrothed to John the Evangelist, but she loses him to the service of Jesus; after she is healed of her diseases, she also joins Jesus' service. As a quasi-apostle she undertakes a career in missionary work, going first to Ephesus and then to Marseilles, where she preaches the faith along with Martha and Lazarus. The *Golden Legend* goes on to have Lazarus become bishop of that city after Mary Magdalene converts the local pagan ruler an his wife and enables them to conceive a child."[120]

Mary Magdalene has always had her "fans." This "Magdalene" craze permeating the media and books is nothing new. Yet according to historical records the only picture available describing the historical Mary Magdalene appears in the NT. To suggest more than that is pure speculation.

Conclusion

By looking at *The Gospel of Philip*, *The Acts of Philip*, *The Gospel of Mary*, and other related texts, it is clear that the inscription *Mariamnē* functions in two ways. First, it operates with a spiritual symbolic meaning equivalent to that of "wisdom." At other times it functions as a key literary figure to promote the Gnostic movement's superiority (validated through special revelation) against historical orthodox Christianity represented by the literary figures of the disciples.

Furthermore there is no consensus among scholars if *Mariamnē* even refers to Mary Magdalene as a literary figure in numerous places. But one thing was obvious in this examination: the Talpiot allegedly *Mariamnē* inscription and similar Gnostic references to this name have nothing to do with the historical NT Mary Magdalene. In addition to the problems presented, we have seen how even the Talpiot inscription reading *Mariamnē* was incorrect. Instead, there are two better readings of this inscription: either it reads "Maria who is also known as Martha," or the inscription refers to two women named "Mariam and Martha," whose bones were gathered in the same ossuary.

From studying the NT picture of Mary Magdalene, one can see how incredulous is the hypothesis that this ossuary includes the bones of Mary Magdalene in a family tomb allegedly belonging to Jesus of Nazareth.

— Chapter 4 —

WAS THOMAS THE UNDERCOVER JUDAS, SON OF JESUS?

> Logically, if Jesus had a wife and son, either they would not have been spoken of at all, or they would have been spoken of in code. Jesus, his family, and his followers were all acutely aware that they were living in a Roman society and that Romans killed all heirs to a contender for kingship in territories they controlled, while often allowing siblings to survive.[1]

Does the New Testament (NT) present evidence that Jesus of Nazareth had a son and was thereby married to Mary Magdalene or someone else? Does the ossuary with the inscription "Judah son of Jesus" prove that Jesus of Nazareth had a son? Could Judas the brother of Jesus (Mark 6:3) really be the undercover son of Jesus named Thomas? What evidence exists that Judas Thomas was the beloved disciple mentioned in John's Gospel? Who is the unnamed beloved disciple in the Gospel of John? To examine and answer the *JFT* book and the *LTJ* documentary all these questions are addressed in this chapter.

NT Evidence of a Possible Son of Jesus?

For the *JFT* book and the *LTJ* documentary to affirm that Jesus Christ had a son, they must show the possibility that He was married. Because of the enormous amount of books published exposing Dan Brown's *Da Vinci Code* fallacy, which claims Jesus was married, this topic need not be covered here. Several scholars have shown decisively that no historical evidence exists to prove that Jesus was ever married.[2]

However the following is a summary of the arguments that show why Jesus was not married.

First, though no explicit text states Jesus' singleness, we can conclude from various passages that He was. Since Jesus argues that some are born with the gift to stay single for the sake of furthering God's kingdom full-time on earth while others may take the necessary steps to do so, it would seem odd for Him to be the Messiah specifically sent by God with this very mission and then, contrary to His own advice, get married and have to divide His time doing other earthly things that could limit His time in being fully devoted to His mission.[3] Not that being a husband is wrong, but it seems to contradict Matthew 19:12, "For there are eunuchs who were born thus from their mother's womb, and there are eunuchs who were made eunuchs by men, and there are eunuchs who have made themselves eunuchs for the kingdom of heaven's sake."[4] Furthermore, why did Paul not mention Jesus' marriage when defending himself against the Corinthians? Gary L. Habermas makes a good point. "If Jesus had been married, this would have been a wonderful clincher to Paul's argument that apostles have the right to bring their wives with them in ministry, although the best Paul could do was to refer to Peter and Jesus' brothers (1 Cor. 9:5). That would have clinched it!" Moreover, "Acts 8:30–34 implies that Jesus had no descendants. At the cross, Jesus committed his mother to John, not to his son (John 19:26). Jesus' brother James is the leader of [the] early church in Jerusalem (Acts 15). But since there is no evidence at all that Jesus was married, it should not be necessary to mention his lack of offspring!"[5]

Second, even if Jesus married, it would not have been wrong. Marriage is part of God's earthly design; it is sacred and is not sinful

(Gen. 1:22, 26–28; 2:21–25). Furthermore this would not diminish His claims to deity any more than His claims to deity make Him any less human.

Third, there is not a single shred of historical evidence to indicate that Jesus was married. Surely if He was married, someone would have recorded such an important piece of information about the person who has had the biggest impact in the world.

Fourth, Darrell L. Bock notes, "One of the few things on which a vast majority of liberal and conservative scholars agree is that Jesus was single. [John Dominic] Crossan in his Beliefnet.com piece did not feel the need to defend the case that Jesus was single. To him, it was that obvious. It is such an unusual situation in the study of Jesus for scholars of all persuasions to agree—when it happens, one should note it."[6]

Thus it seems quite clear that from external historical evidence and internally from the NT, the evidence points to Jesus' singleness. To say otherwise is to go against all available evidence that results in unwarranted speculation. Logically, other arguments do not need to be addressed once having shown clear evidence of Jesus' single status, because all other points depend on Jesus' marital status. However, for the sake of examining evidence undisclosed by the *JFT* advocates, I will continue the journey.

Thomas as Judas Son of Jesus?

The *JFT* advocates allege that Jesus' disciple Thomas was actually named Judas, since Thomas was not a Hebrew name but a word that means "twin." That is, the Aramaic term *tᵉʾômās* translated "Thomas" is rendered by the Greek word *Didymos,* which means "twin" (see John 11:16). Therefore to call someone "Didymos Judas Thomas" is redundantly equivalent to literally saying, "Twin Judas Twin." By pointing to the name of the writer in the first sentence in the Gnostic *Gospel of Thomas* as "Didymos Judas Thomas," they claim, "The name *strongly* suggests that Judas (the brother) and Thomas were indeed one and the same person." They further assert that in the *Gospel of Thomas* saying 11, "On the day when you were one you became two" means Judas was named Thomas, a "strange code that would be impossible to break were it not for an ossuary in Talpiot inscribed 'Judah, son of Jesus.'"7 Hence they suggest the possibility that the word "twin" may perhaps be "an ancient code word for 'junior,'" which was hidden all along in plain sight from the Roman authorities.8

Six points may be noted in response to their allegations. First, while it is true that the Aramaic word *teʾômās* "was never used as a surname" in the Old Testament,9 as is common in the evolution of language, by NT times the name "came to coincide in Greek speaking regions with the Greek name Θωμᾶς [Thomas]."10 Therefore to claim as the *JFT* advocates do that the name Thomas did not exist in the Hebrew, is true but that proves nothing, since by the first century Thomas was a proper name. Numerous NT passages clearly confirm this (Matt. 10:3; Mark 3:18; Luke 6:15; John 11:16; 14:5; 20:24, 26–29; 21:2; Acts 1:13).

Second, there is nothing secret to conceal or nothing "strange" about using the term "Thomas" since it was in fact a proper name of that period. Thus how can one conceal and codify someone's real and proper name?

Third, in the church of Syria, Thomas was known as Judas the brother of Jesus who founded all Eastern churches, "particular of Edessa (in somewhat later tradition, he even travels to India)."11 Unfortunately this erroneous merging in Gnostic tradition of Jesus' brother Judas (also known as Jude, the epistle's author) with one of the twelve apostles named Thomas, called the twin is now repeated by the *JFT* advocates. To believe Judas is Jesus' brother that traveled to India is wrong. Tradition has Thomas, one of the twelve apostles, not Jesus' brother Judas, as the one who traveled to India, as well as to Parthia.12

Thus Thomas, called the twin, and Jesus' brother Judas are not the same individuals. This is also clearly shown in Mark 3:14–19 where Thomas appears as one of the twelve disciples picked by Jesus and just twelve verses later (v. 31) Jesus' brothers and mother are calling Him. In fact none of Jesus' brothers believed in Him prior to His resurrection (John 7:5).

Fourth, the *JFT* advocates also quote the phrase in the *Gospel of*

Thomas saying 11 "when you were one you became two" as if it proves Judas' renaming of Thomas establishes the identity as Jesus' undercover son posing all along as His brother. Thus by the time Thomas wrote his Gospel the cat was out of the bag.

Such an interpretation of saying 11 is foreign to the meaning of the *Gospel of Thomas*. To my knowledge no scholar even considers this interpretation an option.[13] In light of the *Gospel of Thomas's* emphasis on oneness as an "ideal gnostic disciple" characterized by those leaving behind all worldly connections (cf. sayings 4, 16, 23, 30, and 76), and that even promotes women becoming males in order to achieve oneness (cf. saying 114), it seems more likely that the "two" becoming "one" here is negative not positive. Robert M. Grant and David Noel Freedman write, "The third part of the saying describes the condition of the Gnostic believer. Those who were formerly divided have been united; they have worked together (saying 59); they are at peace (49); they have become one (103). Unfortunately, it looks as if becoming 'two' were regarded as the believer's goal. Perhaps it would be best to hold that the present unity of the believers represents their goal, and—in spite of the parallelism of the saying—that the becoming 'two' is something they should avoid. Jesus is not a divider (saying 72), except in the sense that he divides families into Gnostics and non-Gnostics (saying 16)."[14] Therefore saying 11 has nothing to do with revealing a long held secret of Jesus' son.

Fifth, Bock raises another good argument. "If there really had been a Mary and Jesus who had a child and who had a family tomb, those who wrote books in the name of Christian figures—like the Gnostics—who were trying to establish their authority among Christianity would have at some point appealed to one of the relatives coming from the Jesus, Mary and son family that still remained for the basis of their doctrines. Figures not related to Jesus are the referent of many appeals by the Gnostics but certainly if such relatives of Jesus were indeed alive to carry the dynasty many of these writers would have appealed to these figures. But as it stands no such application exist."[15] That is, no Acts of Judah son of Jesus of Nazareth or the Gospel of the daughter of Jesus of Nazareth exist, and no clear statement to Jesus' marriage or any offspring appears in any works of history in or outside the Bible. This looks like an argument *from* silence, but it is not. In such a case it refers more to an argument *about* such silence that screams for an answer to those making such allegations that Jesus' marriage to Mary Magdalene produced offspring, and that one of these children was Judas Thomas, known as the beloved disciple. Surely, we should find at least one of these persons referred to in works by those who one hundred years later were free to reveal the long-held secret. Yet apart from highly questionable, if not impossible, interpretive passages nothing appears in history.

Sixth, the *JFT* book suggests that the inscription *Yehuda son of Yeshua* on ossuary 80.501 refers to Jesus' son whose identity was kept secret for the sake of his survival and thus was named Thomas.[16] That is, *JFT* advocates claim that Rome's policy deterred a specific dynasty from ruling in an absence of an heir by killing immediate family members like father, mother, or children.[17] "But a mere sibling might have a good chance at survival, specifically if he kept a low profile. It was as simple as that."[18] Or is it?

While it is true that Romans killed heirs to the throne and their relatives (fathers, mothers, children, and grandchildren), leaving an opponent's siblings was not much better. Roman history shows how an heir's brother replaced him in office. For example, Gaius Gracchus replaced his brother (Tiberius Gracchus) as "Tribune of the People" after being murdered.[19] One of the greatest persecutors of Christianity, Domitian (A.D. 81–96), replaced his brother Titus as Roman emperor.[20] Flavius Claudius Julianus became Caesar following his half-brother, Flavius Valerius Aurelius Constantinus, after escaping from being killed along with three of his brother's sons and his half brother Constantius Gallus.[21]

Therefore if Rome saw Jesus' alleged son as a threat to claiming the Davidic throne, they would in all likelihood see His siblings as threats too. Yet we see no attempt at hiding or encoding the names of Jesus' brothers or sisters. This exposes the weakness of the *JFT* theory that the name of an alleged son of Jesus was hidden. Also Rome did not see Jesus or any of His family members as a threat to claim the

Davidic throne; or else all of Jesus' immediate family would have been executed. In fact this point seems quite clear and settled at the encounter between Pilate and Jesus, as John 18:33–39 records:

> Then Pilate entered the Praetorium again, called Jesus, and said to Him, "Are You the King of the Jews?" Jesus answered him, "Are you speaking for yourself about this, or did others tell you this concerning Me?" Pilate answered, "Am I a Jew? Your own nation and the chief priests have delivered You to me. What have You done?" Jesus answered, "My kingdom is not of this world. If My kingdom were of this world, My servants would fight, so that I should not be delivered to the Jews; but now My kingdom is not from here." Pilate therefore said to Him, "Are You a king then?" Jesus answered, "You say rightly that I am a king. For this cause I was born, and for this cause I have come into the world, that I should bear witness to the truth. Everyone who is of the truth hears My voice." Pilate said to Him, "What is truth?" And when he had said this, he went out again to the Jews, and said to them, "**I find no fault in Him at all**. "But you have a custom that I should release someone to you at the Passover. **Do you therefore want me to release to you the King of the Jews?**"[22]

There is no evidence whatsoever in the NT of the disciple Thomas being Judas the son of Jesus, and for that matter that Jesus had a son. Harvard professor François Bovon, admits that the idea that Jesus had a son is ridiculous. "I must say that the reconstructions of Jesus' marriage with Mary Magdalene and the birth of a child belong for me to science fiction."[23] Even Talpiot friend and scholar, James D. Tabor, on whom the *JFT* book relied and who appeared on the *LTJ* documentary,[24] admits in his own book, "*The Jesus Dynasty* has no connection to the recently popularized notions that Jesus married and fathered children through Mary Magdalene. While gripping fiction, this idea is long on speculation and short on evidence." Though he now believes differently.[25]

Judas Thomas as the Beloved Disciple?

The *JFT* advocates also allege that Judas Thomas (as Jesus' son) could be the "beloved disciple" in John's Gospel whose identity is purposely ambiguous. They believe that at the cross when Jesus entrusted His mother Mary to the "beloved disciple" to be cared for after His departure (John 19:26–27) this proves that they were family, perhaps "grandmother and grandson." They also claim, "Alternatively, isn't it also possible, as some scholars have suggested, that Mary Magdalene is often replaced in the Gospels by Mary, mother of Jesus, in order to obscure her role in Jesus's [*sic*] life?"[26]

Let me answer the last point first. The *JFT* advocates give no documentation identifying some of these scholars. Also the only place where such a phenomenon seems to appear is in third- to fifth-century Gnostic literature.[27] Furthermore, how can there be any intent to obscure Jesus' mother with Mary Magdalene when the previous verse (19:25) clearly distinguishes both women by name and identifies "his mother" again by using the same phrase in verse 26? Nowhere in the NT or church tradition does one find the merging or replacement of Jesus' mother with the person of Mary Magdalene. So to answer their speculation: *anything is possible* but *highly improbable* since we have no biblical evidence suggesting that such a phenomenon occurs anywhere.

When Jesus told His mother "Woman, behold your son" and to the beloved disciple "Behold your mother," He did not mean they are biological relatives. In fact this proves just the opposite. That Jesus summoned this disciple to care for His mother argues against such an interpretation since the fifth commandment (Exod. 20:12) and Jewish cultural norms assume biological sons would care for their parents.[28] Such a request would be superfluous if they were literally mother and son. Though the disciple looked after the physical well-being of Jesus' mother, a spiritual nuance appears to be more of the emphasis here since at this point His brothers were still unbelievers. J. Carl Laney correctly captures the meaning of Jesus' request. "Jesus' half-brothers were still unbelievers and could not be counted on for spiritual support and encouragement. Jesus' words 'Dear woman, here is your son' may be understood in the sense, 'Consider him as your son.'"[29] Thus

Jesus summoned this disciple to become "his human successor" and take over His responsibilities. To convey this He used the word "son" metaphorically[30] as was commonly done elsewhere (e.g., Matt. 5:9; 8:12; John 12:36; Eph. 2:2; 5:6; 1 Tim 1:2; 2 Tim 2:1; Titus 1:4; Phlm. 10).

Can Judas Thomas as the undercover son of Jesus be identified as the beloved disciple in John's Gospel? Frankly, I have read numerous commentaries and articles trying to identify the beloved disciple in the Gospel bearing the name of John, but I have never encountered this option until I read the *JFT* book. This stretches credulity to another level. From my years of studying and teaching this Gospel, I became convinced that the evidence points to John, the son of Zebedee.

Although John's name is not mentioned in the Gospel, the different names for "John" points to "that disciple whom Jesus loved." This phrase appears three times in John (13:23; 21:7, 20). The same idea is stated in variant forms in John 19:26 "the disciple present whom He loved" (*ton mathētēn parestōta hon ēgapa*) and 20:2 "the other disciple whom Jesus loved" (*ton allon mathētēn hon ephilei ho Iēsous*).[31]

In the NT five men bore the name John. (1) John the Baptist is definitely not the one (John 1:6, 15, 19, 26, 29), because he was beheaded by Herod long before this Gospel was complete (Mark. 6:24–29). (2) John the father of Peter (John 1:42) is also not the one because there is no mention of his name in connection with this Gospel. (3) John Mark, mentioned in Acts 12:12, wrote the second Gospel. He could not be the writer of the Gospel of John because he would have to have been an eyewitness as the Gospel indicates of its author in a number of places where only the twelve or some of the disciples were present. Furthermore, church tradition unanimously attributes authorship of John Mark to Mark's Gospel. (4) John of the Sanhedrin appears only once in Acts 4:5–6 and was an enemy of Christianity. (5) John, the "disciple whom Jesus loved," the son of Zebedee, mentioned in Matthew 4:21, seems to be the best choice by far, though many dispute it.[32] The external and internal evidence favor John the apostle.

External evidence. External evidence points to the apostle John as the author of the fourth Gospel. For example, the early second century church tradition affirmed it as well as universal testimony of the time. Irenaeus (A.D. 130–200) was first to say John wrote this Gospel after the others.[33] His testimony is most important, because he was a pupil of Polycarp who was a friend of the Apostle John. Clement of Alexandria, Clement of Rome, Cyril of Jerusalem, Tertullian, Polycarp, Origen, Papias,[34] Justin Martyr, Augustine, and Jerome all support unanimously that John wrote this Gospel. Eusebius wrote that John's "Gospel which is known to all the churches under heaven, must be acknowledged as genuine… [and further adds] all of the writings of John, his Gospel … and epistles, have been accepted without dispute both now and in ancient times"[35]

Internal evidence. Internal evidence overwhelmingly reveals that the writer was a Jew (John 12:40; 13:18; and 19:37). John's use of language indicates his Jewishness.[36] Furthermore, the details of time, people, custom (2:1–10; 3:25; 11:55) geography (5:2; 11:18) numbers, and minute details demonstrate evidence of an eyewitness (1:14; 2:6; 12:5; 19:33-35; 21:8, 11, 24). The author's statement, "We beheld His glory" (1:14) must have been the report of one who was at the Transfiguration. Peter is referred to by his name in John 1:41, and James was martyred by the time of the fourth Gospel was written. John introduces himself in 13:23 and 19:26, and in mentioning John the Baptist by name ("John"), the internal evidence strongly supports that the author of the Gospel of John is none other than the Apostle John. In addition, since the "disciple whom Jesus loved" is in the Upper Room Discourse and "was leaning on Jesus' bosom," he had to be one of the twelve apostles who were the only ones present and for whom Christ's discourse was meant. Specifically it had to be one of the three in Christ's inner circle of Peter, James, and John. Gary M. Burge sums it up well. "The Synoptics make clear that this meal was reserved for the Twelve (Mark 14:17), and so we may be able to deduce that the beloved disciple must have been an apostle."[37] Finally, since the "disciple whom Jesus loved" (John 19:26) was asked by Christ at the foot of the cross to "Behold your mother" and in Matthew 27:56 one of the ladies happens to be the "mother of the sons of Zebedee," the evidence strongly points to John the Apostle. Furthermore, "This would make John the maternal cousin of Jesus and explain why the apostle is assigned to care for Mary. This connection, however, presupposes that the beloved disciple is a son of Zebedee. At least the logic of this explanation makes for an intriguing explanation of 19:26."[38]

Conclusion

Not a shred of evidence exists to support the notion that Thomas or Judas appears either open or concealed in documents in or outside the NT as the son of Jesus. Even more bizarre is the claim that the "beloved disciple" in John's Gospel, instead of being the author of the fourth Gospel and one of the twelve apostles, was Jesus' son, which is an impossible view in light of the biblical evidence and church tradition.

— Chapter 5 —

MULTIPLE LANGUAGES IN ONE TOMB

Jerusalem, in those days, was an international crossroads of trade under Rome—a condition reflected in the Talpiot tomb cluster, whose names were written in Aramaic, Greek, Hebrew, and Hebrew-inscribed Latin. The tomb appeared to be communicating that Jerusalem in this period was not only bilingual but probably trilingual. Frank Moore Cross had already found the inscription assemblage most remarkable, even in a trilingual city. Something unusual had been recorded in this assemblage.[1]

The *Jesus Family Tomb* (*JFT*) advocates believe that the Talpiot tomb's inscriptions recorded in multiple languages promotes their interpretation of seeing this tomb as belong to a traveling family like that of Jesus, specially since He constantly moved all throughout the region. They claim, "Among the three generations represented in the Tomb of Ten Ossuaries, one would normally have expected (as one normally saw in other tombs) that if these were children burying their parents, they would be using the same language for each burial—unless, the epigrapher guessed, these people traveled widely and came back to

Jerusalem with nicknames of endearment from foreign lands."[2]

Why are there three different languages recorded in the six inscribed ossuaries in the Talpiot tomb? Does this help or hinder the *JFT* view that identifies each of these inscribed bone-boxes as those belonging to Jesus of Nazareth and His family? What reasons could there be for recording names in three different languages in a family tomb? To see whether the *JFT* advocates have accurately disclosed all there is about this issue, these questions will be addressed in this chapter.

Three Different Languages Appear

As one scans the ossuaries of the Talpiot tomb it reveals that six of the bone-boxes appear inscribed in three different languages: Greek, Aramaic, and Hebrew:

1. Greek ossuary inscription: Mariame, also known as (or and) Martha
2. Aramaic ossuary inscriptions: *Jesus son of Joseph* and *Judas son of Jesus*
3. Hebrew ossuary inscriptions: *Maria* (Hebrew letters using the Latinize form) *Matthew, Jose*[3]

The *JFT* people make a positive case on their behalf for a multilingual family tomb, since the norm would be to find "children burying their parents" in family tomb using the "same language." According to them, a family tomb containing inscribed ossuaries using different languages argues for the uniqueness of this tomb and points to such people as travelers of the area who spoke different languages.[4]

While this tomb is no doubt unusual, to find a family tomb with multilingual inscribed ossuaries is not that unique. Rachel Hachlili points to a multilingual family tomb that was discovered at Jericho containing "32 inscriptions written or incised on 14" ossuaries using "Hebrew and Greek names." The reason for this fascinating phenomenon is because "the tomb contained the remains of a family of three generations."[5] Hachlili also notes, "Quite often the inscription was repeated on the ossuary and several were bilingual."[6]

Another family tomb exists with an ossuary that appears inscribed in Hebrew on one side with a further description of the names in

Greek of those interred in it on the other side, along with a translation of the Hebrew word for "Master" in Greek κύριος (*kyrios*).[7] After Rahmani catalogues a number of examples where Hebrew, Aramaic (both of which are not that different), and Greek inscriptions appear in burial chambers, he concludes, "The single conclusion which may safely be drawn from the ossuary inscriptions, most of which are from Jerusalem, is that Jewish script was preferred, though with a heavy admixture of Greek."[8] Thus having a multilingual tomb is not unusual at all. People spoke multiple languages in the Judean region, and therefore it would not be uncommon to find a single family using one tomb for generations containing ossuary inscription names in different languages.[9]

Language Differences Help or Hinder

Examining the facts, we can see that having a multilingual tomb does not necessarily show the uniqueness of this tomb. Hence a multilingual tomb does not necessarily help the case of *JFT* advocates, but in fact, hinders it. Ben Witherington III notices how it does so.

> There is a major problem with the analysis of the names on these ossuaries. By this I mean one has to explain why one is in Hebrew, several are in Aramaic, but the supposed Mary Magdalene ossuary is in Greek. This suggests a multi-generation tomb, not a single generation tomb, and indeed a tomb that comes from A.D. 70 after the Romans had destroyed the temple mount and Jewish Christians fled the city. This tomb is not in old Jerusalem. It is nowhere near the Temple mount, and we already know that the tomb of James was near the Temple Mount.... We have absolutely no historical evidence to suggest Mary Magdalene would have been called by a Greek name before A.D. 70. She grew up in a Jewish fishing village called Migdal, not a Greek city at all. It makes no sense that her ossuary would have a Greek inscription and that of her husband an Aramaic.[10]

Another issue of the multilingual inscriptions found at Talpiot posses a problem to the *JFT* theory. The only way the *JFT* advocates can make a case for interpreting "Mariamne e Mara" to mean "Mary the Master" would be to combine two different languages in one inscription. That is, "Mariamne" is written in Greek while "Mara" appears in Greek letters but is believed by the *JFT* advocates to be a Hebrew name (with a possible meaning "Master"). Someone noticing this problem concluded, "This is preposterous. Since the inscription is in Greek, if it was supposed to say 'Mary the Master' it would have to say 'Mariamne Ho Kurios' [*kurios* being the Greek word for "master"] NOT 'Mariamne e Mara.'"[11] As already argued in chapter three, it may be best to see this inscription containing two women (perhaps sisters, or mother and daughter) named Mary and Martha, which would render the word "Mara" as a shortened form of the name "Martha."

Clearly, having multilingual inscriptions in a family tomb does not help the *JFT* advocates' argument.

Reasons For Multiple Languages

Though a family tomb with multilingual ossuary inscriptions hinders the *JFT* case, there are other good reasons or options that can explain this phenomenon.[12] At least five other alternative explanations answer why there are multilingual family tombs found in the Judean region that were not mentioned in the *JFT* book or the *LTJ* documentary.

Alternative 1: A Multilingual Tomb Points to a Bilingual Family. Similar to what the *JFT* advocates suggest, this may be one family who spoke different languages. However, this does not prove that the phenomenon of having a multilingual family tomb points to people who traveled around the region, like that of Jesus of Nazareth and His followers, or that families who lived in Jerusalem who may have done little traveling did not speak other languages. Jews, with the exceptions of Samaritans who worshiped in Mount Gerizim (John 4:20–22), traveled from all over the Roman Empire to worship in Jerusalem. Therefore, using the *JFT* logic everyone must have been bilingual since most of the Jewish worshipers traveled yearly at the time of Passover to Jerusalem. In addition, it is also difficult to believe Jesus and His followers were the only ones who traveled the region. Suggesting that traveling people may have been bilingual proves nothing.

Furthermore, it appears that at least three languages were spoken in Jerusalem, since the Romans who ruled them spoke Latin, Greek was the commerce language, and Hebrew or Aramaic was the native language of the Jewish people. The condemnation inscription, "JESUS OF NAZARETH, THE KING OF THE JEWS," written in "Hebrew, Greek, *and* Latin" above Jesus' cross (John 19:20) also confirms this.

Alternative 2: A Multilingual Tomb Points to a Multiple Forgeries. Though Dillon Burroughs presents this as a theoretical possibility, he does not believe this to be the case.[13] Though some say the last part of the ossuary inscription "James son of Joseph, *brother of Jesus*" to be a forgery, the circumstances surrounding this bone-box are not identical to the Talpiot tomb. For one thing, the Talpiot tomb has an archaeological context that the James ossuary does not. Second, no scholars debate the authenticity of the Talpiot inscriptions. The debate centers on whether they belong to the family of Jesus of Nazareth.

Alternative 3: A Multilingual Tomb Points To Monetary Issue. The Talpiot tomb was obviously a wealthy man's burial ground. With money and space being an issue at the time, secondary burials of this kind were used (40 B.C. to A.D. 135).[14] Hence one may expect to find a wealthy family who had the privilege of learning various languages, indicated by the multilingual inscriptions, to be buried in this tomb.[15]

Alternative 4: A Multilingual Tomb Points to Multiple Different Families. For example, the Greek inscriptions "Mary and Martha" may refer to one family while the Hebrew inscriptions "Maria" (Hebrew letters using the Latinize form), "Matthew," and "Jose" refer to another family. A possible third family may appear as the Aramaic inscriptions of the father and son relationship indicate: "Jesus son of Joseph" and "Judas son of Jesus." Along with this explanation one needs to account for those buried in the other four noninscribed ossuaries.

Though one may object that nonphysical relatives would not be buried in a family tomb, this objection fails to note two key things. While nonphysical relatives are usually not buried in a family tomb, it is possible to have a large family tomb like that of Talpiot housing various members of distinct families but related within their own family buried in one large tomb. Perhaps various close nonrelated families decided (due to the cost or for friendship reasons) to buy one large tomb to bury all of their close-knit families together. On the other hand, spiritual instead of physical kinship may take precedence among closely related Christians. Hence Witherington suggests, "And what we know about those Christians is that they related to each other as family, even when they were not physically related, and were in some cases buried together, not in clan tombs, because their religious families were more important to them than their physical ones."[16]

Perhaps since secondary-burial practices continued until A.D. 135, according to Rahmani, others from outside the family could have been buried in such a tomb because of money, space, or a number of other factors. In fact, Witherington suggest, "This tomb may reflect that later Christian practice and reality. It would be nice if other ossuaries from the Talpiot tomb could be DNA tested so we could find out if *any* of the folks in this tomb were related. We do not know. But it would not surprise me if *none of them were*. The practice of osslegium [sic], or burial in ossuaries, continued on after A.D. 70 until the Bar Kokhba revolt at least. There is no reason why this Talpiot tomb might not reflect the period between A.D. 70 and 125 or so."[17] Therefore, if this practice was in place longer than expected, then the pool of potential people interred in a given ossuary grows, and the likelihood that we can find the remains of more than a single person in an ossuary also grows, making the assessment of family tombs much more difficult.

All of these options are real possibilities that were not considered by the book or documentary.

Alternative 5: A Multilingual Tomb Points To Multiple Generational Families. Since tombs like that of Talpiot were used for multiple generations of the same family, it seems highly probable that a multilingual tomb points to a multiple generational family burial site. This seems to be the case of the Talpiot tomb according to one of the original excavators, Amos Kloner, who believes this tomb may have contained an estimated 35 people. He writes, "This burial cave was probably used for three or four generations."[18] Such would be the case if this encompassed many years stemming from 20 B.C. to A.D. 135. This would allow for a large family to inscribe ossuaries in multiple languages. Besides, "It was not uncommon for Palestinian Jews to have both Semitic and Greek (or, much less commonly, Latin) names. Using both names together could solve the problem of distinguishing people with very common names."[19] Therefore one could easily see how finding a multilingual family tomb would not be that uncommon since people in the first-century Judean region probably spoke multiple languages. Of the possible alternatives, I favor this last one.

Conclusion

A number of possible views can explain the phenomenon of a multilingual tomb. None of these alternatives were mentioned by the book or documentary. This way of presenting information unfairly slants the case to promote one's personal agenda. Hence Burroughs is correct in concluding, "For a documentary to present only one scenario while neglecting a multitude of additional perspectives and pieces of evidence presents a one-sided viewpoint that comes across as factual although it is in fact misleading."[20]

— Chapter 6 —

DNA ANALYSIS AND OTHER POSSIBILITIES

If these two ossuaries truly belonged to Jesus of Nazareth and Mary Magdalene, DNA tests would reveal that the two people buried within were not related. All Scriptural records—whether canonical or apocryphal—were clear on one genealogical point: Jesus of Nazareth and Mary Magdalene, if their DNA could be read, would be two individuals who had no family ties. But what are the alternatives? People buried in the same tomb were related by either blood or marriage.[1]

With today's scientific technology everyone knows how extremely important DNA analyses can be in solving crime investigations. Taking DNA samples becomes crucial in identifying a suspect by matching DNA blood types with that found at the crime scene. If a pregnant woman has multiple partners, the identity of the father can be determined by matching the DNA of the father and of the baby.

Hence when the *JFT* and the *LTJ* people said that DNA evidence shows that the two ossuaries allegedly belonging to Jesus of Nazareth and Mary Magdalene and that they were married, it caught everyone's attention. They say that since Jesus and Mary did not have identical DNA patterns, they were not related by birth and therefore were married.

However, did the *JFT* book and the *LTJ* documentary examine other possibilities? What kind of test did they do that made them come to such a conclusion? Did they take DNA samples from other ossuaries and test them against the *Yeshua son of Yehosef* and *Mariame kai Mara* ossuaries to see whether similar or different results appear? This and other questions like it are examined in this chapter in order to make a correct analysis.

Limited DNA Analysis

Minimal understanding of how DNA works becomes necessary in order to grasp this argument. By understanding Stephen J. Pfann's simple explanation of how DNA works, we conclude the following.[2] Everyone has two kinds of DNA: nuclear and mitochondrial.

The nucleus DNA splits and becomes what is created first when one is born from the seed of man and woman. This combination determines all the physical characteristics we possess as individuals.

The mitochondrial DNA are small bodies that float in the cells that indicate origin. Even plants have mitochondria in them. There are independent organisms that have their own DNA that can be called orgacells. They nourish the human embryo to foster its growth. One cannot live without them and they cannot exist outside of us.

Mitochondrial DNA does not come from male semen; it exists only within the female's egg. Hence this cell comes solely from mothers. Male and females get them from their mothers. One has 1,000 mitochondrial DNA per every cell. So when looking for DNA samples, one will more likely find mitochondrial DNA.

Furthermore mitochondrial DNA is much more likely than nucleus DNA to survive in ancient materials. Hence this was the only DNA that could be extracted from the *Jesus son of Joseph* and *Mariame kai Mara* ossuaries. Once this type of DNA was extracted from the "Jesus" and the supposedly "Mary Magdalene" ossuaries, the *JFT* advocates concluded that since both were not related through the mother it seems very likely they were married. The following syllogism explains their reasoning.[3]

> **PREMISE 1:** People interred in a family tomb were either related by blood or marriage.
>
> **PREMISE 2:** Mitochondrial DNA found inside the Yeshua and Mariame ossuaries proves they did not have the same mother.
>
> **CONCLUSION:** Then they were related by marriage.

It seems bizarre to test one ossuary and not the others. Even more absurd is to formulate a conclusion without acknowledging the possibilities of these ossuaries containing DNA remains of more than one person that would require testing at least the other 35 individuals who were in all likelihood buried in this tomb.[4] Tombs of this sort commonly "house" a number of multiple people. In fact, Joe Zias, curator of the IAA at the time of the tomb's discovery in 1980, published the finding of a tomb containing 15 ossuaries with remains of 88 people.[5] Gary R. Habermas makes a similar observation, as well.

> A devastating problem for DNA testing is that multiple skeletons were often placed in the same ossuary.... Tabor disputes the presence of 35 people in the Talpiot Tomb, arguing that in the original report by Joseph Gath, there were two or three people outside the ossuaries and "a dozen or so" inside the bone boxes. But even without arguing the specifics, Tabor's total of 14–18 people still makes the point sufficiently well. Thus, Christopher Rollston [Old Testament professor at the Emmanuel School of Religion] rightly notes that, "because of the numbers of burials in the tombs, the practice of interring the skeletal remains of multiple people in a single ossuary,

and the possibility of contamination of laboratory data, the notion that decisive data can be produced seems to me to be difficult." Indeed, without knowing whose bones we are testing, what good is DNA?[6]

Furthermore the book and documentary either forgot or do not know that "sometimes a husband's name appears alone [on the ossuary inscription], even though his nameless wife is buried in the ossuary with him," which strongly hinders the testing of DNA evidence by not considering this fact.[7]

Ben Witherington III notes that having no "DNA control sample" from Jesus' family to compare with the Talpiot tomb DNA samples makes it impossible to know whether this DNA belongs to Jesus. That Jesus and Mariame are not related means nothing since we will never be able to compare the Talpiot DNA with the Jesus of Nazareth DNA.[8] Tabor also admits this. "Such a test, no matter what the results, could not 'prove' that this particular Jesus was the one who became known as the Christ, but they could show whether any of these individuals were offspring of either of the two Mary's, or had a sibling relationship to one another.... it is impossible to prove that this particular tomb was related to Jesus of Nazareth."[9]

All we can know is this. Mitochondrial DNA can tell us whether two individuals come from the same mother, but it has no ability to determine whether these same individuals come from the same father. Knowing whether Jesus and Mariame had different mothers is impossible since we have no way of knowing if multiple individuals were interred in these ossuaries (as customary of that day), thereby corrupting all possible DNA samples.

Other DNA Possibilities Concealed

Consequently, since mitochondrial DNA establishes only whether a motherly relationship existed between two individuals, nowhere do the *JFT* and the *LTJ* people consider other options. For example, though the ossuaries inscribed *Yeshua son of Yehosef* and *Mariame kai Mara* did not have the same mother, that does not mean they could not have had the same father, making *Mariame* the half-sister of *Yeshua*. Considering this option will greatly diminish the likelihood of connecting *Yeshua* and *Mariame* in these two ossuaries by marriage.

Other possibilities were not mentioned either. *Mariame* had been married to someone else in the tomb, such as *Matya, Yehosef, Jose*, or perhaps someone from one of the uninscribed ossuaries? All these possibilities destroy the *JFT* book's argument. Furthermore, we would then need to ask, "Why were Mariame and Martha buried together if *Mariame* was *Yeshua's* wife?" Even if either of both women were married to *Yeshua son of Yehosef* why were they not buried together? If they were husband and wife, one would expect them to buried together.[10] These are relevant questions that were not addressed by the *JFT* and *LTJ* advocates. It appears that they manipulated the evidence to formulate an answer they wished. However, to conclude that because the *Yeshua* and *Mariame* were married simply because they did not come from the same mother is to jump to an illogical and non sequitur conclusion. Hence Carney Matheson, forensic examiner and scientific officer at Lakehead University's Paleo-DNA Laboratory and associate professor in the department of anthropology, Thunder Bay, Ontario, who supervised the DNA test, concluded, "The only conclusions we made was that these two sets were not maternally related [and] to me it sounds like absolutely nothing."[11]

The chart below reveals the assumptions made in the book and the film.[12] Where is the rest of the family according to the names appearing in the first block? According to the second block the only positive connections are between Joseph, Jesus, and Judah. Even the certainty of the name "Jesus," however, since it is not clearly written, causes many scholars to have reasonable doubts.[13] Furthermore, no historical or biblical evidence indicates that Jesus was married or that He fathered children. So even the best possible link between these three ossuaries point to another Jesus other than the Jesus of the New Testament. To connect the rest of the ossuaries a number of assumptions must be made without having any DNA evidence. Even the DNA evidence between the Mariame and the Jesus son of Joseph ossuaries that shows that both of

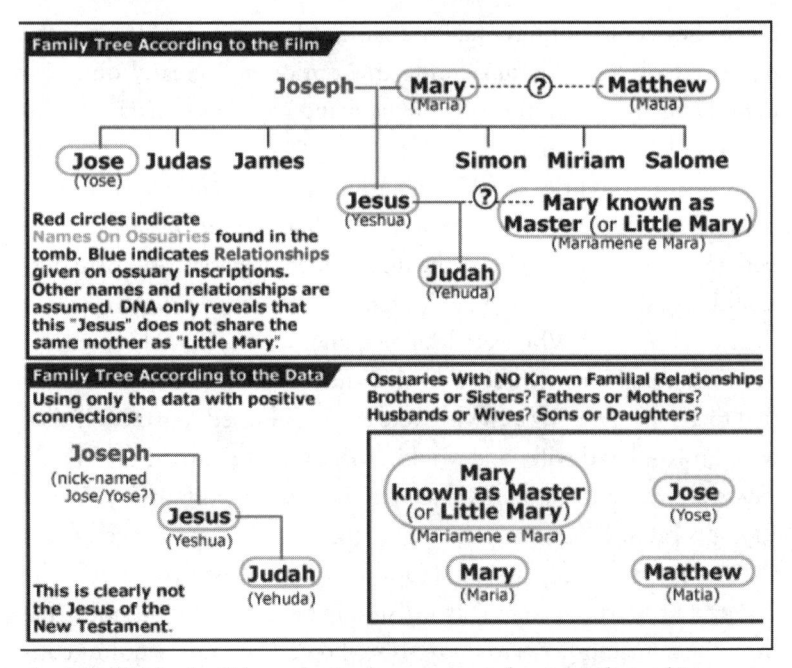

THE JESUS FAMILY TOMB EXAMINED

Family Tree According to the Film

Joseph — Mary (Maria) ······ ? ······ Matthew (Matia)

Jose (Yose), Judas, James | Simon, Miriam, Salome

Jesus (Yeshua) — ? ······ Mary known as Master (or Little Mary) (Mariamene e Mara)

Judah (Yehuda)

Red circles indicate Names On Ossuaries found in the tomb. Blue indicates Relationships given on ossuary inscriptions. Other names and relationships are assumed. DNA only reveals that this "Jesus" does not share the same mother as "Little Mary."

Family Tree According to the Data
Using only the data with positive connections:

Joseph (nick-named Jose/Yose?) — Jesus (Yeshua) — Judah (Yehuda)

This is clearly not the Jesus of the New Testament.

Ossuaries With NO Known Familial Relationships
Brothers or Sisters? Fathers or Mothers? Husbands or Wives? Sons or Daughters?

Mary known as Master (or Little Mary) (Mariamene e Mara) | Jose (Yose)

Mary (Maria) | Matthew (Matia)

these individuals did not have the same mother reveals nothing.

Other reasons are just as likely to answer why both individuals of the ossuaries inscribed *Yeshua son of Yehosef* and *Mariame kai Mara* did not have the same mother. For example, as mentioned above, she could have been married to someone else whose bones are not in that

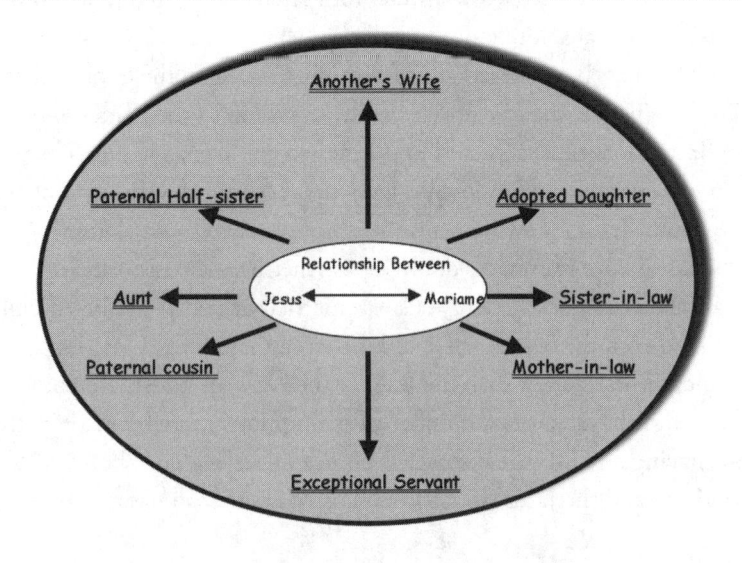

Relationship Between Jesus ↔ Mariame:
- Another's Wife
- Paternal Half-sister
- Adopted Daughter
- Aunt
- Sister-in-law
- Paternal cousin
- Mother-in-law
- Exceptional Servant

– 106 –

tomb. *Mariame* could be the paternal-half sister, sister-in-law, or aunt of *Yeshua*, or she could have been adopted and thus qualified to be buried in the family tomb. Many families adopted in those days. Or she could have been a paternal cousin or someone's mother-in-law. She could have also been an exceptional servant, who was considered as one of the family, and thus was buried with family members. The possible scenarios are numerous.

Conclusion

All these are very real possibilities that must be considered. Thus the DNA testing done by the *JFT* and *LTJ* people is not convincing at all. This is a typical case of manipulating the evidence to fit one's assumed conclusion.[14]

— Chapter 7 —

STATISTICAL COMBINATION OF NAMES: IMPRESSIVE OR INFLATED?

What was ignored all of those years ago was that the names—taken individually—were not the issue. Rather, what should have been examined was the entire cluster of names, which was indeed uncommon.... "And what happens when you do this," the statistician confirmed, "is that even if the individual probability of each particular name is not terribly small, when they are factored all together, they start to build a picture in which the overall tomb assemblage is a very rare event."[1]

Finding a cluster of names like those of the Talpiot tomb appears unusual.[2] This seems to be the strongest evidence presented by the *JFT* and *LTJ* advocates.[3] After reducing all of possible factors by taking a conservative approach and eliminating *Matya* (Matthew) from the equation, the *LTJ* documentary concludes that the odds of the Talpiot tomb belonging to Jesus of Nazareth is 600 to 1.[4] Here is how they get this figure. Professor Andrey Feuerverger, a leading statistician (of the University of Toronto), multiplied each ossuary inscription according to the number of appearances per ossuary in tombs discovered in Jerusalem, totaling about 1,000: (1) There is a 1 in 190 possibility of finding an ossuary with the name "Jesus son of Joseph," (2) a 1 in 160 possibility for "Mariamne", (3) a 1 in 40 possibility for "Matia," (4) a 1 in 20 possibility for "Jose," and (5) a 1 in 4 possibility for "Maria." Multiplying these figures yields a total of 97,280,000:

$$\frac{1}{190} \times \frac{1}{160} \times \frac{1}{40} \times \frac{1}{20} \times \frac{1}{4} = \frac{1}{97,280,000}$$

This seems to be a rare number indeed. By leaving out the ossuary "Judah son of Jesus," the *LTJ* advocates took a more conservative approach. Then they further reduced their figure by dividing the number 97,280,000 by 40, by taking out the Matia ossuary, which reduces the number to 2,432,000. This is reduced to the nearest hundred to 2,400,000. To account for "unintended bias" in the historical sources since other family names of Jesus of Nazareth do not appear in the Talpiot (e.g., Joseph, the father of Jesus, and His other brothers) they further reduced the number 2,400,000 by a factor of 4. This brought the number down to 600,000. Then this number was divided by 1,000, which Feuerverger assumes is the "maximum number of tombs that might have existed in Jerusalem, dating to the first century." The number 600,000 divided by 1,000 yields the figure of 600.[5] We are then left with a chance of one in 600 of finding a first-century tomb with this particular cluster of names.

Could this be correct? Is there more information to this statistical calculation than what the *JFT* book and *LTJ* documentary demonstrate?

Statistical Inflation

While at first the cluster of names found in the Talpiot tomb seems impressive, statistics can be abused if not carefully used. As James R. White says, "Did you know that 87.9% of all statistics are misused? It's true! Well, it's true 78.4% of the time anyway, right?"[6] Doing statistical analysis is not wrong. Mathematics is very precise and helpful. All statistical analysis must begin somewhere, and yet if the starting point is replete with errors, the results from such an analysis will also be flawed.[7]

Even Feuerverger admits this. "The results of any such computations are highly dependent on the assumptions that enter into it. Should even one of these assumptions not be satisfied then the results will not be statistically meaningful."[8] Feuerverger further adds that if the assumed computation of identifying "Mariamenou e Mara" as the historical "Mary Magdalene" is wrong, "this assumption drives the outcome of the computations substantially." This is not to mention the number of other assumptions made on the rest of the inscriptions that must be directly linked to the family of Jesus of Nazareth.[9] Gary R. Habermas also notes, along with New Testament scholar Joseph Fitzmeyer, how many assumptions are often made for the documentary thesis to work. "Joseph Fitzmeyer is typical of many when he argues that the Talpiot Hypothesis contains far too 'iffy' conditionals which basically all must be true in order to arrive at their conclusions. Further, too many rhetorical questions are meant to be answered positively, when a negative answer will change the end result. As he concludes regarding this thesis: 'Speculation is rife.'"[10]

Of the 1,000 ossuaries discovered in Jerusalem about one fourth of them are inscribed. That leaves around 750 ossuaries instead of 1,000 ossuaries noninscribed as the starting point. How could Feuerverger then begin with 1,000 ossuaries when one quarter of them are the only ones inscribed? This leaves 750 ossuaries with names of individuals unknown. I personally counted in Rahmani's catalogue over 230 inscribed ossuaries with questionable ones that I chose not to include.[11] Stephen J. Pfann, president of the University of the Holy Land, corroborates my finding and comments on the problem of trying to formulate a statistic with such limited evidence. "According to L. Y. Rahmani, *A Catalogue of Jewish Ossuaries,* of 917 ossuaries in the collections of the State of Israel, only 231 (25.2%) are inscribed with names. The East Talpiot tomb is unusual in that 6 of its 9 registered ossuaries (66%) were actually inscribed with names. If all tombs contained similar percentages of inscribed bone boxes, then a comparative census between various tombs would be sensible and possible. However this is certainly far from being the case."[12]

Of the 231 ossuaries inscribed, at least two ossuaries have the inscription *Yeshua bar Yehosef* ("Jesus son of Joseph"). This makes a big difference according to Pfann. "That means 1 out of 115½ inscriptions we are going to have one inscribed ossuary with the name '"Jesus son of Joseph."'[13] Even assuming a correct reading of the inscription "Jesus son of Joseph" proves nothing. In fact, there are at least 99 individuals with the name Jesus and another 218 individuals with the name Joseph from this general era (330 B.C. to A.D. 200). Of these names 22 ossuaries have the name Jesus and 45 ossuaries have the name Joseph. These names are so common that Jesus is the sixth most used name of this period and Joseph is the second.[14] So common are these names that two other ossuaries inscribed "Jesus" were discovered in another Talpiot tomb.[15]

Limited Pool of First-Century Names

Furthermore, "if in fact 75 percent of all names come from among 16 Jewish names, one can also take the statistical analysis in another direction, as to how frequently one expects to find the *Yeshua bar Yehosef.* As it turns out, having 10 up to 80 individuals in one tomb, one can expect to find a *Yeshua bar Yehosef* in about three to every eight tombs in this complex.... In fact all of the other names found in the tomb belong to less than the 16 most common Jewish names operative in the first century."[16] Correcting the number of ossuaries taken into account, the number of possible people found in one tomb, and the limited number of names of the first-century changes everything and deflates the seemingly impressive odds of the Talpiot tomb belonging to that of Jesus of Nazareth. Hence Pfann makes the following observation and concludes, "*Remarkably, only 72 different Jewish names are represented among the 286 personal names found on the 231 inscribed ossuaries (bearing in mind that some ossuaries contain two or three names in the formula 'x son of y')!* These 72 personal names include their shortened forms and their Greek or Latin equivalents. What is the implication of this for establishing a statistical probability of occurrence?" Comparing first-century Jewish names, as Pfann does, with the unlimited "pool of individual personal names in use today in North America and Europe, a very small pool of personal names was normally used when naming a child in first century Judea and Galilee. *Again, remarkably, a mere 16 of the 72 personal names account for 75% of the inscribed names (214 in all)*."[17] Pfann then gives a list of the frequency of personal names inscribed on ossuaries, as noted in Rahmani's catalogue:

Names in Rahmani's Catalogue	*Ossuaries Inscribed*
1. Salome (Shalom, Shlomzion)	26
2. Simon (Shim'on)	26
3. Mary (Miriam, Maria)	20
4. Joseph	19
5. Judas (Yehudah)	18
6. Lazarus (El'azar, Eli'ezer)	16
7. Joezer (Yeho'azar)	13
8. John (Yehonan)	12
9. Martha	11
10. Jesus (Yeshua)	10
11. Saul	10
12. Ananias (Hananiah)	10
13. Matthew (Mattitiyahu, Mattai)	8
14. Jonathan (Yehonatan)	6
15. Jacob/James (Ya'aqov)	5
16. Ezekias (Hezekiah)	4
Total names occurring four times or more	214

Pfann concludes, "All of the names that are ascribed in the Gospels to Jesus of Nazareth's father (Joseph), mother (Mary) and brothers (Jacob/'James,' Joseph/Josehs, Simon, and Judas) are found in the list of the 16 sixteen most commonly inscribed names. In fact, four of these names, Simon, Mary, Joseph and Judas are among the top five in the frequency list of names (109 of 286 names: 38% of the entire list of names)."[18]

Names	Total Found	Ossuaries
1. Simon/Simeon	243	59
2. Joseph/Joses	218	45
3. Lazarus (Eleazar)	166	29
4. Judas (Yehudah/Judah)	164	44
5. John (Yohanan)	122	25
6. Jesus (Joshua)	99	22
7. Ananias (Hananiah)	82	18
8. Jonathan	71	14
9. Matthew/Matthias	62	17
10. Manaen	42	4
11. James (Jacob)	40	5
12. Mary (Mariam)	70	42
13. Salome	58	41
14. Shelamzion	24	19
15. Martha	20	17
16. Joanna	12	7
17. Sapphira (Shiphra)	12	9
18. Berenice	8	1
19. Imma	7	6
20. Mara	7	5

As early as 1958, P. B. Bagatti and J. T. Milik composed a list in Italian showing the most common names found in first-century ossuaries in *Dominus Flevit*. This list consists of sixteen names.[19] All of these names are so common that it contains all of the names found in the Talpiot tomb and also appear in most contemporary lists today: Simon, Joseph, Salome, Judas, Maria, John, Eleazar, Jesus, Martha, Matthew, Sapphira, Jonathan, Zechariah, Azariah, Jairus, and Menahem.

So common were these names during the first-century that a mere glance at the top twenty most popular names of the list provided (using also Tal Ilan's computation) by Richard Bauckham, professor of St. Andrews University, will dissuade anyone from thinking anything special about the combinations of the names found at Talpiot:[20]

Interestingly, the name Jesus was so common (not just on ossuaries) that Jewish historian Josephus mentioned fourteen first-century figures with this name,[21] ten of whom "were living at the same time as Christ."[22] In fact, as Bock concludes, "These are just Jesuses who made a historical impact! When we add to this fact the simple, even sloppy, nature of the inscription, the likelihood is that the Jesus whose ossuary was found at Talpiot was not, in fact, Jesus of Nazareth. Every expert I interviewed (Pfann, Kloner, and Ilan) agreed that the names were too common to support the documentary."[23]

Talpiot Ossuary Not Unique

Numerous other elements also point out that the idea that the Talpiot tomb belonged to Jesus of Nazareth and His family is false. A lack of any genealogy found in the first century (except for Jesus' genealogy through Joseph and Mary; see Matt. 1:1–17; Luke 3:23–34) hinders the view of the *JFT* and *LTJ* advocates, since no other list exists by which to compare it. Therefore to speak of any family at all in a statistical fashion becomes problematic since no other genealogical list has survived from the first century.[24] As Pfann says, "For Prof. Feuerverger to make any statement concerning the actual identification of the family is pure speculation, since there are no other complete family lists available for comparison, and is very inappropriate within the rubrics of his discipline."[25]

Therefore statisticians have no say when it comes to the Talpiot tomb discovery since, as correctly noted by Pfann, they have limited resources to work from. For example,

1. It would take another 600 tombs of similar size, form and contents to arrive at one with ossuaries bearing the identical names and numbers of this one. Even for this, there are a number of hurdles to cross:
2. The records of who and how many individuals were actually buried in any given family tomb in 1st century Judea and Galilee cannot be ascertained solely on the basis of examining the extant names on the surviving ossuaries in the tomb. This is due to the following circumstances:
   a) Most tombs have already been visited and looted in antiquity or in recent times, leaving the record of their original contents incomplete.
   b) Not all ossuaries are saved during the excavations so as to be stored and registered. Oftentimes, only ossuaries with inscriptions, decorations or both are kept.[26]

Furthermore since most of the family names of Jesus are mentioned in the Bible, where are they in the tomb? Even if Joseph died in another place, carrying one's bones later to the burial site with those of the family was a common practice as early as the patriarchs (see Gen. 47:29–30; 49:29; 50:5–7, 14). Charles L. Quarles, chair of Christian Studies at Louisiana College, observes, "This statistical analysis also does not reflect the scholarly uncertainty over whether the most important inscription actually reads 'Jesus, son of Joseph.' Nor does this analysis take into account the improbability of a family that resided in Nazareth would be buried in Jerusalem! If one denies the bodily resurrection of Jesus, one would have expected the bones of Jesus to be transferred to Nazareth for interment in a family tomb there. The claim that statistical analysis proves the Jesus of the Ten ossuaries to be the Jesus of the Gospel grossly misinterprets the archaeological and historical evidence."[27] Even taking out Matthew is not enough; one needs to consider subtracting from the statistical analysis even more since other members of Jesus' family expected to be there are not included. This is no small detail. If one claims to have found Jesus' family tomb, one would expect all these names to appear here, especially since this tomb would belong to such an honored person. Statisticians who know this computation must enter the equation if a specific identification is to be made.

Conclusion

Since there are no surviving genealogical records from the first century from anyone (except those in Matthew's and Luke's Gospels), it is a grave mistake to speak of any of the families in a genealogical sense, whether Jesus' or anyone else's. To suggest that this is connected with the Jesus' family tomb presumes that we have an extensive database and unlimited numbers of tombs by which to compare to other families with those names. We have such a small sampling that it is impossible to conclude anything from statistical analysis like what the documentary and book concluded. No statistics on families, therefore, can be formulated because we do not have a complete database on family names from that period.

Furthermore most of the members of the Talpiot family are mentioned by name, but where are the rest of the members of Jesus' family? If this was the tomb of Jesus of Nazareth, the rest of the family ossuaries should be there. Numerous relatives are missing. Where are they?

The occurrences of these names together are not impressive at all since they are "commonly found in the first-century Jerusalem." Many scholars, as Gary R. Habermas notes, acknowledge this point.[28] For example, Tal Ian, the author of one the largest dictionary compilations of Jewish names (*Lexicon of Jewish Names*), is noted by Christopher Mims to "vehemently disagree with the assertion that this could be Jesus' tomb." Ian says such names discovered in tombs "are in every tomb in Jerusalem… these are the most common names you can expect to find anywhere."[29]

Why were these facts not disclosed by the *JFT* book and *LTJ* documentary? If such information were revealed, it would deflate this supposition. The only way the cluster of names appear impressive is if the book and documentary can prove that these inscriptions belong to the family of Jesus of Nazareth, that *Mariamne* refers to Mary Magdalene, that Jose is either Jesus' brother or father, that Matthew is somehow related to them, that Maria is Jesus' mother, and that Judas is Jesus' son. Instead they have assumed their conclusions and have done faulty research in formulating their statistical analysis.[30] Since these are common first-century names, there is nothing unusual about finding a first-century tomb that contains such a cluster of names.

— Chapter 8 —

CONSPIRACY, TENTH OSSUARY, AND PATINA SAMPLES

Statistically speaking, adding "James son of Joseph" to the Talpiot cluster would essentially prove that the Talpiot tomb was the tomb of Jesus of Nazareth. "The additional probability factor that the James ossuary inscription would offer," Feurverger had suggested, "would drive our probabilities down to extremely small numbers: into the one-in-thirty-thousand zone. And that would be very, very remarkable."[1]

Based on the patina encrusted samples taken from inside the letters of the name "James" on the inscription, advocates of the *JFT* book and the *LTJ* film believe "beyond reasonable doubt" that both ossuaries inscribed "James, son of Joseph, brother of Jesus"[2] and "Jesus son of Joseph" were in the same tomb at one point.[3]

Because the tenth ossuary was not documented in L. Y. Rahmani's catalogue of ossuaries the documentary people raised suspicion.

Though the James ossuary surfaced in 2001, the documentary claims this ossuary went missing around the same time the Talpiot tomb was discovered in 1980.[4] Perhaps someone may have stolen it from the site at this time and sold it on the black market, which appears to be about the same time that Oded Golan, an antiquities collector, bought it.

Various arguments are given in an effort to validate this as the missing ossuary. First, James D. Tabor and the Talpiot advocates allege a possible conspiracy cover-up theory to answer the disappearance of the tenth ossuary connecting it with that of the "James, son of Joseph, brother of Jesus" ossuary. The Israel tourist industry tends to lose financially if such a discovery was authentic; for who would travel to see places where hoaxes were fabricated and where many people were lied to for years? Christianity would prove to be false, which would cause a major upheaval in today's religiously dependent civilization. Both of these reasons may cause one to consider a cover-up theory. Second, the time and name connect them to the Talpiot Jesus family. Third, Tabor claimed that the dimensions of the tenth ossuary of Talpiot (80.509) and the "James" ossuary are the same size "to the centimeter."[5] Fourth, patina samples seem to support the idea that both the "James" ossuary and "Jesus" ossuary were in the same family tomb.

Could the James ossuary be the tenth ossuary missing from the Talpiot tomb? Are these four claims without errors and are the *JFT* and *LTJ* people disclosing everything? These fascinating issues are the focus of this chapter.

Conspiracy Cover-up

The folks behind the *JFT* and *LTJ* projects claim that the tenth ossuary mysteriously disappeared.[6] Later Jacobovici theorizes how the disappearance and a possible cover-up conspiracy occurred. "I figure it went missing somewhere between Talpiot and the IAA headquarters at the Rockefeller Museum… What must have happened was that somebody took the ossuary. And the next day Gat and the others had to start explaining why they counted and measured ten and why they brought only nine into the warehouse. So number 509 ends up being written down as broken or damaged, with rounded measurements—

60 by 26 by 30 centimeters with no photo, and with a notation that it was 'plain,' lacking visible inscriptions."[7] Ultimately Jacobovici's desire to add James to the cluster of names would enormously increase the statistics and remove all doubt that was the Jesus family tomb.[8]

Apparently Jacobovici believes that the Talpiot archaeological team lied in their report, and that they guessed on the actual measurements of the tenth ossuary. To add insult to injury Tabor insinuates that Amos Kloner's report in 1996 of the Talpiot tomb is a mere copy of Yosef Gat's (now deceased) original report, as if he was not present.[9]

Numerous errors plague such a theory. As seen in chapter 1, much information exposes the Talpiot discovery for anyone to legitimately claim a cover-up conspiracy. Second, Kloner was one of the original archaeologists present at the 1980 Talpiot tomb, so he did not need to copy from another person's report. In fact Kloner showed Darrell L. Bock original photos taken at the site before the tomb was resealed. Hence Kloner's account of the tenth ossuary is prima-facie evidence even if he took other photos and the front of the cave and not the tenth ossuary.[10]

The *JFT* book conflicts with Tabor's allegation of Kloner's second-hand documentation of the find, and it contradicts itself in various places. The *JFT* book describes how Kloner reached a conclusion after all of the ossuaries were safely guarded against breakage, passed one at a time, and placed it into the bulldozed patio.[11] Kloner personally corroborates this in Bock's interview.[12] How could Jacobovici then claim that the tenth ossuary measurements were rounded of to the nearest centimeter—60 by 26 by 30 cm—after someone allegedly smuggled it when the book admitted earlier that Kloner "reached a conclusion" about all of the ossuaries once out of the Talpiot tomb? How could such a conclusion have been reached without proper measurements of the ossuaries?

Furthermore Tabor also insinuates cover-up by asking, "Was that tenth ossuary stolen after it was catalogued but before the excavation of the tomb was completed?"[13] Kloner directly answers this by explaining that the tenth ossuary was not lost, but instead since it was plain, without inscription or ornamentation, the ossuary was kept together with other plain ossuaries in a closed courtyard of the Rockefeller Museum (IAA) because at the time the basement was filled with ornamented and inscribed ossuaries.[14] Thus plain ossuaries were not discarded or stolen but once stored with similar looking plain ossuaries, it became virtually impossible to find since they all look alike. Normally about 50 percent of all ossuaries discovered are plain.[15] It is senseless to catalogue plain ossuaries with nothing to notice; besides, such a catalogue would be massive and very costly. That is why plain ossuaries like the tenth ossuary in the Talpiot tomb do not get cataloged.

Joe Zias, curator of the Rockefeller Museum at the time, corroborates Kloner's account since he was the person who cataloged the ten ossuaries and formed part of the original team of the Talpiot discovery. In an email on March 1, 2007, to Ben Witherington III, just before the Discovery Channel special aired, Zias clarified the issues surrounding the alleged tenth ossuary mystery, "Amos Kloner is right as I received and catalogued the objects, the 10th [ossuary] was plain and I put it out in the courtyard with all the rest of the plain ossuaries as was the standard procedure when one has little storage space available. Nothing was stolen or missing and they were fully aware of this fact, [it] just didn't fit in with their agenda." Zias then explains why no photos were taken of the tenth ossuary. "There was no photo of the tenth ossuary as there was no reason to photograph it, plain white ossuaries, basically once you have seen one you have seem them all. Time is money and it would be a waste of time to waste resources on something which was put out in the courtyard. Remember these are large, and heavy, not to forget that Kloner has the measurements." Did the *JFT* people know this? They certainly did, but they still went ahead with their documentary since according to Zias, "The conspiracy idea fits in well with their agenda of hyping the film as well as his/their book."[16]

James as the Tenth Ossuary

Before discussing whether the James ossuary is the tenth ossuary of the Talpiot discovery, it helps to know the brief story of how and where the James ossuary surfaced.

On October 21, 2002, Hershel Shanks, editor of *Biblical Archaeology Review*, held a press conference in Washington, D.C., to announce that a limestone ossuary inscribed in Aramaic with the phrase "James son of Joseph brother of Jesus" surfaced in Jerusalem (Figure 9).[17]

Figure 9.

Later it was revealed that private antiquities collector, Oded Golan, had allegedly bought the ossuary fifteen years earlier from an antiquities dealer. He said it came from the Silwan area south of the Old city of Jerusalem. Supposedly Golan was ignorant of the significance of his archaeological possession. When in April 2002 he showed photos of it to André Lemaire, Semitic languages professor, Lemaire immediately recognized its value. When Lemaire told Shank of the find while visiting Jerusalem in May 2002, since it had no archaeological context (i.e., the site was not known), Shank approached the discovery with caution.

However, after the authenticity of the inscription was supposedly confirmed, the press conference took place on October 21, 2002, and immediately it made worldwide headlines. The immediate frenzy took the Israeli authorities by surprise when the IAA had given permission to export the ossuary to Toronto for an exhibition. Immediately Israeli authorities initiated an investigation to see if the ossuary was purchased after 1978, because all archaeological artifacts purchased after that year belonged by law to the Israeli authorities, which meant that Golan had purchased it on the black market illegally.

Once the James ossuary was returned to Israel on February 2003, the IAA confiscated it and assigned a team of fifty experts to determine its genuineness. By June 2003 the verdict by the IAA was in. They determined that the ossuary and part of the inscription "James son of Joseph" was authentic but that the last part of the inscription "brother of Jesus" was added, thereby making it a forgery. Golan was arrested a month later on suspicion of antiquity forgery (Figure 10).[18]

Figure 10.

To this day this issue has not been resolved because the case is still on trial. Whether the entire James ossuary inscription is authentic or not matters little to the examination undertaken here.[19] We are concerned here with the arguments made by those who interpret this ossuary as the tenth ossuary of the Talpiot tomb.

Three arguments are used to support the view that the James ossuary is the tenth ossuary of the Talpiot tomb: the time of appearance, the name inscribed on the ossuary, and dimensions that are similar to an ossuary in the Talpiot tomb.

Regarding the time of its appearance, Tabor claims the time of the James ossuary discovery was about the time that other Talpiot ossuaries were found in 1980.[20] That is interesting because he had said before, along with others, that the James ossuary had come from another "robbed" tomb. Zias notes how some archaeologists changed their stories. "Two members of the *BAR Crowd* who appear prominently in the film had earlier declared that the ossuary had originally come from a robbed tomb which *they* had cleared a few years ago in Silwan and not purchased by the collector decades earlier as he claimed. They clearly had attempted to draw media attention to their robbed tomb in Silwan and when the media attention flagged they now suddenly claim that they were mistaken and the ossuary no longer comes from Silwan but from the Talpiot 'Jesus Family tomb excavated in 1980 by the Israel Antiquities Authority!'"[21]

Moreover, how can the James ossuary belong to the Talpiot tomb discovered in 1980 when at Golan's trial evidence pointed to a date of purchase four years earlier and not when Golan had claimed to buy it? Zias reports, "Well, last week ago a small problem suddenly arose when Oded Golan the owner of the ossuary in question, who is on trial for forging objects, produced a photograph of the ossuary with a time stamp 1976, four years before the Talpiot tomb was accidentally discovered!"[22]

Regarding the inscription, the name on the ossuary reads, "James, son of Joseph brother of Jesus." But is that unique? Not really. "Statistically, according to Lemaire, there could have been as many as twenty people in that period of the time who could have been known as 'James/Jacob son of Joseph brother of Jesus."[23] So even if the James ossuary belonged to the Talpiot family tomb, it would not be that unique.

Tabor claims that the dimensions of the tenth ossuary are "precisely the same, to the centimeter, to those of the James Ossuary."[24] However, Kloner, one of the archaeologists present at the original site, documents the tenth ossuary dimensions as "10. IAA 80.509: 60x26x30 cm. Plain."[25] These dimensions, however, differ remarkably from that of the James ossuary as Lemaire notes. "It is 20 inches long (50.5 cm) at the base and flairs out to almost 22 inches (56 cm) at the top. Although one of the short sides is perpendicular to the base, the other is slanted, giving the box a trapezoid shape. The ossuary is 10 inches (25 cm) wide and 12 inches (30.5 cm) high."[26]

In Bock's interview Kloner completely denied that these ossuaries were the same size. Kloner describes the James ossuary dimensions as 56 cm long at the top and 50.5 cm long, similar to Lemaire's specifications. The bottom measures 30.5 cm high. Kloner adds that one could make a mistake in measurement by half of a centimeter or even a whole centimeter but *not* by measurements of an ossuary measuring 60 cm compared to another measuring 56 cm at the top and 50.5 cm at the bottom rim.[27] Zias supports Kloner's report by adding that someone in "Jerusalem checked the dimensions of the two 'identical' ossuaries and found that the Talpiot plain white 'missing' ossuary is approximately 20% longer than the James brother of Jesus ossuary!"[28]

Once all three arguments are carefully investigated in support of the theory that the "James son of Joseph, brother of Jesus" belongs in the Talpiot tomb, we can safely conclude that it is impossible that this ossuary is from that tomb.

Patina Samples

Two final points remain to be answered, however. Could the patina sample of the James ossuary match the patina samples of the ossuaries found in the Talpiot tomb? If so, does this prove the James ossuary came from the Talpiot tomb?

Patina samples are mineral layers that form in a particular ossuary "unique" to its burial location, thereby pointing to a particular section or tomb that it comes from. This may function like—but not the same as—fingerprints linking a person to the scene of a crime. The way this works is nicely explained by Charles Pellegrino. "A tarnishing piece of metal or a broken chip of china might record changing cooking styles or types of paint used throughout a generation in a single home, just as the patina on the Statue of Liberty has recorded the history of air pollution in New York City. This technique might be applicable for connecting, say, a murder weapon with the chemistry of a particular backyard."[29] This may seem convincing, but one should not be fooled to think this kind of testing even comes close to fingerprints or DNA testing. It does not. Unfortunately that is the impression left by the *LJT* film, and what many viewers were led to believe.

The *terra rosa* soil contains minerals that stick to the ossuaries. If the *terra rossa* soil matches the James ossuary with those of the Talpiot tomb, then Pellegrino could continue to entertain the theory that the James ossuary was the tenth ossuary that was once in the Talpiot tomb. Several of the Talpiot ossuaries were tested to see whether the patinas matched. They did. Then the *JFT* people compared the James ossuary patina results done four years earlier with that of the Talpiot ossuaries, and it indicated a close consistency between them.[30] They concluded that "the ossuaries inscribed 'James, son of Joseph, brother of Jesus' and 'Jesus, son of Joseph' had once resided together inside the same tomb, for millennia."[31] However, while this may impress those who saw the Discovery Channel documentary and read the book, various things were not disclosed which weakens their theory substantially.

First, a "key" component to the patina argument is that similarities do not prove identity. The fact that two things are similar does not prove they are identical.[32]

Second, no other samples were taken from surrounding areas near Talpiot. James White points this out. "Patina from similar tombs (like the one found just north of the Talpiot tomb) where *terra rosa* had entered the tomb around the same time would be needed for a meaningful comparison, and that kind of study was not done."[33] Crime Lab director, Robert Genna, whom Jacobovici and Pellegrino quote in the documentary to validate their theory, did not corroborate their point. After the documentary he said the following in the interview with Ted Koppel.

> The elemental composition of some of the samples we tested from the ossuaries are consistent with each other. But I would never say they're a match…. No scientist would ever say definitely that one ossuary came from the

same tomb as another.... We didn't do enough sampling to see if in fact there were other tombs that had similar elemental compositions.... The only samples we can positively say are a "match" from a single source are fingerprints and DNA.[34]

Genna's comments reveal two problems not conveyed by the documentary and book. Though the patina may help identify similarities between patinas, they cannot be used to detect an identical match like that made by fingerprints and DNA. This poses a major problem to the documentary's theory of placing the James ossuary in the Talpiot tomb. Furthermore, more samples needed to be collected from the surrounding Talpiot area to see whether other *terra rosa* soil patina samples were similar to that of the Talpiot tomb ossuaries.

Forensic scientist, Steven Cox, from the University of the Holy Land, also noted the limited sampling. "The collected samples purported to have been collected from the ossuaries, untraceable to source and unidentified in orientation, indicate the ossuaries could have originated from the same quarry from whence they were hewn. To arrive at a [*sic*] an opinion exhibiting a unique common origin would require more testing of known samples of ossuary stone from numerous quarry sites. This would allow a database which would paint a more confident chemical profile than what was done in documentary." In addition, he observes a number of errors and misinterpretations exhibited in the documentary that are significant.

Observations of Error

Underlying logical errors

A conclusion was formed first through speculation and conjecture, then facts were sought to support the preconceived notion.

Speculation and conjecture are converted into FACTS without supporting logic or confirmed scientific methodology.

Sample collection errors

Sample contamination errors
Sample preparation errors
Sample orientation errors

It should be very evident at this point that the *The Lost Tomb of Jesus* (TLTJ) team's statement is, at best, an overstatement of opinion based on limited fact, poor scientific protocol, unresolved sources of error and shrouded in poor research. In my opinion, one of the greatest tools a forensic scientist learns is not how to operate an instrument. Rather, it is how to logically assess the weight of the result derived from examining evidence or artifacts. In forensic work, someone's life hangs in the scales of justice. Be it a suspect or a victim of crime, the result and the following testimony will effect that persons' life forever. So, a forensic scientist has to take making conclusions and opinions very, very seriously. If this type of conservative and cautious reporting were applied to the TLTJ documentary, the program probably wouldn't have gotten much notice or, at best, it would have produced more responsible journalism.[35]

Given this information, along with other evidence discussed in this chapter, the testing of the patina of the James ossuary and the patina that of the Talpiot tomb ossuaries proves nothing. Consequently this shows to what extent a researcher will go to seek to prove his or her point. Not noticing the likelihood of slanting the evidence to fit our conclusions is a danger we all face when arguing a case. That is why subjecting all research to peer review is essential in order to arrive at the best possible result before drawing a conclusion. This is something the *JFT* and *LTJ* advocates did not do, which is why their research is lacking and continues to receive enormous criticisms from numerous scholars, both liberal and conservative.

Conclusion

After the debris clears three things are certain. The conspiracy idea is farfetched and fits nicely with the agenda of hyping the film as well as the *JFT* book. It is impossible that the "James son of Joseph, brother of Jesus" belongs in the Talpiot tomb since it is approximately 20% longer than the original measurements given of the original tenth ossuary. Furthermore, the testing of the patina of the James ossuary and the patina of the Talpiot tomb ossuaries proves nothing apart from creating more sensationalism.

— Chapter 9 —

OTHER BIZARRE THEORIES AND ALLEGATIONS

When they weren't called "Ebionites," the early followers of the Jesus were called "Nazarenes."...(126) Could it be, Tabor wondered, that the chevron, like the symbol of the fish, was yet another early symbol of Jesus's [sic] first followers?... (129) And it actually makes sense that Jesus's [sic] family would choose the area of modern Talpiot for a family burial cave....(137) Also, if Simcha is right and the symbol on the facade is related to the promise of Jesus—as a Jewish Messiah—to build a Third Temple at the 'end of times,' then even the "Templar" name may be related to the Talpiot tomb....(134) For example, in the Talpiot tomb there is a clear cross-mark on the back of one of the uninscribed ossuaries. Why is it there next to the ossuary of Jesus, son of Joseph?...(196).[1]

Supporters of the *JFT* theory also assert numerous other peculiar claims. (1) The Nazarenes and Ebionites are considered the earliest Jewish followers of Jesus, who established many doctrines in the early church. (2) The chevron sign of a pyramid with a circle could be an early Christian sign depicting an unfinished third temple destined to fall and to be rebuilt in the messianic times. (3) Since the center of early Christianity was in Jerusalem, where James, Jesus' brother, led it, it seems logical to locate the family tomb east of Jerusalem. (4) "By definition ossuaries with single crosses on them don't qualify as ossuaries with mason's marks."[2] Therefore could this be indicative of a Christian cross? (5) Could the Knight Templar be a secret society that knew of Jesus' burial and kept it a secret all these years? These assertions and questions will be examined in this chapter.

Nazarenes and Ebionites

Were the Nazarene and Ebionite groups the real followers of Jesus? Simcha Jacobovici believes so. "I think the original followers of Jesus, variously called Ebionites, Nazarenes, and Judeo-Christians, didn't just 'disappear' at the time of Constantine and the rise of the Gentile church.... In other words, as long as Jerusalem stood, it was the Nazarene/Ebionites who called the theological shots in the Jewish Jesus movement, they seemed indistinguishable from the general Jewish population."[3] These statements are incorrect at best and anachronistic[4] at worst. Furthermore these groups were clearly part of Gnostic groups that flourished in the late second to third centuries and were condemned (by early church followers) because of their heretical views about Jesus Christ.

The name Ebionite comes from the Hebrew word *'ebyônîm* meaning "poor" or "needy." The name Nazarene comes from the place *Nazōraios* where Jesus grew up (Matt. 2:23; Mark 1:24; Luke 4:34). The heretical Gnostic groups that were condemned by Irenaeus, Origen, Epiphanius, and Eusebius were later also known by both of these names. J. A. Fitzmyer says the Ebionites were called as such: "(*a*) because of the poverty of their intelligence (Origen, *De princ.* 4, 22; *Hom. in Gen.* 3, 5; Eusebius, *Hist. Eccl.* 3, 27; Epiphanius, *Pan.* 30,

17); (*b*) because of the poverty of the law which they followed (Origen, *Contra Cels.* 2, 1); (*c*) because of the poverty of the opinions they had of Christ (Eusebius, *Hist. eccle.* 3, 27); (*d*) because they were 'poor in understanding, hope, and deeds' (Epiphanius, *Pan.* 30, 17)."[5] The reader can see reasons why early church tradition considered both of these groups heretical since they deviated from many traditional first-century scriptural teachings.

a) They followed heretics such a Cerinthus and Carpocrates
b) They used only the Gospel of Matthew
c) They deemed Paul a heretic who rejected the Law
d) They practiced circumcision
e) They observed the Sabbath
f) They observed all the Jewish customs and ways of life based on the Law
g) They faced Jerusalem when they prayed (Ebionites)
h) They believed observance of the Mosaic Law is necessary for salvation (Ebionites)
i) They denied the virgin birth of Christ
k) They believed Christ was a mere man
l) They denied Jesus' preexistence as God (Nazarenes)
m) They called Jesus the Son of God (Nazarenes)
n) They maintained Jesus had to merit the title "Christ" by fulfilling the Law
o) They purified themselves with ceremonial bathings (Ebionites)
p) They practiced water baptism (Ebionites)
q) They celebrated the Lord's Supper with unleavened bread and water (Ebionites)
r) They believed Christ annulled the temple sacrifice (Ebionites)
s) They held that God set the devil and Jesus to rule over this world and the one to come (Ebionites)
t) They lived in poverty by giving up all material wealth (Ebionites)
u) They allowed divorce (Ebionites)
v) They accepted some prophets (Abraham, Isaac, Moses, Aaron, Joshua) but denied others (David, Solomon, Isaiah, Jeremiah, Daniel, Ezekiel, Elijah, Elisha) (Ebionites)

w)	They admitted that Christ was alone the prophet of truth (Ebionites)
y)	They abstained from meat like Peter initially said in Acts 10 (Ebionites)
z)	They believe in the resurrection of the dead (Nazarenes)[6]

Though both of these groups did not hold the same doctrines, as seen in this list, they both denied major tenets of the faith (while affirming some Christian beliefs) by rejecting Jesus' deity, salvation by faith alone, and the virgin birth.

Jacobovici incorrectly believes the Ebionites and Nazarenes were the original followers of Jesus. This is impossible since there is no trace whatsoever of such groups mentioned before the late second century (*ca.* A.D. 175) by Irenaeus.[7] Even if both of these groups arose after the destruction of the temple in A.D. 70 and found themselves poor and perhaps were assimilated with the Qumran community, the practice of asceticism as a theology came later in church history.[8] Hence Fitzmyer correctly concludes, "Though it is quite probable they existed as a sect much earlier, there is simply no evidence for their existence in the first century A.D., either before or after the destruction of Jerusalem. Consequently, the simple identification of the Qumran sect and the Ebionites is untenable."[9] Therefore to claim both of these groups were the original followers of Jesus is a theological absurdity and a historical blunder.[10]

Chevron Sign at Talpiot

Another insinuation made by the *JFT* book and *LTJ* film centers on whether the chevron sign over the tomb stood like the Christian fish sign of early Christianity or a sign of an unfinished temple that Jesus predicted will be build in the third millennium ("The Temple of messianic times, of the 'End of Days'"). Jacobovici concludes, "Viewed in this manner, the chevron and circle symbolized, during the last years before the tomb was sealed and the Temple fell, a hoped-for Resurrection for both the Temple and Israel."[11]

This highly questionable interpretation, and the evidence from the Second Temple and first-century burial symbols, shows that this view is not feasible. Chevron signs, like those found in the façade of the Talpiot tomb, are not unique. They seem to stand for both a monument and symbol of the place where the *nefesh* (soul) lives after death, similar to that of Egyptian pyramids (see Figure 11).[12]

Figure 11. The Tomb Façade

Rachael Hachlili defines and explains the use of this symbol as follows:

> The *nefesh*, or funerary marker, consists of a monument, object, stone, stele, or building, and is known from Semitic funerary customs, both from inscriptions and monuments. Among the Syrians and the Nabateans, the *nefesh* was believed to be both a monument as well as the dwelling-place of the spirit after death. Literally, the word *nefesh* means 'soul,' but in a funerary context it is the term applied to a form of funerary monument, the marker on a tomb, a stele or it might indicate the tomb itself, a funerary building or mausoleum.
>
> In Second Temple Period sources, grave markers and pyramid-capped obelisks are mentioned (I Macc. 13:27–29; Ant. 13, 211; 16, 182; 20, 95). In descriptions

of the tombs of the Jewish nobility, the pyramid shape is also emphasized as the mark of a tomb, I Macc. 13:27–30 reads, "... Moreover he set up seven pyramids, one against another for his father and his mother and his four brethren...." The seven pyramids mentioned in this passage are equated with seven nefesh and probably took the form of obelisks. This would imply that nefesh and pyramid were synonymous.[13]

Thus the practice of having a pyramid-like shape of a chevron sign on the Talpiot tomb is not something spectacular, as the *JFT* advocates would have us believe. Evidence suggests that a *nefesh* was used as a "Nabataean custom," and this symbol over a grave seems to have been "adopted by the Jews."[14] A number of first-century ossuaries with their chevron symbol on them are documented by Rahmani (see Figure 12).[15]

Figure 12.

This could hardly be coincidental. The only possible explanation for this fascinating phenomenon is that the Jews adopted the sign of the *nefesh* placed on either a tomb façade or on ossuaries as a symbol where the soul of the dead would rest.

Jesus' Burial at Talpiot

Advocates of the *Jesus Family Tomb* claim, "After all, geographically, Talpiot is about halfway between Jesus's [*sic*] traditional family home in Bethlehem and Jerusalem, which is the seat of power for any family claiming descent from King David."[16] This makes Talpiot, the documentary argues, an ideal location for Jesus' family burial because many of its family members could travel to both cities making the burial site a convenient location to visit.

JFT proponents also argue that after Jesus' departure His brother James became the leader of the Jerusalem church, and so perhaps Jerusalem was the place where James was buried since he probably spent most of his time ministering there. Along with church tradition that asserts James' mother, Mary, was buried in Jerusalem, this seems at first glace to be the best location.

For Jerusalem to be the best location for Jesus' family burial various things must be asserted. However, this theory has numerous problems.

Usually poor classes of Jewish families buried their dead in common individual trenches dug into the ground, much like today. The body would be covered with a blanket then placed into the rectangular hole. Afterward, the trench was filled with earth and sometimes a small rough tombstone would be placed above the site.[17]

Conversely, Joseph of Arimathea initially placed Jesus in his family tomb (Matt. 27:57–60). It appears he did this in order for Jesus to have a proper Jewish burial since according to Jewish Law all burials must take place within 24 hours of death and not on the Sabbath (Deut. 21:23). Probably under normal circumstances Jesus would have been buried in an ordinary trench grave, but there was no time to dig a trench before the Sabbath.

The Sabbath was approaching. Hence Joseph laid Jesus in his rock-cut family tomb that only the rich, unlike Jesus' family, could afford. On Sunday morning followers of Jesus headed to the rock-cut tomb to anoint the body, and perhaps take it to a trench grave or acquire another location because it was uncommon to leave a nonrelative in a family tomb.[18] Thus if Jesus' family did not own a rock-cut tomb there were no ossuaries in which to store bones either, at least not according to the Gospel records (Matt. 28:1–20; Mark 16:1–8; Luke 23:55–56; 24:1-9; John 20:1–10).

So one must ask, "Where would the location of such a family tomb be since Jesus' family lived in Nazareth?" Jesus, of course, was known as a Nazarene (Matt. 2:23).[19] Even if Jesus' family could afford a rock-cut tomb or someone donated it, it would be located in Nazareth, not Jerusalem. Tombs were usually located in the hometown where the families are from. "For example, when Simon, the last of the Maccabean brothers and one of the Hasmonean rulers, built a large tomb or mausoleum for his family, he constructed it in their hometown of Modin. In fact, the Gospel accounts clearly indicate that Jesus' family did not own a rock-cut tomb in Jerusalem—for if they had, there would have been no need for Joseph of Arimathea to take Jesus' body and place it in his own family's rock-cut tomb."[20] Furthermore, if such a family tomb existed for a figure as renowned as Jesus of Nazareth, there would certainly be some evidence recorded in church tradition or in some historical annals, similar to the record of His execution. Yet no such evidence exists. Of course, this does not prove the absence of such a tomb, but it seems highly improbable that if such a tomb existed it could be kept secret since Jesus was so popular and His enemies were so intent on disproving His resurrection claim. If such a tomb existed, all they needed to do is walk over to it and disprove the idea that He rose from the dead. Even if the body was stolen from one location and placed in another, how long could they keep this a secret? How could the disciples steal the body of this famous figure of the day, procure money to buy a family tomb, and then proclaim that Jesus rose from the dead in just three short days after His crucifixion, "knowing all the while that they buried him and his rooted remains [were] in that second tomb?"[21] This poses a huge problem for the Talpiot theory.[22]

Furthermore L. Y. Rahmani, an archaeologist and compiler of all of the ossuaries collected in the state of Israel, observed, "In Jerusalem's tombs, the deceased's place of origin was noted when someone from outside Jerusalem and its environs was interred in a local tomb."[23] Hence Magness correctly concludes the following.

> On ossuaries in rock-cut tombs that belonged to Judean families, it was customary to indicate the ancestry or lineage of the deceased by naming the father, as, for example, Judah son of John (Yohanan); Honya son of Alexa; and Martha daughter of Hananya. But in rock-cut tombs owned by non-Judean families (or which contained the remains of relatives from outside Judea), it was customary to indicate the deceased's place of origin, as, for example Simon Ptolemais; Papias the Bethshanite (of Beth Shean); and Gaois son Artemon from Berenike. Our historical and literary sources (such as the Gospels, Flavius Josephus, among others) often make the same distinctions between Judeans and non Judeans (for example, Galileans, Idumaeans, Saul of Tarsus, Simon of Cyrene, and so on). *If the Talpiyot tomb is indeed Galilean origins, by reading, for example, Jesus [son of Joseph] of Nazareth (or Jesus the Nazarene), Mary of Magdala, and so on. However, the inscriptions provide no indication that this is the tomb of a Galilean family and instead point to a Judean family.*[24]

Joe Zias, curator of the IAA, from 1971–1997, where the ossuaries were stored, corroborates this as well. "The important thing to remember here is that individuals outside of Judea, buried in Judea were named according to their place of origin, whereas in Judea this was not necessary. Had the names [on the ossuaries] been Jesus of Nazareth, Mary of Nazareth, Joseph of Nazareth etc I would have been totally convinced that this may be the family tomb, but as none of the names have place of origin, they are all Judeans."[25]

Thus the burden of proof is on those who claim that the Talpiot family tomb belongs to a Galilean family like that of Jesus of

Nazareth, since the place of origin does not appear on any of the inscriptions found in the Talpiot tomb ossuaries.

Crucifixion Sign on Jesus' Ossuary

The cross (X or +) on Jesus' ossuary may be connected with the "Tao" (ת), the last letter of the Hebrew and Aramaic alphabets, which He spoke, implying a common phrase uttered in Greek by Him in Revelation (22:13), "I am the Alpha and the Omega, the Beginning and the End, the First and the Last." The *JFT* and *LTJ* advocates, along with others, have made the mistake of incorrectly understanding the X mark on ossuaries as a Christian symbol of the cross (see Figure 13).[26]

However, this is nothing more than a mason's mark to align the front part of lid with that of the ossuary that appears on hundreds of first-century bone boxes. Rahmani's catalogue contains about "40%" of "decorated and plain ossuaries" that "bear marks" of crosses, zig-zags, and other markings (see Figure 14).[27]

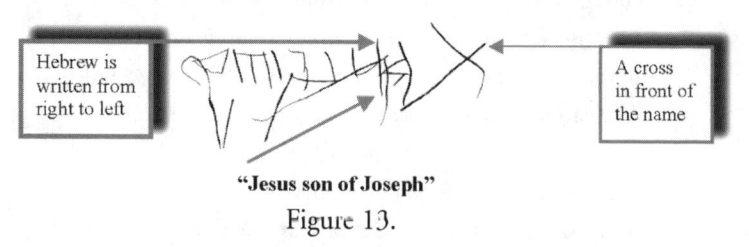

"Jesus son of Joseph"
Figure 13.

He says, "The location of paired marks indicates that *their only function* was to ensure the positioning of the lid for the closest possible fit on the chest."[28]

Interestingly, the *JFT* advocates do not—and simply cannot—sidestep this overwhelming fact. This explains why they choose to

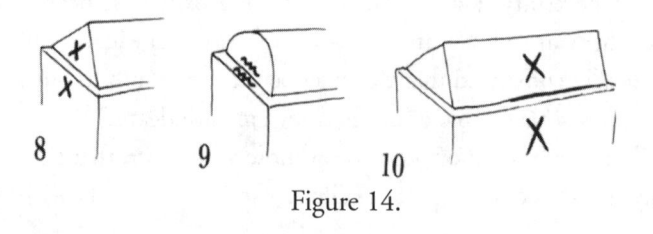

Figure 14.

deflect the opponent's argument by mentioning it sarcastically.

> Had the Romans hanged Jesus from a tree, would his followers have walked around with tiny ornamental gold nooses around their neck? Father Jerome Murphy-O'Connor of the École Biblique in Jerusalem believes it is unlikely that anyone would have worn a cross as a religious symbol at the outset of the Jesus movement. It was a symbol of torture, not redemption.... And what about the hundreds of crosses on ossuaries dating back to the time of Jesus? "They're not crosses, they're mason's marks," is the conventional wisdom.[29]

Instead of going with the enormous amount of evidence against their theory, the *JFT* advocates chose a highly debatable interpretation of a cross-like symbol found in a supposedly religious context appearing as a "shrine" in the city of Pompeii (*ca.* A.D. 79) to argue their point. They acknowledge that scholars explain away the cross-like figure to be "a shelf." More accurately, the cross-like figure was an engraved image in the wall plaster belonging to a bracket that once held a shelf. Everett Ferguson describes this discovery as follows.

> A second floor apartment in Herculaneum (destroyed by Vesuvius in 79) contained a chamber in which on one wall was a rectangular covered with white plaster. In the plaster was engraved a sign in the shape of a Latin cross, 0.43 meter high and 0.365 meter wide. A chest on the floor underneath and slightly to one side of the 'cross' was interpreted as an altar and the room therefore as a Christian cult place. Further consideration, however, has given a more utilitarian purpose: the imprint in the plaster was left by wooden brackets for a wall cabinet or perhaps a shelf mantel with a supporting right piece.
>
> Other supposed "evidence" for Christianity at Pompeii and Herculaneum before A.D. 79 seems similar capable of alternative, more likely interpretations.[30]

If such a symbol signified a Christian cross, similar crosses would clearly be found in other houses throughout Pompeii. However, nothing remotely appearing as a Christian cross has ever been found.[31] Having visited Pompeii in 2004 I do not remember seeing a cross anywhere.

Ferguson also notes how X-shaped crosses occur frequently in "Jewish funerary" monuments and, "On the Jerusalem ossuaries it may have had the utilitarian purpose of marking correspondence of lid and the body of the ossuary." He also acknowledges that because biblical names like those of Jesus' family "were common" this "makes impossible a certain identification with the family of Jesus of Nazareth."[32]

Clearly the evidence shows that until late second century in Tertullian's writings the cross was not necessarily used as a Christian symbol and until Constantine's vision in A.D. 317 it was not used "without restriction as a public symbol of Christian faith."[33] Any interpretation that sees crosses as a first-century Christian symbol (especially on ossuaries) is anachronistic. Crosses on ossuaries, along with other markings, were simply not Christian symbols but mere marks functioning as signals to align ossuary lids with the chest cavity.[34]

Knights Templar Revisited

For those who read Dan Brown's Knights Templar argument in his *Da Vinci Code* and thought that was a ridiculous and dead issue, they may be surprised to find it being referred to in two other books since then, the latest being *The Jesus Family Tomb* (2007).

James White has hit the nail on the head when he said, "Certain groups in history are always rife for a new conspiracy theory. The Knights Templar seems to be at the top of the list when it comes to spawning conspiracy theories."[35] No wonder New York Times bestsellers like Michael Baigent's conspiracy-fraught books *Holy Blood, Holy Grail* (1983) and *The Jesus Papers* (2006), along with Dan Brown's book *The Da Vinci Code* (2003), has used the Knights Templar stories to promote their wild theories and propel sales.

Other Bizarre Theories and Allegations

Unlike Brown's Knights Templar, who defend Jesus' royal linage, Jacobovici's *Jesus Family Tomb's* Knights Templar know a secret which they used to blackmail the Vatican after eliminating most (if not all) of the original Ebionite Jewish-Christians.[36] Here is how the book tells the story:

> Somewhere near the twelfth century, somewhere near this time of Crusaders and Templars, the Tomb of Ten Ossuaries was breached by what would eventually become known as the entry of the "terra rossa people." They were neither local Jews nor local Muslims, for they followed the customs of neither.
>
> The intruders opened the seal of the fifth ossuary niche, removed the northernmost ossuary studied it, and pushed it gently back into place but with one end still protruding. All the ossuaries survived without any signs of being damaged or looted.
>
> In the center of the tomb, the *terra rossa* people left a calling card, of sorts. Three skulls were placed in the chamber in an odd and clearly ceremonial configuration.
>
> Then, by a strange swerve of history, the tomb came to be sealed a second time and was either forgotten or kept secret, once again disappearing into history.
>
> .... It is a fact that the Templar knights were in Jerusalem during the entire century of the First Crusade.... Many speculated that they had something on the church.... It was also said that the Templars performed a secret ceremony in which an initiate was obligated to walk a triangle and circle around a skull and crossbones and that they gained their wealth through the discovery of sacred Jerusalem relics, which bound them together and, for a time, gave them some manner of secret power over the Vatican.[37]

This story is so farfetched that it is laughable. If it were not for many who read and unfortunately believe this, I would not even address it. This is not far from Darrell L. Bock's sentiment and response to Brown's *Da Vinci Code's* outlandish Knight Templar's theory, "There is no good historical reason to discuss these later groups in relationship to a theory about Jesus whose foundation is lacking."[38]

First, there are no accounts of such stories in history books or any other kind of serious works that are nonfiction.

Second, no documentation is given in this story. Therefore how can anyone verify it?

Third, since the Talpiot tomb (discovery in 1980) was left open for a day and a half and eyewitnesses saw children playing with skulls and bones that were scattered in the tomb, how do we know the children were not the ones who did this?[39]

Fourth, similar to Brown's *Da Vinci Code* tactic, mixing fact with fiction to make the story more believable, does not make the account true. It is true that the Templar Knights existed, but here is the *true* story.[40] They were established during the period of the Crusaders in Jerusalem to defend against Muslim bands wanting to control Jerusalem. To protect many pilgrims in their plight to the Holy Land eight or nine French knights (led by Hugues de Payens) took a vow around "late 1119 or early 1120 to devote themselves to their protection and to form a religious community for that purpose." At this time Baldwin II reigned in Jerusalem and gave these knights living quarters in the area where Solomon's temple once stood. This is where they got their name. Though the Templars initially took vows of "poverty and chastity," later they grew enormously, by the "propaganda writings of St. Bernard of Clairvaux" who popularized their way of life, to about 20,000 knights, each of whom wore a white overcoat with a big red cross on it. By the time Pope Innocent II in 1139 headed the church, the knights were relieved from serving any longer a Jerusalem monarch and were placed under papacy authority. Many "kings and great nobles" from Spain, France, and England gave them authority and properties so that by the middle of the twelfth century they diversified and were now able to obtain property and become very wealthy. Though they encountered problems with their military rivals in Europe called the "Hospitalers," their glory days came to a close when the last stronghold to protect Jerusalem was no longer needed after the Muslim ultimate defeat in 1291 in Acre. By 1304 rumors circulated all over Europe about heretical practices due to supposedly secret initiation rites and immoralities, which led to King Philip IV of France arresting all Templars (on October 13, 1307) and confiscating all of their property. Because of political pressure from Philip, French Pope Clement V, also gave orders to arrest all Templars. By 1314 the last Templar, Jacques de Molay, "was burned at the stake." To this day the Knight Templar's guilt and accusations have been a topic of much controversy and debate. Many today believe that they became victims unjustly of "opportunistic persecution."[41]

Compared to the historical facts about the Knight Templar, Jacobovici's story above is purely fictional with some facts sprinkled in it. Yes, they were persecuted but not because of some secret they held over the Vatican. In fact it was King Philip IV, not the Vatican, which began the knight's persecution. It appears that their demise was due more to a political move to remove them from power than because of any religious belief. Even if there were some truth behind the heretical accusations, nothing in the accusations point to the Talpiot tomb or any secret that would supposedly damage Christianity. How does Jacobovici then know the knights broke into the Talpiot tomb, placed three skulls in a "clearly ceremonial configuration," "opened the seal of the fifth ossuary niche, … studied it, and pushed it gently back into place"? He does not. This is pure science fiction.

Conclusion

It becomes clear that *JFT* advocates spin theories based on pure speculations with no documentation or historical veracity backing them up. One of these historical blunders is that the Nazarenes and Ebionites were the earliest Jewish followers who established all the doctrines for the early church.

Another wild theory is that the chevron sign of a pyramid with a circle was an early Christian sign depicting an unfinished third temple destined to fall and to be rebuild in the messianic times. In fact, the evidence strongly suggests that the Jews adopted the chevron sign of the *nefesh* placed on either a tomb façade or on ossuaries as a symbol where the soul of the dead would rest.

Furthermore, since Jesus' family was not from Jerusalem and the ossuaries do not have inscriptions stating where they were from (a normal custom appearing on ossuaries for people buried outside of their hometown), the evidence shows that the Talpiot tomb did not belong to Jesus' family who lived in Nazareth.

Crosses and many other marks on ossuaries are so common that 40 percent of all ossuaries contain them. These marks simply served as signals to align ossuary lids with the chest cavity. That is all that this means.

It is pure nonsense to suggest that the Knight Templar was a secret society that knew of Jesus' burial and kept it a secret for many years. It has no historical foundation. All the issues examined in the *JFT* book and the *LJT* film in this chapter (if not their entire theory) really belong to the literary genre called, "science fiction."

— Chapter 10 —

THE PHYSICAL RESURRECTION A HISTORICAL FACT

> People who believe in a physical Resurrection would not be affected by the discovery of Jesus bone box.... With respect to his Ascension to heaven, the New Testament also does not tell us that its chroniclers believed that Jesus, when he ascended, needed to take his entire body with him. So if you believe in a physical Ascension, the ossuary is a problem. But if you believe in a spiritual one, it becomes an object of veneration.[1]

Most scholars have admitted that early witnesses to Jesus' resurrection believed they really saw Him alive after He had died.[2] But these scholars differ on how they explain what the witnesses saw. They attempt to explain the Resurrection in one of three ways: the natural view, the supernatural view, and the agnostic view.[3] The agnostic view pleads ignorance to what early witnesses saw, while the other two views are each subdivided into two categories.

For example, the natural view seeks to explain Jesus' resurrection by either a subjective *internal* means or objective *external* means.

The subjective internal theory says that the witnesses experienced hallucinations. While many believed they saw Jesus alive, this was just their imagination.[4] Willi Marxsen held that Peter was influenced to believe in the risen Jesus by a vision, whose faith then influenced others to promote the idea that Jesus rose though they themselves did not personally experience the vision. Marxsen adds that it is impossible to know "the actual reality" of what Peter saw.[5] To hold this view, however, one would have to reinterpret the normal meaning of the word "see" when perceiving someone or something objectively, redefine the straightforward testimony of the Gospel accounts of seeing, touching, and eating with the risen Jesus, and reinterpret Paul's terminology in 1 Corinthians 15:1–9 that mentions that a number of people had "seen" the risen Jesus. Hence this view has not been prominent among scholars.

Some who hold to an objective external theory interpret Jesus' resurrection with fantastic explanations. For example, one of the most famous explanations is the "swoon" or "apparent death" view. This view postulates that Jesus merely fainted on the cross, and that after being taken down from the cross and taken to a tomb He somehow survived. Though this view has its advocates, the majority of scholars have rejected this theory since far too many assumptions and exceptions must occur for it to be true, besides having to discard extrabiblical and biblical testimony that says otherwise.[6]

Variations of the naturalistic view exist, but basically this view alleges that Jesus never rose from the dead. Gary R. Habermas concludes, "Each of the naturalistic theories was attacked piece by piece by the liberal scholars in the nineteenth century, as each criticized the other's approaches. In the twentieth century, critical scholarship has largely rejected wholesale the naturalistic approaches to the resurrection."[7]

On the other hand, the supernatural view claims that something actually happened to Jesus after He died. In this view there are also subjective and objective elements as well. The subjective idea of having a personal "vision" was debunked by Theodor Keim, who held that Jesus appeared objectively to the disciples "in the form of heavenly 'telegrams,' revealing his glorified state and convincing them he was alive and well."[8] Although in this view the tomb was not empty, Jesus made supernatural appearances in a noncorporeal way.[9]

Likewise the *JFT* book and *LTJ* film advocates, along with some scholars, believe Jesus' resurrection appearances were spiritual in nature. Hence when interpreting the Resurrection accounts of what the early followers saw, they allege that one should not jump to conclusions that their visions prove that Jesus rose bodily. This helps the *JFT* theory that possessing an ossuary belonging to Jesus of Nazareth is not incompatible with the biblical accounts of the Resurrection or contrary to the historical Christian view of the Resurrection.

Furthermore, some reject the idea that Jesus rose bodily since fallible men wrote the Bible, and since it has a number of errors, who can trust it? This is the allegation made recently by the best-selling author Bart D. Ehrman's *Misquoting Jesus*.[10]

Because many books, monographs, and articles have thoroughly addressed the issue of Jesus' resurrection and whether the Bible is a trustworthy historical document, there is no need to repeat that information exhaustively here.[11] Our scope will be much more limited to address arguments on whether Jesus rose from the dead, and whether He had a spiritual or a physical body.

Before discussing the Resurrection, however, one should first validate the document (the Bible) used to testify of Jesus' resurrection. That is, can the Bible be trusted and thereby give credence to the Resurrection accounts of Jesus of Nazareth?

The Bible as an Accurate Historical Document

A number of scholars agree with the sentiment of Earl Doherty who writes, "We have nothing in the Gospels which casts a clear light on that early evolution or provides us with a guarantee that the surviving texts are a reliable picture of the beginning of the faith."[12] Along with this opinion, people also make an unwarranted assumption: "*difference = contradiction, error, or lack of credibility.*"[13] Another assumption, popularized by Dan Brown's *The Da Vinci Code*, asserts that all of the Bible books were accepted as authoritative on the basis of an unfair vote by the Roman emperor Constantine in the fourth century at the Council of Nicea (A.D. 325).[14]

Before clarifying such allegations of errors, assumptions, and historical blunders, it must be openly stated that showing whether Jesus rose bodily from the grave does not depend on whether one believes in the inerrancy of Scripture. Gary R. Habermas and Michael R. Licona present the "minimal facts" arguments,

> Too often the objection raised frequently against the Resurrection is, "Well, the Bible has errors, so we can't believe Jesus rose." We can quickly push this point to the side: "I am not arguing at this time for the inspiration of the Bible or even its general trustworthiness. Believer and skeptic alike accept the facts I'm using because they are so strongly supported. These facts must be addressed."... Historians recognize that most writings of antiquity contain factual errors and propaganda. They still can identify kernels of historical truth in those sources. If they eliminated a source completely because of bias or error, they would know next to nothing about the past. Thus, [if one rejects]... the inspiration of the Bible, there was still the collection of historical facts that remained to be answered.[15]

These historical facts, which must be answered by those who reject the inspiration of Scripture, are discussed in this chapter to argue for the veracity of the bodily resurrection of Jesus. Having said this, however, the evidence shows the Bible can be trusted as an accurate historical document that conveys the truth of what happened in Jerusalem over two thousand years ago.

It is a colossal historical blunder to allege that all twenty-seven New Testament (NT) books were deemed authoritative by a mere vote that occurred in the Council of Nicea A.D. 325.

First, the Council of Nicea had nothing to do with forming the canon (or the official recognized list of inspired books) of the NT. Instead this Council convened to settle the long-held belief about the deity of Jesus and His relationship to the Father, since a debate arose between two prominent men of the time. Presbyter Arius of Alexander believed Jesus was created and is not of the same nature as God the Father. Conversely Athanasius believed Jesus is distinct from the Father, but is similar in nature as God.[16] After an almost unanimous vote of 316 to 2, the matter was settled and the long-held belief of the church for two hundred years now officially stood: Jesus is God.[17]

Second, within the first century the Bible claimed for itself to be inspired and people trusted it as God's Word (Matt. 5:17; Luke 10:7; 24:27; Acts 2; 17:11; Gal. 6:16; Eph. 2:20; Col. 4:16; 1 Tim. 5:18; 2 Tim. 3:16–17; Heb. 1:1–2; 2 Pet. 1:19–21; 3:16; Rev. 1:3). Almost all scholars date all NT books within the first century, and some even believe they were all written before A.D. 70.[18]

Followers of the apostles, called church fathers, believed that these books were the inspired Word of God. Men like Ignatius of Antioch (A.D. 35–107) and Polycarp, a disciple of the apostle John (A.D. 65–115), and writings including the Epistle of Barnabas (A.D. 120) and the Epistle of Second Clement (A.D. 140) referred to the NT books as "Scripture." Thus by the middle of the second century most of the books were already considered Scripture by church leaders.[19] By the end of the second century most of the NT books appeared in a list called the Muratorian Fragment (Roman origin), except Hebrews, James, and 1 and 2 Peter. These books were still in question, which proves the rigorous process that took place in the early church before accepting any book as authoritative.[20]

Because fast communication systems (airplanes, telephones, and computers) did not exist in those days, it took a while before all twenty-seven books of the NT were recognized and compiled. By A.D. 367, Athanasius was the first to mention the twenty-seven books of the NT as canonical.[21] Later in two councils all twenty-seven books of our present NT were official recognized. This, however, did not occur simply because someone voted them arbitrarily into a list. F. F. Bruce forcefully says,

> One thing must be emphatically stated. The New Testament books did not become authoritative for the Church because they were formally included in a canonical list; on the contrary, the Church included them in her canon because she already regarded them as divinely inspired, recognizing their innate worth and generally apostolic authority, direct or indirect. The first ecclesiastical councils to classify the canonical books were both held in North Africa—at Hippo Regius in 393 and at Carthage in 397—but what these councils did was not to impose something new upon the Christian communities but to codify what was already the general practice of these communities.[22]

Someone said eloquently, "'The church did not create the Canon: the Canon created the church.' In other words, it is the Word of God from the outside, given key moments in history through His chosen messengers, that calls the people of God into existence. In the fourth century, the church merely published for the sake of clarity what it had always believed."[23] To say otherwise is to make a historical blunder.

Another mistake many scholars and laymen make is assuming that "differences" equal "contradictions." Understanding how to interpret history may be a bit complex and requires careful thought, since the way events are recorded may vary according to a writer's perspective.

Darrell L. Bock illustrates this point by asking the name of the worldwide conflict that occurred at the turn of the twentieth century. "Only a few realize that it was initially called 'The Great War' or the 'War to End All Wars.' Both names expressed the scope of the conflict, which was unprecedented up to that time. The name this conflict is known by today is 'The First World War,' a name it could not have until the Second World War took place. Now whether one refers to this event by its original name, The Great War, or by its alternative, The First World War, one is looking at the same set of historical events." Thus sometimes an event may be understood and described by its original name or setting that took place or by its subsequent impact after it occurred. Therefore a historian may record an incident from its original perspective or how it was perceived in the aftermath of the event. Both accounts are true but have different perspectives with one description having more details than the other.[24]

Numerous examples of this sort occur in the Bible.[25] That is, similar accounts of the same event may vary according to the perspective a historian wants to emphasize.

Many books have been written discussing problem passages in the Bible and passages that seem to contradict each other.[26] Two examples will suffice to demonstrate the common erroneous assumption that "differences" equal "contradictions."

Matthew 8:6–9 records a centurion asking Jesus to heal his servant. However, in Luke 7:3–8, messengers are the ones asking Him to heal the centurion's servant. Perhaps these are two similar events that describe different occasions in which a centurion had a slave that needed healing. While that may work, for example, in the accounts described with similar details in the Sermon on the Mount and the Sermon on the Plain (Matt. 5:1; Luke 6:17), it seems incredulous here and in a number of occasions.[27] Another way of resolving the issue is to say these accounts contradict each other and are mistaken. Recording such a contradiction, however, makes no sense if people were trying to forge a godly inspired document. It seems they would want to harmonize the text. The better alternative is to say both are emphasizing different details of the same account. Matthew addresses a Jewish audience in whose culture messengers spoke on behalf of a person as if the person/sender was present.[28] "An example in our culture is when the White House press secretary speaks. What is important is not especially who he is but that he speaks for the president. Ancient culture was similar."[29] Thus Matthew summarizes the event as if the centurion is the one speaking to Jesus (normally understood by his Jewish audience), but since Luke addresses a mixed group of Gentiles he gives more details since they would not understand this way of summarizing the event.

Peter's three denials of Jesus seem to clash in the biblical accounts because those accusing him differ (Matt. 26:69–75; Mark 14:66–72;

Luke 22:55–62; John 18:15–18, 25–27). But again, "It may just be that as the denials proceeded, *more than three people* challenged Peter though different accounts note only *some* of those participants."[30]

What may seem contradictory may be resolved by understanding the different perspectives the historians wanted to emphasize.

Another accusation made against the Bible's trustworthiness appears on three levels, as noted by NT textual critic scholar Bart D. Ehrman. (1) Not only do we not have the original documents the apostles wrote, but we also do not posses copies, or copies of the copies of the primary text. All we have are very late copies of the originals.[31] (2) A number of differences also exist in these copies, so much so that "there are more variants among our manuscripts than there are words in the New Testament."[32] (3) "Orthodox" scribes have altered the text so drastically in a number of places that the meaning of the text changes, which results in having a different doctrinal conclusion.[33]

Ehrman's three objections are noted and answered by Daniel B. Wallace.[34] First, Ehrman has no way of knowing how to determine those late third-or fourth-generation copies. We do have "between ten to fifteen copies within a century of the completion of the New Testament."[35] Hence it seems possible that these third- or fourth-generation copies were made from even earlier manuscripts. Ehrman simply gives a false impression.

Second, differences in manuscripts are sometimes compared to what occurs in a "telephone game."[36] Children sit in a wide circle. At one end a child repeats a secret to the one next to him and so on, until the last child repeats the message which by then is terribly distorted. Wallace, however, clarifies the fallacy of this comparison.

> But the copying of New Testament manuscripts is hardly like this parlor game. Most obviously, the message is passed on in writing, not orally.... Second, rather than one line, multiple lines or streams of transmission are available. These help to function as checks and balances on the wording of the original. A little detective work in comparing, say, three lines of transmission, rather than

reliance solely on the last person's account in one line, would help recover the wording of the original story. Third, textual critics don't rely on just the last person in each line but can interrogate several folks who are closer to the original source. Fourth, writers (known as church fathers) are commenting on the text as it is going through its transmissional history. And when there are chronological gaps among the manuscripts, these writers often fill in those gaps by telling us what the text said in that place in their day. Fifth, in the telephone game, once the story is told by one person, that individual has nothing else to do with the story. It is out of his or her hands. But the original New Testament books most likely were copied more than once and have been consulted even after several generations of copies had already been produced.[37]

Furthermore, do we really have more variations in the manuscript copies than we have words in the NT? Ehrman estimated that 400,000 textual deviations exist in the NT. Compared to the 138,162 words in the standard Greek NT this seems unusually high, and it gives the impression that no one could ever arrive at the original text of the Scriptures.[38] Who can believe the Bible's account of the early witnesses of Jesus' resurrection if the copies were corrupted? But the fact is we can. What Ehrman presents as a huge problem is more apparent than real.

Most textual variations have no bearing on the meaning of the Scripture; no major doctrines are in doubt.[39] Most of the differences simply involve a letter that was omitted in a word or added, or a variant spelling of a word, or a synonym. Even when a different word appears in a passage, which supposedly changes its meaning, so many copies exist along with quotations from church fathers that arriving at the original word and meaning of the text is only a matter of doing the necessary investigative work of comparison: internally in the context and externally by looking at the copies available.[40] In fact, the

Greek NT manuscripts are unrivaled by any other ancient works as the following chart shows:[41]

Authors/Works	Recorded	Dates of Mss.	Time Span	Copies Survived
Caesar	100–44 B.C.	A.D. 900	1,000 YRS	10
Livy	59 B.C.–A.D. 17	A.D. 300	400 YRS	27
Plato	427–347 B.C.	A.D. 900	1,200 YRS	7
Tacitus (*Annals*)	A.D. 56–120	A.D. 800	900 YRS	3
Pliny the Younger (*History*)	A.D. 61–113	A.D. 850	750 YRS	7
Thucydides (*History*)	460–400 B.C.	A.D. 100	600 YRS	20
Suetonious (*De Vita Caesarum*)	A.D. 69–140	A.D. 800	900 YRS	200+
Herodotus (*History*)	484–425 B.C.	A.D. 100	600 YRS	75
Sophocles	496–406 B.C.	A.D. 1000	1,400 YRS	193
Catullus	54 B.C.	A.D. 1550	1,600 YRS	3
Euripides	480–406 B.C.	A.D. 1100	1,500 YRS	9

Authors/Works	Recorded	Dates of Mss.	Time Span	Copies Survived
Demosthenes	383–322 B.C.	A.D. 1100	1,300 YRS	200
Aristotle	384–322 B.C.	A.D. 1100	1,400 YRS	40
Aristophanes	450–385 B.C.	A.D. 900	1,200 YRS	10
Homer	900 B.C.	400 B.C.	500 YRS	643
New Testament	A.D. 35–100	A.D. 100–150	5–30 YRS	5,700

**New Testament copies include (1) fragments, (2) some incomplete copies of the NT, (3) the complete NT, which are all in Greek. Another 10,000+ manuscripts exist in Latin plus more than one million quotations from the church fathers.*

"Besides textual evidence from the New Testament Greek manuscripts and from early versions, the textual critic compares numerous scriptural quotations used in commentaries, sermons, and other treaties by early church fathers. Indeed, so extensive are these citations that if all other sources for our knowledge of the text of the New Testament were destroyed, they would be sufficient alone for the reconstruction of practically the entire New Testament."[42] Hence Wallace concludes, "In sum, New Testament textual critics suffer from an embarrassment of riches when their discipline is compared with other Greek and Latin literature. Although it is true that we don't possess the original documents, to say that we don't have the copies of the copies of the original, without further clarification as to what we *do* have, is misleading. Statements like this reveal one of the fundamental flaws in *Misquoting Jesus*: it's not what Ehrman puts into the book that is so troubling but what he leaves out. And what he leaves out is any discussion of the tremendous resources at our disposal for reconstructing the text of the New Testament."[43]

The Physical Resurrection Accepted Historically

Today some scholars say it is incorrect to speak of Jesus' resurrection as "historical." Marxsen believed this, and "a remarkable number of subsequent scholars have followed him in this assertion."[44] Ehrman, in a debate with William L. Craig, argued that one could believe "theologically" that God raised Jesus from the dead but not historically.

> But this cannot be a historical claim, and not for the reason that he [Craig] imputed to me as being an old, warmed over 18th century view that has been refuted ever since. Historians can only establish what probably happened in the past. The problem with historians is they can't repeat an experiment. Today, if we want proof for something, it's very simple to get proof for many things in the natural sciences; in the experimental sciences we have proof. If I wanted to prove to you that bars of ivory soap float, but bars of iron sink, all I need to do is get 50 tubs of lukewarm water and start chucking in the bars. The Ivory soap will always float, the iron will always sink, and after a while we'll have a level of what you might call predicted probability, that if I do it again, the iron is going to sink again, and the soap is going to float again. We can repeat the experiments doing experimental science. But we can't repeat the experiments in history because once history happens, it's over.[45]

Such a view not only denies the existence of miracles, but also misunderstands how one may refer to "history" in different ways. Noting this kind of error N. T. Wright says, "This proposal appears to be cautious and scientific. It is, however, neither of these things. It involves a rash dismissal of an important question, and a misunderstanding of how science, including scientific historiography, actually works.... This is a classic case of failing to distinguish between the different senses of 'history.'"[46]

Not distinguishing how one may use the word "history" in five different ways has been part of the problem plaguing the "historical Jesus" and the "resurrection of Jesus" debate.[47] Wright succinctly summarizes how the fives senses of the term "history" works, which helps clear the confusion that so often comes with the arguments of those wanting to refute Jesus' physical resurrection.

> First, there is history as *event*. If we say something is "historical" in this sense, it happened, whether or not we can know or prove that it happened.
>
> Second, there is history as *significant event*. Not all events are significant; history, it is often assumed, consists of the ones that are. The adjective that tends to go with this is "historic"; "a historic event" is not simply an event that took place, but one whose occurrence carried momentous consequences.
>
> Third, there is history as *provable event*. To say that something is "historical" in this sense is to say not only that it happened but that we can demonstrate that it happened, on the analogy of mathematics or the so-called hard sciences.[48]
>
> Fourth, and quite different from the previous three, there is history as *writing-about-events-in-the-past*. To say that something is "historical" in this sense is to say that it was written about, or perhaps could in principle have been written about. (This might even include "historical" novels).
>
> Fifth and finally, a combination of (3) and (4) is often found precisely in discussions of Jesus: history as *what modern historians can say* about a topic. By "modern" I mean "post-Enlightenment," the period in which people have imagined some kind of analogy, even correlation,

between history and the hard sciences. In this sense, "historical" means not only that which can be demonstrated and written, but that which can be demonstrated and written *within the post-Enlightenment worldview*. This is what people have often had in mind when they have rejected "the historical Jesus" (which hereby, of course, comes to mean "the Jesus that fits the Procrustean bed of a reductionist world") in favour of "the Christ of faith."[49]

What then is the sense of the word "history" that we ought to understand when the early witnesses claimed to have seen Jesus or when Paul wrote, "He was buried, and ... He rose again the third day according to the Scriptures" (1 Cor. 15:4)? Were they recording a historical event or writing metaphorically? All the early first-century witnesses spoke of Jesus' resurrection as a historical event that actually occurred according to Wright's first point: "history as *event*." Because we speak of Jesus' resurrection as a historical event, this does not mean it cannot be verified. Many things have happened that cannot be proven scientifically according to point number three but can be verified. For example, "The death of the last pterodactyl is in that sense a *historical* event, even though no human witnessed it or wrote about it at the time, and we are very unlikely ever to discover [scientifically] when it took place." Do we then say this is not a true event when all of the circumstantial evidence points to this being the case? "Similarly, we use the word 'historical' of persons or things, to indicate simply and solely that they existed."[50]

We are now left to answer in the rest of this chapter one question: Did the Hebrews and Christians following the apostles understand the Resurrection to be of a spiritual or physical nature?

Hebrew Scriptures' general thought. For ancient peoples (including those in the Middle East) the *Iliad* written by Homer, was to them what the Old Testament (OT) was for the Jews. Along with Homer much of the other Greek classical works (eight to fifth century B.C.) painted a gloomy picture for the dead who could not return.[51] Even the concept of "resurrection" in the world of Egyptian mummification (or any Canaanite or fertility cults) does not have the same biblical sense.[52] Clarifying this difference in Jon Davies'[53] incorrect application of the term, Wright concludes. "The word denotes, as he sees, a further re-embodiment, a return to a this-worldly life, after a period in which the dead person is *not* alive in this way. Mummification and its other attendant practices, however, imply that the person still is 'alive' in some bodily sense, despite appearances." This does not mean a person comes back to a new bodily form of existence (which appears to be the way the NT uses the word "resurrection") but "'continuing existence in a mummified and hence, in that sense, 'bodily' state after death.'"[54]

Homer's view of life after death took an evolutionary turn in Plato's writings (fifth to fourth century B.C.), which the ancient world considered much like that of the NT.[55] Homer viewed the "'self' being the physical body, lying dead on the ground, while the 'soul' flies away to what is at best a half-life, now the 'self,' the true person, is precisely the soul." But "for Plato, the soul is the non-material aspect of a human being, and is the aspect that really matters. Bodily-life is full of delusion and danger; the soul is to be cultivated in the present both for its own sake and because its future happiness will depend upon such cultivation. The soul, being immortal existed before the body, and will continue to exist after the body is gone. Since for many Greeks 'the immortals' were the gods, there is always the suggestion, at least by implication, that human souls are in some way divine."[56] One can see where the Greco-Roman concept and emperors adopted the idea that they were in some form divine.

Contrary to ancient pagan literature, the general thought in the Hebrew Scriptures was based in attaining a bodily resurrection. Though the OT concept of resurrection is minor, however, later Jewish and Christian interpreters noticed "covert allusions" missed by earlier readers, an ability shared by many including Jesus. Although many scholars agree that for most of the OT the concept of a bodily resurrection meant being "deeply asleep," they also believe later revelation brought this idea to the fore.[57]

The concept of resurrection appears to have developed in three common stages. "Many Christians have adopted some kind of theory of progressive revelation, according to which the earlier parts of the Old Testament held little or no belief in life after death, some of the more mature parts began to affirm a life beyond the grave, though without being very specific, and then, right at the end of the Old Testament period, some writers began to proclaim the quite different and radically new belief in bodily resurrection." In other words, "This is routinely seen as a kind of crescendo, beginning with near-silence, as it were, of the grave itself, and moving towards the fully orchestrated statement of the theme which will dominate the New Testament."[58]

Though this general understanding is correct, it needs to be modified. Beginning with the Genesis account of the Fall, God would not be triumphant unless the original physical creation was not in someway renewed. Acknowledging this important feature Bock wrote, "The bodily aspect of Jesus' resurrection is key, because in Judaism the belief in resurrection was a belief in a bodily resurrection involving a redemption of the full scope of what God had created (Rom. 8:18–30)."[59] Similarly Witherington states, "This resurrection is linked to actual environmental renewal of the earth itself (see Rom 8:18–25). The destiny of believers and the destiny of the earth are inexorably linked together."[60] Though not as clear as the third stage that explicitly advocates the concept of physical resurrection, the first stage shows at times the resurrection seed and early plant-life that would later blossom to a mature tree in the New Testament era.[61] However, the Hebrew Scriptures do not concentrate on "life after death" or even "with resurrection."[62]

For example, evidence from numerous passages seems to show, perhaps like that of Homer and other Greek classical writers, that the Hebrew Scriptures described death as the final analysis:

> "For out of it you were taken; for dust you are, and to dust you shall return" (Gen. 3:19).

> "For in death there is no remembrance of you; in the grave who will give you thanks" (Ps. 6:5).

> "The dead do not praise the LORD, nor any who go down into silence" (Ps. 115:17).

"For we will surely die and become like water spilled on the ground, which cannot be gathered up again" (2 Sam. 14:14).

"For the living know that they will die; but the dead know nothing, and they have no more reward, for the memory of them is forgotten. Also their love, their hatred, and their envy have now perished; nevermore will they have a share in anything done under the sun. Go, eat your bread with joy, and drink your wine with a merry heart; For God has already accepted your works. Let your garments always be white, and let your head lack no oil.

Live joyfully with the wife whom you love all the days of your vain life which He has given you under the sun, all your days of vanity; for that is your portion in life, and in the labor which you perform under the sun.

Whatever your hand finds to do, do it with your might; for there is no work or device or knowledge or wisdom in the grave where you are going" (Eccl. 9:5–10).

Many more passages exist that describe the temporal nature of human life without any preview of future hope.[63] Unlike Plato's progressive view of death survived by a bodiless soul, "Death itself was sad, and tinged with evil. It was not seen, in the canonical Old Testament, as a happy release, an escape of the soul from the prison-house of the body." Instead, life, the corollary to death, was to be enjoyed to the fullest.[64]

One should not take from these passages (as the predominant thrust of the OT) that Jews did not believe in a future hope of restoration or the continuation of life after death, since it appears in seed form. Even passages describing the temporal nature of life, the hopelessness, and the ineffective state of the dead were merely ways of depicting life as it is viewed from an earthly perspective, or as the writer of Ecclesiastes, would say: life as seen "under the sun."[65]

However, ancient Israelites knew of other passages that gave them a living hope beyond the grave (e.g., 2 Sam. 7:12–21;[66] Pss. 72:1–12;

89; Isa. 61:1–11).[67] Too many other passages exist, though some are debatable, to simply dismiss the fact that OT Jews had no hope of the dead returning to life (e.g., Gen. 22:5 [cf. Heb. 11:17–19];[68] Job 19:25–27; 33:15–30; Pss. 16:10–11 [cf. Acts 2:23–31]; 22; 49:1–19; 73; Isa. 26:19; 53:10–12; Ezek. 37:1–14).[69] Yet of all OT passages almost all scholars today agree that Daniel 12:2–3 speaks of a concrete bodily resurrection from the dead.[70] "And many of those who sleep in the dust of the earth shall awake, some to everlasting life, some to shame and everlasting contempt. Those who are wise shall shine like the brightness of the firmament, and those who turn many to righteousness like the stars forever and ever."

Though bodily resurrection was not the predominant belief in the OT it does burst forth, as seen above, in various passages. Certainly this is the case in Daniel 12:2–3.

Resurrection in Jewish sources. However, by the second-Temple period, the time of Jesus, and rabbinic writings this position changed (200 B.C. to A.D. 200). By this period almost all Jews believed in some form of bodily resurrection.[71] Those who believed in the resurrection meant life after death in the sense of a two-stage approach. That is when a person died he existed in a place prepared by God where he waited for a future bodily resurrection, not some ghostly or spiritual disembodiment of eternal existence.[72] Sadducees, a Jewish aristocratic group arising in the second century B.C., however, denied any form of resurrection. Many such passages from the *Wisdom of Jesus ben Sirach* (i.e., Ecclesiasticus) appears to support their view that nothing beyond this life awaited anyone.[73] But similar to those passages of the OT, *Wisdom* (and a few intertestamental texts) emphasizes an earthly perspective of the frailty and fleetingness of life so as to encourage obedience while one lives.[74]

Another view—though a minority position—of a disembodied resurrection of the soul existed in this period, like that in Platonic Greek philosophy, which influenced Judaism of the second century B.C.[75] While such passages (1 Macc. 2:49–70; 4 Macc. 3:18; 6:7; 7:19; 9:22; 10:19; 14:5; 16:25; 17:12; 18) appear to promote the disembodied view of the soul, this interpretation can be questioned. Nothing explicitly states in these texts that the soul will live disembodied. Even one of the most used passages, *Jubilee* 23:27–29, frequently cited to argue for the existence of the disembodied souls, says in the following two verses, "rise up," "bones rest," and "spirits increasing joy," which may describe the two-stage expectation of time between a person's death and resurrection (vv. 30–31). Wright believes this is "the probable interpretation." However, this would then be "the only occurrence in the relevant literature of something that looks like the resurrection language being used to denote something other than new bodily existence." And this would be odd.[76]

Another exception to the predominant teaching of this era appears in Philo's writings. Philo, an Alexandrian Jew, was steeped in Hellenistic philosophy like that of Plato and Aristotle, which taught the immortality of the disembodied soul.[77] But this and the previous positions were not majority views in second–Temple Judaism.

Since first-century Jewish Christians testified of Jesus' resurrection, it is necessary to understand the context in which they made such allegations in order to know how to interpret it.

What became the predominant belief of second-Temple Judaism on the Resurrection comes to the fore unambiguously through the martyrs of the Maccabees. As the Syrian oppressor, Antiochus Epiphanes, wanted Jews to defy their laws, by eating pork and worshiping idols, through the story of a mother and her seven sons who are torture to death, they claim to return victoriously in a new body at the resurrection.

> And when he was at his last breath, he said [the second brother], "You accursed wretch, you dismiss us from this present life, but the King of the universe will raise us up to an everlasting renewal of life, because we have died for his laws" (2 Macc. 7:9).

> After him, the third was the victim of their sport. When it was demanded, he quickly put out his tongue and courageously stretched forth his hands, and said nobly, "I

got these from Heaven, and because of his laws I disdain them, and from him I hope to get them back again" (2 Macc. 7:10–11).

"And when he was near death, he [the fourth brother] said, "One cannot but choose to die at the hands of men and to cherish the hope that God gives of being raised again by him. But for you there will be no resurrection to life!" (2 Macc. 7:14).

The mother was especially admirable and worthy of honorable memory. Though she saw her seven sons perish within a single day, she bore it with good courage because of her hope in the Lord. She encouraged each of them in the language of their fathers. Filled with a noble spirit, she fired her woman's reasoning with a man's courage, and said to them, "I do not know how you came into being in my womb. It was not I who gave you life and breath, nor I who set in order the elements within each of you. Therefore the Creator of the world, who shaped the beginning of man and devised the origin of all things, will in his mercy give life and breath back to you again, since you now forget yourselves for the sake of his laws" (2 Macc. 7:20–23).

I [the mother spoke privately to her youngest son] beseech you, my child, to look at the heaven and the earth and see everything that is in them, and recognize that God did not make them out of things that existed. Thus also mankind comes into being. Do not fear this butcher, but prove worthy of your brothers. Accept death, so that in God's mercy I may get you back again with your brothers." [This implies the physical reality of returning since God made the physical world from nothing.] (2 Macc. 7:28–29)[78]

A mere reading of the Jewish text of 2 Maccabees 7 makes it impossible to deny belief in a future bodily resurrection.[79] Another political hero of this era, Judas Maccabeus, discovered that the men who died in battle wore under their robes idolatrous tokens of the idol of Jamnia. He urged those alive to pray that God would forgive them (12:40–42), when they rose again.

> He also took up a collection, man by man, to the amount of two thousand drachmas of silver, and sent it to Jerusalem to provide for a sin offering. In doing this he acted very well and honorably, taking account of the resurrection. For if he were not expecting that those who had fallen would rise again, it would have been superfluous and foolish to pray for the dead (2 Macc. 12:43–44).[80]

Yet another incident occurred to a Jew called Razi, elder of Jerusalem (2 Macc. 14:37). Before being arrested by the enemy Nicanor and the soldiers, he fell on his own sword (v. 41) while hoping to rise one day by the Lord's power.

> But in the heat of the struggle he did not hit exactly, and the crowd was now rushing in through the doors. He bravely ran up on the wall, and manfully threw himself down into the crowd. But as they quickly drew back, a space opened and he fell in the middle of the empty space. Still alive and aflame with anger, he rose, and though his blood gushed forth and his wounds were severe he ran through the crowd; and standing upon a steep rock, with his blood now completely drained from him, he tore out his entrails, took them with both hands and hurled them at the crowd, calling upon the Lord of life and spirit to give them back to him again. This was the manner of his death (vv. 43–46).

Apocalyptic literature of this period, like that of *1 Enoch*, though at times it is not explicitly clear,[81] makes a bold claim for bodily resurrection.

> And in those days shall the earth also give back that which has been entrusted to it, And Sheol also shall give back that which it has received, and hell shall give back that which it owes. For in those days the Elect One shall arise, and he shall choose the righteous and holy from among them: For the day has drawn nigh that they should be saved. And the Elect One shall in those days sit on My throne, and his mouth shall pour forth all the secrets of wisdom and counsel: For the Lord of Spirits hath given (them) to him and hath glorified him. And in those days shall the mountains leap like rams, and the hills also shall skip like lambs satisfied with milk, and the faces of [all] the angels in heaven shall be lighted up with joy. And the earth shall rejoice, and the righteous shall dwell upon it, and the elect shall walk thereon (*1 Enoch* 51:1–5).[82]

Similar to the "Elect One" above, the "Son of Man" together with a righteous remnant will receive a bodily resurrection, which depicts "a judgment scene reminiscent" of Daniel 7:13; 12:2; and Isaiah 52–53.[83]

> And the righteous and elect shall be saved on that day, and they shall never thenceforward see the face of the sinners and unrighteous. And the Lord of Spirits will abide over them, and with that Son of Man shall they eat and lie down and rise up for ever and ever. And the righteous and elect shall have risen from the earth, and ceased to be of downcast countenance. And they shall have been clothed with garments of glory (*1 Enoch* 62:13–15).

First Enoch 91:10 also says, "And the righteous shall arise from their sleep, and wisdom shall arise and be given unto them." Other passages make the same point of the righteous attaining to a future bodily resurrection (*1 Enoch* 96:1–3; 102:4–11; 103:4; 104:1–4; 108:11–15; *Pseudo-Phocylides* 102–105; *Testament of Moses* 10:8–10; *Life of Adam and Eve* 13:3–6; 4; 41:2; 43:2–3; *Sibylline Oracles*

4:179–92; *Testament of Levi* 18:3; *Testament of Judah* 25:4; *Testament of Zebulon* 10:1–3; *Testament of Benjamin* 10:6–9; *4 Ezra* 7:28–44 [Daniel 12:2]; *2 Baruch* 30:1–5; 42:8; 51:5; *Psalms of Solomon* 3:11–16).[84]

In hindsight many Rabbis viewed the Hebrew Scriptures as teaching a bodily resurrection, as seen in the Talmud and the Mishnah.

> How, on the basis of the Torah, do we know about the resurrection of the dead? As it is said, "And you shall give thereof the Lord's heave-offering to Aaron the priest" [Num. 18:28]. And will Aaron live forever? And is it not the case that he did not even get to enter the Land of Israel, from the produce of which heave-offering is given? [So there is no point in Aaron's life at which he would receive the priestly rations.] Rather, this teaches that he is destined once more to live, and the Israelites will give him heave-offering. On the basis of this verse, therefore, we see that the resurrection of the dead is a teaching of the Torah....
>
> R. Simai says, "How on the basis of the Torah do we know about the resurrection of the dead? "As it is said, 'And I also have established my covenant with [the patriarchs] to give them the land of Canaan' [Exo. 6:4]. "'With you' is not stated, but rather, 'with them,' indicating on the basis of the Torah that there is the resurrection of the dead."
>
> Minim asked Rabban Gamaliel, "How do we know that the Holy One, blessed be he, will resurrect the dead?" He said to them, "It is proved from the Torah, from the Prophets, and from the Writings." But they did not accept his proofs. "From the Torah: for it is written, 'And the Lord said to Moses, Behold, you shall sleep with your fathers and rise up' (Deu. 31:16)." *They said to him, "But perhaps the sense of the passage is,* 'And the people will rise up' (Deu. 31:16)?" "From the Prophets: as it is written,

'Thy dead men shall live, together with my dead body they shall arise. Awake and sing, you that live in the dust, for your dew is as the dew of herbs, and the earth shall cast out its dead' (Isa. 26:19)."...

Romans asked R. Joshua b. Hananiah, "How do we know that the Holy One will bring the dead to life and also that he knows what is going to happen in the future?" *He said to them, "Both propositions derive from the following verse of Scripture:* "As it is said, 'And the Lord said to Moses, Behold you shall sleep with you fathers and rise up again, and his people shall go awhorring ...' (Deu. 31:16)." "But perhaps the sense is, '[the people] will rise up and go awhoring' *He said to them, "Then you have gained half of the matter, that God knows what is going to happen in the future." It has also been stated on Amoraic authority:* Said R. Yohanan in the name of R. Simeon b. Yohai, "How do we know that the Holy One, blessed be he, will bring the dead to life and knows what is going to happen in the future? "As it is said, 'Behold, you shall sleep with you fathers, and ... rise again ... (Deu. 31:16)" (*bSanh*. 90).[85]

All Israelites have a share in the world to come ... And these are the ones who have no portion in the world to come: He who says, the resurrection of the dead is a teaching which does not derive from the Torah, (2) and the Torah does not come from Heaven; and (3) an Epicurean (*mSamh*. 10:1).

At one time all blessings in the Temple concluded with "forever." When the heretics corrupted [the practice] and said, "There is but one world [but no world to come]," they ordained that they should say, "forever and ever" [thus suggesting the existence of a world to come] (*mBer*. 9:5).[86]

Jewish leaders also recited daily a common liturgical temple prayer (which perhaps the Sadducees were exempt from repeating). It mentions bodily resurrection as coming from God who gives "life to the dead."[87]

Josephus' (A.D. 37–100) resurrection proclamations have been controversial, but sufficient evidence exists to show that he also followed the common concept of a bodily resurrection.

> Do not you know that those who depart out of this life, according to the law of nature, and pay that debt which was received from God, when he that lent it us is pleased to require it back, enjoy eternal fame? That their houses and their posterity are sure, that their souls are pure and obedient, and obtain a most holy place in heaven, from whence, in the revolution of ages, they are again sent into pure bodies (*The Jewish War* 3.374).

> But every good man hath his own conscience bearing witness to himself, and by virtue of our legislator's prophetic spirit, and of the firm security God himself affords such a one, he believes that God hath made this grant to those that observe these laws, even though they be obliged readily to die for them, that they shall come into being again, and at a certain revolution of things receive a better life than they had enjoyed before (*Apion* 2.218).

Wright correctly says, "Josephus makes the strong claim that belief in the resurrection is supported not only by conscience and the faithfulness of God, but by 'the lawgiver's prophecies.' As we have seen in the rabbis, and shall see in the New Testament, the question of whether the resurrection was prophesied by Moses himself was at the heart of at least some first-century debate on the subject. Josephus is here adopting a clear-cut Pharisaic position, both on the content of the belief and on its biblical basis."[88]

Furthermore the Essenes (Qumran community) described by Josephus appear to have the two-stage approach, in which at death a person's soul survives but later he receives a new body in the Resurrection.[89] Émil Puech's definitive work on the Essenes and their beliefs, especially concerning the Resurrection, is a standard text today.[90] Without having to reduplicate his find, various passages in the Qumran Scrolls bring to bear what the Essenes believed.

> For He shall heal the critically wounded, He shall revive the dead, He shall send good news to the afflicted, (Isaiah 61:1) (4Q521 f2ii+4:12)

> And the Lord will perform marvelous acts such as have never been, as he said; for he will heal the wounded *and will make the dead live*, he will bring good news to the poor, he will lead ... and enrich the hungry ... (4Q521 f2ii+1:10–13)

> ... see all the Lord has made: the earth and all that is in it, the seas and all they contain, and all the reservoirs of waters and torrents ... those who do what is good before the Lord ... like these, accursed. And they shall be for death ... *he who gives life to the dead of his people*. We shall give thanks and announce to you ... of the Lord, who ... (4Q521 f7+5ii:1–7)[91]

> the Reviver [rai]ses the dead of His people. (vacat) Then we shall [giv]e thanks and relate to you the righteous acts of the Lord which[...] thos[e destined to d]ie. And He shall open[the graves ...] and o[pen ...] and[...] and a valley of death [...] and a bridge of de[eps ...] the accursed shall languish (?) [...] and the heavens shall advance[...] (4Q521 f7+5ii:6–14)

> Your holy ones. That bodies, covered with worms of the dead, might rise up from the dust to an et[ernal] council; from a perverse spirit to Your understanding (1QHa 19:15)

> Then the sword of God shall hasten to the time of judgment and all the children of His truth shall awaken to put an end to [the children of] wickedness, and all the children of guilt shall be no more. The hero shall draw his bow, and the fortification shall open [...] as an open country without end. The eternal gates shall open to bring out the weapons of war, and they shall be migh[t]y from one end of the world to the other ... But there is no escape for the creatures of guilt, they shall be trampled down to destruction with no rem[nant. And there is no] hope in the abundance of ... , and for all the heroes of war there is no refuge. (vacat) For [victory belongs] to God Most High [...] Raise the ensign, O you who lie in the dust, and let the worms of the dead lift a banner for [...] they cut [...] in the battles of the arrogant. And He shall cause a raging flood to pass through, which shall not enter the fortified city [...] [...] for plaster and as a beam for [...] truth [....] (1QHa 14:32–40)[92]

Other texts also indicate this, according to Philip Jenkins. "The evidence of the Dead Sea Scrolls shows that at least some Jews had a highly developed concept of the Messiah in the century before Jesus' career, seeing a figure who healed the sick and raised the dead."[93]

Though the main concerns of the Qumran community lie with maintaining "present purity" and with an expectation of better world to come than the present, various texts nevertheless carry the idea of a bodily resurrection; but this was not a point of debate or dogmatically asserted by them.[94]

The *JFT* book and the *LTJ* film promote the view that Jesus of Nazareth could have risen spiritually, thereby making their ossuary discovery of Jesus valid. However, L. Y. Rahmani, one of the leading experts on ossuaries said, "The concept of *ossilegium* was apparently based on the ideas of personal and individual physical resurrection propagated by the Hassidim in the second century BCE. The concepts are explicitly mentioned in late Biblical literature (Dan. 12:2) and exemplified in passages such as II Macc. 7 and 14:46."[95]

Jewish testimony reveals their common belief to be that of a future physical resurrection. Hence Wright said, "The [bodily] resurrection was not simply a doctrine of the Pharisees and their putative successors, the rabbis. All the evidence suggests that, with the few exceptions noted already, it was widely believed by most Jews around the turn of the common era."[96]

Resurrection in Christian sources. Jewish testimony before and during the first-century apostolic era demonstrates that belief in a bodily resurrection was common. But what did the church fathers believe about the Resurrection? Could their view give us a reflection of first-century thought, and do their views reflect similar beliefs of their Jewish predecessors?

Before discussing what the church fathers believed about the resurrection, it is necessary to discount as a predominant view the notion of a fringe group like the "Gnostics," who believed in a symbolic or spiritual Resurrection. First, numerous passages in Gnostic literature explicitly deny bodily resurrection,[97] since according to them the world is evil, and one must return to the prior disembodied state before creation. They believed that a "resurrection" of sorts can occur in this life and that it abides in a person as he gains *gnosis* (knowledge) that will be released on death.[98] Nothing in Gnostic materials agree with Jewish and Christian beliefs about the bodily resurrection, God's goodness, and the orderly creation account.[99] It is clear that nothing in the Gnostic texts reflects what Jewish and first-century sources believed about the future judgment that requires a resurrected body.[100] To suggest that they reflected early Christian thought is wrong and anachronistic since their writings are late (middle second century to the fifth century). Hence it is a mistake to think orthodoxy and Gnosticism were competing beliefs in the first century.[101] Philip Jenkins has correctly said:

> The problem with these reconstructions is the suggestion that both orthodoxy and Gnosticism are equally ancient and valid statements of the earliest Christianity, which

they are not. What became the orthodox view has very clear roots in the first century, and indeed in the earliest discernible strands of the Jesus movement; in contrast, all the available sources for the Gnostic view are much later, and that movement emerges as a deliberate reaction to that orthodoxy....

This point [dating late Gnostic works earlier than they are] is illustrated by the debate over the key concept of the Resurrection, which is so fundamental to Pagel's argument. We recall that the orthodox regarded Jesus' resurrection as a specific event that occurred at a given moment in history, while Gnostics viewed it as a continuing symbolic process. There is no doubt that the orthodox position reflected the ideas of the first century, as all the four canonical gospels had before 100 provided their famous accounts of the resurrection and the various appearances to Jesus' followers. But when did the Gnostic interpretation emerge? Most evidence generally cited in support of such a view dates from well into the second century.[102]

Together with Jenkins one can say, "Finding what Gnostics believed about Jesus might be intellectually interesting … but it brings us no closer to the historical roots of Christianity than does exploring the religious beliefs of nineteenth-century Shakers or Mormons. The Gnostic texts no more than confirm what we already knew about the far fringes of early Christian belief."[103]

The church fathers' beliefs, however, were more in line with Jewish thought but with a slight variance, they taught that a future resurrection is possible because of Jesus' resurrection. Hence we are not surprised that the church fathers, apologists, and later Christians articulated their beliefs in a future Resurrection similar to that of their NT predecessors.

First Clement (first century A.D.) appears to take a two-stage approach of the Resurrection. That is, when Christians die they are temporarily in heaven (see *1 Clem.* 5:4, 7; 6:2; 35:1; 44:5)[104] before receiving a superior resurrection body (*1 Clem.* 24:5 [John 12:24]; 26:1).[105] Clement makes his two-step-postmortem view explicitly in *1 Clement* 50:3–4:

> Those who by God's grace were perfected in love have a place among the godly, who will be revealed when the Kingdom of Christ visits us. For it is written: "Enter into the innermost rooms for a very little while, until My anger and wrath shall pass away, and I will remember a good day and will raise you from your graves."

He says in another passage, "Let us consider, dear friends, how the Master continually points out to us the coming resurrection of which he made the Lord Jesus Christ the firstfruit when he raised him from the dead" (*1 Clem.* 24:1).

Second Clement (second century A.D.) was a sermon written by an anonymous author, but many scholars continue to refer to it as 2 Clement. The homily stresses the reality of the physical resurrection:

> And let none of you say that this flesh is not judged and does not rise again. Understand this: in what state were you saved? In what state did you recover your sight, if it was not while you were in this flesh? We must, therefore, guard the flesh as a temple of God. For just as you were called in the flesh, so you will come in the flesh. If Christ, the Lord who saved us, became flesh (even though he was originally spirit and in that state called us, so also we will receive our reward in this flesh. Therefore let us love one another, that we all may enter into the kingdom of God. (9:1–6).[106]

Ignatius of Antioch (A.D. 35–107) also expounded how believers will likewise be raised from the dead like Jesus.

> [Jesus], moreover, really was raised from the dead when his Father raised him up, who—his Father, that is—in the

> same way will likewise also raise us up in Christ Jesus who believe in him, apart from whom we have no true life. (*Letters of Ignatius to the Trallians* 9:2)

He reiterates in various letters similar sentiment of how Christians must believe in a physical resurrection (*Letters of Ignatius to the Philadelphia* 8:2; 9:2; *to the Smyrnaeans* 1:2; 12:2).

> For he suffered all these things for our sakes, in order that we might be saved; and he truly suffered just as he truly raised himself—not, as certain unbelievers say, that he suffered in appearance only (it is they who exist in appearance only!). Indeed, their fate will be determined by what they think: they will become disembodied and demonic. (*Letters to the Smyrnaeans* 2:1)

> For I know and believe that he was in the flesh even after the resurrection; and when he came to Peter and those with him, he said to them: "Take hold of me; handle me and see that I am not a disembodied demon." And immediately they touched him and believed, being closely united with his flesh and blood. For this reason they too despised death; indeed, they proved to be greater than death. And after his resurrection he ate and drank with them like one who is composed of flesh, although spiritually he was united with the Father. (*Letters to the Smyrnaeans* 3:1–3)

Polycarp (A.D. 69–155), bishop of Smyrna, similarly to Ignatius believed that Christians will rise from the dead just as Jesus rose (*Letter of Polycarp to the Philippians* 2:1–2; 5:2). Waiting to be martyred, he anticipated like many who died before him, eternal life, which he describes in terms "both of soul and of body, in the incorruptibility of the Holy Spirit" (*The Martyrdom of Polycarp* 14:2; see also 19:2).

The *Didache* (early second century A.D.), which means *teaching*, contained instructions for the Christian community. For the *Didache* the physical resurrection is not a central point of debate. However, while discussing the eucharist and end time events, the *Didache* makes it clear that it follows the same beliefs as that of other church fathers.

> Just as this broken bread was scattered upon the mountains and then was gathered together and become one, so may your church be gathered together from the ends of the earth into your kingdom; for yours is the glory and the power through Jesus Christ forever. (*Didache* 9:4)

> And "then there will appear the signs"[46] of the truth: first the sign of an opening in heaven, then the sign of the sound of a trumpet,[47] and third, the resurrection of the dead—but not of all; rather, as it has been said, "The Lord will come, and all his saints with him." Then the world "will see the Lord coming upon the clouds of heaven."[49] (*Didache* 16:6–8)

Barnabas (late first century A.D.) demonstrates in his letter the belief in a physical resurrection since he believes Jesus will come in the flesh.

> The prophets, receiving grace from him, prophesied about him. But he himself submitted, in order that he might destroy death and demonstrate the reality of the resurrection of the dead, because it was necessary that he be manifested in the flesh. (*Letter of Barnabas* 5:6)

He reiterates the belief of Jesus rising from the dead and how there will be a "recompense" for those who will be resurrected (*Letter of Barnabas* 15:8–9; 21:1).

The *Shepherd of Hermas* (mid to second century A.D.) is quite ambiguous in espousing the doctrine of the Resurrection. Only one passage mentions the Resurrection. Though a bit unclear, the references to undefiled "flesh" and "spirit" in order to "live to God" seem to indicate resurrection as the future status of Christians (*Shepherd* 60:1–4 [*Parables* or *Similitudes* 5.7.1–4]).

The *Epistles to Diognetus* (A.D. 150–225),[107] an apologist, comes close to agreeing with the typical Hellenistic dualistic view of the soul versus the body (6:3–5). In the following passage he seems to espouse physical resurrection, but it is difficult to say for sure since it is ambiguous.

> The soul loves the flesh that hates it, and its members, and Christians love those who hate them. The soul is enclosed in the body, but it holds the body together; and though Christians are detained in the world as if in a prison, they in fact hold the world together. The soul, which is immortal, lives in a mortal dwelling; similarly Christians live as strangers amidst perishable things, while waiting for the imperishable in heaven. (*Epistles to Diognetus* 6:6–8)[108]

Papias (A.D. 60–130), bishop of Hierapolis, clearly demonstrated that he believed in a physical resurrection. Three texts demonstrate this.

> Among other things he says that there will be a period of a thousand years after the resurrection of the dead when the Kingdom of Christ will be set up in material form on this earth. These ideas, I suppose, he got through a misunderstanding of the apostolic accounts, not realizing that the things recorded in figurative language were spoken by them mystically. (*Fragments of Papias* 3:12)

> From this it is clear that in the list of names itself there is one John who is placed among the apostles, and another, John the Elder, whom he lists after Aristion. We have mentioned this fact because of the statement made above, which we have recorded on the authority of a considerable number of people, that the two later epistles of John are not the work of the Apostle but of the Elder. He is the one who is said to have promulgated the Jewish tradition of a millennium, and he is followed by Irenaeus, Apollinarius, and others, who say that after the resurrection the Lord will reign in the flesh with the saints. (*Fragments of Papias* 7:3)

> When he says these things he is hinting, I think, at Papias, who was then bishop of Hierapolis in Asia and flourished in the days of the holy evangelist John. For this Papias, in the fourth book of his *Expositions of the Lord*, mentioned food among the sources of enjoyment in the Resurrection. Later on Apollinarius believed this doctrine, which some refer to as the millennium.... and Irenaeus of Lyons says the same thing in the fifth book of his *Against Heresies* and cites in support of his statements the above-mentioned Papias. (*Fragments of Papias* 16:1)

Caroline Walker Bynum's magisterial work, *The Resurrection of the Body*, concludes, "Early Christianity, rabbinic Judaism, and the Koran[109] all speak of the body that rises as bones or a seed.... By the early third century, polemicists for the resurrection of the flesh assumed a dualist anthropology that saw the human being as a union of soul and body.... A theory of bodily return was, to these thinkers, essential."[110] To believe that people would rise bodily from the dead was the predominant view in this period. The evidence makes this an undisputable point.

Conclusion

Before discussing the Resurrection, we looked at the document (the Bible) that testifies of Jesus' resurrection. The evidence demonstrated that the Bible can be trusted as a historical document, and therefore it gives credence to the resurrection accounts of Jesus of Nazareth.

Furthermore, though the Hebrew Scriptures refer in general more to a temporal fleetingness of life that emphasizes an earthly perspective, the seed and early plant form of the doctrine of a future bodily resurrection appears in various passages. During the second-Temple period and in the translation of the Hebrew Scriptures into Greek, the concept of the Resurrection became "much clearer, so that many passages which might have been at most ambiguous became clear, and some which seemed to have nothing to do with resurrection might suddenly give a hint, or more than a hint, in that direction."[111] Thus almost the majority of Jewish literature recorded from 200 B.C. to A.D. 200 emphasized the belief of a future bodily resurrection. Rabbinic literature (Talmud and Mishnah) also exhibited the common expectation of the dead being raised bodily in the future resurrection. This belief continued to be the dominant conviction of the church fathers who followed their apostolic predecessors.

That people would rise bodily from the dead was the predominant view and background of the period when the witnesses of Jesus' resurrection recorded the NT. A reading of the evidence makes this point undisputable.

— Chapter 11 —

PHYSICAL RESURRECTION NOTHING NEW

While speaking of the positive evidence of the Resurrection of our Lord, it may be further urged that the fact, if true, harmonizes all the other facts of His history.[1]

A miracle is "a surprising and welcome event that is not explicable by natural or scientific laws and is therefore considered to be the work of a divine agency: *the miracle of rising from the grave.*"[2] Some people do not believe in miracles for various reasons. However, for those who do, accepting the fact that Jesus of Nazareth rose physically instead of spiritually from the grave is not a shock.

The Jews believed in disembodied spirits of the dead and spirit-angels according to various passages (e.g., 1 Sam. 28:11–20; 2 Kgs. 19:7; Mark 6:49; Luke 24:39; Heb. 1:7, 14). But this belief is never spoken of as "resurrection." Conversely the concept and Hebrew word

היה (*hyh*, "to revive" or "to return life") and the Greek words ἐγείρω (*egeirō*) and ἀνίστημι (*anistēmi*, "rise to life") represent the term "resurrection."[3] This is evident in numerous biblical passages where people were physically raised from the dead back to life (1 Kgs. 17:17–22; 2 Kgs. 4:32–36; 13:20–21; Isa. 26:19; Ezek. 37:3–14; Dan. 12:2–3; Matt. 9:23–25; 27:52–53; Luke 7:11–15; John 11:43–44; Acts 9:36–40; Rev. 11:8, 11).

Some, however, object to calling some of these events (e.g., the raising of Lazarus) "resurrections" because these people (other than Jesus) died again. They prefer to call them "resuscitations." A person who receives CPR (cardiopulmonary resuscitation) after not breathing for a few seconds or minutes may be "revived" or "resuscitated," but this differs from a person who has no vital signs for a long period of time. That person is considered dead and a candidate for resurrection. CPR would not bring this person back from the dead. However, if a person dies for a prolonged period of time and returns to life by a miracle, this may be called a *resurrection*, even though that individual dies again.

All the wicked dead will be raised at the Great White Throne judgment. This is called a "resurrection" even though they will again die after their day in court (Dan. 12:2; Rev. 20:6). Thus the term "resurrection" or "arise" does not imply in itself, apart from qualifiers, *resurrection to everlasting life* (i.e., not to die again), since the word is used of people who return to life to die again. Thus if one is brought back to life by a special miracle, it can be defended biblically as a resurrection. Whether one returns to life and dies again or returns to life never to die again, the person possesses a body, which is a vital element in defining the term "resurrection."

What then is the evidence from the OT and NT passages that preview "the oncoming attraction" of Jesus' physical resurrection? In other words are there passages that show people were raised physically, thereby previewing or hinting that Jesus' physical resurrection was the expected interpretation and nothing new?

Old Testament Resurrection Accounts

Three resurrection accounts testify to the expectancy of a future physical resurrection (1 Kgs. 17:17–22; 2 Kgs. 4:32–36; 13:20–21). Although these individuals died again, these accounts are a preview of the kind of resurrection most Jews anticipated and the way Jesus was expected to rise from the dead, that is, physically instead of spiritually.[4]

Widow's Son. First Kings 17:17–22 records the Bible's first occurrence of a resurrection. Elijah, by God's mandate, met a widowed woman from Zarephath of Sidon who provided nourishment for Elijah in a miraculous way (vv. 17:8–16). While Elijah was there, her son died (vv. 18, 20). Seeing the woman's distraught condition Elijah restored him back to life. "Then the LORD heard the voice of Elijah; and the soul of the child came back to him, and he revived" (v. 22).

Shunammite's Son. Second Kings 4:32–36 also records a resurrection account. A Shunammite woman was distressed when her child died (2 Kgs. 4:25–32). Elisha, successor of Elijah, restored the child back to life. As Elisha lay on the child, the boy "opened his eyes" (v. 35). "The gradual revival of this boy differs from Elijah's method in 1 Kings 17 where there was instant response to the word (as to Christ in Mark 5:41–42; *cf.* Acts 9:40). This was no mere artificial respiration, and Gehazi was a witness both to the child being dead as well as to his revival which became widely known (8:5)."[5]

Unnamed Man. A similar event occurs in 2 Kings 13:20–21. When a dead man was placed "in the tomb of Elisha," he "touched the bones of Elisha" and immediately "revived and stood on his feet."

All three accounts point to a physical resurrection. Regarding these accounts, N. T. Wright says, "The people concerned would die again. Our main interest in these stories—apart from their participation of stories about Jesus—is their implicit assumptions about death. The life-force (*nephes*, always difficult to translate) departs from the child and returns when Elijah revives him. Elisha's servant tells him that the child has not 'woken up.' This language anticipates some of the key ideas that are used in connection with resurrection itself."[6] That is, though the modes used to revive the children and the dead man in these accounts differs, the stories nevertheless end in the same conclusion: *all were resurrected from the dead.*

The following accounts vary from those of 1 and 2 Kings in that these seem to point to some being permanently resurrected. Various OT passages teach that a group of people in the future will be resurrected physically never to die again, while others will die again.

Decayed Body. Job 19:25–27 seems to reflect a belief that Job expected to see God in the future resurrection. These verses have too many interpretive issues for the scope of this book.[7] Regardless of one's interpretation, however, one important point may be noted.

Verse 26 can be translated in three ways, resulting in completely different meanings:

> "And after my skin has been destroyed, yet *in my flesh* I will see God" (NET)

> "and after my skin has been thus destroyed, then *from my flesh* I shall see God" (RSV)

> "And after my skin, even this body, is destroyed, then *without my flesh* shall I see God" (ASV)[8]

Since the Hebrew preposition מִן (*min*) can be translated "in," "from," or "without," it is difficult to know what Job meant. If one translates the preposition מִן along with the phrase as "*in* or *from* my flesh," Job referred to seeing God once he was restored physically in this life.[9] This translation may also be understood as Job referring to seeing God in his final "new bodily resurrection" after his present deteriorated "skin [i.e., body] is destroyed," which would mean Job reached a level of extraordinary faith.

However, if the correct translation is "*without* my flesh," Job may mean he expected to see God in some kind of a postmortem state, perhaps in his spirit. Perhaps Job refers to "figuratively the eyes of his soul."[10]

Verse 26 reflects a common Hebrew figure of speech called parallelism, where the second line corresponds in some sense with the first line. However, what kind of correspondence these lines have is the question. All possible interpretations fit the category known as "antithetical parallelism," where the second line contrasts the idea of the first line in some sense. But that contrast remains a mystery. Does it contrast the temporal destruction of Job's body to his being restored physically in this life as shown in chapter 42? Does it contrast the total destruction of Job's body to his seeing God when he will receive a new body in the resurrection? (Perhaps Job 33:15–30 refers to the bodily resurrection for which Job longed.) Or perhaps, 19:26 contrasts the total destruction of Job's body to his seeing God after death in his disembodied spirit.[11]

Job seems to have viewed life from a temporal perspective as is typical of wisdom literature and most of the OT (Job 7:7–10; 14:1–14; 16:22). However, since Hebrews 11:17–19 states that Abraham believed in a physical resurrection of some kind (according to Gen. 22:5) perhaps Job's claim is an exception. In fact, many commentators believe that. "Though the passage probably does not itself refer explicitly to resurrection, it was 'built on the same logic' that eventually led to the early Christian viewpoint. Those who still maintain that the passage envisages a post-mortem vindication ... [suggest], in a careful and sensitive argument, that Job makes a 'leap of faith' to a 'life beyond physical decay.'"[12] Whether Job meant he would see God after being restored to health in this life or in his resurrected body, or his disembodied spirit, we cannot be sure. But what is certain is that regardless of Job's present state, he was sure to "see God" who would ultimately vindicate him. This is very comforting for people who now read "explicit passages" referring to the Resurrection, since they, like Job, can have confidence that they will see God who will vindicate them at the resurrection of the dead.

Dust Dwellers Will Live. Isaiah 26:19 mentions a resurrection. But does it refer figuratively to the nation returning from captivity, or literally to the final bodily resurrection of Israelites, or both?

> LORD, in trouble they have visited You. They poured out a prayer when Your chastening was upon them. As a woman with child is in pain and cries out in her pangs, when she draws near the time of her delivery, so have we been in Your sight, O LORD.

> We have been with child, we have been in pain; we have, as it were, brought forth wind; we have not accomplished any deliverance in the earth,
>
> Nor have the inhabitants of the world fallen. **Your dead shall live; together with my dead body they shall arise. Awake and sing, you who dwell in dust; for your dew is like the dew of herbs, and the earth shall cast out the dead.** Come, my people, enter your chambers, and shut your doors behind you; hide yourself, as it were, for a little moment, until the indignation is past. For behold, the LORD comes out of His place to punish the inhabitants of the earth for their iniquity; the earth will also disclose her blood, and will no more cover her slain (Isa. 26:16–20).

Whether one interprets verse 19 (above in bold letters) as referring figuratively to a national "resurrection" from captivity[13] or to a future physical resurrection, one cannot discount the analogy of the pregnant woman giving birth, which pictures actual "deliverance" for those of the earth who have fallen (i.e., died) and who will participate in a bodily resurrection.[14] This is the proper interpretation of verse 19 if one notes the entire context. J. Alec Motyer does just that. "First, the (mere) continuance of the community [figurative resurrection of the nation] as such does not meet the problems that the poem describes. The world has not come to new birth. The continuance of the community does nothing to solve this. Second, relating this passage to its parallel in verses 5–6, it is the inhabitants of the 'lofty city' who *dwell in the dust*. The Lord's people already inhabit the city of salvation.... It is others who need to be drawn in. In this connection *your dead* is more likely to mean 'the dead you are concerned about.'... It is, then, a promise of life for the world: the counterpart of the vision of 25:6–10a. But 25:7–8 looked forward specifically to the abolition of death itself. If we view 26:19 in its context in this way (as in deed we must), then its terms go beyond any figurative significance to the literal sense of a full resurrection."[15] Wright also concludes, as do numerous other scholars, "The original Hebrew refers literally to bodily resurrection, and this is certainly how the verse is taken in the LXX and at Qumran. It is still possible, of course, that here resurrection is, as ... in Ezekiel, a metaphor for national restoration; but the wider passage, in which God's renewal of the whole cosmos is in hand, opens the way for us to propose that the reference to resurrection is intended to denote actual concrete events."[16]

Dry Bones. Ezekiel used the image of resurrection as a metaphor (or metonymy) to illustrate the literal restoration of the nation from captivity (37:11). In chapter 36 God promised to restore Israel and He complied with that promise in the vision given to Ezekiel. Almost all scholars agree with this view.[17] Though this passage does not refer *directly* to a literal bodily resurrection, it does *indirectly* show that Jews must have believed in a future bodily resurrection of the dead. That is, if the OT Jews did not believe in a literal bodily resurrection, as in Isaiah 26:19 and Daniel 12:2–3, then how would they understand the literal return of the nation depicted through the resurrection metaphor? In other words, if there is no corresponding reality of a literal bodily resurrection, there can be no corresponding return of the nation illustrated by the resurrection metaphor. The metaphor is only as effective as the reality it illustrates. If there is no real bodily resurrection, then there is no real return of the nation of Israel.[18]

Dead Rising at the End. Daniel 12:2–3 says, "And many of those who sleep in the dust of the earth shall awake, some to everlasting life, some to shame *and* everlasting contempt. Those who are wise shall shine like the brightness of the firmament, and those who turn many to righteousness like the stars forever and ever."

The word "sleep" is a common metaphor referring to literal death when the body returns to the "dust of the earth."[19] It does not refer to soul sleep.[20] Since the metaphorical word "sleep" means physical death, the metaphorical word "awake" "points to *bodily* resurrection, not simply a renewal of the soul."[21] Two types of resurrections will occur. Those who trusted in God's plan of salvation will be resurrected bodily to receive "everlasting life" and those who did not will be resurrected bodily to receive "everlasting contempt."

Verse 3 portrays "two parallel similes to describe the final state of the resurrected righteous."[22] The resurrected righteous will "shine like the brightness of the firmament," and "like the stars forever and ever." Some writers suggest that this refers to some "astral immortality," or that the righteous in their final state will literally "become stars" at the resurrection. This is incorrect. As Wright correctly suggests, "The two clauses are similes: the passage predicts that the righteous will be *like* stars, not that they will *turn into* stars, nor even that they will be *located among* them."[23]

This is the clearest OT passage on bodily resurrection.[24] Wright said, "There is little doubt that this refers to concrete, bodily resurrection."[25] Similarly John J. Collins observes, "Virtually unanimous agreement [exists] among modern scholars that Daniel is referring to the actual resurrection of individuals from the dead."[26]

New Testament Resurrection Accounts

Six NT resurrection accounts testify to the common physical resurrection Jews witnessed (Matt. 9:23–25; 27:52–53; Luke 7:11–15; John 11:43–44; Acts 9:36–40; Rev. 11:8, 11). Although these individuals would die again, the accounts show what kind of resurrection most Jews anticipated: a physical resurrection not a spiritual one.

Jairus's Daughter. Matthew 9:23–25 describes Jesus' power over death by resurrecting a girl.[27] The girl's father told Jesus that his daughter had died (v. 18), and he petitioned to Jesus to lay a "hand on her and she will live." A funeral procession was already under way as the flutes sounded and the crowed wailed.[28] This clearly shows, along with terms like "dead," contrast to "live" (v. 18) that the twelve-years-old girl (Luke 8:42) was dead.[29] While the word "sleep" sometimes refers to literal sleep as in Luke 22:46, the term "sleep" (as in the OT) also expressed euphemistically "death."[30] Besides Luke adds that the crowd knew "she was dead" (8:53). "Jesus was not denying that she was actually dead. He was simply comparing her dead condition to sleep. Like sleep, her death was temporary, and she would rise from it."[31]

Widow's Only Son. Luke 7:11–15 also describes a dead man being raised to life by Jesus. While the funeral procession was on its way to bury the dead man, Jesus had compassion on him and "touched the open coffin" and called the dead to "arise" (as He did to Jairus's daughter and Lazarus [Luke 8:54; John 11:43]). Consequently, "So he who was dead sat up and began to speak" (Luke 7:15). Clearly this illustrates another example of a dead person being raised to life physically.

Lazarus of Bathany. John 11:43–44 is perhaps the most telling of all Jesus' miracles. The fact that Lazarus was dead is undisputed. When Jesus asked that "the stone" covering the burial chamber be removed, Martha replied, "Lord, by this time there is a stench, for he has been *dead* four days" (v. 39). Nevertheless to show God's glory in being able to raise the dead to physical life, Jesus "cried with a loud voice, 'Lazarus, come forth!'" And Lazarus "who had died, came out bound hand and foot with graveclothes, and his face was wrapped with a cloth. Jesus said to them, 'Loose him, and let him go'" (vv. 43–44).

Many Saints. Matthew 27:52–53 records one of the most baffling historical event ever witnessed. "The graves were opened; and many bodies of the saints who had fallen asleep were raised; and coming out of the graves after His resurrection, they went into the holy city and appeared to many." Carson suggests, "Matthew does not intend his readers to think that these 'holy people' were resurrected when Jesus died and then waited in their tombs till Easter Sunday before showing themselves.... The 'holy people were raised, came out of the tombs, and were seen by many after Jesus rose from the dead."[32] There must have been a good number of people alive when Matthew recorded this. Thus if this event were not true, many people could have denied it. Many people who witnessed this event may have been included in the "five hundred brethren ... of whom the greater part remain to the present" who witnessed the physical resurrection of Christ and were still alive when Paul wrote 1 Corinthians around A.D. 54-55. "Most likely [these resurrected saints]... were on the earth until the point when Jesus first ascended to His Father following the Resurrection or at least by the time of His final ascension (Acts 1), fifty[33] days later."[34] Therefore it is erroneous to think that Christ's ascended spiritually instead of bodily. "This [ascension] is not the mere ascent of a soul. A bodily ascension fits the Jewish background, especially after a physical resurrection."[35]

Dorcas. Acts 9:36–40 records a bodily resurrection of a gracious lady named "Tabitha, which is translated Dorcas." She "became sick and died" (v. 37). Two men summoned Peter to come (v. 38). When Peter arrived he found many widows crying, but he "put them all out, and knelt down and prayed. And turning to the body he said, 'Tabitha, arise.' And she opened her eyes, and when she saw Peter she sat up" (vv. 39–40). This event is similar to Elisha who resurrected a dead boy (2 Kgs. 4:35) and Christ who resurrected Jairus's daughter (Luke 7:15; 8:54–55). "The parallel is no accident. Peter's ministry shows that Jesus is still at work."[36] The connection reflects the glory of Christ (see John 11:4, 40; cf. vv. 25–27) raising people from the dead bodily.

Two Witnesses. Revelation 11:8, 11 mentions two witnesses of God who will be killed by a satanic messenger (v. 7). After their bodies will be left exposed in the open "three and a half days" for all to see (v. 9), "the breath of life from God entered them, and they stood on their feet" (v. 11). This clearly indicates a bodily resurrection. Robert L. Thomas notes that "the clear allusion is to Ezekiel 37:5, 10, where God sends the breath of life into dead bones, making them live again and stand on their feet (cf. 2 Kings 13:20–21)."[37]

Conclusion

The evidence from the OT and NT passages is overwhelming in giving a "preview of the oncoming attraction" of Jesus' physical resurrection. Numerous passages show that people were raised physically, thereby previewing Jesus' physical resurrection as the expected interpretation.

— Chapter 12 —

OLD AND NEW TESTAMENT PROPHECIES OF THE RESURRECTION

Peter Stoner in *Science Speaks* [shows] that coincidence is ruled out by the science of probability. Stoner says that by using the modern science of probability in reference to eight prophecies... "We find that the chance that any man might have lived down to the present time and fulfilled all eight prophecies is 1 in 10^{17}." That would be 100,000,000,000,000,000.[1]

Josh McDowell notes that an estimated 300 Old Testament (OT) references were fulfilled in some sense or other in the person of Jesus of Nazareth.[2] To get an idea of just how impossible it is to suggest that this is mere coincidence, McDowell acknowledges Stoner's equation of probabilities of just eight of these prophecies coming true in Jesus. "Stoner illustrates it by supposing that 'we take 10^{17} silver dollars and lay them on the face of Texas. They will cover all of the state two feet deep. Now mark one of these silver dollars and stir the whole mass thoroughly, all over the state. Blindfold a man and tell him that he can travel as far as he wishes, but must pick up one silver dollar and say that this is the right one. What chance would he have of getting the right one? Just the same chance the prophets would have had of writing ... eight prophecies and having them all come true in any one man, from their day to the present time, providing they wrote them in their own wisdom."[3] If the number increased just a bit, such as forty-eight prophecies being fulfilled in Jesus, the number according to Stoner jumps to ten followed by one hundred and fifty seven zeros.[4] The number is staggering.

We noted in the previous chapter that people being raised from the dead was nothing new, and their resurrections preview the fact that Jesus rising physically was nothing strange or unexpected. However, are there any OT passages that specifically predict the resurrection of Jesus of Nazareth that were fulfilled in the New Testament (NT)? Yes! At least two such prophecies clearly predicted the resurrection of Jesus of Nazareth.

Psalms 16:8–11 and Acts 2:25–32

A complete analysis of this passage is beyond the scope of this book. However, enough details exist that many scholars interpret it as David prophesying of the resurrection of the Messiah, which Peter confirms in Acts 2:25–32.

OT Passage: Psalm 16:8–11

> I have set the LORD always before me; because He is at my right hand I shall not be moved. Therefore my heart is glad, and my glory rejoices; my flesh also will rest in hope. For You will not leave my soul in Sheol, nor will You allow Your Holy One to see corruption. You will show me the path of life; in Your presence is fullness of joy; at Your right hand are pleasures forevermore.

NT Passage: Acts 2:25–32

For David says concerning Him:

> "I foresaw the LORD always before my face,
> For He is at my right hand, that I may not be shaken.
> Therefore my heart rejoiced, and my tongue was glad;
> Moreover my flesh also will rest in hope.
> For You will not leave my soul in Hades,
> Nor will You allow Your Holy One to see corruption.
> You have made known to me the ways of life;
> You will make me full of joy in Your presence.'

"Men and brethren, let me speak freely to you of the patriarch David, that he is both dead and buried, and his tomb is with us to this day. Therefore, being a prophet, and knowing that God had sworn with an oath to him that of the fruit of his body, according to the flesh, He would raise up the Christ to sit on his throne, he, foreseeing this, spoke concerning the resurrection of the Christ, that His soul was not left in Hades, nor did His flesh see corruption. This Jesus God has raised up, of which we are all witnesses."

Numerous views seek to explain how Psalm 16:8–11 was used by Peter in Acts 2:25–32.[5] However, Gregory V. Trull has argued convincingly that although Psalm 16 refers primarily to David's confidence in Yahweh, because of the covenant relationship (2 Sam. 7:12–16; Acts 2:30), in Psalm 16:10b "David employed the term חָסִיד [Holy One] to refer to a later recipient of the dynastic covenant, the Messiah. The description of a resurrection before does not depict David's experience. So one may conclude that he spoke of another. This other One was linked to David through the enduring promise of the dynastic covenant. So they were related, yet distinct. David spoke of the resurrection of חָסִיד, Messiah, the ultimate recipient of David's promise."[6] David spoke of himself in general terms of a resurrection in 10a, "You will not leave my soul in Sheol." Then he referred to the physical resurrection of the Messiah in 10b, "nor will You allow Your Holy One to see corruption."[7] Several facts argue indisputably that David's prophecy of the Messiah's physical resurrection was fulfilled in Jesus according to Peter's sermon in Acts 2:25–32.

(1) "In the psalm David shifted from a first-person pronoun in verse 10a ('my soul') to the third [sic, second] person חָסִיד [Holy one] in verse 10b. The word חָסִיד extends beyond David to his seed, the Messiah, and the resurrection also extends beyond David to the unique experience of Christ."[8]

(2) The LXX translation διαφθοράν ("corruption") of the Hebrew word שַׁחַת ("pit") is not wrong since it is consistently rendered "corruption" elsewhere in the Hebrew Scriptures by the translators of the LXX. Hence David was not referring to imminent physical deliverance from death but to a deliverance from bodily corruption/decay from the dead by the Messiah rising bodily from the grave.[9]

(3) Chapter ten and eleven of this book, as well as Trull's dissertation chapter three, shows that David could have believed in a bodily resurrection,[10] which concept is the predominant thought in Judaism at the time Peter cited Psalm 16:10 in Acts 2:27.[11]

(4) Peter said David spoke of "Him" (i.e., Jesus Christ) as a "prophet," and thus he knew God would not leave Jesus' body in the grave. Thus Peter consciously spoke prophetically that God would raise the Messiah according to his straightforward and literal use of language in Acts 2:25–32.[12] If one does not discount the miraculous nature of prophecy, one can see how David could have spoken prophetically of Jesus' bodily resurrection in the OT (cf. 1 Pet. 1:10-11; 2 Pet. 1:19–21).

(5) David's tomb was moved to Jerusalem where all could witness it, according to Peter's words in Acts 2:29.[13] Hence David could not have referred literally, as Peter also confirmed, to escaping bodily decomposition in the grave. Hence David and Peter refer to Jesus Christ as the one who was raised bodily from the grave.

(6) Paul's sermon in Acts 13 also reflects similar ideas as that of Peter's use of Psalm 16.[14]

Thus we conclude that David prophesied—with limited knowledge—in Psalm 16:8–11 that the future Messiah would be bodily resurrected, which ultimately guaranteed his covenant relationship of an eternal dynastic ruler and his eternal life before God who was at his "right hand" ([יְמִינִי], i.e., "God's proximity to him ... to protect him," which terms form the brackets in vv. 8, 11).[15] Furthermore Peter affirmed that David spoke in Psalm 16:8–11 of Messiah's physical resurrection.

> Peter's commentary on Psalm 16:8–11 reveals important insights into the understanding of this key Old Testament passage. Verse 10b is a prophecy by David of Messiah's resurrection. As a prophet David had foresight of the Messiah's resurrection, and as a recipient of the Davidic Covenant he had insight into its ultimate fulfillment in Messiah's rule. The phrase Peter used to introduce the quotation, "David spoke concerning Him," shows that Psalm 16:10b focused on the Messiah rather than himself. The distancing of David from the referent of the psalm becomes even clearer through Peter's words about David's tomb. The decay of David's body attested to Peter's point that David spoke not of himself but of the Messiah. Clearly then in Acts 2:25–32 Peter quoted Psalm 16:8–11, specifically the single line in verse 10b, as a direct prophecy from David concerning the Messiah's resurrection.[16]

This proves in NT times believing that Jesus rose bodily was nothing new.[17] In fact it was prophesied and fulfilled in Jesus of Nazareth

Isaiah 53:10–12

> Yet it pleased the LORD to bruise Him; He has put Him to grief. When You make His soul an offering for sin, He shall see His seed, He shall prolong His days, And the pleasure of the LORD shall prosper in His hand.
>
> He shall see the labor of His soul, and be satisfied. By His knowledge My righteous Servant shall justify many,

for He shall bear their iniquities.

Therefore I will divide Him a portion with the great, and He shall divide the spoil with the strong, because He poured out His soul unto death, and He was numbered with the transgressors, and He bore the sin of many, and made intercession for the transgressors.

Few would debate that a clear reference to resurrection appears in this passage. Hence John N. Oswalt concludes, "The point is to say in the most vivid language that the Servant's life will not be futile after all…. But whether Isaiah intends to speak of resurrection or not, this much is clear, as Westermann points out: it is only on the other side of the Servant's death that the deliverance and ours may be realized."[18] As N. T. Wright wrote, "There is no explicit mention of resurrection itself, and only an oblique statement of what will happen to the servant after his death (53.11). But it is clear that the servant (a) dies and is buried (53.7–9), and (b) emerges in triumph, however densely expressed (53.10–12)"[19]

Though one may argue that words in Romans 4:25; 1 Corinthians 15:3; and Galatians 1:4 may refer to Jesus' substitutionary atonement indicated by Paul's use of the formula "according to the Scriptures,"[20] how can this not include the victory of the resurrection that follows the suffering Servant mentioned by Isaiah 53:10–12?[21] Paul certainly included the resurrection following Jesus' atonement for sin in Romans 4:25, and this is very similar to that of Isaiah 53:10–12.[22] The clauses, "He shall see His seed, He shall prolong His days" and "He shall divide the spoil with the strong" (vv. 10, 12) reflect the Servant's physical resurrection.

Various scholars have noticed an implicit picture of physical resurrection in Isaiah 53:10–12. Merrill C. Tenney said, "The prophet, speaking of the Servant, presents contrasting pictures of suffering and triumph. The two cannot be simultaneous; one must follow the other. In the given sequence the triumph follows the suffering, thereby implying resurrection."[23] John A. Martin views the clause "He shall see His seed" as a reference to Jesus' physical resurrection.[24] G. W.

Grogan says that after the Servant's suffering "comes vindication ... [by] the opening of a new life beyond that death."[25] Luke 22:37 quotes part of the last section in Isaiah 53:12 as being fulfilled in Jesus, which quotation in part may be suggestive of the entire Isaiah 53 passage. This prophecy fits perfectly with what was recorded in the Gospels and the letters of the NT about Jesus' death and bodily resurrection. Moreover, Norman L. Geisler and Ronald M. Brooks write, "Also, the Old Testament teaches the Resurrection by logical inference. There is clear teaching that the Messiah was to die (cf. Ps. 22; Isa. 53) and equally evident teaching that He is to have an enduring political reign from Jerusalem (Isa. 9:6; Dan. 2:44; Zech. 13:1). There is no way to reconcile these two teachings unless the Messiah who dies is raised from the dead to reign forever. Jesus died before He could begin to reign. Only by His resurrection could prophecies of the messianic kingdom be fulfilled."[26]

The OT indirectly testifies of a Servant's death and resurrection that cannot fit anyone else other than Jesus Christ. That Isaiah's passage points to a physical resurrection is indicated by verses 10–12 and is also verified by the fact that Israel in the OT period believed God can and would resurrect the righteous bodily from the grave.[27]

Conclusion

Clearly two OT passages specifically predict the resurrection of Jesus of Nazareth that were verified as fulfilled in the NT. There are other passages that implicitly or explicitly[28] refer to the Jewish expectation of physical resurrection, but I have taken a conservative approach in showing only two in order to show that the OT did predict the physical resurrection of Jesus of Nazareth, which are fulfilled in the NT.

— Chapter 13 —

DEATH BEFORE RESURRECTION

> If the Gospels afforded us no assistance we would have to imagine how Jesus contrived to give the impression of death, and suggest a way in which his body could have been secured by his friends. It is by no means a novel theory that Jesus was not dead when taken from the cross, and some will have it that he subsequently recovered.... There is no cause to doubt the crucifixion of Jesus, or that he had an assistant to aid him in his bid for survival.[1]

The *JFT* book and the *LTJ* film claim that Jesus was resurrected spiritually. However, since they claim to possess the ossuary that contained Jesus' bones, why did no one provide the corpse when the disciples preached His physical resurrection?

That Jesus really died on the cross needs to be established for various reasons. If Jesus did not die—which is a necessary prelude to rising physically—there can be no forgiveness of sins and eternal life for all who believe in Him (Rom. 6:1–23; 1 Cor. 15:12–23). Furthermore, the OT Law illustrated the necessary shedding of blood in order to forgive sins as seen in its sacrificial Levitical system. If Jesus faked His death, the Christian message is void and worthless, since John testified of Jesus, "Behold! The Lamb of God who takes away the sin of the world!"[2]

One of the best-known books denying that Jesus rose bodily from the grave is *The Passover Plot*, by Hugh J. Schonfield.[3] He argues that Jesus did all He could to fulfill the Old Testament prophecies but that He did not intend to die. Instead He plotted to survive the Crucifixion. Though Schonfield's fictional *Passover Plot* theory was analyzed and found completely wanting,[4] this has not stopped others from making similar allegations.

Another conspiracy theory denying Jesus' death on the cross is *The Jesus Conspiracy*, by Elmar R. Gruber. He claims, "A detailed analysis shows that the term used in the Greek original for the thrust of the soldier, *nyssein*, means a light scratch, puncture or stab to the skin, not a thrust with full force, let alone a deep penetration.... Even Origen (185–254), who did actually believe Jesus was dead at the time when the blood and water came out from the wounds, pointed out that corpses do not bleed."[5] Recently best-selling author Michael Baigent claims in *The Jesus Papers*, "Pilate took steps to ensure that Jesus would survive. He spoke with a member of the Sanhedrin and friend of Jesus, the wealthy Joseph of Arimathea."[6]

Could these allegations be true? Was Jesus lightly tortured, thereby making it possible for Him to endure the cross? Did He really die or was He resuscitated instead of resurrected? How does one deal with an empty tomb, or was it not empty, after all?

Jesus Tortured Short of Death

Before Jesus faced the death sentence of crucifixion, Pilate had Him "flogged/scourged" (Matt. 27:26; Mark 15:15; Luke 23:25; John 19:16). Even before being flogged, Jesus underwent six trials and in some of them He was beaten. (see following chart).

Religious Trials	Scripture References
Before Annas Before Caiaphas Before the Sanhedrin	John 18:12–14 Matthew 26:57–68 Matthew 27:1–2
Civilian Trials	**Scripture References**
Before Pilate Before Herod Before Pilate	John 18:28–38 Luke 23:6–12 John 18:39–19:6

Before Jesus ever reached the civil trials He was already punched and slapped in His first religious trial, according to Mark 14:65. "Then some began to spit on Him, and to blindfold Him, and to beat Him, and to say to Him, 'Prophesy!' And the officers struck Him with the palms of their hands."[7]

When Jesus was finally turned over to the Roman guards to be flogged, He was probably already in some physical pain. But what condition was He in after the Roman guards finished?

Before a person received a Roman execution, he was given a preliminary legal flogging, all except women, Roman senators, and soldiers.[8] Though Mel Gibson's movie *The Passion of the Christ* has Hollywood embellishments, one of the things Gibson got correct was perhaps the most gruesome and bloodiest scene, next to the crucifixion, of the flogging of Jesus. Roman guards would inflict just the right amount of pain without killing the victim facing capital punishment. Victims were forcefully stripped of their clothes and tied to a post. Then the guards administered one of the most painful and cruel scourgings ever imaginable. Hebrew Law did not allow more than 40 lashes, but the Romans placed no limitation on them (Deut. 25:3). The scourging instrument was called a flagrum. This was sometimes called the Cat of Nine Tails because it had nine pieces of leather with pieces of sharp bones and metal attached that would "greatly lacerate human flesh" (Figure 15).[9]

The following article describes graphically the medical evidence showing the gruesome torture endured by a crucifixion victim.

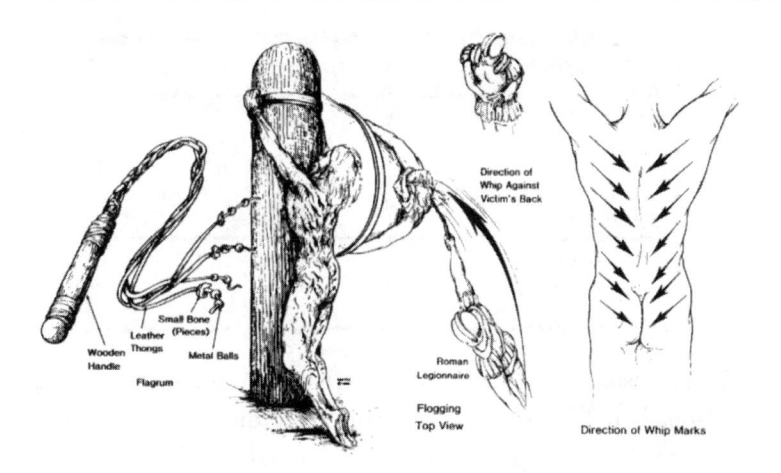

Figure 15. Scourging

As the Roman soldiers repeatedly struck the victim's back with full force, the iron balls would cause deep contusions, and the leather thongs and sheep bones would cut into the skin and Subcutaneous tissues. Then, as the flogging continued, the lacerations would tear into the underlying skeletal muscles and produce quivering ribbons of bleeding flesh. Pain and blood loss generally set the stage for circulatory shock. The extent of blood loss may well have determined how long the victim would survive on the cross.

At the Praetorium, Jesus was severely whipped. (Although the severity of the scourging is not discussed in the four gospel accounts, it is implied in one of the epistles [1 Peter 2:24]. A detailed word study of the ancient Greek text for this verse indicates that the scourging of Jesus was particularly harsh.) It is not known whether the number of lashes was limited to 39, in accordance with Jewish law. The Roman soldiers, amused that this weakened man had claimed to be a king, began to mock him by placing a robe on his shoulders, a crown of thorns on his head, and a wooden staff as a scepter in his right hand.

Next, they spat on Jesus and struck him on the head with the wooden staff. Moreover, when the soldiers tore the robe from Jesus' back, they probably reopened the scourging wounds.[10]

John P. Mattingly's observes correctly, "The phrase 'And they bring unto the place of Golgotha' (Mark 15:22a) would also indicate that Christ, unable to walk under His own power, had to be literally brought or borne along the place of execution. Thus, the revolting and horrifying pre-cross sufferings were brought to a close, and the crucifying began" (Figure 16).[11]

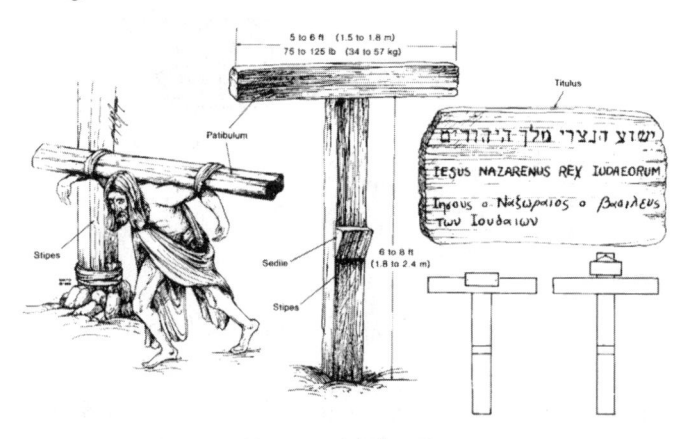

Figure 16. The Cross

In view of these intense suffering how could anyone argue that Jesus survived the crucifixion?

Did He Really Die?

Since skeptics cite the Koran (Surah 4:157) as evidence that Jesus merely pretended to die on the cross, it is necessary to investigate whether He actually died. If He did not die, then He merely resuscitated and was not resurrected. That is not, however, what the biblical and extrabiblical records claim.

Biblical Records. The Scriptures present several facts about Jesus' death. First, as already noted, Jesus was critically injured before He was crucified. After the flogging a crown of thorns was placed on His head, which most certainly intensified the bleeding (Matt. 27:29).

Second, besides being in serious condition before He was put on the cross, Jesus "suffered five major wounds between nine in the mourning and just before sunset (cf. [Mark 15] vv. 25, 33). Four of these were nails used to fix Him on the cross. We know from remains of Palestine crucifixion victims that these nails were five to seven inches long and about three eights inch square."[12] These knife-size nails would certainly result in death (Figure 17).[13]

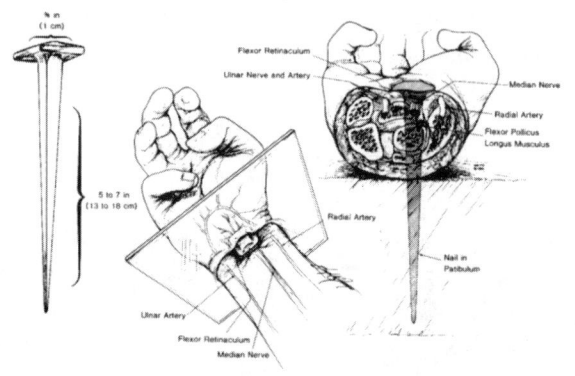

Figure 17. Nails and Crucifixion

Third, Roman soldiers often crucified convicts. Therefore the odds of allowing one to survive crucifixion are zero. In fact they made sure the two criminals crucified with Jesus were dead by breaking their legs. This was necessary since the Sabbath day was approaching and Jewish Law did not permit anyone to remained crucified overnight (Deut. 21:22–23; Mark 15:42). But when the soldiers "came to Jesus and saw that He was already dead, they did not break His legs" (John 19:32–33). Breaking the legs caused a crucifixion victim to suffocate since he could not push himself up to get air (Figure 18).

As Gary R. Habermas describes, "It was typical for a person to hang on the cross for days. However, on occasion when the Romans desired to speed up the process they would employ the *crurifragium*, the act of breaking the legs with a heavy club or mallet. This would prevent the victim from pushing up and exhaling. The cause of death for a crucified

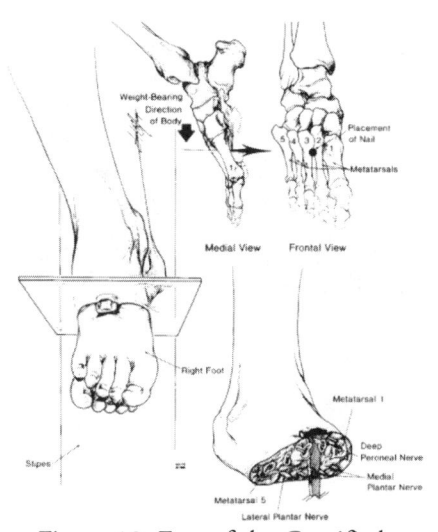

Figure 18. Feet of the Crucified

victim was simple—he could not breathe." Were the soldiers mistaken in thinking that Jesus was dead? "The soldiers had seen hundreds of men executed by crucifixion. It was routine to know when the victim was dead. He was not pushing up any longer for air."[14]

Furthermore, to insure that Jesus was dead the guards "pierced His side with a spear, and immediately blood and water came out" (John 19:34). The Greek word νύσσω ("pierced") does not refer to a mere "light scratch, puncture or stab to the skin," as Elmar R. Gruber argues.[15] The degree of the "stab" depends on the description given in the context not the word itself.[16] In this case the context clearly attests to Jesus' death. Pilate also verified this according to the biblical record. "Pilate marveled that He was already dead; and summoning the centurion, he asked him if He had been dead for some time" (Mark 15:44). Thus the stabbing was deep enough to penetrate the skin and rupture something since according to John "blood and water came out" (John 19:34; Figure 19).

Three medical doctors describe what the spear did and the medical results of what probably occurred. "Clearly, the weight of historical and medical evidence indicates that Jesus was dead before the wound to His side was inflicted and supports the traditional view that

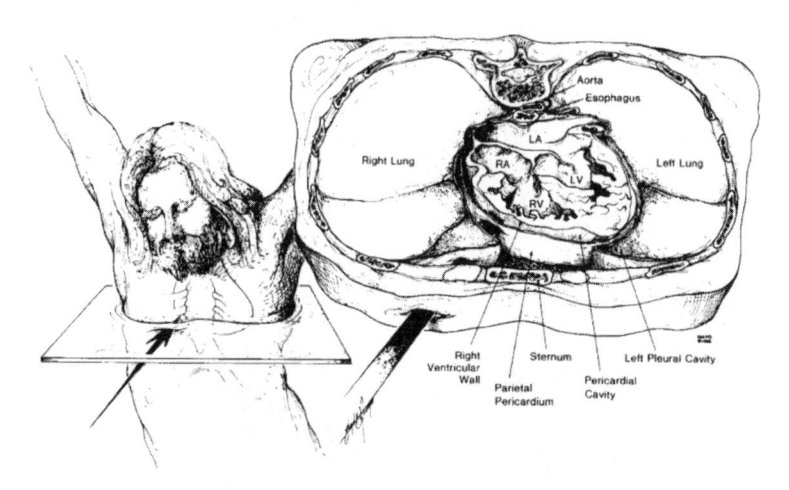

Figure 19. Piercing

the spear, thrust between His right ribs, probably perforated not only the right lung but also the pericardium and heart and thereby ensured his death. Accordingly, interpretations based on the assumption that Jesus did not die on the cross appear to be at odds with modern medical knowledge."[17]

Gruber also argues that people do not bleed after death. But this wrongly assumes Jesus was dead for a long time. Jesus was pierced in the "sac" surrounding the heart that contains plenty of blood for a person to bleed even if the heart is not pumping blood.[18]

Fourth, anointing a body with about 75 to 100 pounds of spices, then wrapping it tightly in "strips of linen," and placing it in a cold slab tomb-rock would definitely guarantee asphyxiation or some other form of death if it did not occur on the cross. Imagine the scenario if Jesus had survived the cross? Such is the portrait Habermas paints by explaining liberal scholar David F. Strauss's critique and decisive blow to the swoon theory.

> Strauss' [sic] most convincing point concerned Jesus' condition upon reaching his disciples. Very few would doubt that he would be in sad physical shape, limping badly, bleeding, pale and clutching his side. He would obviously

be in need of physical assistance and, at any rate, would not appear to be the resurrected and glorified Lord of Life! As Strauss pointed out, the disciples would have gone for a doctor's help rather than proclaim Jesus the risen Son of God! Strauss asserted that even if the swoon theory was conceivable, it still could not account for the disciples' belief in the risen Jesus. Since they did proclaim him to be the resurrected and glorified Lord, the swoon theory is not able to account for the facts.[19]

In fact we know more about Jesus' burial than that of any other historical figure of the past. Wilbur M. Smith wrote, "We know more about the burial of the Lord Jesus than we know of the burial of any single character in all of ancient history. We know infinitely more about His burial than we do the burial of any Old Testament character, or any king of Babylon, Pharaoh of Egypt, any philosopher of Greece, or triumphant Caesar."[20] Yet we do not find anyone questioning whether these individuals died. That is because those who questioned Jesus' death know those who followed these leaders were not claiming they were resurrected. Therein lies the issue, not whether Jesus died but on whether He was bodily resurrected. Therefore denying Jesus' death is just another way of refuting His physical resurrection.

People just did not survive crucifixion. "Survival of crucifixion was unknown, just as surviving the firing squad, the electric chair, a lethal injection, or the gas chamber is unheard of today. Because the law had decreed the prisoner's death, even if a first attempt failed, procedures would be repeated until the decree was carried out. But death from crucifixion was as certain as any modern method of execution. There was no escape."[21]

Extrabiblical Records. A number of sources outside the Bible also attest to the common Roman practice of crucifixion.[22] The cruel form of punishment of first-century crucifixion is also well documented by scholars.[23] Josephus, Cicero, Tacitus, Lucian of Samosata, Mara Bar-Serapion, the Babylonian Talmud, and even critical scholars testify of Jesus' death.

Josephus wrote, "And when Pilate, at the suggestion of the principal men amongst us, had condemned him to the cross, those that loved him at the first did not forsake him, for he appeared to them alive again the third day, as the divine prophets had foretold these and ten thousand other wonderful things concerning him; and the tribe of Christians, so named from him, are not extinct at this day."[24]

Tacitus describes, "Nero fastened the guilt [of the burning of Rome] and inflicted the most exquisite tortures on a class hated for their abominations, called Christians by the populace. Christus, from whom the name has its origin, suffered the extreme penalty during the reign of Tiberius at the hands of one of our procurators, Pontius Pilatus."[25]

Lucian of Samosata, a Greek satirist, stated, "The Christians, you know, worship a man to this day—the distinguished personage who introduced their novel rites, and was crucified on that account."[26]

Mara Bar-Serapion said, "Or [what advantage came to] the Jews by the murder of their Wise King, seeing that from that very time their kingdom was driven away from them?"[27]

The Babylonian Talmud records, "On the eve of the Passover Yeshu was hanged. For forty days before the execution took place, a herald went forth and cried, 'He is going forth to be stoned because he has practiced sorcery and enticed Israel to apostasy. Any one who can say anything in his favor, let him come forward and plead on his behalf.' But since nothing was brought forward in his favor he was hanged on the eve of the Passover!"[28] The name *Yeshu* is the equivalent Hebrew name for "Joshua," or Greek *Iēsous*, translated in English as "Jesus." The Jews believed that if a person "hung on a tree," the equivalent terminology for crucifixion, he was "accursed of God" (Deut. 21:23).

Critical scholar John Dominic Crossan also believes Jesus died on the cross. "That he [Jesus] was crucified is as sure as anything historical can ever be."[29]

NT critic, Gerd Lüdemann said, "Jesus' death as a consequence of crucifixion is indisputable."[30]

Even *JFT* advocate James D. Tabor concludes, "None of these theories appear to have any basis whatsoever in reliable historical sources. I think we need have no doubt that given Jesus' execution by Roman crucifixion he was truly *dead* and that his temporary place of burial was discovered to be empty shortly thereafter."[31]

The Empty Tomb

Many theories are suggested to explain the empty tomb, such as the "swoon theory" which has been mentioned already. The strongest issue that critics of Jesus' physical resurrection have to contend with is that of the empty tomb. Since no one was able to produce the body of Jesus, in order for proponents to disprove the Resurrection, it remains a key argument that points to Jesus' physical resurrection. Hence Smith said, "No man has written, pro or con, on the subject of Christ's resurrection, without finding himself compelled to face this problem of Joseph's empty tomb. That the tomb was empty on Sunday morning is recognized by everyone, no matter how radical a critic he may be."[32]

William L. Craig presents eight reasons why the empty tomb points to Jesus' physical resurrection.[33]

"*The Historical Reliability of the Account of Jesus' Burial Supports the Empty Tomb.*" As Smith mentioned above, we know more about Jesus' burial than the burial of any other historical figure. How does this relate to an empty tomb and a risen Jesus? First, the disciples would not believe in Jesus' resurrection if a body laid in the tomb. Second, even if they were deceived, others living in Jerusalem would not be, since a stroll to the tomb would show that the disciples idea was a hoax. Third, the Roman authorities could easily disprove the Resurrection by exhuming the corpse. "Thus, you see, if the story of Jesus' burial is true, then the story of the empty tomb must be true as well."[34]

"*Paul's Testimony Implies the Fact of the Empty Tomb.*" Paul believed in the empty tomb. The statement, "He was buried" followed by the remark "He was raised" refers to an empty tomb. N. T. Wright also defends this point from critics who accused Paul of not mentioning the empty tomb. "The fact that the empty tomb itself, so prominent in the gospel accounts, does not appear to be specifically mentioned in this passage [1 Cor 15:4], is not significant; the mention here of 'buried then raised' no more needs to be amplified in that way than one would need to amplify the statement 'I walked down the street' with the qualification 'on my feet.' The discovery of the empty tomb in the gospel accounts is of course significant because it was (in all the stories) the first thing that alerted Jesus' followers to the fact that something extraordinary had happened; but when the story was telescoped into a compact formula it was not the principal point. The best hypothesis for why 'that he was buried' came to be part of this brief tradition is simply that the phrase summarized very succinctly that entire moment in the Easter narratives."[35]

Furthermore Paul's witness recorded in 1 Corinthians 15:3–5 was the earliest creed (like the Apostles Creed). Creeds are pithy ways to transmit oral information that is easy to memorize. Numerous scholars believe three years after Paul's salvation (A.D. 33 or 36)[36] or later when he visited Jerusalem and met with James and Peter (Gal. 1:18–19), he received this "creedal" information. Even if he received it later, it could not have surpassed A.D. 51, which is when he first arrived at Corinth.[37] Thus he wrote, "For I delivered to you first of all that which I also received" (1 Cor. 15:3a). Habermas states, "At minimum, we have source material that dates within two decades of the alleged event of Jesus' resurrection and comes from a source that Paul thought was reliable. Dean John Rodgers of Trinity Episcopal School for Ministry comments, 'This is the sort of data that historians of antiquity drool over.'"[38] Therefore Paul's words in 1 Corinthians 15:3–5 testify that he believed and incorporated the message of the empty tomb, and they also show that the earliest creed could not have been "a late legendary development."[39]

"*The Empty Tomb Story Is Part of Mark's Source Material and Is Therefore Very Old.*" If one considers Mark's source (perhaps Peter) to be early, the inclusion of the empty tomb at the end of Mark's Gospel that appear to be grammatically and linguistically linked is telling. If one considers Caiaphas's occupation from A.D. 18 to 37, Mark's source of information comes within only seven years of Jesus' death. Why would anyone circulate a story of a buried man instead of an empty tomb?[40] They would not. Hence this strongly points to the validity of an empty tomb.

"*The Phrase 'The First Day of the Week' Is Very Ancient.*" Contrasting Paul's term "on the third day" (1 Cor. 15:3, NASB) are the women who found the empty tomb "on the first day of the week" (Mark 16:2). Since Paul's "on the third day" creedal statement is accepted to be one of the earliest repeated credos by the church, it seems that if Mark's account was late and legendary, promoters would want to smooth these statements out. This shows that Mark's creedal statement "on the first day of the week" is perhaps earlier than that of Paul's, thereby removing any doubt of the authenticity of the empty tomb account.[41]

"*The Story Is Simple and Lacks Legendary Development.*" Other than including or excluding various small details because of the Gospel writers different perspectives, the four Gospel accounts on Jesus' burial agree and record a simple and straightforward testimony (Matt. 27:57–28:8; Mark 15:42–16:8; Luke 23:50–24:10; John 19:38–20:8). By contrast, the Gnostic *Gospel of Peter* has embellishments that are obviously legendary; it describes scribes, elders, Pharisees, a number of soldiers, and a huge crowd witnessing "a loud voice in heaven, ... the heavens opened, ... two men come down from there in a great brightness and draw night to the sepulcher. That stone ... started of itself to roll ... both the young men entered in.... And ... three men come out from the sepulcher, and two of them sustaining the other, and the cross following them, and the heads of the two reaching to heaven, but that of him who was led of them by the hand overpassing the heavens. And they heard a voice out of the heavens crying, 'Hast thou preached to them that sleep?' and from the cross there was heard the answer, 'Yea.'"[42] The straightforward and simple explanations of the event in the Gospels argue for the authenticity of the Gospel accounts of the empty tomb.[43]

"*The Tomb Was Discovered Empty by Women.*" Women were the first to witness the empty tomb.[44] Yet in Jewish society women were not considered credible witnesses.

> But let not a single witness be credited; but three, or two

at the least, and those such whose testimony is confirmed by their good lives. But let not the testimony of women be admitted, on account of the levity and boldness of their sex, nor let servants be admitted to give testimony on account of the ignobility of their soul; since it is probable that they may not speak truth, either out of hope of gain, or fear of punishment. But if anyone be believed to have borne false witness, let him, when he is convicted, suffer all the very same punishments which he against whom he bore witness was to have suffered (Josephus, *Antiquities* 4.219 [4.8.15.219]).[45]

It is not possible to have a world without either males or females, but happy is the one whose children are males, and woe for him whose children are females (Talmud, bPesahim 65a [5.10.10.1]).[46]

This is the governing principle: Any evidence that a woman [gives] is not valid, also they are not valid [to offer]. Thus any evidence that a woman [gives] is valid, also they are valid [to offer]. Said Rab Ashi, "This is to say that a person who, by their [that is, Rabbinical] standards, is a robber is valid to offer testimony [normally allowed] of a woman" (Talmud, Rosh Hashanah 22a [1:8]).

As Rosh Hashanah's statement shows, the witness of a woman was viewed as no more reliable than that of a thief. Perhaps this sheds light on why the Jewish disciples did not immediately believe the women's witness of the empty tomb.[47] "And their words seemed to them like idle tales, and they did not believe them" (Luke 24:11). Romans too shared contempt toward women. "Whereas men and women hitherto always sat together, Augustus confined women to the back rows even at gladiatorial shows: the only ones exempt from this rule being the Vestal Virgins, for whom separate accommodation was provided."[48]

Thus, if one were to invent the account of the empty tomb, women would not be the best witnesses to use. Why would someone record the most incredible event in history and risk the chance of embarrassment by using questionable witnesses to verify it? Hence Habermas concludes, "If the Gospel writers had originated the story of the empty tomb, it seems far more likely that they would have depicted men discovering its vacancy and being the first to see the risen Jesus. Why would they not list the male disciples Joseph of Arimathea and Nicodemus and avoid the female issue altogether? If the account of the empty tomb had been invented, it would most likely *not* have listed the women as the primary witnesses, since in that day a woman's testimony was not nearly as credible as a man's. Thus the empty tomb appears to be historically credible in light of the principle of embarrassment."[49]

"*The Disciples Could Not Have Preached the Resurrection in Jerusalem Had the Tomb Not Been Empty.*" As mentioned earlier, if the tomb was not empty a brief stroll to the Jerusalem tomb would have resolved the issue and would have silenced the disciples once for all. But since no one produced a corpse, the preaching of the disciples was clearly based on the fact that Jesus' tomb was empty.

"*The Earliest Jewish Propaganda against the Christians Presupposes the Empty Tomb.*" An early skeptic's attempt to refute the empty tomb appears in Matthew 28:11–15.

> Now while they were going, behold, some of the guard came into the city and reported to the chief priests all the things that had happened. When they had assembled with the elders and consulted together, they gave a large sum of money to the soldiers, saying, "Tell them, 'His disciples came at night and stole Him away while we slept.' And if this comes to the governor's ears, we will appease him and make you secure." So they took the money and did as they were instructed; and this saying is commonly reported among the Jews until this day.

By the last phrase, "This saying is commonly reported among the Jews until this day," Matthew recorded an effort in his day to try to refute the physical resurrection of Jesus. In the zealous attempt, however, of those who tried to refute the physical resurrection of Jesus, they did not deny the empty tomb because they admitted, "His disciples came at night and stole Him away." They could not have it both ways: an empty tomb and a nonresurrected Jesus. "The Jewish propaganda did not deny the empty tomb, but instead entangled itself in a hopeless series of absurdities trying to explain it away. In other words, the Jewish propaganda that the disciples stole the body presupposes that the body was missing. Thus, the Jewish propaganda itself shows that the tomb was empty."[50]

Besides, this theory is full of problems. Could the disciples have overpowered Roman guards and stolen the body? Not a chance. Just hours before, they were all scared and abandoned Jesus; and the most fearless, Peter, became fearful and denied Him three times.[51] In addition how could the guards know who took the body since they were sleeping? The best they could do was say, "Someone stole the body?" Even believing this is problematic. How can anyone sleep through the removal of a rock covering the tomb heavy enough that took a number of men to move? Assuming the thieves were successful, the guards would never claim such a thing because by Roman law they would deserve the death penalty for falling asleep and allowing grave robbers to steal a body on their watch.[52]

Without answers to all these eight reasons pointing to an empty tomb, one must continue to believe that Jesus of Nazareth rose bodily, not spiritually, as the *JFT* and the *LTJ* advocates claim.

Conclusion

Jesus was not lightly tortured. He underwent such a severe mode of torture and execution that it would have been impossible for Him to have survived the cross.

The biblical records verify Jesus' death on the cross, and extrabiblical sources do so as well. Josephus, Cicero, Tacitus, Lucian of Samosata, Mara Bar-Serapion, the Talmud, and even critical scholars, all testify of Jesus' death.

Eight good reasons show that the tomb was empty. It was not empty because Jesus did not die, or because the disciples stole the body. Such theories create more problems than they solve. In fact

Craig notes that NT critical scholar and resurrection researcher, Jacob Kremer provides names of twenty-eight scholars (including his) who acknowledge the empty tomb:

> Blank, Blinzler, Bode, von Campenhausen, Delorme, Dhanis, Grundmann, Hengel, Lehmann, Léon-Duffour, Lichtenstein, Manek, Martini, Mussner, Nauck, Rengstorff, Ruckstuhl, Schenke, Schmitt, Shcubert, Schweizer, Seidensticker, Strobel, Stuhlmacker, Trilling, Vögtle, and Wilckens.' [He adds] I can think of at least sixteen more that he failed to mention: Benoit, Brown, Clark, Dunn, Ellis, Gundry, Hooke, Jeremias, Klappert, Ladd, Lane, Marshall, Moule, Perry, Robinson, and Schnackenburg. Perhaps most amazing of all is that even two Jewish scholars, Lapide and Vermes, have declared themselves convinced on the basis of the evidence that Jesus' tomb was empty.[53]

The fact is that Jesus died, and the tomb was empty because He rose physically from the dead. A number of witnesses and various accounts verify this, which is the subject of the next chapter.

— Chapter 14 —

HE ROSE PHYSICALLY

The certainty of the apostles was founded on their experience in the factual realm. To them Jesus showed Himself alive "by many infallible proofs" (Acts 1:3). The term Luke uses is "tekmerion," which indicates a demonstrable proof. The disciples came to their Easter faith through inescapable empirical evidence available to them, and available to us through their written testimony. It is important for us, in an age that calls for evidence to sustain the Christian claim, to answer the call with appropriate historical considerations.[1]

Since the *JFT* and *LTJ* advocates claim Jesus rose spiritually, they say Christians should venerate the Jesus ossuary belonging to His family tomb discovered in 1980.[2] However, chapters 10 and 11 presented compelling evidence that first-century Judaism believed in a bodily resurrection. Would Jesus' resurrection be an exception to the rule?

New Testament (NT) accounts report that Jesus appeared on numerous occasions after His resurrection. He appeared ten times (or eleven counting Paul's witness in Acts 9:1–9) in forty days to different people highlighted in eighteen steps.[3] How one understands the nature of Jesus' resurrection largely depends on how one interprets His postmortem appearances which were witnessed by many people.

Could all these witnesses have been deceived in thinking they saw Jesus? Assuming they saw Him, did He possess the same physical body that came out of the tomb or a totally different body? These and other questions are discussed in this chapter.

Appeared Sunday Morning[4]

Before Jesus rose from the dead Matthew records that angels moved the stone from Jesus' tomb (28:2–4). The other Gospels simply mention the stone was rolled away from the tomb but do not say who did it (Mark 16:4; Luke 24:2; John 20:1), although one assumes "the two men" who "stood by them in shinning garments" were the angels who removed the stone (Luke 24:4; cf. Mark 16:5).

Removing the stone proves Jesus rose physically, not spiritually. Why? Because an incorporeal "body" could have walked through the rock just as spirits pass through doors. The removal of the stone also points to a physical resurrection of the same body that entered the tomb. If Jesus' new physical body had no continuity from the old body that entered the tomb, there would be no need to remove the stone. God could have created a new body while discarding the previous one by leaving it in the grave or simply taking it as He did with the body of Moses (Jude 9). Those who argue for a spiritual resurrection need to address this important detail of the stone's removal, which is mentioned in each of the four Gospels.

While there is continuity in Jesus resurrected body with His old body, there is also discontinuity from that body. This makes Jesus' resurrection body unique from the old one. Both elements of Jesus' resurrection body are clearly evident in the NT.

That same Sunday morning the women (Mary Magdalene, Mary the mother of James, and Salome) "bought spices, that they might come and anoint" Jesus, but found no body (Mark 16:1). Two points may be noted here. First, why use women to verify the empty tomb if they were not considered credible witnesses in Jewish society?[5] If one were making this up, another scenario would make a better argument to further the lie. Second, if Jesus rose "spiritually," why highlight the point that the tomb was empty (Luke 24:3)? If He had been raised spiritually, the tomb could just as well have contained Jesus' dead body for a long time. A number of critical scholars acknowledge the empty tomb, but what of the resurrection body? An empty tomb does not fit a spiritual body hypothesis, unless one assumes a scenario like that of Moses. Jesus' resurrection appearances in the Gospels debunk this view.

John chose to highlight how Mary Magdalene left, perhaps before seeing the angels as the other two women did (Mark 16:5–7), to tell Peter and John. They ran to the tomb and verified (at about 6:30 a.m.)[6] Mary Magdalene's testimony, found the tomb empty with "the linen cloths lying" in the grave and the "handkerchief that had been around His head ... folded together in a place by itself." Once John arrived he "saw and believed." Then the Greek explanatory conjunction "for" (*gar*) begins verse 9 as a clarification of how they had not yet understood that Scripture prophesied that Jesus "must rise again from the dead" (John 20:1–9). J. Carl Laney notes how both of these disciples did not understand that a number of Old Testament (OT) prophecies verified this (cf. Ps. 2:7; 16:10; Isa. 52:10; 53:10–12).[7] However, other prophecies they failed to apprehend may also include Jesus' prediction of His death and resurrection (John 12:27–32; Mark 8:31; 9:31; 10:33–34).[8] Chapters 11 and 12 discussed how people in the OT expected and prophesied that the Messiah would rise physically.

Jesus' *first appearance* occurred when Mary Magdalene encountered Him on her return to the tomb at about 7:00 a.m.[9] Mary went ahead of the other women, found the tomb empty, and ran to tell the disciples before the other women got there. Later she returned before any of the other first group of women saw Jesus. Unlike John, who believed He had risen just by seeing the empty tomb, Mary sat outside the tomb crying. Suddenly Jesus appeared to her and she tried clinging to Him. Jesus, however, did not allow her to do so. Again this demonstrates the physical nature of Jesus' resurrection. One can tell the difference between a physical and a spiritual disembodied being. Thus how could Mary want to "cling" to a spirit (John 20:11–18; Mark 16:9–11)?[10]

Jesus' *second appearance* occurred when another group of women returned to the sepulcher and saw and "held Him by the feet and worshiped Him" (Matt. 28:9). How could these women hold the "feet" of a spirit?

Furthermore we described in chapter 13 the problems with the story of the Jewish leaders and guards and concluded that such a story is impossible to believe (Matt. 28:11–15). The soldiers could not have been asleep to see who took the body, and if they admitted that the disciples took the body they would receive the death penalty under Roman law for falling asleep on guard duty or allowing a prisoner to escape (Acts 12:19; 16:25–27). An empty tomb here argues for a raised body.[11]

Appeared Sunday Afternoon

Jesus' *third appearance* (about 4:00 p.m.) was to Peter. On Sunday afternoon Peter saw Jesus but that is all of the information given. If they talked or did something else together is unknown. All the Bible says is, "The Lord is risen indeed, and has appeared to Simon!" (Luke 24:34; cf. 1 Cor 15:5). Since all the other accounts highlight the physical nature of Jesus' resurrection, we have no reason to think the phrase "the Lord has risen" refers to a spiritual resurrection. Usually the Greek term *egeirō* ("raise") refers to physical resurrection (e.g., Matt. 27:52; John 11:12; 1 Cor. 15:15, 29, 32, 35, 52).[12] Hence Peter witnessed a physically risen Jesus.

Jesus' *fourth appearance* on resurrection Sunday afternoon occurred on the road to Emmaus to Cleopas and an unnamed companion (Mark 16:12–13; Luke 24:13–32). As both men were on their way to Emmaus, a city "seven miles from Jerusalem, … Jesus Himself drew near and went with them" but they did not recognize Him because "their eyes were restrained" (Luke 24:13, 15–16). While walking with them, Jesus elicited an explanation regarding their sad state of affairs regarding the Jerusalem headlines of the day: the death, burial, and resurrection of Jesus of Nazareth (24:17–24). If Jesus' bones had been in the grave or removed, someone would have known. But that is not the case. News travels quickly in a small place, and both of these disciples of Jesus were informed of the events, yet they doubted. Even this account rings authentic, for it shows the human incredulity of people who were present when those things took place, and heard firsthand witnesses but doubted. Without recognizing Jesus yet, He sought to remove their doubts by showing how all that transpired to Jesus of Nazareth was taught, predicted, and accomplished according to the OT.

> Then He said to them, "O foolish ones, and slow of heart to believe in all that the prophets have spoken! Ought not the Christ to have suffered these things and to enter into His glory?" And beginning at Moses and all the Prophets, He expounded to them in all the Scriptures the things concerning Himself (Luke 24:25–27).

Jesus' admonition, "O foolish ones, and slow of heart to believe," only makes sense if both disciples should have known and believed what the Hebrews Scriptures ("Moses and all the Prophets") taught, but they did not. Hence one cannot claim—according to Jesus' very words—that His suffering, death, and resurrection were not known. Responsible ignorance cannot replace revealed truth according to Jesus. While numerous passages come to mind of what Jesus may have mentioned in this walk-along Bible study, those passages discussed in chapters 10–13 may well have been discussed (Gen. 12:3; 15:6; 22:5 [cf. Heb. 11:17–19]; 2 Sam. 7:12–16; Pss. 16:8–11; 22; 89; Isa. 53:1–12).

Since both men did not seem startled when talking to this unknown person (Jesus) as they would be to a spirit, their conversation was to a man with a corporeal body. This is further confirmed when Jesus stayed with them that "evening" and revealed Himself to them and they finally understood the Scriptures. But once this occurred "He vanished from their sight" (Luke 24:29–32). Obviously Jesus' disappearance does not detract from the reality of His possessing a body. Philip, the apostle, was guided by God's Spirit to instruct an Ethiopian eunuch about Jesus being the one prophesied in Isaiah 53, and then he disappeared similar to the way Jesus disappeared.[13] "Now when they came up out of the water, the Spirit of the Lord caught Philip away, so that the eunuch saw him no more; and he went on his way rejoicing" (Acts 8:39). Yet Philip had not died, and he continued ministering, as seen later in Acts 8:40 and 21:8. If this occurred to a person not yet resurrected, how much more so it could have occurred to Jesus, who regained His glorified state when He was resurrected (John 17:5; Rom. 1:4)?[14] Though Jesus had a body, it was now a glorified body after the resurrection with newfound powers not limited to matter, time, and space.

Appeared Sunday Evening

Jesus' *fifth appearance* occurred on resurrection Sunday evening when both of the Emmaus disciples returned to Jerusalem and were gathered with the ten apostles. Thomas was absent (John 20:24). As the Emmaus disciples recounted their story, "Jesus Himself stood in the midst of them, and said to them, 'Peace to you.' But they were terrified and frightened, and supposed they had seen a spirit" (Luke 24:33–37; John 20:19–20).

Here is one of the strongest argument against believing Jesus rose spiritually instead of physically. If ever there was a time to clarify someone's mistaken interpretation about the nature of Jesus' resurrection, it was now when the disciples believed that when they saw Jesus they encountered a spiritually resurrected being. Notice Jesus' clarification:

> And He said to them, "Why are you troubled? And why do doubts arise in your hearts? Behold My hands and My feet, that it is I Myself. Handle Me and see, for a spirit does not have flesh and bones as you see I have." When He had said this, He showed them His hands and His feet. But while they still did not believe for joy, and marveled, He said to them, "Have you any food here?" So they gave Him a piece of a broiled fish and some honeycomb. And

He took it and ate in their presence (Luke 24:38–43; cf. John 20:19–25).

Jesus pointed to His hands and feet to show them the crucifixion marks, which argues for interpreting His resurrection body as possessing a certain continuity with that of His former state but without diminishing any of the dissimilarity of His newly glorified state. Jesus summoned then to "handle" (i.e., to touch) Him and see that it was physically He since "a spirit does not have flesh and bones as you see I have" (Luke 24:39). Darrell L. Bock explains this as follows.

> Luke 24:39 is the only text that describes the resurrected body as having flesh and bones. This is not a phantom or a vision.... It is the raised Jesus whose body has been brought back to life. It has characteristics of the physical body, though it carries those characteristics in a way that the old body could not (e.g., this new body will not perish and it can appear and vanish) and in ways that make his initial appearance startling, not the appearance of merely another disciple.[15]

Even after the disciples touched Jesus, "they still did not believe for joy, and marveled" (v. 41). This can mean either that they remained in disbelief, or that what they were witnessing was so incredible to them that they are amazed. "In other words, this does not express doubt but overwhelming and paralyzing realization (the servant's response to Peter in Acts 12:14 shows a similar paralysis of natural action resulting from joy)."[16] This shows how Luke used the term "marvel." "Luke uses θαυμάζω (*thaumazō*, to marvel) to express reaction to miraculous events or to teaching (cf. Luke 1:63; 2:18; 4:22; 7:9; 8:25; 9:43; 11:14; 20:26). The combination of joy and amazement suggests the second option."[17]

But in case any suspicion remained whether a ghost was talking, "Jesus removed all doubt and freed them from any sense of terror at his presence by asking for something to eat.... A meal shows that it is Jesus and not a phantom, and it also indicates table fellowship and oneness."[18] Spirits do not eat meals. This passage along with the following one should dispel any notion that Jesus did not rise physically.

Appeared the Following Sunday

Jesus' *sixth appearance* occurred a week later on the following Sunday when all eleven apostles were present. Since Thomas had not believed the report of the ten disciples, he said, "Unless I see in His hands the print of the nails, and put my finger into the print of the nails, and put my hand into His side, I will not believe" (John 20:25). Then, "after eight days His disciples were again inside, and Thomas with them. Jesus came, the doors being shut, and stood in the midst, and said, 'Peace to you!'" (v. 26). Now comes the telling part. To prove to Thomas, similarly as to the ten disciples, that He was not a ghost, Jesus told him, "Reach your finger here, and look at My hands; and reach your hand here, and put it into My side. Do not be unbelieving, but believing." To which Thomas replied, "My Lord and my God!" (vv. 27–28). No one reading this account can dispute that Jesus' revelation to Thomas dispels any notion that He possesses a corporeal body similar to the body that entered the tomb, since the crucifixion marks were visible, but yet it was still unique since He could appear and disappear. As C. K. Barrett notes, "John was evidently of the opinion that the resurrection body, though it could pass through closed doors, could also be handled; it was physically 'real.'"[19] This is the same body that was buried and rose. Thus one cannot believe in the resurrection of Jesus and still hold the notion that an ossuary contained the bones of Jesus of Nazareth.

Appeared Thirty-two Days Following

Jesus' *seventh appearance* occurred thirty-two days later when He appeared to seven disciples by the Sea of Tiberias as they were fishing (John 21:1–14). Verse 4 records, "Jesus stood on the shore; yet the disciples did not know that it was Jesus." Baiting them for a response that would allow Him to perform one last miracle and reveal Himself, He asked them, "'Children, have you any food?' They answered Him, 'No'" (v. 5). He replied, "'Cast the net on the right side of the boat, and you will find some.'" So they cast, and now they were not able to draw it in because of the multitude of fish." Once they were all on the shore with Jesus after having recognized Him, Jesus served as host. Having prepared breakfast He "took the bread and gave it to them, and likewise the fish." That Jesus appears bodily here is obvious. A spirit would not prepare and eat a breakfast. His preparing breakfast serves as a transition to the following incident in which He commissioned Peter to the work of the ministry.[20]

Jesus' *eighth appearance* happened within those thirty-two days when He commissioned the eleven disciples in a mountain in Galilee (Matt. 28:16–20; Mark 16:15–18). However, perhaps "a large crowd accompanied them, and many scholars believe this would be the occasion for the five hundred witnesses Paul references (1 Cor. 15:6)."[21] In Matthew 28:17 there seems to be a change in subject indicated by the Greek grammatically construction *hoi de* ("but some") from the previous clause "they worshiped." Hence the "some" who "doubted" (which refers more to *hesitate* than to *unbelief*)[22] were perhaps the five hundred witnesses that "were less sure how to react,"[23] which was the typical response of those who first encountered the resurrected Jesus. Regardless, everyone saw Jesus, not some ghostly apparition.

In Jesus' *ninth appearance* He appeared to His half-brother James (1 Cor. 5:7). Surely James saw something compelling that made him become a believer in Jesus, whom he had denied up to the Resurrection (John 7:5). N. T. Wright notes how "James is not mentioned as a follower of Jesus at any point of the gospel narratives."[24] Perhaps Jesus' physical resurrection convinced James to believe in Him as the Messiah.

In Jesus *tenth appearance* at Jerusalem, He instructed His disciples to wait for the coming of the Holy Spirit ten days later (Luke 24:44–49; Acts 1:3–8). In Luke 24 Jesus seems to have repeated the Great Commission He gave earlier in Matthew 28:19–20.

While on the Mount of Olives, Jesus ascended in a cloud. In fact Jesus' physical return is only as good as His physical departure according to Scripture. "Now when He had spoken these things, while they watched, He was taken up, and a cloud received Him out of their sight. And while they looked steadfastly toward heaven as He went up, behold, two men stood by them in white apparel, who also said, 'Men of Galilee, why do you stand gazing up into heaven? This same Jesus, who was taken up from you into heaven, will so come in like manner as you saw Him go into heaven'" (Acts 1:9–11). Since the Messiah, Jesus, will return physically according to numerous OT passages, certainly He departed physically. If He did not depart physically, how could He return physically so that "His feet will stand on the Mount of Olives" (Zech. 14:4)?

Apparent or Actual Physical Resurrection: 1 Corinthians 15:44

Regarding the resurrection bodies of believers Paul wrote, "It is sown a natural body, it is raised a spiritual body. There is a natural body, and there is a spiritual body" (1 Cor. 15:44).[25] Interestingly this passage actually says the opposite of what most people claim. Many wrongly interpret the words "spiritual body" to mean an "immaterial" body (i.e., composed of "spirit") or a body composed of a semi-spiritual "light substance."[26]

The Gospel accounts of Jesus' resurrection show that He possesses a body with continuity and discontinuity of His former state. Now Paul made the same point in 1 Corinthians 15:1–50. "Jesus' own appearances, in which he eats and is seen and touched by others, reveal the first-century Christians who held to Christianity held to a resurrection hope. The model was Jesus, the firstborn from the dead (Col. 1:15–20). In fact, this clear teaching of the Gospels necessitates a *physical* resurrection."[27]

Paul argued contextually from what people witnessed in the Gospels about Jesus' bodily resurrection. They were now witnesses taking the stand to bolster Paul's argument from 15:1–8. Paul obviously witnessed the resurrected Jesus on the road to Damascus (Acts 9:1–9). Whether he had other encounters with Jesus cannot be known for sure (e.g., 2 Cor. 12:2). Furthermore Paul contrasted how resurrection overcomes death, which can only mean in Judaism *physical resurrection*, or else Adam's curse on the whole creation that brought physical death to mankind has really not been overturned (1 Cor. 15:12–23; Gen. 3:1–22).[28]

In 1 Corinthians 15:35, Paul rhetorically asked, "How are the dead raised up? And with what body do they come?" He explains it by a metaphor through the seed sprouting (vv. 36–38) and by numerous contrasting analogies that the resurrection body contains continuity but discontinuity from one's former earthly existence. He says,

> All flesh is not the same flesh, but there is one kind of flesh of men, another flesh of animals, another of fish, and another of birds. There are also celestial bodies and terrestrial bodies; but the glory of the celestial is one, and the glory of the terrestrial is another. There is one glory of the sun, another glory of the moon, and another glory of the stars; for one star differs from another star in glory (vv. 39–41).

Paul could not mean the resurrection body is "immaterial," because that would argue against the point he made that all matter (flesh) is not of the same "kind" of substance. The contrasts in the analogies are not denoting two different substances of human existence ("immaterial-spirit" vs. "material-flesh") but two different "kinds" of material substance ("material-spirit-controlled" vs. "material-fleshly-controlled").[29] All these analogous comparisons have different "kinds" of matter; hence the same is true of the resurrection body. It will not be of the same kind of material substance that we now possess but will nevertheless be of some bodily material substance.

Three parallel negative terms also indicate modes of existence, not substance: "corruption" (decay), "dishonor" (disgrace), and "weakness" (vv. 42–43).[30] Hence Wright observes,

> In the concluding section of the chapter, Paul will stress the distinction between a body which is corruptible, i.e., which can and will decay, die and ultimately disintegrate altogether, and a body of which none of this is true (verses 50b, 52b, 53, 54). This contrast of corruption/incorruption, it seems,

> is not just one in a list of differences between the present body and the future one, but remains implicit underneath the rest of the argument, not least between the present humanity in its *choikos* ('earthly') state, ready to return to dust, and the new type of humanity which will be provided in the new creation. The fundamental leap of imagination that Paul is asking the puzzled Corinthians to make is to a body which cannot and will not decay or die: something permanent, established, not transient or temporary.[31]

In fact Paul's use of the adjectives "natural" (*psychikos*) and "spiritual" (*pneumatikos*) in the Corinthian letter do not refer to objects or persons composed of immaterial or material substance.[32] Instead he employed the terms to emphasize what kinds of powers are controlling a person.[33] Either a person is controlled by a *fleshly, carnally*, or *humanly* force, or he is controlled by the *Spirit* (1 Cor. 2:13, 15; 3:1; 14:37).[34] Believers in Corinth were failing to live according to the Spirit. And so in 1 Corinthians 15:44 Paul epitomized the ultimate victory over the *fleshly* (*psychikos*) nature that controls unbelievers (2:14) but that can also drive believers to act in similar ways (3:1).[35] Hence in 1 Corinthians 15:44 Paul seemed to follow his early use of *pneumatikos*.[36] In addition, it seems that if Paul wanted to indicate that the resurrection body was an "immaterial-spiritual" entity, he would have used the adjective *pneumatinos*, whose ending *nos* emphasizes the body's spiritual nature.[37]

All "exegetical, theological, and lexicographical evidence" goes against saying the words "spiritual body" refers to an "immaterial body."[38] Instead, as seen by the overwhelming majority of commentators, "Paul is speaking in v. 44 of a *mode and pattern of intersubjective life directed by the Holy Spirit*."[39] F. F. Bruce points to the fact that verse 45 refers to the life-giving Spirit.[40] C. K. Barrett says the "spiritual body" is "the new body animated by the Spirit of God."[41] Two points of contrasts, belonging to two different realms, controlled by two different drives are what Paul conveyed in v 44.[42]

The "natural body" refers to the complete person composed of matter and spirit that belongs to this fallen Adamic realm where two controlling powers (the "flesh" and the "Spirit" in Gal. 5–6) are fighting to gain control of a believer. Conversely, the "spiritual body" refers to the complete person composed of a uniquely powerful material-sinless body and a renewed spirit (cf. Rom. 6:6)[43] that is Christlike and belongs to His redeemed realm.[44] Thus the resurrection body will be perfectly suited to obey God in everything through a body controlled by the Spirit.[45] That is the goal of the "spiritual body."

A link then exists between Jesus' resurrected body and the kind of body that believers will possess. That is, "This provides a constructive connection between the salvific and ethical character of the body directed by the Holy Spirit and character of Christ's own raised body in later traditions of the canonical Gospels as 'more' but not 'less' than an earthly physical body. In these resurrection traditions Jesus Christ was not always immediately 'recognized (John 20:14, 15; 21:12; Luke 24:13–20) but his personal identity was recognized in terms of sociophysical gestures and characteristics (Luke 24:31; John 20:16, 20, 27–28; action, voice, hands, side)."[46] Similar to Christ, believers will have a body unique that will function marvelously under the new realm but will also be able to be recognized as the person he or she was before.[47]

Conclusion

All the witnesses in the NT clearly believed and give evidence that they saw Jesus. Also they touched, ate, and conversed with Him after He rose bodily from the dead. Believers were able to examine Jesus with their five senses. Hence no doubt should remain in concluding that Jesus possessed a physical body. His resurrected body was similar in some sense to the one in which He was buried, but also it was uniquely different since now time and spatial barriers do not limit it.

Similarly Paul argued in 1 Corinthians 15:1–58 that believers will possess a uniquely physical body called a "spiritual body," because it will be perfectly suited to obey God through the power of the Spirit.

After examining the evidence of all the accounts of Jesus' resurrection and Paul's explanation of the resurrection, the NT clearly validates that Jesus rose physically.

— Chapter 15 —

TRANSFORMATION AS EVIDENCE OF THE RESURRECTION

That "something" was so dramatic it completely changed eleven men's lives, so that all but one died a martyr's death. That something was an empty tomb! An empty tomb that a 15-minute walk from the center of Jerusalem would have confirmed or disproved. Even after two thousand years since that time, mankind hasn't forgotten the empty tomb nor the resurrection appearances of Jesus Christ.[1]

We are living in an age where many things are believable without thinking critically or investigating the validity of a truth claim. Hence many cults dupe people into giving up their time, talents, and treasures for a lie in the name of religion. Conversely and equally true, in our scientific and postmodern era few things are believable unless they can be verified in a laboratory. In such an age Josh McDowell's words resonate more than ever in regards to Jesus' resurrection. "If you wish to rationalize away the events surrounding Christ and His resurrection, you must deal with certain imponderables."[2]

These "imponderables" are the enormous evidence not easily dismissed that argues for Jesus' resurrection, which in turn guarantees the future of all who believe in Him alone. This chapter covers these "imponderables" regarding Jesus' resurrection that no amount of pedigrees, rationalization, or coincidence can explain away.

The Resurrection Does Not Contradict Science

James B. Conant, a former president of Harvard University, defines science as follows. "Science is an interconnected series of concepts and conceptual schemes that have developed as a result of experimentation and observation, and are fruitful of further experimentation and observations."[3] In a scientific-explosion age many people refuse to believe anything not tested numerous times in a controlled environment that results in a fixed and stable outcome. McDowell affirms a similar sentiment today. "Many people advocate that nothing can be accepted as true unless it can be proven scientifically. When speaking on the historical aspects of the resurrection in a university classroom, I am constantly confronted with the question, 'Can you prove it scientifically?' I immediately reply, 'No.' The modern scientific method does not apply when researching the factuality of the events surrounding the *death, burial and resurrection of Jesus Christ. Science is unable to investigate it.*"[4]

Correctly defined, science then also disqualifies macroevolution (as a valid explanation of the origins of all species) since no one has ever scientifically showed one kind of species changing into another (e.g., a fish changing into a bird). Origins and destinies are always outside the realm of science since they cannot be reproduced in a laboratory.

However, there is a difference between scientific proof and historical proof. Since most people have not seen a dead person rise, they conclude dead people do not rise. But such a conclusion limits reality and truth to the mind of what an individual can perceive. This results in setting people as the ultimate arbiter of what can and cannot happen based on experiments done today. Logically this does not follow. If we have not seen, touched, or experienced something, that does not mean it did not occur in the past (since we were not there to witness it) or that it will not occur in the future (since we are waiting to validate it). At worst, one should be an agnostic (saying "I am not sure" or "I do not know") about the resurrection of Jesus. At best, one can arrive at a certain conclusion about the resurrection of Jesus of Nazareth by studying the circumstantial evidence just as we study other historical events, and examine the impact the event has had historically.

People accept our legal system's way of arriving at the truth regarding criminals and whether they will be incarcerated or freed, or executed or allowed to live. And yet people refuse to apply the same criteria to ascertain whether Jesus was or was not raised from the dead. McDowell's lucid explanation strikes at the heart of the matter in how to distinguish scientific and circumstantial legal evidence necessary to arrive at an informed conviction of the truth.

> Testing the truth of a hypothesis by the use of controlled experiments is one of the key techniques of the modern scientific method. For example, somebody says, "Ivory soap doesn't float." So I take the person to the kitchen, put eight inches of water in the sink at 82.7°, and drop in the soap. Pluck. Observations are made, data are drawn, and a hypothesis is empirically verified: Ivory soap floats.
>
> Now if the scientific method was the only method of proving something, you couldn't prove that you went to your first hour class this morning or that you had lunch today. There's no way you can repeat those events in a controlled situation.
>
> Now here's what is called the legal-historical proof, which is based on showing that something is fact beyond a reasonable doubt. In other words, a verdict is reached on the basis of the weight of the evidence. That is, there's no reasonable basis for doubting the decision. It depends upon three types of testimony: oral testimony, written testimony, and exhibits (such as a gun, bullet, notebook). Using the legal method of determining what happened, you could pretty well prove beyond a reasonable doubt

that you were in class this morning: your friends saw you, you have your notes, the professor remembers you.

The scientific method can be used only to prove repeatable things; it isn't adequate for proving or disproving many questions about a person or event in history. The scientific method isn't appropriate for answering such questions as "Did George Washington live?" "Was Martin Luther King a civil rights leader?" "Who was Jesus of Nazareth"? "Was Robert Kennedy attorney general of the U.S.A.?" "Was Jesus Christ raised from the dead?" These are out of the realm of scientific proof, and we need to put them in the realm of legal proof.[5]

N. T. Wright points out the ultimate reason people reject the bodily resurrection of Jesus. "Not that science has disproved Easter, but that Easter challenges the social and political pretensions of modernism, both right wing and left wing" to respond ethically to "submit to the kingdom of God."[6] Whether consciously aware of it or not, ulterior motive can drive people to think irrationally or to be dishonest about the evidence confronting them. Anyone investigating the resurrection of Jesus can be convinced without a doubt whether the claims of Scripture are true or false.[7] The credibility of the evidence will cause one either to reject this truth that lies outside the scientific realm or accept it.

Logical Testimony of the Resurrection

Scripture records the words of Jesus' enemies taking steps to prevent His resurrection. "On the next day, which followed the Day of Preparation, the chief priests and Pharisees gathered together to Pilate, saying, 'Sir, we remember, while He was still alive, how that deceiver said, "After three days I will rise." Therefore command that the tomb be made secure until the third day, lest His disciples come by night and steal Him away, and say to the people, "He has risen from the dead." So the last deception will be worse than the first.' Pilate said to them, 'You have a guard; go your way, make it as secure as you know how.' So they went and made the tomb secure, sealing the stone and setting the guard" (Matt. 27:62–66).

Resurrection Enemies Validate It. "In fact, you might say that both the Jews and the Romans outwitted themselves when they took so many precautions to make sure Jesus was dead and remained in the grave. These 'security precautions'—taken with the trial, crucifixion, burial, entombment, sealing and the guarding of Christ's tomb—make it very difficult for critics to defend their position that Christ did not rise from the dead!"[8] Jewish leaders could have produced a body but did not. "Instead, they continually resisted the apostle's teaching, but never attempted to refute it."[9] Why? Because there was no physical body to present, they had no excuse, and they could not accuse the disciples of stealing Jesus' body since they took all the necessary measurements to stop the Resurrection from happening. Hence the enemies of the Resurrection argue strongly in favor of the validity of the event.

Rome, the Seal, and the Stone Validate It. Rome's silence also argues for the validity of the event. If Jesus did not rise and the disciples made up the story, there should be at least one historical Roman document denying the event since His resurrection was widely heralded across the empire. Even in Jerusalem we hear of nothing from Rome, other than Pilate's amazement at Jesus' speedy death (Mark 15:44). John R. Stott also concludes that the silence of the enemies of Christ is "as eloquent a proof of the resurrection as the apostles' witnesses."[10]

What about the seal placed on the tomb? A. T. Robertson explains that the sealing was done "probably by a cord stretched across the stone and sealed at each end as in Dan. 6:17. The sealing was done in the presence of a Roman guard who was left in charge to protect this stamp of Roman authority and power."[11] In fact, "The consequences of breaking the seal were severe. The FBI and CIA of the Roman Empire were called into action to find the man or men responsible. When they were apprehended, it meant automatic execution by crucifixion upside down. Your guts ran into your throat."[12] Would the frightened disciples who abandoned Jesus hours before (Mark 14:50) and who knew the penalty behind breaking a Roman-burial seal do this?

The Romans "did their best to prevent theft and the resurrection ... but they overreached themselves and provided additional witness to the fact of the empty tomb and the resurrection of Jesus."[13] How could anyone overpower the guards and break the Roman seal?

The stone was another problem. As shown in chapter 14, what impressed Sunday-morning witnesses was that the stone was rolled away. Their shock came not only because of the missing corpse but also because of their concern over who moved the stone. All four Gospels mention the stone (Matt. 28:2; Mark 16:3–4; Luke 24:2; John 20:1) because it was a significant barrier to the physical resurrection of Jesus. The stone probably weighed anywhere from 200 pounds to two tons, which would mean several people would be needed to move it. Furthermore the stone may have been in an inclined position, which would have made it all the more difficult to move.[14] Nevertheless the fact that all four Gospels state that it was moved and no record exists to dispute it argues strongly for Jesus' physical resurrection.

Who Moved the Body: Man, Satan, or God? By logical deduction we can answer this question. What man would challenge Rome and dare tamper with a Roman seal? Enemies of Jesus would not want to steal the body. They wanted to disqualify Him as a prophet since they remembered His resurrection predictions (Matt. 12:38–40; 27:62–67; John 2:18–22). Jewish leaders took all precautions to prevent the tomb from being broken into. Therefore they would not steal the body.

Satan wanted Jesus to remain dead for various reasons. First, Jesus is Satan's enemy and who probably knew of the ancient prophecy of his defeat by the Messiah, who he now knows is Jesus (Gen. 3:15; Rom. 16:20). Second, Jesus' resurrection would mean His sacrifice was accepted as a valid payment to redeem mankind (Rom. 3:21–4:25; 1 Cor 15:12–26). Third, Jesus' resurrection would give hope and increase the number of His followers. Would Satan want all of this? Keeping Jesus dead and entombed would be a decisive victory for the prince of darkness; therefore he would not steal the body or deceive anyone about Jesus' resurrection.

God is the one responsible for raising Jesus from the dead. To be more precise, the entire Trinity raised Jesus from the dead. Peter and Paul said God the Father raised Jesus from the dead (Acts 2:24; 3:15; 4:10; 10:40; 13:23, 30, 37). Paul also noted that God the Holy Spirit raised Jesus from the dead (Rom. 8:11). And Jesus claimed to raise Himself from the dead. "No one takes it from Me, but I lay it down of Myself. I have power to lay it down, and I have power to take it again. This command I have received from My Father" (John 10:18). All three members of the Trinity were involved in the physical resurrection of Jesus Christ.

Transformation as Evidence of the Resurrection

The Disciples. At Jesus' trials the disciples abandoned Jesus (Mark 14:50). However, something miraculously happened to them. Peter denied Jesus three times (vv. 65–72). But fifty days later he defied the Jewish leaders when asked not to preach the Resurrection and salvation in Jesus' name (Acts 2–4; 10:1–4). How could one account for this extraordinary change apart from the physical resurrection of Jesus? Many of Jesus' followers witnessed boldly for Jesus. In fact most of them were martyred because of their witnessing for Jesus.

(1) Stephen was the first martyr of the church. His death came around A.D. 35. The Jews stoned him to death (Acts 7:59).

(2) James, the son of Zebedee and the brother of the Apostle John, was the first of the twelve apostles to be martyred. He was executed by king Herod Agrippa I of Judea in A.D. 44 (Acts 12:1–2).

(3) Matthew is said to have traveled to Ethiopia and associated with Candace (see Acts 8:27). "Some writings say he was pinned to the ground and beheaded with a halberd in the city of Nadabah (or Naddayar), Ethiopia, in circa A.D. 60."

(4) James, the less, was Jesus' half brother who wrote the NT letter. Before the Resurrection and throughout Jesus' ministry, it is very probable he did not believe in Jesus as the Messiah (see John 7:5). Yet, he became a believer and also the leader of the Jerusalem church (Acts 12:17; 15:13–29; 21:18–24). He died about A.D. 66. Josephus records

that Ananus ordered James to be put to death by stoning. However, "Hegesippus, an early Christian writer, quoted by the third-century Christian historian Eusebius, says James was cast down from the Temple tower. This version of his death further states that he was not killed by the fall, and so his head was smashed in with a fuller's club, which may have been a club used to beat clothing, or a hammer used by blacksmiths."

(5) Matthias took the place of Judas Iscariot (Acts 1:15–26). Later he was stoned and beheaded in Jerusalem. (His year of death is unknown.)

(6) Andrew, Peter's brother, according to tradition preached the gospel in Asiatic nations. While in Edessa he was killed by crucifixion on an X-shaped cross that later became known as "St. Andrew's Cross." (His year of death is unknown.)

(7) Mark, who wrote the Gospel, according to tradition was "dragged to pieces by the people of Alexandria when he spoke out against a solemn ceremony for their idol Serapis." (His year of death is unknown.)

(8) When Peter, the brother of Andrew, left Rome, Jesus, according to Hegesippus, appeared to him and told him to return because he was to glorify Jesus through a similar death (cf. John 21:19). Nero around A.D. 64 then captured Peter. He asked to be crucified upside down since he did not consider himself worthy to die as Jesus did.

(9) Paul was arrested for the second time around A.D. 64 (about the same time Peter was arrested). When fire broke out in Rome, many believed Nero started it, but he blamed the Christians. Paul was beheaded around A.D. 66.

(10) Jude, brother of James and half brother of Jesus, who wrote the little letter in the New Testament (NT), was crucified at Edessa (like Andrew) around A.D. 72.

(11) Bartholomew, according to tradition, preached in various countries, and "then translated the Gospel of Matthew into the language of Easy-Indian and taught it in that country. His pagan enemies cruelly beat and crucified him." (His year of death is unknown.)

(12) Thomas spread the gospel in "Persia, Parthia, and India. In Calamina, India, he was tortured by angry pagans, run through with spears, and thrown into the flames of an oven." (His year of death is unknown.)

(13) Luke was probably a Gentile who was Paul's companion on many missionary journeys. He wrote the Gospel of Luke and the Book of Acts. Though no one knows for sure how or when he died, an "early source says that he went to Greece to evangelize, and was there martyred by being hung from an olive tree in Athens in A.D. 93."

(14) John the apostle, and brother of James, gets credit for the establishing the seven churches in Revelation: Ephesus, Smyrna, Pergamum, Thyatira, Sardis, Philadelphia, and Laodicea. From Ephesus John was arrested and sent to Rome where he was thrown into a caldron of boiling hot oil. Still alive afterward, Emperor Domitian then banished him to the Island of Patmos, where he penned the Book of Revelation. After leaving Patmos, John returned to Ephesus, where he died a non-martyr's death, becoming the only one of these fourteen who did not die violently.[15]

The fact that they were willing to die for what they believed validates that what they saw and believed was true. Logically this in itself does not prove that what they believed was correct or right. Other people with different beliefs have died for what they believed to be true. That does not make their beliefs credible or true.

Agreed, but this misses the point: The disciples' willingness to suffer and die for their beliefs *indicates that they certainly regarded those beliefs as true.* The case is strong that they did not willfully lie about the appearances of the risen Jesus. Liars make poor martyrs.

> No one questions the sincerity of the Muslim terrorist who blows himself up in a public place or the Buddhist monk who burns himself alive as a political protest. Extreme acts do not validate the truth of their beliefs, but willingness to die indicates that they regarded their beliefs as true. Moreover, there is an important difference between the apostle martyrs and those who die for their beliefs today. Modern martyrs act solely out of their trust in beliefs that others have taught them. The apostles died for holding to their own testimony that they had *personally* seen the risen

Jesus. Contemporary martyrs die for what they *believe* to be true. The disciples of Jesus died for what they *knew* to be either true or false.[16]

It would be senseless for the disciples to die for a lie since they were the actual witnesses of their claims, not what someone else told them. Hence their testimony and martyrdom argues strongly for the validity of the bodily resurrection of Jesus.

Saul the Christian Persecutor to Paul the Christian Propagator

What can be said of Saul of Tarsus, later called Paul, who persecuted the Christians and then became a propagator of the Christian message? In the Book of Acts (7:58; 8:1–3; 9:1–19; 22:1–16; 26:9–23) Luke recorded how Paul not only consented to the stoning of Stephen but also persecuted the church in order to extinguish its members and promoters. He was a Pharisee and a strict observer of the Law of Moses (Acts 22:9–11; Gal. 1:22–23); but when on the road to Damascus to persecute Christians everything changed for him in one instant when he saw the risen Jesus. After that point until his martyrdom, he began preaching, "Jesus is the Christ" (Acts 9:1–22).

In Philippians 3:1–10 Paul gives a pithy biographical testimony of his conversion that is related to Jesus' resurrection. Paul became the apostle to the Gentiles and he also led many Jews to faith in Christ (Rom. 1:16; 11:13). He also wrote no less than thirteen letters that form part of the NT.[17]

What could have made a man change so drastically from a foe to a friend, from a persecutor to a promoter, and from Saul the murderer for the Sanhedrin to Paul the messenger of the Savior? One simple answer: Paul met the risen Jesus! "Certainly a skeptic may comment that Paul's conversion is no big deal, since many people have converted from one set of beliefs to another. However, the cause of Paul's conversion makes his different. People usually convert to a particular religion because they have heard the message of that religion from a secondary source and believed the message. Paul's conversion was based on what he perceived to be a personal appearance of the risen Jesus. Today we might believe that Jesus rose from the dead based on secondary evidence, trusting Paul and the disciples who saw the risen Jesus. But for Paul, his experience came from primary evidence: the risen Jesus appeared directly to him. He did not merely believe based on the testimony of someone else."[18]

Psychologically people do not change in a blink of an eye, unless something radical happens to them. One cannot explain the historical account of what happened to Paul psychologically apart from his seeing the risen Christ. What selfish motive would he have in going from a highly educated, wealthy, and respected member of the Sanhedrin to join a persecuted group, become a blue-collar worker, receive beatings, remain on the run throughout his life, and become almost certain to end as a martyr? People lie for their best interests not to bring problems and calamity on themselves. Paul did not lie; he told the truth, and that often leads to persecution, especially when one preaches Jesus Christ (Mark 4:17; Acts 11:19; 13:50; Gal. 5:11; 6:12; 2 Tim. 3:12).

Paul's conversion may perhaps be the most compelling evidence that validates the Christian faith and Jesus' resurrection. Elias Andrews said, "Many have found in the radical transformation of this 'Pharisee of the Pharisees' the most convincing evidence of the truth and power of the religion to which he was converted, as well as the ultimate worth and place of the Person of Christ." In fact Archibald MacBride, former professor at Aberdeen University, wrote, "Besides his [Paul's] achievements ... the achievements of Alexander and Napoleon pale into insignificance."[19] Paul's radical change and lifelong commitment to promote Christianity in spite of persecution also argues strongly for the bodily resurrection of Jesus.

The Church and Changed Lives

How could the Christian church continue to thrive today as it has throughout the centuries without having solid evidence and believing the primary apostolic testimony of the resurrection of Jesus? Norval Geldenhuys said it best. "It is historically and psychologically impossible that the followers of Jesus, who at His crucifixion were so completely despondent and perplexed, would within a few weeks thereafter enter the world (as they did) with such unheard-of joy, power and devotion, if it had not been for the fact that He had risen from the dead, had appeared to them, and had proved that His claims to be the Son of God were genuine."[20]

The early church of the first and second centuries knew most of the men who witnessed the resurrection of Jesus (e.g., Polycarp was a disciple of the Apostle John), which in turn influenced them to become martyrs in order to promote the message of the gospel that propelled the church to exponential growth. Someone has correctly said, "The seed of the church was built on the blood of the martyrs."[21] Such was the building blocks of the church. In just a couple of centuries six million martyrs forged the edifice of the building that Jesus, the prophets, and the apostles founded (Eph. 2:20).

One cannot account for the changed lives of Jesus' disciples unless they experienced something radical. My own testimony is a case in point.

I cannot attest to ever seeing the resurrection of Jesus, but I can attest to experiencing His resurrection power that changed my life forever. Unfortunately before I became a Christian in my early twenties, I grew up in the "*locumi* religion" (also known in the Cuban community as "Santeria"). This is a mixture of Roman Catholicism with African voodoo. Supernatural occurrences were easy for me to believe. As a teenager I saw numerous supernatural occurrences that defy scientific laws (e.g., the law of gravity). Once a high priest of the religion came to my house and did numerous religious rites, supposedly to rid the place of bad spirits. I do not know if the spirits left, but once seeing various pieces of irons go up a flight of stairs and land in front of my mother and me, a chicken faint and rise at the sound of the man's voice, and seeing a coconut float in the air, I wanted to leave. This might sound comical, but it is true. I witnessed it with my own eyes. Yes, I could have been fooled, but what about the other three people in the room with me who saw the same thing? Furthermore this was just one day's occurrence. There were many more bizarre things I witnessed in that religion. I believed in the supernatural and that God existed. This religion, however, did nothing to change and make me a better person.

In my late teens and early twenties I became worse. My track record read like a bad grocery list: burglary (arrested five times), grand theft, petit theft, theft (three times), loitering, possession of burglary tools, trespass (three times), defrauding innkeeper (two times), evading transit fare, cocaine possession (two times), forced strong-arm robbery (three times), dealing in stolen property (two times), petit larceny (three times), obstruction of police officer (three times), resisting arrest (two times), battery on a police officer, alcohol violation and four drug rehabilitation programs. All of this occurred between 1986 and 91.

I could not make sense of life. But then when I met Jesus Christ the direction of my life changed. He became the ultimate key that unlocked the enormous amount of questions in my soul that nothing and no one could open. True, some people change apart from a relationship with Jesus Christ. But they do not change *radically* without Him. Furthermore, as I looked into many other religions, philosophies, and scientific ideas, nothing made sense other than what Jesus' resurrection represented for everyone who simply believes in Him receives eternal life.

Now that I had purpose in life through my relationship with Christ, my "grocery list" began to change—and radically. I earned a B.A. with high honors from Trinity International University, where I later served as an adjunct faculty member for three years. I earned a Th.M. with honors from Dallas Theological Seminary, where I am currently a Ph.D. candidate. I was on the National Dean's List twice and also given twice the Outstanding Young Man of America award for professional achievement, superior ability, and exceptional community service. At Dallas Seminary I was also awarded the J. Dwight Pentecost Ph.D. scholarship for excellence in Bible Exposition. I have also been pastoring for the past ten years.

All these things—wonderful as they are—are rubbish compared to the surpassing knowledge of Jesus Christ, who changed me. I share them to show the contrast of what I was before and what God has made of me. The radical change began when I simply *believed in Christ's promise that I could receive eternal life* (John 1:12; 3:16; 5:24; 6:40, 47; 11:25-27). Jesus did a miracle of radical proportions in changing my life, and He can do it with anyone, because He died for our sins and rose again on the third day according to the Scriptures (Isa. 53:1–12; Rom. 4:24–25; 1 Cor. 15:3–4).[22]

Conclusion

Once we understand how to distinguish scientific and circumstantial legal evidence, we can then arrive at an informed conviction about the resurrection of Jesus.

Having looked at some of these evidences, the following points are clear. Enemies of the Resurrection actually helped solidify the testimony that validates its authenticity. For example, the empty tomb, the broken seal, the removal of the large stone, and the silence of Rome in not producing a body can only be logically and historically explained by the physical resurrection of Jesus.

That is not all. The disciples' transformed lives validate Jesus' resurrection. From running scared to proclaiming boldly the Resurrection that resulted in most of them being martyred argues for the authenticity of their having seen the risen Jesus.

Furthermore, how does one account for the change in Saul, the most antagonist person of the Christian faith to becoming an advocate of it? Only the risen Jesus appearing to Paul can explain this change.

In fact, because Jesus had met many believers and had directly spoken to the apostles after His resurrection, early church followers were willing to face martyrdom. Exponentially the church grew because of this, which continues to thrive today.

I have witnessed various supernatural things. Those things are as real as the words on these pages. More real than that, however, is the impact Jesus Christ had in my life in changing me from a "train wreck" to a "trusted worker" for Him, who willingly gave Himself for me and rose from the dead—so that all who by faith alone in Him believe His promise of eternal life can be sure they possess it (John 1:12; 3:16; 5:24; 6:40, 47; 11:25–27; Rom. 3:21–4:25; Eph. 2:8–9).

— Chapter 16 —

CONCLUSION: OUR RESPONSE

> The lessons here include that when one of these sensations breaks (and surely we will see more in the future), (1) those who underwrite it should be careful to put their names behind it and to vet it carefully, soliciting feedback from people with a variety of views, and (2) the public should be patient to let any public scrutiny of such a story play itself out, whether on the Internet in real time or in circles where those with relevant backgrounds can weigh in, taking their time to work through the tangle of arguments. After all, the claim of today often becomes the refuse of tomorrow.[1]

For those who think this issue is going away, they should think again. First, on March 2008 Simcha Jacobovici came out with a revised and updated version of the *The Jesus Family Tomb* book, with a new subtitle: from *The Discovery, the Investigation, and the Evidence That Could Change History* to *The Evidence Behind the Discovery No One Wanted to Find*.

– 245 –

Second, James Charlesworth, recognized expert on "Jesus" and professor of New Testament language and literature at Princeton Theological Seminary, chaired a four-day symposium in January 2008 from Jerusalem, in which fifty scholars rigorously debated the issue of the "Talpiot Tomb."[2] Unanimously the scholars voted that the tomb should be reopened to examine the findings more carefully. The symposium "considered the evidence and is opening the door for further research." "Simcha Jacobovici, the filmmaker of *The Lost Tomb of Jesus*, said, 'It's time that the world seriously considered that the Jesus family tomb may very well have been located.'"[3] He also added in an interview with TIME magazine, "I feel vindicated. It's moved from 'it can't be the Jesus' family tomb' to 'it could be.'"[4]

To add fuel to the flames, the widow of the late Joseph Gat, the original chief archaeologist of the team that excavated the tomb in 1980, confessed at the symposium, "My husband believed that this was Jesus's [sic] tomb, but because of his experiences as a Holocaust survivor, he was worried about a backlash of anti-Semitism and he didn't think he could say this."[5]

Professors Eric Meyers (of Duke University) and Jodi Magness (of University of North Carolina at Chapel Hill) said that the media slanted their report to favor Simcha Jacobovici (producer) and James Cameron (Hollywood director) of the "The Lost Tomb of Jesus" documentary. However, "Nothing further from the truth can be deduced from the discussion and presentations that took place on January 13-17, 2008." Both professors conclude by clarifying the issues and posting the names of the scholars who were present at the symposium and who disagreed with the *LTJ* documentary's conclusion.

> To conclude, we wish to protest the misrepresentation of the conference proceedings in the media, and make it clear that the majority of scholars in attendance—including all of the archaeologists and epigraphers who presented papers relating to the tomb - either reject the identification of the Talpiot tomb as belonging to Jesus' family or find this claim highly speculative.

Signed,
> Professor Mordechai Aviam, University of Rochester
> Professor Ann Graham Brock, Iliff School of Theology, University of Denver
> Professor F.W. Dobbs-Allsopp, Princeton Theological Seminary
> Professor C.D. Elledge, Gustavus Adolphus College
> Professor Shimon Gibson, University of North Carolina at Charlotte
> Professor Rachel Hachlili, University of Haifa
> Professor Amos Kloner, Bar-Ilan University
> Professor Jodi Magness, University of North Carolina at Chapel Hill
> Professor Lee McDonald, Acadia Seminary
> Professor Eric M. Meyers, Duke University
> Professor Stephen Pfann, University of the Holy Land
> Professor Jonathan Price, Tel Aviv University
> Professor Christopher Rollston, Emmanuel School of Religion
> Professor Alan F. Segal, Barnard College, Columbia University
> Professor Choon-Leong Seow, Princeton Theological Seminary
> Mr. Joe Zias, Science and Antiquity Group, Jerusalem
> Dr. Boaz Zissu, Bar-Ilan University[6]

After the four-day Jerusalem symposium, Charlesworth (also a Methodist minister) concluded, "I don't think it will undermine belief in the resurrection, only that Jesus rose as a spiritual body, not in the flesh." Furthermore he added, "Christianity is a strong religion, based on faith and experience, and I don't think that any discovery by archaeologists will change that."[7] Biblical faith, however, is based on historical facts. So if the facts say Jesus did not rise bodily, Christians need to reassess their faith, because according to Scripture if Jesus did not rise bodily believers are still in their sins (1 Cor. 15:16–17). If that is not what Paul argued in 1 Corinthians 15, then how should we interpret what first-century Judaism and the primitive church believed—since the evidence clearly points to people who expected and believed in a bodily resurrection?

Charlesworth is seeking to gain permission to attain the necessary permits from the Jerusalem Municipality to reopen the tomb. The Israel Antiquities Authorities agreed to support him.[8]

An ongoing dialogue, and "heated" exchange at times, continues on the Jesus family tomb discovery in the Biblical Archaeology Society website.[9] Therefore we have not seen the end of this drama. But how should we respond to these and future issues to come? Here is some advice to follow.

Be patient. Darrell L. Bock suggests that people should be calm. By letting the discussion "play itself out" in the public square numerous scholars can opine about these issues and give cogent answers. When the *Jesus Family Tomb* book and the *Lost Tomb of Jesus* film were released, many people were anxious. If someone attacks our faith, we need to be patient and not react irrationally but respond intelligently at the right time.

Be controlled. Though one can be patient, sometimes it is difficult not to be emotional, especially if people attack the way one thinks, how one lives, and the very hope that carries one from day to day. Attacking people who disagree with us does not help. "The Media Research Center, a conservative media group, called for the Discovery Channel not to broadcast the misleading documentary. While this was not necessarily a bad choice, those who have had a more effective outreach on this issue have been those who have stepped up to address the issues presented rather than trying to deny airtime to the broadcast."[10]

When one reacts, instead of reasoning through the issues, he or she will end up making mistakes by either insulting their opponents or appearing ignorant. Scripture teaches that self-control is a fruit of the Spirit (Gal. 5:23). Nothing turns away an unbeliever more than a believer getting belligerent and hostile in an argument.

Be informed. Truth must always be validated through investigation. Some Christians have a misinformed notion that faith is a feeling apart from facts. That cannot be further from the truth. God gave us brains to use. Many people quickly discard a point of view—without minimal consideration—simply because they do not agree with it. Not only is this dangerous but it is regressive to physical and spiritual growth. People need to exercise their intellects. Cults teach people not to think for themselves, but Scripture encourages testing all things to see whether they qualify as truth (1 Thess. 5:21; 1 John 4:1). Blindly following pastors, preachers, teachers, the media, books, or anyone without testing theories will bring disaster. That is how people become victims. Considering opposing views, though we might not agree, may teach us something new and show us mistakes to correct, though we may disagree with the views. Furthermore we will never be able to help others unless we know how they think.

Be evangelistic. By our being patient, controlled, and informed God will open many doors. Far too many believers are inactive for Jesus. The *Jesus Family Tomb* book became a *New York Times* best seller not because people are not interested but because people are. Many people in churches are clueless on this issue. Because they have not heard of the *JFT* book or film, they think it will blow over and it does not matter. That is how the book *The Da Vinci Code* began until it blew over and "swallowed" many people. The *JFT* book has a lot more going for it than Dan Brown's book since this is a real historical find, uses theology, history, statistics, science, and archaeology. God does not need us but He chooses to use us. The more we know about the Bible and the issues of the day the better God can use us. As a result we will be a blessing to others, and we will be blessed now and throughout eternity. Be evangelistic.

Be at peace. The family tomb that was found in Jerusalem in 1980 is not the tomb of Jesus of Nazareth. Even if five or perhaps six out of ten ossuaries in the tomb contained a cluster of names similar to those related to Jesus, all these names were very common in the first century. During that period there was a limited pool of about sixteen names to draw from. Nothing unique exists in having this cluster of names.

The inscription name *Mariamne* does not refer to Mary Magdalene but to another Mary of the first century. DNA testing disproving motherly kinship between the *Jesus son of Joseph* ossuary and the *Mariamne* ossuary does not prove anything since no other DNA testing was done to compare *Mariamne* with other ossuaries. Thus we cannot determine whether Jesus and *Mariamne* were husband and wife, or that she was this Jesus' half-sister, cousin, or a beloved servant who was interred in the family tomb. None of these possibilities was considered by the *LTJ* film or by the *JFT book*. DNA testing of ossuaries with high probabilities of having more than one person's bones is impossible to conduct, and so this makes the DNA testing of the Jesus tomb worthless.

The tenth ossuary was never "missing." Since Amos Kloner documented the ossuary as plain and noninscribed, they treated it like other plain ossuaries by putting it outside in the IDAM yard together with other plain ossuaries.

How does one answer the statistical analysis of six hundred to one that shows impressive odds of a cluster of names, starting with Jesus' name and five or possibly six other names appearing in the same tomb, which present a good probability that this is the Jesus of Nazareth's family tomb? We do not. This analysis is only as good as the assumption behind the formulas used to create it. That is, if one piece of the formula fails, it all falls apart. According to the *JFT* proponents, *Mariamne* has to be Mary Magdalene. *Jesus son of Joseph* has to be Jesus of Nazareth. Jesus has to have been married and to have had a son named Judah. Jose has to be Jesus' brother. Mary has to be His mother. In other words for this combination to qualify as being the family tomb of Jesus a number of dots need to connect. But if one of the assumptions made to connect these dots is wrong, the entire theory crumbles. The evidence shows the fallacy behind these assumptions.

The Bible, which records Jesus' resurrection, is a valid and trustworthy historical document. We can trust the Bible's account that Jesus rose from the dead. Judaism and the early Christian church also exhibited the common expectation of a future bodily resurrection.

Hence the Gospel accounts that mention Jesus' resurrection should not be understood as speaking of a spiritual resurrection, especially when the Gospels record that Jesus ate and was touched by people. Interpreting Jesus' resurrection as spiritual misreads the very point Paul made in 1 Corinthians 15:16–17, "For if the dead do not rise, then Christ is not risen. And if Christ is not risen, your faith is futile; you are still in your sins!"

Jesus' resurrection was the power that changed the apostles, earlier followers, and will continue to change anyone who simply believes in Him for the free gift of eternal life.

— Appendix A —

EFFORTS TO DISPROVE THE BIBLICAL JESUS

> Now while they were going, behold, some of the guard came into the city and reported to the chief priests all the things that had happened. When they had assembled with the elders and consulted together, they gave a large sum of money to the soldiers, saying, "Tell them, 'His disciples came at night and stole Him away while we slept.' And if this comes to the governor's ears, we will appease him and make you secure." So they took the money and did as they were instructed; and this saying is commonly reported among the Jews until this day (Matt. 28:11-15).

Trying to disprove the biblical Jesus is nothing new. Matthew records that immediately after the news broke in Jerusalem that Jesus' body was missing, Jewish leaders formulated a story to invalidate the resurrection. Could the biblical account be a conspiracy cover-up by Jesus' disciples? Could the account, in Matthew 28:11-15, be a later insertion by church fathers to promote Jesus' resurrection, knowing full well that He did not rise? Or was the early church simply deceived by following an early tradition begun by Jesus' early followers? Such questions have prompted numerous scholars throughout the centuries to continue to search for Jesus' bones, hoping that one day something will turn up.

Many argue today that such a "prophecy" has indeed been fulfilled by the discovery in 1980 of a family tomb in Talpiot, a suburb of Jerusalem, where Jesus' name appears with five other biblical names related to Him in one way or another. This news, however, does not surprise scholars—though it may shock the uniformed public—since for a long time now the media, numerous movements, and a plethora of published manuscripts have sought to redefine the historical and biblical Jesus. Yet as we have seen, this is nothing but a false alarm.

Past Efforts to Disprove the Biblical Jesus

Art galleries always use proper lighting, a stellar frame, and prepare the best location for a painting before displaying it. Such things bring to light elements on a canvas painting that otherwise would be missed. In examining the claims of *The Lost Tomb of Jesus* documentary and *The Jesus Family Tomb* book, setting the frame becomes necessary before placing the picture on display. "Setting the frame" means setting the context by showing the long-standing efforts to disprove the biblical Jesus. This will allow the reader to understand the historical context of present allegations, and thereby be better prepared to make a better judgment.

Though many have tried to redefine the biblical Jesus during the first 1,500 years after His life, the real "explosion" came after the Reformation.[1] This explosion came in ten new philosophical approaches to the Bible that evolved through time. These ten are inductivism, materialism, rationalism, deism, skepticism, agnosticism, romanticism, idealism, evolution, and existentialism.[2] Today numerous books draw directly from one or more of these philosophies that seek to redefine the biblical Jesus and at times go beyond that and create their own radical theories.

Inductivism. Sir Francis Bacon (1561-1626), a lawyer, orator, writer, philosopher, and scientist, became Lord Chancellor in England in 1618 and published his magnum opus *Novum Organum* in 1620.[3] Basically in this work Bacon postulated that experiment and experience are the bases for discovering truth, which became known as the *inductive* method. Obviously this view resulted in separating science from faith, which would later lead to a mythological understanding of Scripture and perhaps influencing the writings of David F. Strauss and Rudolf Bultmann.[4] Under this new system science is at odds with Scripture. The inductive method is not wrong, for how else do we examine facts but to test them? Instead of interpreting science to oppose Scripture, we should understand both as working harmoniously with each other. But under this new system science sits in judgment of Scripture and is the exclusive arbiter of truth, and it accepts Scripture as a valid judge only on spiritual matters.

Materialism. Thomas Hobbes (1588-1679) worked for Francis Bacon for a while and became the promoter of materialism as explained in his work *Leviathan*.[5] He said all reality consists of matter and the visual, and that the spiritual realm is nonexistent. Going one step further than Bacon, Hobbes's ultimately ended in diminishing the Scriptures' relevancy and authority for everyone. Hence Farnell correctly concludes, "Reason now ascends the throne"[6] in a total sense.

Rationalism. Baruch de Spinoza (1632-1677), Jewish born, was expelled from the synagogue for his heretical views.[7] Repulsive to Jews and Christians alike, Spinoza was described at times as a "hideous atheist." In reality he was a "rationalistic pantheist,"[8] which is not technically the same thing. Rationalism interprets all things through reason, not experience, as the primary means to understanding. Natural science is an a priori system by which to measure all truth, and truth is discovered through mathematical equations. This philosophy led to the Enlightenment period. However, unlike many philosophers of that period (e.g., Descartes and Leibniz), Spinoza believed God was in all things (pantheism). Therefore one could not have a loving personal relationship with such a God since He is part of the essence of all creation. Thus Spinoza's system defines "religion as 'the Mind's intellectual love of God.'"[9] Such ideas obviously reveal why he was not popular with Jews and Christians since it contradicts Scripture that teaches God is not like a man nor are His thoughts our thoughts (Num. 23:19; 1 Sam. 15:29; Isa. 55:8-9).

Deism. Herbert of Cherbury (1583-1648), whose ideas were later advanced by Charles Blount (1654-1693), believed that God is separate from creation but that He does not intimately interact with it. Like other philosophical movements, Deists reject any claims to supernatural revelation since God does not reveal Himself in any way other than through creation. Thus natural law, rejecting all forms of miracles, reigns supreme[10] and runs counter to Jewish and Christian thought.

Skepticism. David Hume (1711-1776), though influenced by the three major Enlightenment philosophies of rationalism, deism, and empiricism that preceded him, went beyond them to postulate that all reality exists in the mind and is perceived through the five senses.[11] He influenced many future theologians such as David F. Strauss (1808-1874), F. E. D. Schleiermacher (1768-1834), Ernst Renan (1823-1892) and Adolph Harnack (1851-1930). As Farnell wrote of Hume, "We perceive the data of our senses, but cannot know that there is anything beyond. In Hume's thought, one could not even prove the existence of the human self."[12]

Agnosticism. Influenced by Hume's system Immanuel Kant (1724-1804) went beyond it in trying to synthesize the philosophy of empiricism and rationalism into one system: agnosticism. Nothing, he said, is knowable for sure. Kant distinguished external experience and reality as something existing outside of self, apart from one's internal mechanism that subjectively interprets this reality based on personal bias. Thus the receptor of the mind processes external experiences it perceives according to its own mechanism. That is, "the mind does not perceive these things as they actually are in themselves, for the mind reshapes what it perceives ... In other words, the mind conditions (perhaps better 'colors') everything that it encounters.... One can know only what appears (*phenomenal*), not what really is (*noumenal*). The thing-in-itself is unknowable."[13] Such statements are self-defeating and nonsensical, because if the proposition (nothing is knowable) were true, it predicates something that can be known. But how can it be known when the very statement negates what it purports to know? All religious people who believe God communicates through supernatural revelation reject such a system (including *skepticism*) because it denies the foundation by which a system can be validated and believed, namely, *that God communicates knowable truth based on people's ability to perceive it for what it really is.*

Romanticism. F. E. D. Schleiermacher (1768-1834) is the person most identified with this movement.[14] In response to the intellectual and unemotional philosophy derived from the Enlightenment, Romanticism emphasized feelings, sensualism, fantasy, experience, the individual over the universal, freedom of expression against the order and the controlled. Farnell summarizes the incompatibility between Romanticism, the Bible, and the Jesus of Scripture:

> In summary, for Schleiermacher the Bible may not be propositional authoritative revelation or historically accurate, but it still conveyed religious "experience" relevant to people. He did not speak about the Jesus of history but about the Christ of faith and about the search for the "historical Jesus." In terms of historical-critical interpretation, "what it means to me in my present situation" (namely, eisegesis and application) was more important for Schleiermacher than the original meaning of Scripture (exegesis and interpretation).[15]

Idealism (transcendentalism). G. W. Hegel (1770-1831) was the most influential advocate who promoted *absolute idealism,* which states that mental and spiritual values are more essential to life than matter.[16] Idealism became "the opposite of realism—the view that things exist independently of being perceived—and of naturalism that explains the mind and spiritual values via materialism.... In other words, history, nature, and thought are aspects of the Absolute Spirit coming to self-consciousness."[17] How that happens seems to be mystical. Again, it is impossible to know the historical-biblical Jesus in this system apart from a reconstruction of the available data, but Hegel and its followers eliminated all miracles and advocated that virtue is the ultimate end of religion that enters the mind by means of the Spirit in mystical form.

Evolution. Charles Darwin (1809-1882) popularized this philosophy through two major works, *The Origin of Species* (1859) and *The Descent of Man* (1871).[18] However, he was not the originator of the evolutionary theory since the naturalistic philosophies espoused by him existed long before him.[19] Evolution leaves God out of the picture in assessing reality and asserts that everything that exists (i.e., matter) stems from a natural process that arose by chance and evolves from a simple form of life to a more complex organism. This system has permeated the scientific community. But it has also influenced theological thought by rejecting the Mosaic authorship of the first five books of the Bible and interpreting a gradual development of biblical revelation that stems from the simple to the more complex.[20]

The evolutionary view resulted in rejecting the uniqueness of monotheism (one God), supernatural revelation, and ultimately the biblical Jesus. Hence Wilhelm Bousset (1865-1920) advocated that biblical concepts evolved and were based on ideas stemming from other religions (e.g., Egyptian, Babylonian, mystery religions, and other ancient myths).[21] However, this system contradicts the second law of thermodynamics, which states that all things go from a state of order to disorder. Also evolutionary philosophy ends in a system that believes—without evidence—that all matter appeared out of nothing by chance. The mathematical possibility of this occurring is staggering and is hard to accept. In fact, it takes more faith to believe in that system than in a system that holds that all design must have a Designer.

Existentialism. Søren Kierkegaard (1813-1855) is considered the father of existentialism. Unfortunately, defining existentialism is not easy because others like "Karl Jaspers (1883-1969), Gabriel Marcel (1889-1973) represent the theistic branch. Jean-Paul Sartre (1905-1980), Martin Heidigger (1889-1976, and Albert Camus (1913-1960) represent the atheistic branch."[22] Kierkegaard believed that biblical truths are attained through subjective means, and he disregarded objective means as a path of arriving at religious truth. This, however, does not mean he did not believe in objective truth but that this form of it could not aid one in becoming a person of faith. Thus Kierkegaard wrote, "And so I say to myself: I choose; that historical fact means so much to me that I decide to stake my whole life upon it.... That is called risking; and without risk faith is an impossibility."[23] His paradoxical position describes where his views end in regard to the historicity of the Bible and Christ: "Kierkegaard never denied that Christianity was objectively or historically true, but he felt that the results of historical research are uncertain. Though asserting his personal belief in the historicity of the Bible and Christ, he maintained that objective truth is not essential to Christianity."[24] Perhaps he believed this way since faith was a step beyond historical facts that could not be proven absolutely. However, to believe in something absolutely one does not need to touch or study it in a laboratory. Many people believed George Washington existed and was the first president of the United States, but no one alive saw or touched him in an absolute way. Historical evidence exists that proves this. Part of the problem occurs when many fail to differentiate between the distinctive senses of "history," which is discussed in chapter 10.

One can appreciate Kierkegaard's fervor for having faith and desiring to experience a personal relationship with God and/or Christ. Yet how can one enter into such a relationship or experience Christ apart from the only objective means (the Bible) that conveys that truth? The contradiction is obvious.

Recent Efforts to Disprove the Biblical Jesus

All of these philosophical thoughts have somehow influenced contemporary writers. Today many of these movements and authors directly seek to redefine the biblical Jesus by posing radical theories with meager evidence to support them. These include the (1) *Jesus Seminar* movement; (2) the *National Geographic* television program about the *Gospel of Judas* that supposedly clarifies the relationship between Jesus and Judas, who was wrongly accused of betraying Jesus; (3) Bart Ehrman's *Misquoting Jesus*; (4) James D. Tabor's *The Jesus Dynasty*; and (5) Michael Baigent's *The Jesus Papers*.[25]

The Jesus Seminar began in 1985 with its founder and chairman Robert Funk along with a group of more than seventy liberal New Testament scholars.[26] Its purpose was to determine which words of Jesus in the Gospels were actually His. As a result of a vote from these scholars, using colored beads they decided which were the authentic words of Jesus. Each of the beads had a color that meant something. For example, *red*: "That's Jesus," *pink*: "Sure sounds like Jesus," *gray*: "Well, maybe," and *black*: "There's been some mistake."[27] Ultimately this resulted in publishing a volume *The Five Gospels: The Search for the Authentic Words of Jesus*, which concluded that 82 percent of what Jesus supposedly said was not authentic, 18 percent was somewhat doubtful, and only 2 percent of what the New Testament Gospels record were the words Jesus actually said.[28] Furthermore the Seminar did not regard the New Testament as superior to any other literature of the church or other writings of the day (the Gospel of Thomas is the fifth Gospel as noted in the book title).[29] The Seminar used seven rules called "pillars" in deciding what to accept as authentic. While all seven pillars have numerous logical flaws and have been thoroughly evaluated elsewhere,[30] I would like to answer two of these rules to show the unscholarly biased and flawed system of these scholars.[31]

How can modern scholars existing more than two thousand years after Jesus be better judges in determining Jesus' authentic words than Jesus' contemporaries who wrote the Gospels? Efforts made by contemporary scholarship that seeks to better understand the ancient world are good. But to dismiss early witnesses as easily as the Seminar does is severely problematic. Furthermore, the church fathers, who lived just one to two hundred years after Jesus, testified to the authenticity and authorship of the four Gospels. Unless solid evidence appears to contradict this, one should not dismiss their testimony.

Jesus Seminar scholars reverse the criteria in how to judge the authenticity of a historical document. They assert that *the Gospels are unhistorical until proven otherwise*. That is like saying in the jurisprudence system that a person is guilty until proven innocent. If we used these criteria, we would be left doubting the majority of all historical documents we now possess. Hence on both of these issues Gregory A. Boyd concludes:

> These twentieth-century scholars imagine that they are in a better position to compose the Bible than was the early church of the second and third centuries. If that strikes you as a bit presumptuous, you are not alone. After all, the early church knew all of this literature well, and was in a much better position than we are to know who wrote it and to judge its accuracy.... And despite the presumptuous claims of the Jesus Seminar, most historical scholars argue that the burden of proof should generally lie with the historian who wants to argue that what an ancient document is reporting is *not* true. A historian, in other words, must generally prove that an ancient account is *wrong*, not that what an ancient document reports is *right*.[32]

The discovery of the *Gospel of Judas* was made public on Thursday, April 6, 2006, when the National Geographic Society held a press conference at its headquarters in Washington, D.C. This was a little more than a year before *The Lost Tomb of Jesus* was aired on the Discovery Channel on March 4, 2007. In a packed room of more than one hundred news personnel the society announced the discovery of the *Gospel of Judas*. Three days later on Sunday, April 9, 2006, a two-hour documentary on the National Geographic channel was televised. Why all the hype? This new document not only asserts that Judas Iscariot was Jesus' best disciple, who was taught by Him in private more than the others,[33] but it also reveals that Jesus urged Judas to betray Him so that Jesus could get out of the flesh (physical body) and into the spirit realm.[34]

While the document is authentic (i.e., it was written around the fourth-century A.D. and is not a contemporary forgery), numerous facts argue against its being a book authorized by the apostles.

First, the church fathers never mentioned such a book.

Second, this Gospel is written in Coptic, whereas Greek is the language of all four canonical Gospels recorded in the first century A.D.

This betrays a late date—to which all scholars agree—and one of the reasons why it could not have been approved by the apostles.

Third, the *Gospel of Judas* follows a practice called "pseudonymity" (falsely attributing a name to a document that was actually written by someone else). Obviously this was done in order to gain acceptance by the public.

Fourth, the *Gospel of Judas* sounds like a document with a similar name that Irenaeus, around A.D. 180, condemned.[35] If this is the same document, then this work was already condemned by the late second-century A.D.

While the document can illuminate the church's historical context when Gnosticism flourished, it contributes nothing to understanding more about Jesus or Judas since this document does not date back to the first century A.D. As Ben Witherington III concludes, "To say otherwise is an argument entirely from silence, not from hard evidence."[36]

Misquoting Jesus was written by Bart D. Ehrman in 2005. In it he reiterates much of the material of an earlier work of his, *The Orthodox Corruption of Scripture* (1993).[37] Basically Ehrman believes humans corrupted the text of the Scriptures. He writes, "The Bible began to appear to me as a very human book."[38] He believes that errors in the extant copies of the Scriptures discredit the verbal inspiration and inerrancy of the Bible. Though we only have copies, the function of textual criticism is to compare the 5,700 complete New Testament copies available, plus over 10,000 more copies in Latin, and more than one million quotations from church fathers to arrive at a very precise reading of the original documents.[39]

Ehrman asserts that more than minor differences exist.[40] For example, he cites 1 John 5:7b, which has an alternative reading based on a scribal alteration of the text.[41] However, one can readily arrive at the original reading—when more than one reading appears—by simply doing some comparisons.

Furthermore, contrary to Ehrman, in such places where alternative readings occur *no major doctrines are at stake.* Hence Witherington says, "There is a reason that both Ehrman's mentor in text criticism and mine, Bruce Metzger, has said that there is nothing in these variants that really challenges any Christian belief: they don't. I would like to add that other experts in text criticism, such as Gordon Fee, have been equally emphatic about the flawed nature of Ehrman's analysis of the significance of such textual variants."[42]

In *The Jesus Dynasty* James D. Tabor seeks to define the historical Jesus by postulating that Jesus' true royal dynasty continued through James, his brother, and not Paul (hence the book's title). Tabor claims that Paul, not James, elevated Jesus to divinity.[43] Tabor uses an inconsistent criterion in interpreting passages by choosing those that support his premise, ignoring those that do not, and superimposing his own meaning on others.[44]

Tabor occupies a faculty position at the University of North Carolina at Charlotte and is a trained theologian (with an interest in archaeology) who received his Ph.D. degree from the University of Chicago. Tabor has interesting and helpful archaeological information. His book is well written and easy to read. As Witherington wrote, "Absent from this study are wild theories about Gnostic gospels being our earliest and best sources about the life of Jesus.... Equally refreshing is Tabor's willingness to take serious the historical data not just in the synoptics but also in the Gospel of John."[45] However, I have the same concern as that of Evans who wrote, "I worry about nonexperts who read it and fail to see how tenuous some of the speculation and conclusions are."[46] Interestingly, though Tabor differs from Baigent and Brown on numerous points,[47] all three of them claim that twenty-first-century theories are closer to the truth than the New Testament records written in the first century A.D.

Since Tabor begins with a premise that discounts the supernatural, many of Jesus' miracles are explained away by natural means.[48] For example, he argues that Jesus could not have been born of a virgin since virgins do not bear children.[49] And Jesus could not have risen physically from the dead since dead people do not rise bodily. Tabor simply follows a philosophical bias called "uniformitarianism" (the present is the key to the past).[50]

His method of research to validate a biblical account is extremely flawed. Here are some examples. John the Baptist was also one of two

Messiahs.[51] But this position clearly contradicts the Baptist's own admission in John 1:20, "I am not the Christ." Tabor, however, fails to mention this text. This is not surprising since Tabor views numerous accounts in John's Gospel (especially accounts in chapters 1 and 3) as having been altered later by Christians.[52] When presenting evidence why Matthew's name appears in the Talpoit tomb along with Jesus' bones and therefore belonging to Jesus' family, Tabor accepts Luke's account as evidence that Mary's genealogy merged with the line of Levi, thereby showing how a person named Matthew could appear in Jesus' family tomb.[53] This shows how selective and inconsistent are his methods, and how his bias permeates the entire book. He repeatedly accepts one reading of a New Testament text above another without explanation.

While denying the virgin birth Tabor also believes Mary became illegitimately pregnant by a Roman soldier named Pantera, and that she ultimately had sex with not one but three men.[54] Part of Tabor's supposed evidence comes from a second-century A.D. philosopher named Celsus who wrote against Christianity, whose work *Contra Celsum*, is quoted in various places in a rebuttal by Origen, a church father of the third century A.D. He also believes a tombstone inscription bearing the name Pantera discovered in 1859 in Bingerbrück, Germany, may possibly be the father of Jesus who at one time lived in Sidon. Hence he believes Mark 7:24 suggests why Jesus secretly visited that city ("And He entered a house and wanted no one to know it"). He also supports this by noting that some church fathers[55] accepted the point about Pantera. Evans, however, says, "Tabor thinks this supports the historicity of the tradition. Otherwise, why would the church fathers such as Epiphanius take it so seriously? But Epiphanius and later Christian writers are simply trying to fend off slur, and to do so they throw out various proposals, some having more merit than the allegations themselves." In fact Evans correctly concludes that one cannot allege from fourth-century A.D. rebuttals that an earlier tradition for Pantera proposed by Celsus existed other than the time that Celsus himself lived (in the second century A.D.).[56] Tabor has presented no archaeological evidence whatsoever to link Pantera to Jesus. Discovering a Roman tombstone and proposing various outlandish theories does not qualify as credible evidence. These are highly improbable views that go against all the enormous weight of evidence that tilt the scale in the other direction.

Tabor also believes in a *spiritual* rather than a *physical* resurrection,[57] similar to what *The Lost Tomb of Jesus* documentary and *The Jesus Family Tomb* book claim.[58]

Tabor accepts the premise of the *Jesus Seminar* (without mentioning it) that equally recognizes the second-century A.D. Gnostic *Gospel of Thomas* as equal to or perhaps better than the other Gospels.[59] He suggests that there is a "cryptic" clue in Saying 105 that echoes Jesus' illegitimate birth: "One who knows his father and his mother will be called *the son of a whore*."[60] It has been acknowledged by numerous scholars that the *Gospel of Thomas* was written too late (in the second half of the second-century A.D.) to give a clear picture of Jesus, is replete with mystic and condemned Gnostic teachings, and was never accepted as an apostolic Gospel, as the first four hundred years of church tradition clearly shows.[61] To be fair, however, Tabor does not believe all Gnostic accounts are equally valid since he considers the "Infancy Gospel" and other manuscripts that purport to have Jesus' lost years as late and legendary (second to fourth centuries A.D.) and as being entertaining other than informative.[62] Tabor's book has helpful archaeological information, but he fails miserably as a theologian-lawyer who presents a very weak case. Many of his theories are more than speculative and biased; they are unsubstantiated and incredible.

The Jesus Papers appears as Michael Baigent's latest book similar to his conspiracy-fraught tomes of the *Holy Blood, Holy Grail* (1983) and *The Dead Sea Scrolls Deception* (1992). Baigent holds a M.A. degree in mysticism from the University of Kent in England. He claims that Jesus survived the crucifixion and wrote a set of letters in A.D. 45 denying His deity. Baigent says these letters were buried for two thousand years and were finally unearthed in 1960 from a cellar in a house in Jerusalem. Baigent professes to have seen these letters but are lost today.[63] "What evidence does he have?" one may ask.

Baigent alleges that a number of people saw the letters, but he has not produced any evidence of such individuals.

Why should anyone believe Baigent's story?

Baigent admits he does not read Aramaic.[64] However, he wants everyone to believe that he knows for sure what the letters said. The only way he could know the contents of the letters is to have them translated. And if they were translated, how would he know if the translators were lying since only a few people were able to examine the contents of these alleged letters?

It is impossible for any papyrus letter to survive two thousand years in a cellar of a house in Jerusalem, as Evans correctly notes. "I might also mention that Baigent neglects to mention that archaeologists and papyrologists will tell you that no papyrus (plural: papyri) can survive buried in the ground, in Jerusalem, for two thousand years. The only papyrus documents that have survived from antiquity have been found in climates, such as the area surrounding the Dead Sea and the sands of Egypt. No ancient papyri have been found in Jerusalem itself. Jerusalem receives rainfall every year; papyri buried in the ground, beneath houses or wherever decompose quickly. So whatever Baigent saw, they were not ancient papyri found beneath somebody's house in Jerusalem, and they were not letters Jesus wrote."[65]

If the other points are detrimental to Baigent's case, this last point nails the coffin shut on the bizarre assertion that Pilate conspired with Jesus to fake the crucifixion.[66] Why? Because, as Witherington explains, "Baigent's work ... requires that [he] explain away all the evidence we have from Paul (our earlier New Testament writer), from the canonical gospels, from Josephus, and from Roman sources (such as Tacitus and the later Suetonius) that Jesus suffered the extreme penalty and died from crucifixion under and at the hands of Pontius Pilate." Hence, "Not many people are taking seriously Baigent's attempts at revisionist history. It goes against every shred of first-century evidence, Christian or otherwise, that we have about Jesus's [*sic*] demise."[67]

Conclusion

Thus the historical quest to disprove the biblical Jesus and search for His bones that started two thousand years ago continues to thrive today. And although many have tried redefining Jesus as He appears in the first-century A.D. New Testament documents, the real upsurge of this attempt came after the Reformation, as seen in the ten philosophical approaches discussed earlier (inductivism, materialism, rationalism, deism, skepticism, agnosticism, romanticism, idealism, evolution, and existentialism).

A number of books today have adopted one or more of these philosophies and seek to redefine the biblical Jesus through bizarre and radical theories void of any scholarly evidence. This is the context and current atmosphere in which *The Lost Tomb of Jesus* documentary and *The Jesus Family Tomb* book appear.

— Appendix B —

THE JFT ONE YEAR LATER: ANSWERS TO OBJECTIONS AND OUR RESPONSE

One year has passed since the book *The Jesus Family Tomb* was first published. The subtitle of the book has been reworded, and comments by Simcha Jacobovici and answers to objections by James D. Tabor have been added.[1] Jacobovici's portion simply recounts unknown events that occurred on February 26, 2007, and the aftermath once the documentary and book were released. Tabor, however, answers (from pages 219–34) a number of objections that scholars have made against the film and the book. Below are his answers to objections and our responses to his answers, as well as the final word to-date on the Talpiot tomb's statistical calculation.

Our First Response
Tabor said, "In terms of Christian faith… the Resurrection of Jesus does not have to be understood as a literal 'flesh and bones'

event, with Jesus ascending to heaven as a physical being."[2]

First, Tabor misses the point that if Jesus only rose spiritually it does not overturn the spiritual and physical curse that fell on humanity and the earth at creation.[3] Furthermore, second-Temple Judaism, the apostolic fathers, and Christians understood the Resurrection as a physical event, as extensively argued in chapter 10. Tabor presents no evidence to the contrary other than suggesting the common argument from 1 Corinthians 15:44 (already clarified in chapter 14). However he adds a new twist that Jesus' physical body can be viewed as similar to that of angels who on occasions assumed what appeared to be a human body. That is, angels were seen eating with Abraham in Genesis 18 but yet they possessed a spiritual nature. While that is true, Tabor fails to note that the materializing of angels is not the same as a person being born, dying, and rising from the dead (something angels do not experience).

We have already shown in part two of this book that the terminology "rising" and "resurrection" was always understood as the entire person physically rising not solely the immaterial part of man. Thus it will be with Abraham, Isaac, and Jacob, since they were made physical literal promises of a land (Gen. 15:18–21; Heb. 11:8–10) to be enjoyed in some physical sense. Furthermore, according to Hebrews 11:17–19, Abraham believed in a physical resurrection (Gen. 22:5) as he viewed the receiving of Isaac as if he was dead.

To say that the materializing of angels is the same as Jesus' resurrection body is to compare apples with oranges, since angels do not die and by their very nature are spiritual not physical beings. Conversely, Jesus took on a human nature. Thus what governs Jesus is not what governs angels. Moreover, similarities do not prove identity. That is, because Jesus can materialize and dematerialize at will does not prove He rose spiritually. All that this proves is that His resurrection body is now not limited to time, matter, and space, as was His former body. But it is a body nonetheless with special powers at its disposal. Much like angels can venture into the material world while maintaining their original ties to the spiritual world, Jesus and all resurrected Christians can venture into the spiritual world while maintaining their original ties to the material world. All that Tabor proves by mentioning that angels can materialize and eat is that they can materialize. That, however, fails to prove that Jesus rose spiritually. To say Jesus rose spiritually because angels are spiritual beings that can materialize is a non sequitur and faulty logic.

Our Second Response

Tabor answers the objection that Jesus' family was poor and could not afford a family tomb by proposing the following hypothesis. "Although they arose from peasant origins, it is not at all clear that Jesus and his family were destitute or poor in later life." He adds that Jesus' "family had artisan skills" and had supported their families and mother. Furthermore He had loyal followers who financially supported Him (Luke 8:1–3). Besides, Joseph of Arimathea could have donated a tomb.[4] However, no evidence of such a donation exists, which most likely would not go unnoticed if such were the case.[5] Why does Tabor not address the Holy Sepulcher burial place of Jesus instead of positing such a highly improbable hypothesis? He also assumes his conclusion that Jesus rose spiritually in order to formulate his view that His women supporters mentioned in Luke 8:1–3 could have donated a family tomb. Why would such a donation exist if Jesus rose physically from the dead? The answer is obvious. One has to assume no physical resurrection for such a "tomb donation hypothesis" to work. This is simply a case of assuming one's conclusion.

Along with James and Jude, probably all of Jesus' family became believers after His resurrection. Thus, if they were not rich before becoming believers, it seems the chances of becoming wealthy after becoming believers is less since they would most likely be involved in the ministry (e.g., Acts 15 and the letters of James and Jude). Since Christians were harshly treated in Jerusalem, once a Jew made an open profession of Christ, making a living became harder, not easier. Perhaps that is what gave rise to the letter to the Hebrews. Jewish-Christians were under peer pressure to return to Judaism and many where abandoning Christianity. In addition the evidence suggests that poor saints were in the Jerusalem church and needed financial help, a need Paul helped meet (2 Cor. 8–9; Rom. 15:25–27).

Our Third Response

Tabor correctly claims, "The reading 'Yeshua, son Yehosef,' or 'Jesus, son of Joseph,' has been confirmed by several of the world's leading epigraphers, including Dr. Frank Cross of Harvard University."[6] However, what he does not admit is that many scholars have acknowledged the reading *Yeshua* but with doubts.[7]

He further tries to deemphasize the scrappy handwriting of the name *Yeshua* on this inscription by stating that this is typical of inscriptions since even the inscription of "Joseph, son of Caiaphas, the wealthy and influential high priest who resided over the trial of Jesus, is quite difficult to read."[8] Not only is the opposite true (for a picture of Caiaphas' inscription see chapter 2 [fig. 8]), but most ossuaries documented in Rahmani's catalogue are clearly readable unlike the *Yeshua* inscription. This is why, unlike most others, it has a question mark next to its name.

Tabor also claims "more formal and theological designations such as 'Jesus of Nazareth' and 'Jesus the Christ' became popular decades later."[9] Yet the evidence in Rahmani's catalogue shows otherwise. Furthermore all experts (Joe Zias, Jodi Magness, and L. Y. Rahmani) have said, regardless of the period, "In Jerusalem's tombs, the deceased's place of origin was noted when someone from outside Jerusalem and its environs was interred in a local tomb."[10] Tabor, however, does not provide a shred of evidence for his claim.

Our Fourth Response

Tabor does not believe that the names found in the Talpiot tomb are all that common. "The Rahmani collection does not include all inscribed ossuaries found in the Jerusalem area for the period, but the name frequencies and distributions appear to be fairly representative of our large body of data."[11] He refers to the 231 inscribed ossuaries in Rahmani's catalogue. Not only have all onomastic experts said these names are common, thus contradicting Tabor, but also 231 inscribed ossuaries are a fairly small number according to the estimated 80 thousand Jerusalem residents of the time. If we include the four million residents of the region, this makes the number 231 almost insignificant. Pointing to the limited amount of documented ossuaries in Rahmani's catalogue hinders instead of helps Tabor's point.

Our Fifth Response

Tabor objects to the view that "Mariamne and Mara" could refer to two women, Mariam and Martha, but he does not cite any evidence in support that the names refer to one individual. A careful analysis arguing that two individuals could be the best reading of the inscription of this ossuary was given in chapter 3. Tabor simply restates that *Mara* meant in Aramaic "lord" or "mistress," and that this "could very well fit a woman such as Mary Magdalene."[12] Asserting a statement does not make it true. Where is the evidence other than what the book already states? Tabor's answer does not add anything new.

Our Sixth Response

Tabor originally denied that Jesus was married and called it a "gripping fiction" that is "short on evidence."[13] He has now changed his mind saying, "Jesus was married."[14]

The only so-called "strong evidence" he claims is Paul's lack of reference to Jesus' singleness when recommending celibacy, which would have clinched Paul's argument.[15] However, Tabor fails to recognize three points. First, Paul calls celibacy a "gift from God" (1 Cor. 7:7), which allows one to devote more time and effort to the Lord's work (vv. 32–35). Is not that the whole purpose for Jesus' coming to earth (see John 18:37)?[16]

Second, Paul did not need to refer to Jesus when speaking of celibacy because Jesus had spoken of this already in Matthew 19:10–12. That is why Paul wrote that the revelation from 1 Corinthians 7:12 and following is being added by him ("But to the rest I, not the Lord"), since Jesus did not speak about mixed marriages among believers and nonbelievers. Paul did not need to mention Jesus' singleness because it was common knowledge that Jesus promoted that the ultimate state of existence to do the Lord's work necessitated remaining single (Matt. 19:12). Would Jesus promote celibacy as the highest form of existence to serve the Lord and do less Himself? Hence Paul also promoted celibacy.

Third, Tabor says 1 Corinthians 9:5 does not mention the names of Jesus' brothers wives, or children, which suggests that they were not celibate. Thus "silence does not equal celibacy."[17] True, but this is not silence. In fact this works against Tabor's point, for if Paul wanted to strengthen his point, mentioning Jesus' marriage would have clinched the argument. Instead Paul mentioned the marriage of apostles, Jesus' brothers and Peter's, but not Jesus' marriage. Tabor then actually reverses the logic and point of the passage.

Final Statistical Note
Everyone knows the majority of scholars rejected the statistical analysis from Prof. Andrey Feuerverger, because of the enormous unsubstantiated assumptions (given to him by Jacobovici) needed for his calculations to work. The most recent statistical analysis done by Randall Ingermanson gives a more reasonable number of a 2% probability that the Talpiot tomb belongs to Jesus and His family.[18]

Ingermason arrives at a 2% probability by first noting that there were an estimated 128 men at that time in Jerusalem that were named "Jesus son of Joseph." This leaves 1 in 128 (1%) that the Jesus of Talpiot is Jesus of Nazareth.

Being conservative, Ingermason qualified some of the previous assumptions made by Feuerverger, some of them worked for and some worked against the Talpiot hypothesis. Thus he concluded the name Maria was far too common to help the Talpiot hypothesis. The name "Yoseh" is a customary contraction of "Yehosef," one of the most common names of that period. Besides the "New Testament data asserts that Jesus was buried in a tomb very close to the execution site (a couple of miles from Talpiot [John 19:41])." A number of other observations made by Ingermason were anticipated in this book.[19] Though most scholars at the January 2008 symposium gave no chance of this being the tomb of Jesus of Nazareth, the best Talpiot hopefuls can say is what Ingermason concluded. "My best estimate is that the probability of authenticity is less than 2%. Based on my best understanding of what the scholars say, the probability may well be much lower than 2%. But I don't believe it is higher than 2%."[20]

Conclusions

Jacobovici and Tabor add nothing new that makes their case more believable. Other points made by Tabor have already been anticipated in this book and answered. Most of the information, especially pages 228–34, of the revised book are rehashing previous arguments but without any supporting materials. The revised and updated volume adds nothing compelling to their arguments, other than make various logical fallacies and restate former ideas with various twists.

SELECTED BIBLIOGRAPHY

Ankerberg, John, and Dillon Burroughs. *What's the Big Deal about Jesus?* Eugene, OR: Harvest House Publishers, 2007.

Ankerberg, John, and John Weldon. *The Passion and the Empty Tomb.* Eugene, OR: Harvest House Publishers, 2005.

Bauckham, Richard. *Jesus and the Eyewitnesses: The Gospels as Eyewitness Testimony.* Grand Rapids: Wm. B. Eerdmans Publishing, 2006.

Blomberg, Craig L. "Where Do We Start Studying Jesus?" In *Jesus Under Fire: Modern Scholarship Reinvents the Historical Jesus*, ed. Michael J. Wilkins and J. P. Moreland, 17-50. Grand Rapids: Zondervan Publishing House, 1995.

Bock, Darrell L. *Can I Trust the Bible?* Norcross, GA: Ravi Zacharias International Ministries, 2001.

Bock, Darrell L. *Breaking the Da Vinci Code: Answers to Questions Everyone's Asking.* Nashville: Thomas Nelson, 2004.

Bock, Darrell L. *The Missing Gospels: Unearthing the Truth Behind Alternative Christianities.* Nashville: Thomas Nelson, 2006.

Bock, Darrell L., and Daniel B. Wallace. *Dethroning Jesus: Exposing Popular Culture's Quest to Unseat the Biblical Christ.* Nashville: Thomas Nelson, 2007.

Boyd, Gregory A. *Jesus Under Siege.* Wheaton, IL: Victor Books, 1995.

Burroughs, Dillon. *The Jesus Family Tomb Controversy: How the Evidence Falls Short.* Ann Arbor, MI: Nimble Books LCC, 2007.

Bynum, Caroline Walker. *The Resurrection of the Body in Western Christianity, 200–1336*, 1995.

Crossan, John Dominic, and Jonathan L. Reed. *Excavating Jesus: Beneath the Stones, Behind the Texts: Revised and Updated.* 1st ed. San Francisco: HarperSanFrancisco, 2001.

Evans, Craig A. *Jesus and the Ossuaries.* Waco, TX: Baylor University Press, 2003.

Evans, Craig A. *Fabricating Jesus: How Modern Scholars Distort the Gospels.* Downers Grove, IL: InterVarsity Press, 2006.

Farnell, F. David. "Philosophical and Theological Bent of Historical Criticism." In *The Jesus Crisis: The Inroads of Historical Criticism into Evangelical Scholarship*, ed. Robert L. Thomas and F. David Farnell, 85-131. Grand Rapids: Kregel Publications, 1998.

Habermas, Gary R. *The Historical Jesus: Ancient Evidence for the Life of Christ.* Joplin, MO: College Press Publishing, 1996.

Habermas, Gary R. *The Secret of the Talpiot Tomb: Unravelling the Mystery of the Jesus Family Tomb.* Nashville: Broadman & Holman Publishing, 2007.

Habermas, Gary R., and Michael R. Licona. *The Case for the Resurrection of Jesus.* Grand Rapids: Kregel Publications, 2004.

Hachlili, Rachael. "Hebrew Names, Personal Names, Family Names and Nicknames of Jews in the Second Temple Period." In *Families and Family Relations: As Presented in Early Judaisms and Early Christianities: Texts and Fictions*, ed. Jan Willem Van Henten and Athalya Brenner. Studies in Theology and Religion, vol. 2, 83–115. Netherlands: Deo Publishing, 2000.

Hachlili, Rachael. *Jewish Funerary Customs Practices and Rites in the Second Temple Period.* Supplements to the Journal for the Study of Judaism, ed. John J. Collins, vol. 94. Leiden: E. J. Brill, 2005.

Jenkins, Philip. *Hidden Gospels: How the Search for Jesus Lost Its Way.* Oxford: Oxford University Press, 2001.

Quarles, Chales L., ed. *Buried Hope or Risen Savior: The Search for the Jesus Tomb.* Nashville, TN: Broadman & Holman Publishing, 2008.

Sausa, Don. *The Jesus Tomb: Is It Fact or Fiction? Scholars Chime In*, ed. Jeffrey Clark. Fort Myers, FL: Vision Press, 2007.

Witherington III, Ben. *The Gospel Code: Novel Claims about Jesus, Mary Magdalene and Da Vinci.* Downers Grove, IL: InterVarsity Press, 2004.

Witherington III, Ben. *What Have They Done with Jesus? Beyond Strange Theories and Bad History—Why We Can Trust the Bible.* San Francisco: HarperSanFrancisco, 2006.

Wright, N. T. *The Resurrection of God.* Christian Origins and the Question of God, vol. 3. London: SPCK, 2003.

Yamauchi, Edwin M. "Tammuz and the Bible." *Journal of Biblical Literature* 84 (September 1965): 283–90.

ENDNOTES

Preface

[1] There are two acceptable spellings for the name of the city where the tomb was found: either Talpiyot (a transliterated Hebrew word) or Talpiot. The latter will be used throughout the book unless the former (Talpiyot) appears in a quote.
[2] Simcha Jacobovici and Charles Pellegrino, *The Jesus Family Tomb: The Discovery, the Investigation, and the Evidence That Could Change History* (San Francisco: HarperSanFrancisco, 2007).
[3] James R. White, *From Toronto to Emmaus: The Empty Tomb and the Journey from Skepticism to Faith* (Birmingham, AL: Solid Ground Christian Books, 2007), 7.
[4] Gary R. Habermas and Michael R. Licona, *The Case for the Resurrection of Jesus* (Grand Rapids: Kregel Publications, 2004), 14 (italics theirs).
[5] Jacobovici and Pellegrino, *Jesus Family Tomb*, 70-71.

Chapter One

[1] Amos Kloner, "A Tomb with Inscribed Ossuaries in East Talpiyot, Jerusalem," *Atiquot* 29 (1996): 15. A report of the discovery first appeared in the journal *Hadashot Arkheologiyot* in 1981.
[2] Most of the details in this section are taken from the detailed account by Simcha Jacobovici and Charles Pellegrino, *The Jesus Family Tomb: The Discovery, the Investigation, and the Evidence That Could Change History* (San Francisco: HarperSanFrancisco, 2007), 1-24.
[3] The pictures of the Talpiot tomb along with the sketch drawings inside the tomb are used with permission of Amos Kloner, which appear in the article "Inscribed Ossuaries in East Talpiyot, Jerusalem," 15–22.
[4] Jacobovici and Pellegrino, *Jesus Family Tomb*, 5.

[5] These drawings were used with permission and appear in Kloner, "Inscribed Ossuaries in East Talpiyot, Jerusalem," 15. The type of chambers used here are also called loculi, which are rows of burial compartments that encompass the length of a body. Such bodies could be placed in them—instead of the arcosolia (resting places made of a bench in the center or outside the *loculi*)— until the body decomposed which would take about a year. Then the bones would be put in a bone-box (ossuary) and placed in the *loculi* (i.e., *kokh*).

[6] Ibid., 15-16. The drawings are also in the article by Kloner.

[7] See Jacobovici and Pellegrino, *Jesus Family Tomb*, 1-24. Other books recounting this event—that give a rebuttal to the *Jesus Family Tomb* book— basically depend on either Jacobovici's detail account or the description by Kloner, "Inscribed Ossuaries in East Talpiyot, Jerusalem," 15-22. He summarizes what took place and reports the dimensions, details of the names and pictures of each of the ten ossuaries. As already noted, another article titled "The Tomb that Dare Not Speak Its Name" was published in a British newspaper, *The Sunday Times*, on March 31, 1996. A week later a BBC television documentary titled "The Body in Question" aired in the series *Heart of the Matter*. Just recently the Discovery Channel aired a documentary on March 4, 2007, also describing details the Talpiot tomb discovery.

[8] Joseph Gat, "East Talpiyot," *Hadashot Arkheologiyot* 76 (1981): 24-25.

[9] Levy Yitzhak Rahmani, *A Catalogue of Jewish Ossuaries in the Collections of the State of Israel*, ed. Ayala Sussmann and Peter Schertz (Jerusalem: Israel Antiquities Authority, 1994), 222-24. Rahmani did not include the tenth ossuary because it was not inscribed or ornamented.

[10] Courtesy of *The Sunday Times*, London.

[11] See http://orion.huji.ac.il/orion/archives/1996a/threads.html#00145. This was also noted by Don Sausa, *The Jesus Tomb: Is It Fact or Fiction? Scholars Chime In*, ed. Jeffrey Clark (Fort Myers, FL: Vision Press, 2007), 34.

[12] John Dominic Crossan and Jonathan L. Reed, *Excavating Jesus: Beneath the Stones, Behind the Texts: Revised and Updated*, 1st ed. (San Francisco: HarperSanFrancisco, 2001), 19-20. Also see http://www.sbl-site.org/Article.aspx?ArticleId=657 where Jonathan L. Reed said, "My letter to the *SBL Forum* attacks the documentary, which, along with the book, the producers' statements at the press conference and in subsequent interviews, make the misleading claim that no one ever thought through the issue. The Talpiot ossuaries were allegedly forgotten and buried deep inside the bowels of the IAA. My point is that all serious scholars who know about ossuaries knew about this discovery. Many scholars had read Kloner's report and Rahmani's catalogue. Why is there no lengthy bibliography? No one, including fine New Testament scholars like Evans and McCane, thought that denying the tomb's connection to

Jesus of Nazareth merited a serious, in-depth article. Based on the inscriptions, the use of statistics, the DNA, and the patina analysis, in short, every bit of evidence that the documentary and book produce, I still do not think a lengthy article is warranted. I am sorry, but the documentary's suggestion relies on too much speculation to be historically plausible."

[13] Jacobovici and Pellegrino, *Jesus Family Tomb*, 35, claim that, "Looking at the Judeo-Christian was—and is—an exercise fraught with potential controversy. It's likely to get you into hot water with both Jews *and* Christians, because it involves shedding light in the dark corners of the so-called Judeo-Christian tradition. It's certainly not something that the Kloners of this world want to get involved with. Why should the Judeo-Christian perspective pose such a problem?" See also pages 36-46. The book and documentary are filled with secrecy and conspiracy-type implications in almost every chapter.

[14] *Ad hominem* refers to attacking an opponent's character instead of his arguments, which tends to divert attention away from the point of contention.

[15] Jeff Shannon, *Titanic* (http://www.imdb.com/title/tt0120338/amazon, 1997, accessed September 5, 2007).

[16] See Jacobovici and Pellegrino, *Jesus Family Tomb*, xii-xiii; Sausa, *Jesus Tomb*, 20, also notes this.

[17] James Cameron, *Why Go to Mars?* (http://www.space.com/sciencefiction/cameron_ why_mars_825.html, August 25, 1999, accessed September 5, 2007); Cornelia Dean, *Evolution on Film? Cut!* (http://www.iht.com/articles/2005/03/20/business/imax.php, March 21, 2005, accessed September 5, 2007); Jacobovici and Pellegrino, *Jesus Family Tomb*, xii. In the address to the International Mars Society Cameron said, "We need this, or some kind of challenge like it, to bring us together to all feel a part of something and to have heroes again. The problem is there's no challenge on our horizon like Mars. If we rise to a challenge, we're gonna redefine ourselves, and we're gonna ratchet ourselves up another notch in the evolutionary ladder. In return, Mars will reward us with answers to profound questions and with a renewed sense of self-worth as a species" (*Why Go to Mars?*).

[18] Various well-known scholars in the field of archaeology rejected the premise of the film as Sausa, *Jesus Tomb*, 20, also notes. See Christopher Heard, *The Exodus Decoded: An Extended Review, part 1* (http://www.heardworld.com/ higgaion/?p=60, August 26, 2006, accessed September 5, 2007); Hershel Shanks, *The Exodus Debated* (http://www.biblicalarchaeology.org/bswbOOexodus.html, October 13, 2006, accessed September 5, 2007).

[19] Sausa, *Jesus Tomb*, 22.

[20] Charles R. Pellegrino, *Author* (http://www.harpercollins.com/authors/17997/Charles_R_Pellegrino/index.aspx, accessed September 5, 2007) (Italics added).

21 Sausa, *Jesus Tomb*, 24-25.

22 See the Appendixes A and B for an explanation of his view.

23 Sausa, *Jesus Tomb*, 26-27.

24 See the Appendix A for an account that shows how many have tried to redefine the biblical Jesus.

25 Tomb-burial inscriptions and artifacts attest to this as many scholars have indicated. See Craig A. Evans, *Jesus and the Ossuaries* (Waco, TX: Baylor University Press, 2003), 26. See Theodor Mommsen and et al., eds., *Corpus Inscriptionum Latinarum* (Berlin: G. Reimer, 1862–?), 1.2.1222. 4.2965; 6.889; A. E. Gordon, *Illustrated Introduction to Latin Epigraphy* (Berkley, CA: University of California Press, 1983), 96, 107-8; L. J. Keppie, *Understanding Roman Inscriptions* (Baltimore: John Hopkins University Press, 1991), 98; P. Shore, *Rest Lightly: An Anthology of Latin and Greek Tomb Inscriptions* (Wauconda, IL: Bolchazy-Carducci, 1997), 34. Crossan and Reed, *Excavating Jesus*, 279, specify, "Unlike the Roman tradition of cremation, which was one of the common customs alongside interring the deceased in body-sized sarcophagi, Jewish tradition strictly forbade the burning of bodies. Instead, Jewish burial practices included the long standing Semitic tradition of secondary burial, in which the body was laid in the tomb for about a year and then the bones were gathered up and redeposited."

26 I. Gafni, "Reinterment in the Land of Israel: Notes on the Origin and Development of a Custom," in *Jerusalem Cathedra: Studies in the History, Archaeology, Geography, and Ethnography of the Land of Israel*, ed. L. I. Levine, vol. 1 (Jerusalem: Yad Izhak Ben-Zvi Institute; Detroit, MI: Wayne State University Press, 1981), 96-104; L. Y. Rahmani, "Ossuaries and Ossilegium (Bone-Gathering) in the Second Temple Period," in *Ancient Jerusalem*, ed. H. Geva (Jerusalem: Israel Exploration Society, 1994), 193 94; N. A. Silberman, "Ossuary: A Box for Bones," *Biblical Archaeological Review* 17 (1991): 73-74. These are noted in Evans, *Jesus and the Ossuaries*, 26.

27 Rahmani, *Catalogue of Jewish Ossuaries*, 53.

28 Ibid., 54. In the Jerusalem Talmud Rabbi Meir attests to the necessary requirement of the decomposition of the body before the bones are collected and placed in the ossuary and the sinless state attained (*Mo'ed Katan* 80c). Rabbi Akiva seems to attest to these twelve months of decay and purification for perfection by his comment, "[T]he judgment of the wicked in Gehenna is twelve months" (Mishnah *'Eduyyot* 2:10F). See also the Babylonian Talmud which further describes this (*Rosh Hashshanah* 17a).

29 Crossan and Reed, *Excavating Jesus*, 282, 287.

30 However, Crossan and Reed note that Jewish secondary burial was practiced for "nearly a millennium" before the first century by placing the *family*

bones or *clan* "in a pit or cavity, called a charnel pile." Charnel piles were, however, used less often in the first century (ibid., 280-81). Burial differences with that of their neighbors centered on whether previous remains stayed in these charnels and whether people outside the family could be buried in the same pit, making it a "communal charnel" (Rahmani, *Catalogue of Jewish Ossuaries,* 53).

31 Ibid.

32 Ibid. Though Jews did not adopt such a belief of having to attend to the dead as did people in their neighboring countries, several Bible verses may shed light on another reason for *ossilegium* practice mentioned by Evans, *Jesus and the Ossuaries,* 28. "One of the interesting features of *ossilegium* is that it likely reflects the belief that the dead are still with the living and, perhaps, still able to be of some influence. In other words, the dead are not completely dead, but diminished and weakened.... They mutter as shades (Isa. 8:19; 29:4) and feel worms gnawing at them (Job 14:22; Isa. 66:24). Indeed, mere contact with the bones of Elisha, who was a powerful 'man of God,' restores life to a dead man (2 Kgs. 13:21). The idea that some life still lingers in the bones of the deceased may help us understand better Ezekiel's vision of the dry bones (Ezek. 37), bones that are still capable of returning to a full life." This does suggest agreement with the possible Jewish first-century interpretation of these passages. As Evans correctly points out, at the very least it may help us understand partly why they practiced ossilegium. Chapter 10 discusses the concept of Jewish and Christian resurrection.

33 See chapter 3 for evidence showing how two people are buried in one ossuary.

34 Stephen J. Pfann, *Interview by Darrell L. Bock of Stephen J. Pfann to Help Identify Inscriptions* (online: http://media.bible.org/mp3/bock/profpfann 030807.mp3, 2007, accessed April 4, 2007).

35 Rahmani, *Catalogue of Jewish Ossuaries,* 11.

36 Ibid.

37 Jodi Magness, *Has the Tomb of Jesus Been Discovered* (online: http://www.sbl-site.org/Article.aspx?ArticleId=640, 2007, accessed October 15, 2007). "A plain ossuary would not have been too expensive—an inscription prices one at a drachma and four obols, or just over a day's wages for a skilled laborer, and the style, decorations, and workmanship of the James ossuary in no way imply that extraordinary wealth was available. The more prohibitive factor was the plot of land for the burial in shafts and secondary burial in ossuaries.... But not every family in first-century Jerusalem had a parcel of land with a burial chamber, nor could many afford an ossuary. For every one of the hundreds of ossuary and kokhim burials examined by

archaeologists, we must assume thousands of bodies were deposited in shallow graves without any protection from decomposition and disintegration in the soil" (Crossan and Reed, *Excavating Jesus*, 282, 288). Therefore, although plain ossuaries were not too expensive poor families like that of Jesus of Nazareth could not afford them, and even less afford a family tomb. See Appendix B.

[38] Rahmani, *Catalogue of Jewish Ossuaries*, 22-23.

[39] See L. Y. Rahmani, *A Catalogue of Roman Byzantine Lead Coffins From Israel* (Jerusalem: Israel Antiquities Authority, 1999). Rahmani, *Catalogue of Jewish Ossuaries*, 23. His chart on page 22 points out the type of materials used.

[40] Jacobovici and Pellegrino, *Jesus Family Tomb*, 26, "As I was to learn later, scholars have no real idea how the ossuary ritual began. But we know why it stopped. It came to a fiery end when Roman troops destroyed Jerusalem in 70 C.E." See Eric M. Meyers, "Second Burials in Palestine," *Biblical Archaeology* 33 (1970): 16–18.

[41] Evans, *Jesus and the Ossuaries*, 28. See the Jerusalem Talmud *Semahot* 12–13 and *m. Sanhedrin* 6:6.

[42] Erwin Ramsdell Goodenough, *Jewish Symbols in the Greco-Roman Period*, Bollingen Series, 37, vol. 2 (New York: Pantheon Books, 1953), 63; Goodenough, *Jewish Symbols in the Greco-Roman Period*, 1:115; Meyers, "Second Burials in Palestine," 24 n. 35.

[43] Evans, *Jesus and the Ossuaries*, 29–30, notes that Josephus mentions Herod's use of limestone and employment of a number of stonecutters from that period until A.D. 64 (*Jewish Antiquities* 15.11.2 §390; 15.11.2 §399; 20.9.7 §219). In fact Evans may be right in connecting the rebellion that played a part in precipitating the later Jewish wars ending in the destruction of the temple in A.D. 70 (see also Josephus, *The Jewish Wars* 7.2.2 §26-27).

[44] Rahmani, *Catalogue of Jewish Ossuaries*, 60.

Chapter Two

[1] Simcha Jacobovici and Charles Pellegrino, *The Jesus Family Tomb: The Discovery, the Investigation, and the Evidence That Could Change History* (San Francisco: Harper SanFrancisco, 2007), 77. Italics are oringinal.

[2] See chapter 7 for discussion and a chart showing the common and limited pools of names found in the first century A.D.

[3] A similar observation appears in Don Sausa, *The Jesus Tomb: Is It Fact or Fiction? Scholars Chime In*, ed. Jeffrey Clark (Fort Myers, FL: Vision Press, 2007), 67.

4 Levy Yitzhak Rahmani documents all of the inscriptions as follows: *Mariamene e Mara* (701–80-500), *Yehuda son of Yeshua* (702–80.501), *Matya* (703–80.502), *Yeshua son of Yehosef* (704–80.503), *Yose* (705–80.504), *Marya* (706–80.505), and the remaining ones are non-inscribed ossuaries (707–80.506, 708–80.507, 709–80.508, and 710–80.509). (*A Catalogue of Jewish Ossuaries in the Collections of the State of Israel*, ed. Ayala Sussmann and Peter Schertz [Jerusalem: Israel Antiquities Authority, 1994], 222-24). The last ossuary does not appear in Rahmani's catalogue because it was not inscribed or ornamented. However, one of the original archaeologist present at the Talpiot tomb in 1980 documents it in his article (Amos Kloner, "A Tomb with Inscribed Ossuaries in East Talpiyot, Jerusalem," *Atiqout* 29 [1996]: 21).

5 Rahmani, *Catalogue of Jewish Ossuaries*, 223.

6 Kloner, "Inscribed Ossuaries in East Talpiyot, Jerusalem," 19. See also http://www.jesusfamilytomb.com/essential_facts/1980_discovery.html. Though Aramaic and Hebrew are related languages, both co-existed independently as North West Semitic dialects. Neither of them sprung from the other. I am grateful to my friend and OT scholar Eugene H. Merrill who pointed this out.

7 Jacobovici and Pellegrino, *Jesus Family Tomb*, 75. The ratio may "actually be 1 in 358.2" according to the chair of Christian Studies at Louisiana College, Charles L. Quarles (*Buried Hopes or Risen Savior: Is the Talpiot Tomb the Burial Place of Jesus of Nazareth?*[online: https://www.lacollege.edu/ifl/jesus_tomb.pdf, March 4, 2007, accessed October 18, 2007]). He notes, "These statistics conflict with those now published on the Discovery website which calculates that 1 in 190 had the name Jesus, son of Joseph. The discrepancy likely resulted from doubling the number so that women were included in the calculation and then rounding the number. This is a questionable inflation since a woman would not have a masculine name like Yeshua or be identified as the 'son of' anyone. Since there was a 1 in 2 chance that Jesus could have been feminine, the second element of the ratio was doubled. This seems to distort the results of the calculation" (ibid.).

8 Quarles notes, "Even if the inscription reads 'Jesus, son of Joseph' this would not be shocking. We know of at least 99 different individuals with the name Jesus from this general period (330 B.C. to 200 A.D.) and at least 218 different individuals with the name Joseph. In fact, Joseph was the second most common name among Palestinian Jewish males from the period, second only to Simon. Jesus was the sixth most common name from the period" (ibid.). See also Richard Bauckham, *Jesus and the Eyewitnesses: The Gospels as Eyewitness Testimony* (Grand Rapids: Wm. B. Eerdmans Publishing, 2006), 85.

[9] Rahmani, *Catalogue of Jewish Ossuaries*, 77, no 9 for photo.
[10] Eleazar Lippa Sukenik, *Jüdische Gräber Jerusalems um Christi Geburt* (Jerusalem: Azriel, 1931), 19.
[11] Craig A. Evans, *Jesus and the Ossuaries* (Waco, TX: Baylor University Press, 2003), 94.
[12] Kloner, "Inscribed Ossuaries in East Talpiyot, Jerusalem," 19.
[13] Jacobovici and Pellegrino, *Jesus Family Tomb*, 194-95.
[14] This picture appears in Craig A. Evans' website http://www.craigaevans.com/tombofjesus.htm. Courtesy of the IAA.
[15] Though initially Quarles reserved final judgment until expert epigraphers had a chance to examine whether the first word of the inscription reading "Yeshua" was correct, what he originally heard has not changed. "I have heard rumors that well-known experts in Aramaic script have disputed the original transcription. If it turns out that this ossuary belonged to a son of Joseph bearing a name other than Yeshua, the effort to connect this tomb with Jesus of Nazareth quickly collapses" (Quarles, *Buried Hopes or Risen Savior: Is the Talpiot Tomb the Burial Place of Jesus of Nazareth?* [accessed]).
[16] Kloner says, "The first name following the X mark is difficult to read. In contrast to other ossuaries of this tomb, the incisions are here superficial and cursorily carved" ("Inscribed Ossuaries in East Talpiyot, Jerusalem," 18).
[17] Rahmani, *Catalogue of Jewish Ossuaries*, 223.
[18] Stephen J. Pfann, *Interview by Darrell L. Bock of Stephen J. Pfann to Help Identify Inscriptions* (online: http://media.bible.org/mp3/bock/profpfann030807.mp3,2007, accessed April 4, 2007).
[19] Ibid. (accessed).
[20] Sausa, *Jesus Tomb*, 68 (italics his). See also the following site where Pfann believes the word *Yeshoshua* [Jesus] on the inscription may best be rendered as "Hanun or something" (Mati Milstein, *Jesus' Tomb Claim Slammed By Scholars* [online: http:// news.nationalgeographic.com/news/2007/02/070228-jesus-tomb_2.html, February 28, 2007, accessed June 20, 2007]).
[21] Sausa, *Jesus Tomb*, 69-70. This quote appears in an email sent to Sausa, and the brackets in the quotation are original.
[22] David Horowitz, *Editor's Notes: Giving 'Jesus' the Silent Treatment* (online: http://www.jpost.com/servlet/Satellite?cid=1171894551868&pagename=JPost%2FJPArticle%2FShowFull, March 3, 2007, accessed June 21, 2007). All the quotes in this paragraph appear in this article, and are also noted in Sausa, *Jesus Tomb*, 70.
[23] I do not know who began using this phrase; however, a number of scholars use it to describe the sloppily written inscription.
[24] This photo of the Caiaphas ossuary was used with permission: Courtesy of

the IAA.

25 Rachael Hachlili, *Jewish Funerary Customs Practices and Rites in the Second Temple Period*, Supplements to the Journal for the Study of Judaism, ed. John J. Collins, vol. 94 (Leiden: Brill, 2005), 304.

26 Pfann, *Identify Inscriptions* (accessed).

27 Personal email on November 3, 2007. He has also made this public in the SBL letter, see François Bovon, *The Tomb of Jesus* (online: http://www.sbl-site.org/Article.aspx? ArticleId=656, 2007, accessed November 1, 2007).

28 Rahmani, *Catalogue of Jewish Ossuaries*, 222.

29 Kloner, "Inscribed Ossuaries in East Talpiyot, Jerusalem," 17.

30 Jacobovici and Pellegrino, *Jesus Family Tomb*, 19, 76.

31 Ibid., 19, 102.

32 Hachlili, *Jewish Funerary Customs Practices*, 316.

33 Rahmani, *Catalogue of Jewish Ossuaries*, 15. See, for example, ossuaries nos. 13, 24, 821.

34 Ibid., 223.

35 Kloner, "Inscribed Ossuaries in East Talpiyot, Jerusalem," 18.

36 Tal Ilan, *Lexicon of Jewish Names in Late Antiquity: Part I: Palestine 330 BCE–200 CE*, TSAJ, ed. Martin Hengel and Peter Schäfer, vol. 91 (Tübingen: Mohr Siebeck, 2002), 55–56. This is a slightly different figure from Kloner's article since Ilan has updated the study since 1987. See Kloner, "Inscribed Ossuaries in East Talpiyot, Jerusalem," 18.

37 Ilan, *Lexicon of Jewish Names* 55–56. There is also a different count in Bauckham, *Jesus and the Eyewitnesses*, 70. He has Judah appearing as the fourth most popular name (164 times) but Joshua still as the sixth most popular name (99 times). Hachlili has yet another count ranking Judah (96 times) as the fourth most common name used and Joshua (60 times) as the sixth most common name, see Rachael Hachlili, "Hebrew Names, Personal Names, Family Names and Nicknames of Jews in the Second Temple Period," in *Families and Family Relations: As Presented in Early Judaisms and Early Christianities: Texts and Fictions*, ed. Jan Willem Van Henten and Athalya Brenner, Studies in Theology and Religion, vol. 2 (Leiderdorp: Deo Publishing, 2000), 114.

38 It is commonly accepted that around A.D. 66 the estimated population in Jerusalem was about 80,000 people. See Hershel Shanks and Ben Witherington III, *The Brother of Jesus: The Dramatic Story and Meaning of the First Archaeological Link to Jesus & His Family* (San Francisco, CA: HarperSanFrancisco, 2003), 57. And four million can be safely estimated to be the number of population in the region. See Darrell L. Bock and Daniel

B. Wallace, *Dethroning Jesus: Exposing Popular Culture's Quest to Unseat the Biblical Christ* (Nashville: Thomas Nelson, 2007), 207.

[39] See http://www.jesusfamilytomb.com/essential_facts/1980_discovery.html.

[40] Daniel B. Wallace, *The Lost Tomb of Jesus* (online: http://www.bible.org/page.php? page_id=4894, March 5, 2007, accessed June 3, 2007), (italics his). In a conversation with Wallace, he stressed how personal the naming of one's child is, and thereby the unlikelihood of such an event taking place, assuming for the sake of argument that Jesus was married and fathered children.

[41] Rahmani, *Catalogue of Jewish Ossuaries*, 223.

[42] Kloner, "Inscribed Ossuaries in East Talpiyot, Jerusalem," 20.

[43] Jacobovici and Pellegrino, *Jesus Family Tomb*, 77.

[44] Kloner, "Inscribed Ossuaries in East Talpiyot, Jerusalem," 19.

[45] Jacobovici and Pellegrino, *Jesus Family Tomb*, 78.

[46] Ibid., 75.

[47] Ibid.

[48] Rahmani, *Catalogue of Jewish Ossuaries*, 90.

[49] P. B. Bagatti and J. T. Milik, *Gli Scavi del Dominus Flevit (Monte Oliveto—Gerusalemme)*, Studium Biblicum Franciscanum: Collectio Maior No. 13 (Jerusalem: Franciscan Printing Press, 1958), 89, no 20 fig. 21, 4; Rahmani, *Catalogue of Jewish Ossuaries*, 90, 176, 202; Victor A. Tcherikover and A. Fuks, *Corpus Papyrorum Judaicarum* vol. 1 (Cambridge, MA: Harvard University Press, 1957-1964), 1:4.

[50] Luke 3:29 appears only as a variant reading in the Majority Text.

[51] Rahmani, *Catalogue of Jewish Ossuaries*, 223–24.

[52] Ilan, *Lexicon of Jewish Names* 20.

[53] Even the *JFT* advocates admit this. See http://www.jesusfamilytomb.com/essential_ facts/ 1980 _discovery.html.

[54] See chapter 7, n. 20. Based on this information Dillon Burroughs asks, "Why should it be assumed that such a common name is Mary mother of Jesus? What proof exists? The documentary claims this is the same Mary based on the *other ossuaries*, not solely on the Maria inscription. Therefore, its strength stands or falls based on analysis of the other names in the tomb." (*The Jesus Family Tomb Controversy: How the Evidence Falls Short* [Ann Arbor, MI: Nimble Books LCC, 2007], 13).

[55] For a statistical analysis of all of the names in the Talpiot tomb ossuary inscriptions see chapter 7.

[56] Rahmani, *Catalogue of Jewish Ossuaries*, 223.

[57] Kloner, "Inscribed Ossuaries in East Talpiyot, Jerusalem," 20.

[58] Jacobovici and Pellegrino, *Jesus Family Tomb*, 78; James D. Tabor, *The Jesus*

Dynasty: The Hidden History of Jesus, His Royal Family and the Birth of Christianity (New York: Simon & Schuster, 2006), 52-56.
59 See chapter 7 for a complete analysis.
60 Rahmani, *Catalogue of Jewish Ossuaries*, 224. See the photos in plate 101, numbers 707–9.
61 Kloner, "Inscribed Ossuaries in East Talpiyot, Jerusalem," 21.
62 See chapter 8 for a detail discussion of the tenth ossuary as the possible "James, son of Joseph, brother of Jesus" ossuary.

Chapter Three

1 Simcha Jacobovici and Charles Pellegrino, *The Jesus Family Tomb: The Discovery, the Investigation, and the Evidence That Could Change History* (San Francisco, CA: Harper SanFrancisco, 2007), 95-96.
2 The inscription appears in Levy Yitzhak Rahmani, *A Catalogue of Jewish Ossuaries in the Collections of the State of Israel*, ed. Ayala Sussmann and Peter Schertz (Jerusalem: Israel Antiquities Authority, 1994), 222.
3 Jacobovici and Pellegrino, *Jesus Family Tomb*, 97 (Italics theirs).
4 Ibid., 100.
5 Stephen J. Pfann said, "The name 'Mariamene' is of central importance to the story line of the documentary *The Lost Tomb of Jesus* and its companion book. Since 'Mariamene' is unique (and likewise, 'Mariamne,' is rare) among the ossuaries, this name is also highly significant when creating statistics and probabilities concerning the uniqueness of the Talpiot cave and its inscribed ossuaries" (*Mary Magdalene Is Now Missing: A Correct Reading of Rahmani Ossuary CJO 701 and CJO 108* (online: http://sbl-site.org/Article.aspx?ArticleId=653, 2007, accessed April 23, 2007). James R. White makes a similar observation. "In my opinion, if the argument fails here, the rest of the entire film and book are left without any basis or foundation." (*From Toronto To Emmaus: The Empty Tomb and the Journey from Skepticism to Faith* [Birmingham, AL: Solid Ground Christian Books, 2007], 47).
6 Jacobovici admits, "From the beginning, we focused on this particular ossuary because it seemed to be the key to the whole story. Everything depended on this unique artifact. Nonetheless, we did not learn its secrets right away. They were revealed slowly over time" (*Jesus Family Tomb*, 204).
7 A number of other books have already treated this topic thoroughly. See Darrell L. Bock, *Breaking The Da Vinci Code: Answers to Questions Everyone's Asking* (Nashville: Thomas Nelson, 2004), 61-98; idem, *The Missing Gospels: Unearthing the Truth Behind Alternative Christianities* (Nashville: Thomas Nelson, 2006); Craig A. Evans, *Fabricating Jesus: How Modern Scholars*

Distort the Gospels (Downers Grove, IL: InterVarsity Press, 2006), 52-100; Philip Jenkins, *Hidden Gospels: How the Search for Jesus Lost Its Way* (Oxford: Oxford University Press, 2001); J. Ed Komoszewski, M. James Sawyer, and Daniel B. Wallace, *Reinventing Jesus: How Contemporary Skeptics Miss the Real Jesus and Mislead Popular Culture* (Grand Rapids: Kregel Publications, 2006), 151-66; Ben Witherington III, *The Gospel Code: Novel Claims about Jesus, Mary Magdalene and Da Vinci* (Downers Grove, IL: InterVarsity Press, 2004), 21-25, 32-38, 81-109, 113-18; *idem, What Have They Done with Jesus? Beyond Strange Theories and Bad History—Why We Can Trust the Bible* (San Francisco: HarperSanFrancisco, 2006), 27-51; Darrell L. Bock and Daniel B. Wallace, *Dethroning Jesus: Exposing Popular Culture's Quest to Unseat the Biblical Christ* (Nashville: Thomas Nelson, 2007), 77–130, 193–213.

[8] Bock, *Missing Gospels*, 15. "The term *Gnosticism* is not ancient. The Protestant Henry More coined the term in 1669 as a polemical name for heresy. More used it to complain about Catholic theology.... It is likely the name came from Irenaeus's complaint in circa AD 180 about views he was writing against in his work known as *Against Heresies*" (ibid., 15-16, and also see pages 17–21).

[9] Five characteristics are present in Gnostic literature that describe their belief as pointed out by Kurt Rudolph, *Gnosis: The Nature and History of Gnosticism*, trans. Robert McLachlan Wilson (Edinburgh: T & T Clark, 1983), 57-59. These are also noted by Bock, *Missing Gospels*, 18-20. (1) *Dualism*. Dualism refers to the mixture of good and evil in man that did not necessarily come from the true God but the god of creation. Thus the god of creation in Genesis and the true God are not one and the same. The god of creation "botched the job." (2) *Cosmogony*. Creation has a dualistic nature as seen in terms of "light versus darkness." The god of Genesis sees himself as the only god known as a *Demiurge* (i.e., "maker") of the known material world, which is evil and in contrast to the good and spiritual God who is the Father. Thus dualism teaches that "matter" is evil and "spirit" is good. Points one and two go against the biblical God understood in Judeo-Christian theology. (3) *Soteriology*. Salvation does not come through faith in Jesus alone who died on the cross and rose physically from the dead (John 3:16; 5:24; 6:47; Rom. 3:21–4:25; Eph. 2:8-9). It comes by "knowledge" about Gnostic truths. The Christ of Gnosticism is too pure to suffer on the cross. Thus Jesus died on the cross, but He is different from the Christ who could not die on the cross because of His purity. Furthermore there is no bodily resurrection from the dead in Gnosticism since all forms of the flesh are evil. This contradicts John 1:1-18; Romans 3:21–5:11; 1 John 1:1-4; 5:6-8. (4) *Eschatology*. The

last days are headed toward a pure spiritual world totally separate from any form of a physical world. (5) *Cult Worship.* This group had rites beyond baptism that they practiced. (6) *Women.* Bock adds (which Rudolph does not mention) by describing how women were encouraged to "experience revelation and be leaders in the community." One must keep in mind that these same Gnostics are the one's claiming in the *Gospel of Thomas* 114 that "females" had to become "males" in order to enter the kingdom of God. See Bock, *Breaking The Da Vinci Code*, 84-85.

10 Karen King says that one cannot "support a single, monolithic definition" that describes Gnosticism as a single unison movement (*What Is Gnosticism?* [Cambridge, MA: Harvard University Press, 2003], 226). While that is true, one may, however, classify a Gnostic work by a number of similar characteristics in it. As seen in note 9, Rudolph lists five traits that one can use to classify whether a work is Gnostic or not. See Bock, *Missing Gospels*, 18-20.

11 Both of the following works of renowned figures take such a view. Bart D. Ehrman, *Lost Christianities: The Battles for Scripture and the Faiths We Never Knew* (New York: Oxford University Press, 2003); Elaine Pagels, *The Gnostic Gospels* (New York: Random House, 1979).

12 Dan Brown, *The Da Vinci Code: A Novel* (New York: Doubleday, 2003), 231 (Italic his).

13 "The new school claims that Irenaeus 'won' and was the key architect of orthodoxy. The claim is that this orthodoxy (or the claim of a defined, legitimate Christianity) emerged even more clearly in the third and fourth centuries. So the new school argues that the Christianity we know has roots that do not really go back to the time of Jesus or even to the apostles in a way that precludes other alternative views of Christianity" (Bock, *Missing Gospels*, xxiv-xxv). See chapter 10 for a fuller discussion.

14 James M. Robinson, ed., *The Nag Hammadi Library in English*, 3rd rev. ed. (Leiden: E. J. Brill, 1978; reprint, New York: HarperCollins Publishers, 1990), XIII. The collections of these lists by others do not even come close. "The collection of *The Gnostic Scriptures* by Bentley Layton has just short of forty works, three of which bear the title *gospel* and overlap with the Nag Hammadi list. In fact, most of these works were not gospels. The most generous count of extrabiblical documents appears in Harvard Professor Helmut Koester's *Introduction to the New Testament*. That count stands at sixty, excluding the twenty-seven books in the New Testament. However, a vast majority of these works were not gospels" (Bock, *Breaking The Da Vinci Code*, 62). Thus, even if one includes the *Gospel of Bartholomew* (fifth or sixth century), the *Gospel of Judas* (second century), the *Gospel of Peter* (mid-second century), the *Gospel of the Savior* (second century), and the *Gospel of Thomas*

the Contender (early to mid-third century), as listed by Bock, *Missing Gospels*, 218-19, this list does not come close to eighty gospels.

15 Bock, *Missing Gospels*, 5.

16 Hans-Josef Klauck, *The Religious Context of Early Christianity: A Guide to Greco-Roman Religions*, trans. Brian McNeil, Studies of the New Testament and Its World (Edinburgh: T & T Clark, 2000), 458. This is quoted by Bock, *Missing Gospels*, 24-25.

17 When thinking of Gnosticism as a unison group, one must keep in mind the following: "The key point is that *Gnosticism was not a singular connected movement but more a way of seeing the world that produced a myriad of viewpoints on the themes tied to its definition.* However, in this varied form it was never a clear alternative to the earliest expression of Christianity until a variety of Gnostic schools began to emerge, which each tried distinctly to organize Gnostic thinking. Yet—and this is crucial—there was never a 'Gnostic church,' only a conglomeration of disconnected schools that disagreed with each other as well as with the traditional Christians" (Bock, *Missing Gospels*, 23 [italics his]).

18 What Gnosticism did was cause church fathers to form a more orthodox creed of the early church's belief. That is, "This proliferation of alternatives caused the apologist to write detailed assessments of these movements, showing that the name *heresiologist* reflects the thrust of their work. These writings developed full arguments that formed what became the details of orthodox faith" (ibid., 11).

19 Bock, *Breaking The Da Vinci Code*, 63.

20 The bulk of Gnostic writings are dated from late second to third century A.D. See Bock, *Missing Gospels*, 7. Furthermore, "There is material in Codex VII which shows that it was produced after A.D. 348, giving us a potential starting date, and the codices were probably placed in their storage jar somewhere in the fourth or fifth century, judging by dating of its lid" (Witherington III, *What Have They Done with Jesus?* 37).

21 Bock illustrates this point. "For example, the *Gospel of Peter* is not from Peter nor does it give teaching preserved by those familiar with his teaching; it is simply a name given to lend authority to a work written much later. Almost every scholar agrees with this view of this gospel. This situation stands in contrast to Mark or Luke in that neither writer of these gospels was an apostle, yet many accept that Mark and Luke had access to the apostles and were aware of what they taught. For Mark, the contact was Peter, while Luke likely had contact with several of the apostles and traveled with Paul" (*Missing Gospels*, 7).

22 Ibid., 8. Witherington also concludes, "In fact one could make a case for

more critical scrutiny being applied to texts, the further removed in time they are from the subjects they are written about. But when you actually undertake such scholarly enterprise, you realize pretty quickly that the Gnostic documents do not reveal anything about the historical Jesus that could not be deduced from the canonical material itself, and in the places they disagree with the canonical material, they are surely not more authentic witnesses to Jesus and his movement than the NT documents" (*What Have They Done with Jesus?* 34). For a description of Gnostic belief in comparison to Judeo-Christian see note 12. All of the NT books were completed at least one hundred to fifty years even before the supposedly earliest Gnostic document, the *Gospel of Thomas*. For further discussion see Evans, *Fabricating Jesus*, 52-122.

[23] Brown, *The Da Vinci Code*, 246; Jacobovici and Pellegrino, *Jesus Family Tomb*, 99.

[24] Bock also notes this (*Breaking The Da Vinci Code*, 21).

[25] Wesley W. Isenberg, "The Gospel of Philip (II, *3*)," in *The Nag Hammadi Library in English*, 148. When words appear bracketed it means there is a lacuna in the text but that the words could be constructed with a fair amount of certainty. However, when three dots appear inside brackets, the text could not be constructed.

[26] Looking at the entire sentence in context it is not hard to make out the missing words and interpret the sentence: "Daniel grabbed his glove and bat and drove to the park to play ball with his friends."

[27] The Coptic language is a form of Egyptian that adopted the Greek alphabet in the first century. Hence it is easy to see how the Coptic language uses loan words from Greek.

[28] Walter Bauer et al., *A Greek English Lexicon of the New Testament and Other Early Christian Literature*, rev. and ed. Frederick William Danker, 3rd ed. (Chicago: University of Chicago Press, 2000), 209-10, cf. 554. The following writers note this point: Bock, *Breaking The Da Vinci Code*, 23; Witherington III, *Gospel Code*, 24; idem, *What Have They Done with Jesus?* 41. See the *Gospel of Philip* 59:9-10 where it also refers to this Mary as Jesus' "companion."

[29] Witherington III, *What Have They Done with Jesus?* 41.

[30] Karen L. King, *The Gospel of Mary Magdala: Jesus and the First Woman Apostle* (Santa Rosa, CA: Polebridge Press, 2003), 145-46, 249 n. 50. Although Mary could have been kissed on the mouth, in no way this implies sexual intimacy but a mere pop-kiss instead of the more romantic passionate kiss between lovers. For an excellent explanation behind the concept of "kissing," see Craig S. Keener, "Kissing," in *Dictionary of New Testament Background*, ed. Craig

A. Evans and Stanley E. Porter (Downers Grove, IL: InterVarsity Press, 2000), 628–29.

[31] Bock, *Breaking The Da Vinci Code*, 22-23.

[32] Therefore, even if King believes Jesus kissed Mary on the mouth (which seems unlikely), she suggests that in the *Gospel of Philip* it seems best to interpret Mary as a symbol for "Wisdom." She makes a fascinating observation that validates this interpretation. "In the *Gospel of Philip*, for example, Mary Magdalene is explicitly mentioned as one of three Mary's [see *GPhil* 59:6-11].... This formulation is intriguing for at first it distinguishes three distinct Marys: Jesus' mother, her sister (i.e., his aunt), and his companion, who is explicitly identified as the Magdalene. Yet the next sentence suggests that there is only a single Mary, one who is the mother, his sister, *and* his companion. The *Gospel of Philip* wants its readers to see that these figures are more than literal, historical characters.... Mary Magdalene, too, is the companion of the Savior because he loved her more than the rest of the disciples. If Mary is understood as Wisdom, that explains how she is at once mother, sister, and companion. She is the mother of angels, his spiritual sister (since the son does not have children but siblings), and his female counter part." See King, *Gospel of Mary Magdala*, 144-46. Perhaps this is why the phenomenon of merging Mary Magdalene with Mary of Bethany occurs since the symbolic meaning of the text and not the historical figure is what the Gnostics intended to convey. Mary, the sister of Martha (Luke 10:38-42; John 11:1–12:8), gets "merged in the *Acts of Philip*," See François Bovon, "Mary Magdalene in the Acts of Philip." In *Which Mary? The Marys of Early Christian Tradition*, ed. Christopher R. Matthews and F. Stanley Jones, Society of Biblical Literature Symposium Series: no 19 (Atlanta, GA: Society of Biblical Literature, 2002), 79, 82 n. 20, 33. It also seems to occur in the *Gospel of Philip* (François Bovon, *New Testament Traditions and Apocryphal Narratives*, trans. Jane Haaoiseva-Hunter, Princeton Theological Monograph Series; vol 36, ed. Dikran Y. Hadidian [Allison Park, PA: Pickwick Publications, 1995], 153).

[33] Witherington III, *Gospel Code*, 24.

[34] Witherington III, *What Have They Done with Jesus?* 41.

[35] Evans, *Fabricating Jesus*, 94 (italic his).

[36] *The Gospel of Philip* 81:34–82:19 says, "No [one can] know when [the husband] and the wife have intercourse with one another except the two of them. Indeed marriage in the world is a mystery for those who have taken a wife. If there is a hidden quality to the marriage of defilement, how much more is the undefiled marriage a true mystery! It is not fleshly but pure. It belongs not to desire but to the will. It belongs not to the darkness or the

night but to the day and the light. If a marriage is open to the public, it has become prostitution, and the bride plays the harlot not only when she is impregnated by another man but even if she slips out of her bedroom and is seen. Let her show herself only to her father and her mother and to the friend of the bridegroom and the sons of the bridegroom. These are permitted to enter every day into the bridal chamber."

[37] Isenberg, "Gospel of Philip," 140.

[38] Witherington III, *What Have They Done with Jesus?* 42. See also Witherington III, *Gospel Code*, 24, 28-37.

[39] Bock, *Breaking The Da Vinci Code*, 24.

[40] This is something I have heard from scholars on several television specials. See also Bock and Wallace, *Dethroning Jesus*, 204, and chapter 4.

[41] On *The Today Show*, February 26, 2007, James Cameron said, "To be fair to them, there was a critical piece of information they didn't have available. They said, 'Oh, well there's a second Mary here. You know, Mariamne is a diminutive of Mariam, which is Mary. But they didn't have the information from the Acts of Philip which *definitely* identifies Mary Magdalene as Mariamne. If they'd had that information, they might have looked at the whole name cluster differently in 1980. Simcha found that information" (quoted in White, *Empty Tomb*, 44-45).

[42] Jacobovici and Pellegrino, *Jesus Family Tomb*, 96, 204.

[43] Acts 1–9 can be accessed in http://www.gnosis.org/library/actphil.htm. Acts 15 and the Martyrdom existed separately "in many recessions," which can now be accessed in http://www.ccel.org/ccel/schaff/anf08.vii.xxviii.i.html.

[44] Ken Gewertz, *Women Priests, Vegetarianism—An Early Christian Manuscript Holds Some Surprises* (online: http://www.news.harvard.edu/gazette/2000/02.03/apocrypha. html, February 3, 2000, accessed November 1, 2007).

[45] Here is how Peter H. Desmond succinctly describes these other practices: "Among the revelations turned up in this unexpurgated *Acts of Philip*, especially in the story of a visit to Hell, are glimpses of a heretical community whose members may have written or transmitted the text. Devoted to ascetic practices, the group flourished in Asia Minor during the fourth century A.D. Members were to eat no meat, drink no wine, shun wealth, and abstain from sexual intercourse. Both sexes wore men's clothing made only from plant fibers. Even the sacrament of the Eucharist was modified, with water replacing wine. Sect members believed that this level of purity not only guaranteed salvation after death, but allowed them to 'talk with God' in this life. Within the community, women as well as men served at all levels. One list mentions 'presbytides' (female elders, or priestesses) alongside 'presbyters' (male elders, or priests). Deaconesses are paired with deacons, as are virgins

with eunuchs. (It is unknown whether the latter rank required surgery or merely celibacy.)" (*Fourth-Century Church Tales: Women Priests, Vegetarians, and Summer Dresses* [online: http://www.harvardmagazine.com/on-line/0500113.html, May-June 2000, accessed November 1, 2007]). See also Bovon, "Mary Magdalene in the Acts of Philip," 80-89.

[46] See Jacobovici and Pellegrino, *Jesus Family Tomb*, 96.

[47] Ibid., 205.

[48] Ibid.

[49] Origen's *Contra Celsum* 5.62.14-17 reads: Κέλσος μὲν οὖν οἶδε καὶ Μαρκελλιανοὺς ἀπὸ Μαρκελλιανοὺς καὶ Ἁρποκρατιανοὺς ἀπὸ Σαλώμης καὶ ἄλλους ἀπὸ Μαριάμμης καὶ ἄλλους ἀπὸ Μάρθας· ἡμεῖς δὲ οἱ διὰ τὴν κατὰ τὸ δυνατὸν ἡμῖν φιλομάθειαν οὐ μόνα τὰ ἐν τῷ λόγῳ καὶ τὰς διαφορὰς τῶν ἐν αὐτῷ ἐξετάσαντες, ἀλλ' ὅση δύναμις καὶ τὰ τῶν φιλοσοφασάντων φιλαλήθως ἐρευνήσαντες οὐδέ ποτε τούτοις ὡμιλήσαμεν.

[50] Unfortunately the Greek word was translated *Mariamne* by Alexander Roberts and James Donaldson, eds., *The Ante-Nicene Christian Library: Translations of the Writings of the Fathers Down to A.D. 325*, vol. 4 (New York: Christian Literature, 1885), 570. Similarly White also notes this (*Empty Tomb*, 60).

[51] I say allegedly because this too has been challenged. Antti Marjanen said, "While many features of the earlier consensus were shaken [in regards to understanding how Mary Magdalene, women and certain common Gnostics teachings] in the course of the 1990's one thing remained untouched. Mary of the so-called Gnostic texts was still identified as the Magdalene. But even this could not go unchallenged when the new century commenced. In his paper at the 2000 Society of Biblical Literature Meeting, Stephen Shoemaker presented a thesis that Mary of the so called second- and third-century Gnostic texts—with the exception of some texts in the *Gospel of Philip and Pistis Sophia*—was not Magdalene but the mother of Jesus." Though Marjanen argues against this view, he admits, "Nevertheless, Shoemaker is right when he insists that there are second- and third-century Greek texts in which *mariam* or *mariammē* is used for the mother of Jesus. In addition, Shoemaker correctly emphasizes that even the Sahidic translation of the NT can employ a form of the name *mariham* when speaking about the mother of Jesus (Matt 13:55)" ("The Mother of Jesus or the Magdalene? The Identity of Mary in the So-Called Gnostic Christian Texts," in *Which Mary? The Marys of Early Christian Tradition*, ed. Christopher R. Matthews and F. Stanley Jones, Society of Biblical Literature Symposium Series, no. 19 [Atlanta, GA: Society of Biblical Literature, 2002], 32-33).

⁵² Bovon, "Mary Magdalene in the Acts of Philip," 80. "The figure of Μαριάμνη (spelled sometimes Μαριάμμη in one or two manuscripts ...." (see also ibid., 80 n. 21). Specifically the texts mentioned by Bovon are *The Acts of Philip* 6:13, *The Acts of Philip Martyrdom* 35:6, and other fragments.
⁵³ Having said this, however, some may argue, as Bovon probably would, that Mary Magdalene and Mary of Bethany, Martha's sister, are merged in Gnostic literature.
⁵⁴ While Bovon sees the merging of these two Mary's in *The Acts of Philip* as one and the same, his intent of studying these texts are not to prove or disprove whether this is the NT Mary Magdalene. Hence he says, "To be clear, I am not interested here in the reconstruction of the historical figure of Mary Magdalene, but in her portrayal in the literary texts, particularly in the *Acts of Philip*" ("Mary Magdalene in the Acts of Philip," 79-80, 82 n. 20, 33). White makes the same observation. "The Gnostic Magdalene is an argument, a theology, not a human being who lived and witnessed the resurrection of Christ" (*Empty Tomb*, 62, see also 62 n. 32).
⁵⁵ White makes similar observations in this paragraph and adds, "In any case, Origen is thin ground upon which to make such connection, as a brief reading of the text would prove. Might this be why Jacobovici and Tabor do not bother to give us the citation? One truly wonders" (ibid., 60).
⁵⁶ James D. Tabor, *The Jesus Dynasty: The Hidden History of Jesus, His Royal Family and the Birth of Christianity* (New York: Simon & Schuster, 2006), 4. However, Tabor now believes Jesus was married. See Appendix B.
⁵⁷ White, *Empty Tomb*, 60-61.
⁵⁸ Marjanen, "The Mother of Jesus or the Magdalene?" 40 (quoted in White, *Empty Tomb*, 61).
⁵⁹ G. R. S. Mead, *Pistis Sophia: A Gnostic Miscellany: Being for the Most Part Extracts from the Books of the Saviour, to Which Are Added Excerpts from a Cognate Literature: Englished* (London: J. M. Watkins, 1921), 20.
⁶⁰ See *Pistis Sophia* 116:21-126:11-16, and the arguments made by Marjanen, "Mother of Jesus or the Magdalene?" 33, 36-37. Also see Ann Graham Brock, "Setting the Record Straight—The Politics of Identification: Mary Magdalene and Mary the Mother in *Pistis Sophia*," in *Which Mary? The Marys of Early Christian Tradition*, 43-52.
⁶¹ King, *Gospel of Mary Magdala*, 144. "In the third-century text *Pistis Sophia*, Mary again appears to be preeminent among the disciples, especially in the first three of the four books. She asks more questions than all the rest of the disciples together, and the Savior acknowledges that: 'You are she whose heart is more directed to the Kingdom of Heaven than all your brothers' [see *PiSo* 26:17–20; 199:20–200:3; 232:26–233:2; 328:18–19; 339:8–9]. Indeed,

Mary steps in when the other disciples are in despair and intercedes with the Savior for them [*PiSo* 218:10–219:2]. Her complete spiritual comprehension is repeatedly stressed" (ibid.).

62 Bock, *Breaking The Da Vinci Code*, 147.

63 George W. MacRae, R. McL. Wilson, and Karen L. King, "The Gospel of Mary (BG 8502, *1*): BG 7, 1-19, 5," in *The Nag Hammadi Library in English*, 524.

64 See note 32 and King, *Gospel of Mary Magdala*, 144-46.

65 Similarly White concludes, "The Mary Magdalene of Gnosticism a hundred and fifty years later has precious little to do with Mary Magdalene of Scripture who happens to be the Mary Magdalene of history. The Gnostic Magdalene is a fictional character without roots in Judaism, without a real existence in Judea. The Gnostic Magdalene is an argument, a theology, not a human being who lived and witnesses the resurrection of Christ" (*Empty Tomb*, 62). Stephen J. Pfann also notes how the sources used by the *JFT* book and the *LTJ* documentary to identify the Talpiot Mariamne as Mary Magdalene are two, three, and four centuries too late" (*Interview by Darrell L. Bock of Stephen J. Pfann to Help Identify Inscriptions* [online: http://media.bible.org/mp3/bock/profpfann0308 07.mp3, 2007, accessed April 4, 2007]).

66 Jacobovici and Pellegrino, *Jesus Family Tomb*, 97, 100 (italics his).

67 Ibid., 100, see also p. 18 (italics his).

68 François Bovon, *The Tomb of Jesus* (online:http://www.sbl-site.org/Article.aspx?ArticleId=656, 2007, accessed November 1, 2007).

69 This is documented in a personal email between Bovon and me on November 3, 2007, and is used with his permission.

70 This is exactly what the reader is led to perceive upon reading pages 100-102.

71 Regarding this debate Marjanen says: "In light of this, it has to be admitted that, generally speaking, the use of the name *mariham* (*mē*) is not a conclusive argument for maintaining that in instances where this particular form of the name is used it must refer to Mary Magdalene. On the other hand, one cannot close one's eyes to the fact that at least in the so-called second- and third-century Gnostic texts it is much more common to style the mother of Jesus *maria* than *mariham* (*mē*), whereas the latter form of the name is used relatively often for Mary Magdalene" ("Mother of Jesus or Magdalene?" 33-34). The entire book of essays document numerous positions on this issue, which validates how highly debatable this issue is.

72 Bock and Wallace, *Dethroning Jesus*, 204.

73 Montague Rhodes James, *The Apocryphal New Testament: Being the*

ENDNOTES

Apocryphal Gospels, Acts, Epistles, and Apocalypses (Oxford: Clarendon Press, 1924), 446 (bold words added for emphasis). See the online article http://www.gnosis.org/library/act phil.htm.

74 Pfann similarly adds, "Furthermore, the Mary of the Acts of Philip clearly refers to the Mary related to Martha the relatives Lazarus in the Gospel of John, not Mary Magdalene. This is merely a stretching of the story to make this work" (*Identify Inscriptions* [accessed]).

75 See note 32 and 53.

76 Brown, *The Da Vinci Code*, 245-48; Jacobovici and Pellegrino, *Jesus Family Tomb*, 99.

77 MacRae, Wilson, and King, "Gospel of Mary," 525-27 (italics theirs).

78 Ibid., 524.

79 Bock, *Breaking The Da Vinci Code*, 147.

80 Ibid. See also King's similar conclusion in note 32.

81 Evans, *Fabricating Jesus*, 94.

82 Rahmani, *Catalogue of Jewish Ossuaries*, 222-23.

83 All of the pictures of the ossuary inscription 701–80.500 and others in this chapter are used by permission from Pfann, *Mary Magdalene Is Now Missing* (accessed), Kloner's article, or the IAA.

84 Tal Ilan, *Lexicon of Jewish Names in Late Antiquity: Part I: Palestine 330 BCE–200 CE*, TSAJ, ed. Martin Hengel and Peter Schäfer, vol. 91 (Tübingen: Mohr Siebeck, 2002), 392. The *JFT* advocates do not give this reference, but I included it here for those wanting to do further research.

85 Jacobovici and Pellegrino, *Jesus Family Tomb*, 76.

86 Ibid.

87 Rahmani, *Catalogue of Jewish Ossuaries*, 16.

88 Ibid.

89 Ibid., 222-23. For a complete bibliography list and citations of who and where the different forms of the Hebrew name *Miriam* appear and how it is used see Bovon, "Mary Magdalene in the Acts of Philip," 75-89, specifically note 2-7, 20, 32.

90 Amos Kloner, "A Tomb with Inscribed Ossuaries in East Talpiyot, Jerusalem," *Atiquot* 29 (1996): 17.

91 Rahmani, *Catalogue of Jewish Ossuaries*, 15, 222. "Contracted names…occur frequently. In some cases, both the *plene* and the contracted forms of the name appear on the same ossuary, e.g., 'Yeshu'a' and 'Yeshu' (No. 9), 'Mathathya' and 'Mathya' (No. 42) and 'Martha' and 'Mara' (No. 468 [and No. 701]). This clearly indicates that contractions were forms of endearment used by relations and friends which sometimes became the only name by which a person was known" (ibid., 15).

92 Ibid., 14. Similar use of *os kai* ("who is also called") appears to be how Maurice Robinson (of Southeastern Baptist Theological Seminary) renders the form *e kai* as "also known as," which would mean, "Mary, who is also known as Martha," as noted by White, *Empty Tomb*, 48. See how the same construction *os kai* is used in Luke 6:14.

93 Rahmani, *Catalogue of Jewish Ossuaries*, 14, see ossuary nos. 31, 95, 477, 868 on pp. 82-83, 101, 183-84, 258-59.

94 Ibid., 14. See also another example in Rachael Hachlili, *Jewish Funerary Customs Practices and Rites in the Second Temple Period*, Supplements to the Journal for the Study of Judaism ed. John J. Collins, vol. 94 (Leiden: E. J. Brill, 2005), 319.

95 Maurice Robinson takes a similar interpretation of this inscription. "Robinson believes it is better to recognize a common form for 'also known as' between the normative form Mariam (found often in the New Testament) and the name Mara. Likewise, there are NT grounds for reading η και in this fashion. This reading then would be, 'Mary, who is also known as Martha'" (White, *Empty Tomb*, 48).

96 He emailed this to me on November 3, 2007.

97 He admits this on a personal email sent on January 4, 2008. Used by permission of François Bovon.

98 Pfann, *Mary Magdalene Is Now Missing* (accessed). All of the color inscriptions in this section were graciously provided and are used by permission from Professor Pfann.

99 Ibid.(accessed).

100 Ibid.(accessed).

101 Ibid.(accessed).

102 Ibid.(accessed). Pfann mentioned the same thing in his interview with Bock (*Identify Inscriptions* [accessed)]). See also note 80.

103 Pfann, *Mary Magdalene Is Now Missing* (accessed). He says, "Due to the fact that (1) an ossuary would often contain more than one individual's bones and (2) these two names are among the most common personal names of the first century, the combination of these two names together on an ossuary is not unique." This was also the case in another tomb according to Hachlili. "Usually, each ossuary contained the bones of one individual, but in one tomb there were several instances of more than one individual in an ossuary" (*Jewish Funerary Customs Practices*, 462, also see 481).

104 Noted by Pfann, *Mary Magdalene Is Now Missing* (accessed). See P. B. Bagatti and J. T. Milik, *Gli Scavi del Dominus Flevit (Monte Oliveto—Gerusalemme)*, Studium Biblicum Franciscanum: Collectio Maior No. 13 (Jerusalem: Franciscan Printing Press, 1958), 75, 77-79, see Ossuary 7.

ENDNOTES

[105] Kloner, "Inscribed Ossuaries in East Talpiyot, Jerusalem," 22 n. 2. See also Amos Kloner, *Interview by Darrell L. Bock to Amos Kloner to Help Identify Talpiot Discovery Issues* (online: http://media.bible.org/mp3/bock/profkloner 030807.mp3, 2007, accessed April 4, 2007).

[106] Bagatti and Milik, *Gli Scavi del Dominus Flevit*, 91, 97-98, see Ossuary 37; Pfann, *Mary Magdalene Is Now Missing* (accessed).

[107] This is also what Pfann believes. See Pfann, *Identify Inscriptions* (accessed).

[108] Checking a concordance or doing a computer search in any Bible program shows that this is the case. Daniel B. Wallace also notes this as well. (*The Lost Tomb of Jesus* [online: http://www.bible.org/page.php?page_id=4894, March 5, 2007, accessed June 3, 2007]).

[109] The Hebrew name is מִרְיָם (Exod. 15:20–21; Num. 12:1, 4–5, 10, 15; 20:1; 26:59; Deut. 24:9; 1 Chr. 4:17; 6:3; Mic. 6:4), but may also be spelled "Mariam," as a transliteration of the Greek name Μαριάμ (e.g., Luke 1:30).

[110] Ilan, *Lexicon of Jewish Names*, 57.

[111] Bock makes a similar observation of the lists of Mary's and further says, "Often a male is the distinguishing feature.... Such a connection reflected the patriarchal first-century culture; that is, it was culturally centered on the male. This frequent naming of females with a male connection will be a significant point when we consider whether Jesus was married" (*Breaking The Da Vinci Code*, 15).

[112] A similar structure appears in Ibid., 16-19.

[113] Ibid., 17.

[114] Though scholars are divided on whether Mark 16:9–20 was originally part of the Gospel, that issue does not play any significant part here.

[115] Bock, *Breaking The Da Vinci Code*, 18.

[116] Bock concludes, "In other materials from the Fathers, there is nothing particularly outstanding about Mary. Such texts describe her in terms that parallel what the biblical Gospel tell us" (ibid., 21).

[117] Ibid., 20–21. Mark Goodacre also notes, "We do not know who Mariamne is in the Naassenes discussed by Hippolytus," (*Mariamne and the "Jesus Family Tomb"* [online: http://ntgateway.com/weblog/labels/Naassenes.html, February 28, 2007, accessed September 6, 2007]). Wallace says, "The name Mariamne, in fact, never occurs in the NT. The earliest possible identification found that might use this name for Mary Magdalene is Hippolytus, *Haereses* 5.7, though there is not enough information in the context to make a positive identification with Mary Magdalene" (*Lost Tomb of Jesus* [accessed]).

[118] Bock, *Breaking The Da Vinci Code*, 29.

[119] Darrell L. Bock, *Luke 1:1—9:50*, Baker Exegetical Commentary New Testament, ed. Moisés Silva (Grand Rapids: Baker Books, 1994), 695.

120 Witherington III, *What Have They Done with Jesus?* 48.

Chapter Four

1 Simcha Jacobovici and Charles Pellegrino, *The Jesus Family Tomb: The Discovery, the Investigation, and the Evidence That Could Change History* (San Francisco, CA: HarperSanFrancisco, 2007), 105.
2 Some of these works include Darrell L. Bock, *Breaking The Da Vinci Code: Answers to Questions Everyone's Asking* (Nashville: Thomas Nelson, 2004); James L. Garlow and Peter Jones, *Cracking Da Vinci's Code* (Colorado Springs, CO: Victor, 2004); J. Ed Komoszewski, M. James Sawyer, and Daniel B. Wallace, *Reinventing Jesus: How Contemporary Skeptics Miss the Real Jesus and Mislead Popular Culture* (Grand Rapids: Kregel Publications, 2006); Edwin W. Lutzer, *The Da Vinci Deception* (Wheaton, IL: Tyndale Publishing House, 2004); Lee Strobel and Gary Poole, *Discussing the Da Vinci Code: Examining the Issues Raised by the Book & Movie* (Grand Rapids: Zondervan Publishing House, 2006); Ben Witherington III, *The Gospel Code: Novel Claims about Jesus, Mary Magdalene and Da Vinci* (Downers Grove, IL: InterVarsity Press, 2004). See particularly the detailed arguments by Bock, *Breaking The Da Vinci Code*, 31–45.
3 Of course, before reaching the age of thirty, when Jesus began His public ministry, He was living as a normal and ordinary member of a family and worked as a carpenter. This, however, does not disprove my point because that was a necessary part of His mission to prepare Him in His humanity, since He also grew and learned (Luke 2:52).
4 Unless otherwise noted, all Scripture references are from the NKJV. Gary R. Habermas admits that arguing from silence is not the best argument but passages like Matthew 19:12 implicitly seem to indicate Jesus' singleness: "Arguments from silence are notoriously weak, so we cannot place too much emphasis on this point, but is worth mentioning Jesus' teaching about being single for the kingdom of heaven (Matt. 19:12) is also a pointer" (*The Secret of the Talpiot Tomb: Unravelling the Mystery of the Jesus Family Tomb* [Nashville, TN: Broadman & Holman Publishing, 2007], 31).
5 Ibid.
6 Bock, *Breaking The Da Vinci Code*, 33. John Dominic Crossan notes how ridiculous it is to believe that Jesus was married. He says comically, "There is an ancient and venerable principle of biblical exegesis which states that if it looks like a duck, walks like a duck, and quacks like a duck, it must be a camel in disguise. So let's apply that to whether or not Jesus was married. There is no evidence that Jesus was married (looks like a duck), multiple indications that

he was not (walks like a duck), and no early texts suggesting wife or children (quacks like a duck)...so he must be an incognito bridegroom (camel in disguise)." For the rest of the article see John Dominic Crossan, *Why Jesus Didn't Marry* (online: http://www.beliefnet.com/story/135/story_13529_1.html, 2003, accessed September 9, 2007).

[7] Jacobovici and Pellegrino, *Jesus Family Tomb*, 107–8 (italics theirs).

[8] Ibid., 108.

[9] The term appears in the Masoretic Text only three times (Gen. 25:24; 38:27; Song 4:5), but never as a proper name.

[10] Walter Bauer et al., *A Greek English Lexicon of the New Testament and Other Early Christian Literature*, rev. and ed. Frederick William Danker 3rd ed. (Chicago: University of Chicago Press, 2000), 463.

[11] Helmut Koester, "The Gospel of Thomas (II, 2)," in *The Nag Hammadi Library in English*, ed. Douglas M. Parrott, trans. Thomas O. Lamdin (Leiden: E. J. Brill, 1978; reprint, New York, NY: HarperCollins Publishers, 1990), 124.

[12] Eusebius, *Historical Ecclesiastical* 3.1.1. See Craig L. Blomberg, "Gospel of Thomas," in *The International Standard Bible Encyclopedia*, ed. Geoffrey W. Bromiley, vol. 4 (Grand Rapids: Wm. B. Eerdmans Publishing, 1988), 842.

[13] See scholars comments on the Gospel of Thomas saying 11 at http://www.earlychristianwritings.com/thomas/gospelthomas11.html.

[14] Robert M. Grant and David Noel Freedman, *The Secret Sayings of Jesus*, trans. William R. Schoedel, 1st ed. (Garden City, NY: Doubleday, 1960), 130.

[15] Amos Kloner, *Interview by Darrell L. Bock to Amos Kloner to Help Identify Talpiot Discovery Issues* (online: http://media.bible.org/mp3/bock/profkloner 030807.mp3, 2007, accessed April 4, 2007).

[16] Jacobovici and Pellegrino, *Jesus Family Tomb*, 107.

[17] Ibid., 105-7.

[18] Ibid., 106.

[19] Gaius Gracchus, *Gaius Gracchus (159-121 B.C.)* (online: http://www.roman-empire.net/republic/gai-gracchus-index.html, accessed June 18, 2007).

[20] Domitian, *Titus Flavius Domitianius Augustus (A.D. 51–96)* (online: http://www.roman-empire.net/emperors/emp-index.html, 2007, accessed June 18, 2007).

[21] Flavius Claudius Julianus, *Julian the Apostate (A.D. 331–363)* (online: http://www.answers.com/topic/julian, accessed June 19, 2007).

[22] Bold was added for emphasis to show that Pilate clearly thought Jesus was not a threat to Rome, and hence he wanted to release Him.

23 François Bovon, *The Tomb of Jesus* (online: http://www.sbl-site.org/Article.aspx? ArticleId=656, 2007, accessed November 1, 2007).
24 Jacobovici and Pellegrino, *Jesus Family Tomb*, 205.
25 James D. Tabor, *The Jesus Dynasty: The Hidden History of Jesus, His Royal Family and the Birth of Christianity* (New York: Simon & Schuster, 2006), 4. See Appendix B.
26 Jacobovici and Pellegrino, *Jesus Family Tomb*, 208-9.
27 See chapter 3 where I discuss the phenomenon in Gnostic literature of merging Mary, the mother of Jesus, and Mary of Bethany with Mary Magdalene.
28 J. Carl Laney, *John*, Moody Gospel Commentary, ed. Paul Enns (Chicago, IL: Moody Press, 1992), 348.
29 Ibid.
30 Andrew T. Lincoln, *The Gospel According to Saint John*, Black's New Testament Commentaries, ed. Morna D. Hooker (Peabody, MA: Hendrickson Publishers, 2005), 476–77. Noting how metaphorical language appears as a normal convention of communication of those days, Lincoln observes, "A partial parallel is provided by 1 Macc. 2.65, where, as Mattathias is on the point of death, he makes provision for his children by announcing, 'Look, your brother Simeon who, I know, is wise in counsel; always listen to him; he shall be your father.' He passes over his first-born son and makes Simeon, the second son, his successor as a metaphorical father, who in the role of wise teacher is to secure his descendants allegiance to the covenant. While Simeon succeeds Mattathias as father, the Beloved Disciple succeeds Jesus as son, yet is to have a similar role as successor by instructing Jesus' future followers about authentic allegiance to Jesus."
31 Donald Guthrie, *New Testament Introduction* (Downers Grove, IL: InterVarsity Press, 1990), 246. He notes that "patristic writers without question accepted the designation 'the beloved disciple' as a reference to the apostle John."
32 Gary M. Burge gives a brief history of those who reject Johannine authorship (*Interpreting the Gospel of John* [Grand Rapids: Baker Book House, 1992], 15–40). Though a number of views exist that attempt to identify the author of this Gospel, Laney is correct in his assessment, "There are two major views regarding the authorship of the fourth gospel. Most evangelicals believe that the book was written by John the apostle. A slight modification of this view is that John the apostle was the witness of events recorded but some other person actually wrote the gospel. Others have held that the author was certain 'John the elder' mentioned by Papias. The most prominent view among nonevangelicals today is that the author of John is unknown" (*John*, 13).
33 *Against Heresies*, 2.22.5; 5.3.3-4. See Eusebius, *Historical Ecclesiastical* 3.23.3.

34 Some scholars suggest that Papias's (bishop of Hierapolis, A.D. 70–155) mention of "John the elder" was the author of the Gospel who was "later confused with the apostle." Laney gave four excellent reasons why referring to John the apostle by the title "elder" would not be wrong or strange. Then he concludes, "A careful reading of Papias reveals that he used 'elder' in an apostolic sense and that both references to John are to the same individual. John is seen in two situations: first associated with the other apostles and presumably laboring in Palestine, and then accessible to Papias at a time when the other apostles had passed from the scene. It may well be that this shadowy figure 'John the Elder' may 'never have existed at all'" (*John*, 14-15).

35 Ibid., 3.24.1, 17.

36 Burge notes, "In 1924 Abraham, a rabbinic scholar at Cambridge and orthodox Jew, addressed stunning news to the university's theological society: 'To us Jews, the Fourth Gospel is the most Jewish of the four!'" (*Interpreting the Gospel of John*, 20).

37 Ibid., 40.

38 Ibid., 41.

Chapter Five

1 Simcha Jacobovici and Charles Pellegrino, *The Jesus Family Tomb: The Discovery, the Investigation, and the Evidence That Could Change History* (San Francisco, CA: HarperSanFrancisco, 2007), 100.

2 Ibid., 100–1.

3 The different languages attributed to these inscriptions were also noted by Jacobovici (ibid., 16–18, 100). See also their website http://www.jesusfamily tomb.com/essential_ facts/1980 _discovery.html.

4 Ibid., 100–1.

5 Rachael Hachlili, "Hebrew Names, Personal Names, Family Names and Nicknames of Jews in the Second Temple Period," in *Families and Family Relations: As Presented in Early Judaisms and Early Christianities: Texts and Fictions*, ed. Jan Willem Van Henten and Athalya Brenner, Studies in Theology and Religion, vol. 2 (Leiden: Deo Publishing, 2000), 83, see also pp. 84-99.

6 Rachael Hachlili, *Jewish Funerary Customs Practices and Rites in the Second Temple Period*, Supplements to the Journal for the Study of Judaism ed. John J. Collins, vol. 94 (Leiden: E. J. Brill, 2005), 463.

7 Levy Yitzhak Rahmani, *A Catalogue of Jewish Ossuaries in the Collections of the State of Israel*, ed. Ayala Sussmann and Peter Schertz (Jerusalem: Israel Antiquities Authority, 1994), 16. The ossuary is no. 560. See also no. 559.

⁸ Ibid., 13. See also pages 12–14.
⁹ See for example Ibid., 13.
¹⁰ Ben Witherington III, *Problems Multiply for Jesus Tomb Theory* (online: http://benwitherington.blogspot.com/2007_02_01_archive.html, February 28, 2007, accessed September 9, 2007).
¹¹ *Archeological Identity Theft: The Lost Tomb of Jesus Fails to Make the Grade*, (online: http://www.extremetheology.com/2007/02/index.html, February 26, 2007, accessed September 9, 2007).
¹² I am indebted to the following writer for some of the contents found in this section. Dillon Burroughs, *The Jesus Family Tomb Controversy: How the Evidence Falls Short* (Ann Arbor, MI: Nimble Books LCC, 2007), 22–25.
¹³ Ibid., 24.
¹⁴ See chapter one.
¹⁵ Burroughs notes, "If space was an issue (which could have been the case with as many as 900 tombs within a two-mile radius in Talpiot), then it may have functioned like modern cemeteries, where space is given to those with money to afford it" (*The Jesus Family Tomb Controversy*, 23).
¹⁶ Witherington III, *Problems Multiply for Jesus Tomb Theory* (accessed).
¹⁷ Ibid. (accessed). Italics are original.
¹⁸ Amos Kloner, "A Tomb with Inscribed Ossuaries in East Talpiyot, Jerusalem," *Atiquot* 29 (1996): 21–22.
¹⁹ Richard Bauckham, *Jesus and the Eyewitnesses: The Gospels as Eyewitness Testimony* (Grand Rapids: Wm. B. Eerdmans Publishing, 2006), 83.
²⁰ Burroughs, *The Jesus Family Tomb Controversy*, 25.

Chapter Six

¹ Simcha Jacobovici and Charles Pellegrino, *The Jesus Family Tomb: The Discovery, the Investigation, and the Evidence That Could Change History* (San Francisco, CA: HarperSanFrancisco, 2007), 167-68.
² Stephen J. Pfann, *Interview by Darrell L. Bock of Stephen J. Pfann to Help Identify Inscriptions* (online: http://media.bible.org/mp3/bock/profpfann030807.mp3, 2007, accessed April 4, 2007).
³ The idea of the syllogism comes from Gary R. Habermas, *The Secret of the Talpiot Tomb: Unravelling the Mystery of the Jesus Family Tomb* (Nashville: Broadman & Holman Publishing, 2007), 12.
⁴ Pfann notes the same thing in his interview with Bock, (*Identify Inscriptions* [accessed]). Advocates who believe that at least 35 people were buried in the Talpiot Tomb are listed in Amos Kloner, "A Tomb with Inscribed Ossuaries in East Talpiyot, Jerusalem," *Atiquot* 29 (1996): 22; Amos Kloner, *Interview by Darrell L. Bock to Amos*

Kloner to Help Identify Talpiot Discovery Issues (online: http://media.bible.org/ mp3/bock/profkloner030807.mp3, 2007, accessed April 4, 2007); Pfann, *Identify Inscriptions* (accessed).

[5] Joe Zias, *Deconstructing the Second and Hopefully Last Coming of Simcha and the BAR Crowd* (online: http://www.joezias.com/tomb.html, March 7, 2007, accessed September 10, 2007).

[6] Habermas, *The Secret of the Talpiot Tomb*, 36–37.

[7] Rachael Hachlili, *Jewish Funerary Customs Practices and Rites in the Second Temple Period*, Suplements to the Journal for the Study of Judaism, ed. John J. Collins, vol. 94 (Leiden: E. J. Brill, 2005), 232.

[8] Ben Witherington III, *The Jesus Tomb? 'Titanic' Talpiot Tomb Theory Sunk From the Start* (online: http://benwitherington.blogspot.com/2007/02/jesus-tomb-titanic-talpiot-tomb-theory.html, February 26, 2007, accessed September 7, 2007).

[9] James D. Tabor, *The Jesus Dynasty: The Hidden History of Jesus, His Royal Family and the Birth of Christianity* (New York: Simon & Schuster, 2006), 26–27. See also Habermas, *The Secret of the Talpiot Tomb*, 37.

[10] Usually husbands and wives are buried together and their names may be inscribed on the ossuary. See Rachael Hachlili, "Hebrew Names, Personal Names, Family Names and Nicknames of Jews in the Second Temple Period," in *Families and Family Relations: As Presented in Early Judaisms and Early Christianities: Texts and Fictions*, ed. Jan Willem Van Henten and Athalya Brenner, Studies in Theology and Religion, vol. 2 (Leiden: Deo Publishing, 2000), 87; Hachlili, *Jewish Funerary Customs Practices*, 232; Levy Yitzhak Rahmani, *A Catalogue of Jewish Ossuaries in the Collections of the State of Israel*, ed. Ayala Sussmann and Peter Schertz (Jerusalem: Israel Antiquities Authority, 1994), 15.

[11] Cited in Stephen J. Pfann and UHL Staff, *Cracks in the Foundation: The Jesus Family Tomb Story: The Experts Weigh In and Bow Out Disclaimers from the Film's Own Experts ON THE RECORD* (online: http://www.uhl.ac/Lost_Tomb/CracksInTheFoun dation.html, March 2007, accessed September 10, 2007).

[12] This chart is used by permission from David R. Pensgard who designed it. It also appears in the website of Gary R. Habermas (http://www.garyhabermas.com/articles/The_Lost_Tomb_of_Jesus/losttombofjesus_response.htm).

[13] See chapter 2.

[14] Many scholars have also made the observation that the *JFT* book and *LTJ* documentary were biased. See Mark Goodacre, *The Statistical Case for the Identity of the "Jesus Family Tomb"* (online: http://ntgateway.com/weblog/2007/03/statistical-case-for-identity-of-jesus.html, March 1, 2007, accessed July 25, 2007); Stephen J. Pfann, *The Improper Application of Statistics in "The Lost Tomb of Jesus"* (online: http://www.uhl.ac/JudeanTombsAnd

Ossuaries.html, accessed September 5, 2007); Pfann and Staff, *Cracks in the Foundation* (accessed). Habermas mentions a host of others scholars who make similar observations (*The Secret of the Talpiot Tomb*, 23–62).

Chapter Seven

[1] Simcha Jacobovici and Charles Pellegrino, *The Jesus Family Tomb: The Discovery, the Investigation, and the Evidence That Could Change History* (San Francisco, CA: HarperSanFrancisco, 2007), 111-12.

[2] These are the standard works on Jewish names: P. B. Bagatti and J. T. Milik, *Gli Scavi del Dominus Flevit (Monte Oliveto—Gerusalemme)*, Studium Biblicum Franciscanum: Collectio Maior No. 13 (Jerusalem: Franciscan Printing Press, 1958); Richard Bauckham, *Jesus and the Eyewitnesses: The Gospels as Eyewitness Testimony* (Grand Rapids: Wm. B. Eerdmans Publishing, 2006), 67-92; Tal Ilan, *Lexicon of Jewish Names in Late Antiquity: Part I: Palestine 330 BCE–200 CE*, TSAJ, ed. Martin Hengel and Peter Schäfer, vol. 91 (Tübingen: Mohr Siebeck, 2002); Rachael Hachlili, "Hebrew Names, Personal Names, Family Names and Nicknames of Jews in the Second Temple Period," in *Families and Family Relations: As Presented in Early Judaisms and Early Christianities: Texts and Fictions*, ed. Jan Willem Van Henten and Athalya Brenner, Studies in Theology and Religion, vol. 2 (Leiden: Deo Publishing, 2000), 83–115.

[3] Mark Goodacre notes this but concludes, "The major part of the case that the Talpiot tomb is Jesus' family tomb is based on a statistical claim. It is thought to be so unlikely that this cluster of names, so familiar from the New Testament record, would show up by accident that the identification of this tomb with the family of Jesus is on firm ground. What are the chances, they ask, that one would find a Jesus son of Joseph together with a Maria, a Mariamne and a Jose? Their answer is that the chances are something like 600:1 on a conservative estimate. The identification between this tomb and Jesus' family is all but certain" (*The Statistical Case for the Identity of the "Jesus Family Tomb"* [online: http://ntgateway.com/weblog/2007/03/statistical-case-for-identity-of-jesus.html, March 1, 2007, accessed 2007 July 25]).

[4] Jacobovici and Pellegrino, *Jesus Family Tomb*, 114.

[5] Ibid.

[6] James R. White, *From Toronto To Emmaus: The Empty Tomb and the Journey from Skepticism to Faith* (Birmingham, AL: Solid Ground Christian Books, 2007), 81.

[7] See also ibid., 81. See Appendix B.

[8] Andrey Feuerverger, *Dear Statistical Colleagues* [online: http://fisher.

utstat.toronto.edu/andrey/OfficeHrs.txt, March 12, 2007, accessed July 25, 2007]).

[9] Ibid. (accessed). He admitted the following in an interview of scholars by Ted Koppel that he had to "work with the interpretations given" to him, and the validity of the calculations are strongly based on the assumptions that enter the equation. For example, if the inscription "Maria" reads as just another common person of the first century, the "calculations... and statistical significance would wash out considerably" Ted Koppel, "The Lost Tomb of Jesus: A Critical Look," in *Discovery Channel Interview with Ted Koppel* [online: http://www.mininova.org/tor/613599, March 4, 2007]).

[10] Gary R. Habermas, *The Secret of the Talpiot Tomb: Unravelling the Mystery of the Jesus Family Tomb* (Nashville: Broadman & Holman Publishing, 2007), 46.

[11] Levy Yitzhak Rahmani, *A Catalogue of Jewish Ossuaries in the Collections of the State of Israel*, ed. Ayala Sussmann and Peter Schertz (Jerusalem: Israel Antiquities Authority, 1994).

[12] Stephen J. Pfann, *The Improper Application of Statistics in "The Lost Tomb of Jesus"* [online: http://www.uhl.ac/JudeanTombsAndOssuaries.html, 2007, accessed September 5, 2007]).

[13] Stephen J. Pfann, *Interview by Darrell L. Bock of Stephen J. Pfann to Help Identify Inscriptions* [online: http://media.bible.org/mp3/bock/profpfann 030807.mp3, 2007, ac–cessed April 4, 2007]).

[14] Bauckham, *Jesus and the Eyewitnesses*, 85. See also Charles L. Quarles, *Buried Hopes or Risen Savior: Is the Talpiot Tomb the Burial Place of Jesus of Nazareth?* [online: https ://www.lacollege.edu/ifl/jesus_tomb.pdf, March 4, 2007, accessed October 18, 2007]).

[15] Rachael Hachlili, *Jewish Funerary Customs Practices and Rites in the Second Temple Period*, Supplements to the Journal for the Study of Judaism ed. John J. Collins, vol. 94 (Leiden: E. J. Brill, 2005), 262. For very indebt mathematical treatment showing the statistical fallacies of the *JFT* advocates see William A. Dembski and Robert J. Marks II, "The Jesus Tomb Math," in *Buried Hope or Risen Savior? The Search For the Jesus Tomb*, ed. Charles L. Quarles (Nashville, TN: Broadman & Holman Publishing, 2008), 113–151.

[16] Pfann, *Identify Inscriptions* (accessed).

[17] Pfann, *Improper Application of Statistics* (accessed) (Italics his).

[18] Ibid.(accessed). Other names used less frequently are "3x: 'Amah, Hanan, Shalum, Shappira; 2x: 'Azaviah, 'Ahai, Haniah, Hanin/Hanun, Yatira, 'Ezra, Qariah, Shamai, Seth." I produced the chart with the details Pfann provided.

[19] Bagatti and Milik, *Gli Scavi del Dominus Flevit*, 108. The following site contains the Italian list for all to see: http://biblelight.net/DF-pg-108.gif.

20 This combined list appears separate under males and females in Bauckham, *Jesus and the Eyewitnesses*, 85, 89. See also Ilan, *Lexicon of Jewish Names*, 54–57. A similar list with slight variations also appears in Hachlili, "Hebrew Names," 114–15. These lists verify all common names. The following are the percentages of each name is used according to the total references. At the present time the total of male names discovered is 2625 and female references are 328, both of which appear in Bauckham, *Jesus and the Eyewitnesses*, 88–89. Based on this, all percentages of male and female names on the chart above are calculated as follows: Simon (9.3%), Joseph (8.3%), Eleazar (6.3%), Judas (6.2 %), John (4.6%), Jesus (3.8%), Hananiah (3.1%), Jonathan (2.7%), Matthew (2.4%), Manaen (1.6%), James (1.5%), Mary/Mariame (21.3%), Salome (17.7%), Shelamzion (7.3%), Martha (6.1%), Joanna (3.7%), Sapphira (3.7%), Berenice (2.4%), Imma (2.1%), and Mara (2.1%). Mara could be "an abbreviated form of Martha" (ibid., 89 n. 86).

21 Ibid., 85. When Darrell L. Bock mentions the number of times Josephus refers to the name of Jesus, he really meant 14, not 22. The latter is the total of inscribed ossuaries next to the total number of times Josephus mentions Jesus (Darrell L. Bock and Daniel B. Wallace, *Dethroning Jesus: Exposing Popular Culture's Quest to Unseat the Biblical Christ* [Nashville, TN: Thomas Nelson, 2007], 203).

22 Bock and Wallace, *Dethroning Jesus*, 203.

23 Ibid., 203–4.

24 Pfann, *Identify Inscriptions* (accessed).

25 Pfann, *Improper Application of Statistics* (accessed).

26 Several elements were changed the way the quotation appears in ibid.(accessed).

27 Quarles, *Buried Hopes or Risen Savior: Is the Talpiot Tomb the Burial Place of Jesus of Nazareth?*(accessed).

28 Habermas, *The Secret of the Talpiot Tomb*, 25.

29 Christopher Mims, *Special Report: Has James Cameron Found Jesus's* [sic] *Tomb or Is It Just a Statistical Error?* [online: http://www.sciam.com/article.cfm?id=14A3C2E6-E7F2-99DF-37A9AEC98FB0702A&page=2, March 2, 2007, accessed September 5, 2007]). See also Ilan, *Lexicon of Jewish Names*, 54–57.

30 Their leading statistical consultant admitted to some extent much of what is said here. He acknowledged that he went beyond his expertise in making allegations that the documentary makes. "As a result, the calculations made by Feuerverger and others rest on premises that must be decided by historians and archaeologists, who are still far from agreement on even the basics of

the Talpiot tomb." Feuerverger then says, "I did permit the number one in 600 to be used in the film—I'm prepared to stand behind that but on the understanding that these numbers were calculated based on assumptions that I was asked to use.... These assumptions don't seem unreasonable to me, but I have to remember that I'm not a biblical scholar" (Mims, *Jesus's* [sic] *Tomb* [accessed]). See Appendix B.

Chapter Eight

[1] Simcha Jacobovici and Charles Pellegrino, *The Jesus Family Tomb: The Discovery, the Investigation, and the Evidence That Could Change History* (San Francisco: HarperSanFrancisco, 2007), 189.

[2] Instead of writing the entire name of "James, son of Joseph, brother of Jesus," every time, whenever mentioning this ossuary in this chapter, the shorter referent "James ossuary" is used.

[3] Jacobovici and Pellegrino, *Jesus Family Tomb*, 189.

[4] Ibid., 15, 51–53. See also James D. Tabor, *The Jesus Dynasty: The Hidden History of Jesus, His Royal Family and the Birth of Christianity* (New York: Simon & Schuster, 2006), 32.

[5] Tabor, *Jesus Dynasty*, 32.

[6] Jacobovici and Pellegrino, *Jesus Family Tomb*, 15.

[7] Ibid., 91.

[8] Ibid., 92.

[9] Tabor, *Jesus Dynasty*, 31, says, "Since Kloner was not the original excavator he is merely writing up his report based on the notes of the now-deceased Gath."

[10] Amos Kloner, *Interview by Darrell L. Bock to Amos Kloner to Help Identify Talpiot Discovery Issues* (online: http://media.bible.org/mp3/bock/profkloner 030807.mp3, 2007, accessed April 4, 2007).

[11] Jacobovici and Pellegrino, *Jesus Family Tomb*, 15. The book also claims, "Amos Kloner, soon joined the team" of Shimon Gibson and Yosef Gat (ibid., 7).

[12] Kloner, *Interview by Darrell L. Bock to Amos Kloner to Help Identify Talpiot Discovery Issues* (accessed).

[13] Tabor, *Jesus Dynasty*, 32.

[14] Ibid. (accessed).

[15] Ibid. (accessed).

[16] Ben Witherington, *The Smoking Gun—Tenth Talpiot Ossuary to Be Blank* (online: http://benwitherington.blogspot.com/2007/03/smoking-gun-tenth-talpiot-ossuary_9874. html, 2007, accessed August 20, 2007).

[17] For an accurate and complete description of the James ossuary discovery see Hershel Shanks and Ben Witherington III, *The Brother of Jesus: The Dramatic Story and Meaning of the First Archaeological Link to Jesus and His Family* (San Francisco: HarperSanFrancisco, 2003), 3–22; Tabor, *Jesus Dynasty*, 15–23. The James ossuary picture was used with permission and by the courtesy of the Biblical Archaeology Society (Washington, D.C.).

[18] The James ossuary picture was used with permission and by the courtesy of the Biblical Archaeology Society (Washington, D.C.).

[19] For various arguments for and against the authenticity of the James ossuary see http://www.bib-arch.org/. See also Shanks and Witherington, *Brother of Jesus*.

[20] Tabor, *Jesus Dynasty*, 32.

[21] Joe Zias, *Deconstructing the Second and Hopefully Last Coming of Simcha and the BAR Crowd* (online: http://www.joezias.com/tomb.html, March 7, 2007, accessed September 10, 2007).

[22] Ibid. (accessed).

[23] William D. Barrick, "Curiosities or Evidence? The James Ossuary and The Jehoash Inscription," *Master's Seminary Journal* 14 (spring 2007): 2-3. See André Lemaire, "Burial Box of James the Brother of Jesus," *Biblical Archaeological Review* 28/6 (Nov/Dec 2002): 33.

[24] Tabor, *Jesus Dynasty*, 32.

[25] Amos Kloner, "A Tomb with Inscribed Ossuaries in East Talpiyot, Jerusalem," *Atiquot* 29 (1996): 21.

[26] Lemaire, "Burial Box of James," 27-28.

[27] Kloner, *Interview by Darrell L. Bock to Amos Kloner to Help Identify Talpiot Discovery Issues* (accessed).

[28] Zias, *Deconstructing the Second and Hopefully Last Coming of Simcha and the BAR Crowd* (accessed).

[29] Jacobovici and Pellegrino, *Jesus Family Tomb*, 178.

[30] Ibid., 178-80.

[31] Ibid., 189.

[32] James R. White, *From Toronto To Emmaus: The Empty Tomb and the Journey from Skepticism to Faith* (Birmingham, AL: Solid Ground Christian Books, 2007), 94.

[33] Ibid.

[34] Robert Genna, *Cracks in the Foundation: The Jesus Family Tomb Story: The Experts Weigh In and Bow Out Disclaimers from the Film's Own Experts on the Record* (online: http://www.uhl.ac/Lost_Tomb/CracksInTheFoundation.html, 2007, accessed August 28, 2007).

[35] Steven Cox, *Cracks in the Foundation: The Jesus Family Tomb Story: The Experts Weigh In and Bow Out Disclaimers from the Film's Own Experts on the

Record (online: http://www.uhl.ac/Lost_Tomb/CracksInTheFoundation.html, 2007, accessed August 28, 2007).

Chapter Nine

[1] Simcha Jacobovici and Charles Pellegrino, *The Jesus Family Tomb: The Discovery, the Investigation, and the Evidence That Could Change History* (San Francisco: HarperSanFrancisco, 2007), 126, 129, 134, 137, 196.
[2] Ibid., 196.
[3] Ibid., 125, 127.
[4] Anachronistic interpretation is reading back wrongly a meaning of a person, period, or thing into another period.
[5] Joseph A. Fitzmyer, *The Semitic Background of the New Testament*, Biblical Resource Series, ed. Astrid B. Beck and David Noel Freedman (Grand Rapids: William B. Eerdmans Publishing, 1997), 438.
[6] Ibid., 441-43.
[7] Irenaeus *Against Heresies*, 1.26.2. Both of the following scholars also make the same assessment: Fitzmyer, *Semitic Background of the New Testament*, 447; W. W. Wessel, "Ebionites: Ebonism," in *The International Standard Bible Encyclopedia*, ed. Geoffrey W. Bromiley, vol. 2 (Grand Rapids: Wm. B. Eerdmans Publishing, 1982), 10.
[8] Wessel, "Ebionites: Ebonism," 9.
[9] Fitzmyer, *Semitic Background of the New Testament*, 447.
[10] Wessel agrees with both of these observations: "(1) the Ebionites appear too late to be identified with the Qumrân sect (the earliest mention of the Ebionites is *ca.* A.D. 175): and (2) the religious background of the Ebionites, though heretical, is definitely Christian, whereas that of the people of Qumrân is pre-Christian and oriented to the OT, not the NT" ("Ebionites: Ebonism," 10). I would modify Wessel's last point by saying the Ebionites adopted some Christian teachings but do not qualify to be called Christians since they deny some of the most fundamental tenets of the Christian faith. Furthermore, since the Qumrân community existed in the first century where the apostolic Christian church began after Christ' death, burial, and resurrection, it is best to label the Qumrân community as a non-Christian community instead of a "pre-Christian" community since they seemed to exist at a time when Christianity emerged and was in full force.
[11] Jacobovici and Pellegrino, *Jesus Family Tomb*, 130.
[12] Rachael Hachlili says, "Past research has emphasized the pyramid as the most important and necessary element of the *nefesh*. It is believed that this shape symbolized the dead man's soul according to local custom coming orig-

inally from Egypt, but continuing in use through the Hellenistic Romans Period in the Eastern Mediterranean. At Souceida the remains of first century BCE square structure with Doric columns and architrave surmounted by a stepped pyramid were discovered, with an inscription in Greek and Nabatean mentioning a *nefesh*. It means that this kind of solid structure is a *nefesh*. In Nabatean art the obelisk and the shape of the pyramid became a symbol for the *nefesh*. The Nabateans used a similar shape of a square base topped by the pyramid or a cone, engraved on the rock at Petra, sometimes with a Nabatean inscription mentioning a *nefesh*" (*Jewish Funerary Customs Practices and Rites in the Second Temple Period*, Supplements to the Journal for the Study of Judaism, ed. John J. Collins, vol. 94 [Leiden: E. J. Brill, 2005], 350). The picture was used with Amos Kloner's permission and appears in "A Tomb with Inscribed Ossuaries in East Talpiyot, Jerusalem," *Atiquot* 29 (1996): 15.

[13] Hachlili, *Jewish Funerary Customs Practices*, 339. See also Levy Yitzhak Rahmani, *A Catalogue of Jewish Ossuaries in the Collections of the State of Israel*, ed. Ayala Sussmann and Peter Schertz (Jerusalem: Israel Antiquities Authority, 1994), 31-32.

[14] Hachlili, *Jewish Funerary Customs Practices*, 350. Although N. Avigad "believes that the evidence in support of this view is insufficient," I would have to agree with E. Littmann and M. Gawlikowski that believe otherwise.

[15] Rahmani, *Catalogue of Jewish Ossuaries*, 31-32, see the photos of ossuaries 14, 37, 151, 208, 229, 231, 311R, 346, 392, 597, 654. See also Hachlili, *Jewish Funerary Customs Practices*, 339-54.

[16] Jacobovici and Pellegrino, *Jesus Family Tomb*, 137. Though this picture appears in Rahmani's catalogue by the no. 597: *R*, it was taken from Joe Zias, *Deconstructing the Second and Hopefully Last Coming of Simcha and the BAR Crowd* (online: http://www.joezias.com/tomb.html, March 7, 2007, accessed September 10, 2007).

[17] Jodi Magness, *Has the Tomb of Jesus Been Discovered* (online: http://www.sbl-site.org/Article.aspx?ArticleId=640, 2007, accessed October 15, 2007), 1-2.

[18] Ibid. (accessed), 1. Seeing the matter in a similar light Magness concludes, "It is therefore possible that followers or family members removed Jesus' body from Joseph's tomb after the Sabbath ended and buried it in a trench grave, as it would have been unusual (to say the least) to leave a non-relative in a family tomb. Whatever explanation one prefers, the fact that Jesus' body did not remain in Joseph's tomb means that his bones could not have been collected in an ossuary, at least not if we follow the Gospel accounts" (ibid.). Now Tabor believes Joseph could have donated the tomb and that Jesus' family could

have been wealthy. See Appendix B.

[19] See Matthew 21:11; 26:71; Mark 1:9, 24; 10:47; 14:67; 16:6; Luke 2:39; 4:16, 34; 24:19; John 1:45-46; 18:5, 7; 19:19; Acts 2:22; 3:6; 4:10; 6:14; 10:38; 22:8; 26:9.

[20] Magness, *Tomb of Jesus* (accessed), 2.

[21] Darrell L. Bock and Daniel B. Wallace, *Dethroning Jesus: Exposing Popular Culture's Quest to Unseat the Biblical Christ* (Nashville: Thomas Nelson, 2007), 200.

[22] For an excellent discussion of these issues see ibid., 199–200.

[23] Rahmani, *Catalogue of Jewish Ossuaries*, 17.

[24] Magness, *Tomb of Jesus* (accessed), 1 (italics added).

[25] Zias, *Deconstructing the Second and Hopefully Last Coming of Simcha and the BAR Crowd* (accessed), 2.

[26] See Jacobovici and Pellegrino, *Jesus Family Tomb*, 195-97. In another Talpiot tomb Jesus' name also appears with the + in front of it and was also misunderstood to stand for a Christian symbol. Such an erroneous interpretation, however, was corrected and noted by Hachlili, *Jewish Funerary Customs Practices*, 262. "Sukenik … incorrectly interpreted these inscriptions and the cross-marks as an expression of lamentation for the crucifixion of Christ." See the inscriptions in Rahmani, *Catalogue of Jewish Ossuaries*, 106-7.

[27] Far too many ossuaries appear bearing crosses, zigzags and other markings (which at times used even Greek and Jewish letters) designating where the lid aligned with the right part of the ossuary chest. Even inscriptions were repeated on rims of ossuary chests to align the lid with it "similar to direction marks" (Rahmani, *Catalogue of Jewish Ossuaries*, 12, 19).

[28] Ibid., 19 (italics added).

[29] Jacobovici and Pellegrino, *Jesus Family Tomb*, 195.

[30] Everett Ferguson, *Backgrounds of Early Christianity*, 3rd ed. (Grand Rapids: Wm. B. Eerdmans Publishing, 2003), 590.

[31] See for further study L.W. Barnard, "The 'Cross of Herculaneum' Reconsidered," in *The New Testament Age: Essays in Honor of Bo Reicke*, ed. William C. Weinrich (Macon, GA: Mercer University Press, 1984); L. de Bruyne, "La 'crux interpretum' di Ercolano," *Revisita di Archeologia Cristiana* 21 (1945): 281; P. de Jerphanion, "La Croix d'Herculaneum?" *Orientalia Christiana Periodica* 7 (1941): 5.

[32] Ferguson, *Backgrounds of Early Christianity*, 591.

[33] David G. Burke clarifies how this came about. "With the death of Jesus on the cross a new significance was attached to the figure [of the cross]. It became the primary symbol of the Christian religion and has been elaborated in a profuse variety of forms in Christian art. It was not,

however, until the time of Constantine that the cross could be used without restriction as the public symbol of Christian faith. Constantine's sanction was doubtless the result of the vision of A.D. 317 in which he claimed to have seen a flaming cross in the sky with the accompanying words *en toútô níka*, 'by this [sign] conquer' (Eusebius *Vita Constantini* i.28), and of the story of the discovery of the true cross by his mother. Tertullian (*De corona* 3) reveals the extent to which the sign of the cross was employed among the faithful as a gesture by the late 2nd cent.: 'At each journey and progress, at each coming in and going out, ... at meals, ... at bedtime, ... we mark the brow with the sign of the cross'" ("Cross; Crucify," in *The International Standard Bible Encyclopedia*, ed. Geoffrey W. Bromiley, vol. 1 [Grand Rapids: Wm. B. Eerdmans Publishing, 1979], 827).

[34] See for further study Erich Dinkler, "Comments on the History of the Symbol of the Cross," *Journal of the Theology and the Church* 1 (1965): 124–46; Duncan Fishwick, "Talpioth Ossuaries Again," *New Testament Studies* 10 (October 1963): 49–61; J P. Kane, "The Ossuary Inscription of Jerusalem," *Journal of Semitic Studies* 23 (Autumn 1978): 268–82; Robert H. Smith, "The Cross Marks on Jewish Ossuaries," *Palestine Exploration Quarterly* 106 (January-June 1974): 53–66; Eleazar Lipa Sukenik, "The Earliest Record of Christianity," *American Journal of Archaeology* 51 (October-December 1947): 3–30.

[35] James R. White, *From Toronto To Emmaus: The Empty Tomb and the Journey from Skepticism to Faith* (Birmingham, AL: Solid Ground Christian Books, 2007), 95.

[36] Jacobovici and Pellegrino, *Jesus Family Tomb*, 131–32.

[37] Ibid., 123, 131, see also pp. 133-34 (italics his).

[38] Darrell L. Bock, *Breaking The Da Vinci Code: Answers to Questions Everyone's Asking* (Nashville: Thomas Nelson Publishers, 2004), 154.

[39] This and other similar facts were also noted by White, *Empty Tomb*, 95.

[40] The following entire historical account comes from Robert McHenry, ed., *The New Encyclopaedia Britannica*, ed. Robert McHenry (Chicago: Encyclopaedia Britannica, 1993), 623–24.

[41] Ibid.

Chapter Ten

[1] Simcha Jacobovici and Charles Pellegrino, *The Jesus Family Tomb: The Discovery, the Investigation, and the Evidence That Could Change History* (San Francisco: HarperSanFrancisco, 2007), 70–71.

[2] Gary R. Habermas, "Mapping the Recent Trend toward the Bodily

Resurrection Appearances of Jesus in Light of Other Prominent Critical Positions," in *The Resurrection of Jesus: John Dominic Crossan and N. T. Wright in Dialogue*, ed. Robert B. Steward (Minneapolis: Fortress Press, 2006), 79–81.

3 These categories and explanations that follow are derived from ibid., 82–92.

4 German liberals promoted this view beginning the second half of the nineteenth century and into the twentieth century. See Gerd Lüdemann, *The Resurrection of Jesus: History, Experience, Theology*, trans. John Bowden (Minneapolis: Fortress Press, 1994); Gerd Lúdemann and Alf Ozen, *What Really Happened to Jesus: A Historical Approach to the Resurrection*, trans. John Bowden (Louisville, KY: Westminster John Knox Press, 1995).

5 Willi Marxsen, *The Resurrection of Jesus of Nazareth*, trans. Margaret Kohl (Philadelphia: Fortress Press, 1970), 88, 94, 96–97. He says the disciples "were all like Thomas and so an appearance was necessary. But this answer will hardly be thought satisfactory. Alternatively one might say that appearances really happened, so why should they not be reported? This may be admitted. But it is essential to add that an appearance was not necessary in order that the ten should believe; for they believed before. And this means that their faith too was dependent on the appearance to Peter. We can therefore now answer the question put earlier. Since the appearance to Peter led others to faith, the functional aspect was bound up with first appearance from the very beginning.... So although the functional aspect is not expressly named in the formula ('Jesus appeared to Peter'), the function is none the less implicit and is to be read into it" (ibid., 90).

6 See chapter 13 for an analysis of this view.

7 Habermas, "Recent Trend toward the Bodily Resurrection Appearances of Jesus," 86. For or an impressive list of scholars who reject the naturalistic view see p. 202 n. 41.

8 This is the explanation succinctly given by Habermas (ibid., 87 n. 43).

9 Hans Grass, *Ostergeschehen und Osterberichte*, 2nd ed. (Göttingen: Vandenhoeck and Ruprecht, 1962), 93, 118–19, 242, 279. This appears in Habermas, "Recent Trend toward the Bodily Resurrection Appearances of Jesus," 87 n. 44.

10 Bart D. Ehrman, *Misquoting Jesus: The Story Behind Who Changed the Bible and Why* (San Francisco: HarperSanFrancisco, 2005). In this book Ehrman asserts that the Bible cannot be trusted because it has numerous errors. In a debate between William Lane Craig and Bart D. Ehrman at College of the Holy Cross, Worcester, Massachusetts, on March 28, 2006, Craig said, "Sadly, Dr. Ehrman came to radically different conclusions as a result of his studies.

In his most recent book he poignantly describes how he came to lose his teenage faith. I'm not sure, based on Dr. Ehrman's writings, whether he still believes in Jesus' resurrection or not. He never denies it. But he does deny that there can be historical evidence for Jesus' resurrection. He maintains that there *cannot* be historical evidence for Jesus' resurrection. Now this is a very bold claim, and so naturally I was interested to see what argument he would offer for its justification. I was stunned to discover that the philosophical argument he gives for this claim is an old argument against the identification of miracles which I had studied during my doctoral research and which is regarded by most philosophers today as demonstrably fallacious" (p. 3, italic his). Later in the debate Ehrman admitted, "I'm a historian dedicated to finding the historical truth. After years of studying, I finally came to the conclusion that everything I had previously thought about the historical evidence of the resurrection was absolutely wrong" (p. 9). Ehrman does not deny the resurrection nor does he affirm it. He is agnostic about it since he believes the concept of the Resurrection as a miracle cannot be verified in history. Whether that is true will be discussed later in this chapter. He says, "What about the resurrection of Jesus? I'm not saying it didn't happen; but if it did happen, it would be a miracle. The resurrection claims are claims that not only that Jesus' body came back alive; it came back alive never to die again. That's a violation of what naturally happens, every day, time after time, millions of times a year. What are the chances of that happening? Well, it'd be a miracle. In other words, it'd be so highly improbable that we can't account for it by natural means. A theologian may claim that it's true, and to argue with the theologian we'd have to argue on theological grounds because there are no historical grounds to argue on. Historians can only establish what probably happened in the past, and by definition a miracle is the least probable occurrence. And so, by the very nature of the canons of historical research, we can't claim historically that a miracle probably happened. By definition, it probably didn't. And history can only establish what probably did. I wish we could establish miracles, but we can't. It's no one's fault. It's simply that the canons of historical research do not allow for the possibility of establishing as probable the least probable of all occurrences. For that reason, Bill's four pieces of evidence are completely irrelevant. There *cannot* be historical probability for an event that defies probability, even if the event did happen. The resurrection has to be taken on faith, not on the basis of proof" (p. 12 italics his). For a complete analysis of the debate see William Lane Craig and Bart D. Ehrman, *Is There Historical Evidence for the Resurrection of Jesus? A Debate between William Lane Craig and Bart D. Ehrman* (online transcript: http://www.holycross.edu/departments/crec/website/resurrection-debate-transcript.pdf, March 28, 2006, accessed

November 5, 2007), 3, 9, 12.

[11] We need not duplicate here the enormous number of tomes written on Jesus' resurrection. For a good bibliography (though not exhaustive) of primary and secondary references of works on the Resurrection see Gary R. Habermas and Michael R. Licona, *The Case for the Resurrection of Jesus* (Grand Rapids: Kregel Publications, 2004); N. T. Wright, *The Resurrection of God*, Christian Origins and the Question of God, vol. 3 (London: SPCK, 2003).

[12] Earl Doherty, *Challenging the Verdict* (Ottawa, ON: Age of Reason, 2001), 39. Some of those scholars are Bart D. Ehrman, *The Orthodox Corruption of Scripture: The Effect of Early Christological Controversies on the Text of the New Testament* (Oxford: Oxford University Press, 1993); *idem, Lost Christianities: The Battles for Scripture and the Faiths We Never Knew* (New York: Oxford University Press, 2003); *idem, Misquoting Jesus*; Robert W. Funk, Roy W. Hoover, and the Jesus Seminar, *The Five Gospels: The Search for the Authentic Words of Jesus*, ed. R. Funk and J. V. Hills (New York: MacMillian Publishing, 1993).

[13] Darrell L. Bock, *Can I Trust the Bible?* (Norcross, GA: Ravi Zacharias International Ministries, 2001), 18.

[14] Dan Brown, *The Da Vinci Code: A Novel* (New York: Doubleday, 2003), 233–35.

[15] Habermas and Licona, *Case for the Resurrection of Jesus*, 44–45.

[16] The Council of Nicea of A.D. 325 recorded the following: "We believe in one God, the Father All-sovereign, maker of heaven and earth, and all things visible and invisible; And in one Lord Jesus Christ, and the only-begotten Son of God, Begotten of the Father before all ages, Light of Light, true God of true God, begotten not made, of one substance with the Father, through whom all things were made; who for us men and for our salvation came down from the heavens, and was made flesh of the Holy Spirit and the Virgin Mary, and became man, and was crucified for us under Pontius Pilate, and suffered and was buried, and rose again on the third day according to the Scriptures, and ascended into the heavens, and sits on the right hand of the Father, and comes again with glory to judge living and dead, of whose kingdom there shall be no end: And in the Holy Spirit, the Lord and the Lifegiver, that proceeds from the Father, who with the Father and Son is worshipped together and glorified together, who spoke through the prophets: In one holy catholic and apostolic church: We acknowledge one baptism unto remission of sins. We look for resurrection of the dead and the life of the age to come."

[17] James L. Garlow and Peter Jones respond to the ridiculous allegation of

Brown in, *The Da Vinci Code*, 233, in which he claimed this was a close vote of 316 to 2 (*Cracking Da Vinci's Code* [Colorado Springs, CO: Victor, 2004], 95). Correctly, Darrell L. Bock points out that what occurred at Nicea was not a vote to make Jesus God. "This council and the creed represented what a sizable number of Christian communities had believed for more than two hundred years.... The vote at Nicea, rather than establishing the church's beliefs, affirmed and officially recognized what was already the church's dominant view" (*Breaking the Da Vinci Code: Answers to Questions Everyone's Asking* [Nashville: Thomas Nelson, 2004], 102.

[18] Out of a number of scholars that date all New Testament books within the first century John A. T. Robinson seems to make the best argument (*Redating the New Testament* [Philadelphia: The Westminster Press, 1976]). A. Harnack, C. E. Raven, and a number of contemporary scholars today also believe all NT books were written before A.D. 70.

[19] F. F. Bruce, *The New Testament Documents: Are They Reliable?* 6th ed. (Grand Rapids: Wm. B. Eerdmans Publishing, 1981), 25. Garlow and Jones also observe this in *Cracking Da Vinci's Code*, 139.

[20] This fact goes against a current popular opinion that believes competing Christianities and other religious "Gnostic" books existed and were also considered inspired.

[21] Bruce, *New Testament Documents*, 25.

[22] Ibid., 27.

[23] Garlow and Jones, *Cracking Da Vinci's Code*, 141. For an easy to read explanation of how the books of the Bible were formed, authoritatively accepted, and historically reliable see Josh D. McDowell, *The New Evidence that Demands a Verdict* (Nashville: Thomas Nelson, 1999), 17–68; Norman L. Geisler and William E. Nix, *A General Introduction to the Bible: Revised and Expanded* (Chicago: Moody Press, 1986).

[24] Bock, *Can I Trust the Bible?* 18–19.

[25] A number of these examples are explained by Bock (ibid., 19–28).

[26] Formidable volumes addressing these issues are Robert Anderson, *Misunderstood Texts of the New Testament* (Grand Rapids: Kregel Publications, 1991); Gleason L. Archer, *Encyclopedia of Bible Difficulties* (Grand Rapids: Zondervan Publishing House, 1982); F. F. Bruce, *The Hard Sayings of Jesus*, The Jesus Library, ed. Michael Green (Downers Grove, IL: InterVarsity Press, 1983); J. Carl Laney, *Answers to Tough Questions From Every Book of the Bible: A Survey of Problem Passages* (Grand Rapids: Kregel Publications, 1997).

[27] For example see Jesus' baptism (Matt. 3:17; Mark 1:11; John 1:30–34), temptation (Matt. 4:1–11; Luke 4:1–13), and other places described in the books mentioned in note 26.

[28] The following volumes point out how messengers can speak on behalf of others and can be addressed as if they are the person who sent them. J. C. L. Gibson, *Canaanite Myths and Legends*, ed. G. R. Driver (Edinburgh: T. & T. Clark 1978), 42; Samuel A. Meier, *The Messenger in the Ancient Semitic World*, Harvard Semitic Monographs, ed. Frank Moore Cross, vol. 45 (Atlanta, GA: Scholars Press, 1988), 184.

[29] Bock, *Can I Trust the Bible?* 19.

[30] Ibid., 21 (italics his).

[31] Ehrman, *Misquoting Jesus*, 10.

[32] Ibid., 90.

[33] Ibid., 208.

[34] Darrell L. Bock and Daniel B. Wallace, *Dethroning Jesus: Exposing Popular Culture's Quest to Unseat the Biblical Christ* (Nashville: Thomas Nelson, 2007), 38–76. Other scholars mentioned in Appendix A also expose a number of Ehrman's errors. See Craig A. Evans, *Fabricating Jesus: How Modern Scholars Distort the Gospels* (Downers Grove, IL: InterVarsity Press, 2006), 25–31; Ben Witherington III, *What Have They Done with Jesus? Beyond Strange Theories and Bad History—Why We Can Trust the Bible* (San Francisco: HarperSanFrancisco, 2006), 7.

[35] Bock and Wallace, *Dethroning Jesus*, 43–44.

[36] Ibid., 44.

[37] Ibid., 44–45. Wallace, interestingly, documents how Tertullian, an early church father, reprimanded someone for doubting the original manuscripts of Scripture and pointed the skeptic to visit the churches where the "very thrones," or place, where the apostles read the text in "their own *authentic writings*." Debatable as it is, this could refer to either the original text or copies of it (ibid., 45, [italics his]).

[38] This type of thinking is all too prevalent in postmodernism. Interestingly Wallace said, "To be skeptical about the text of the New Testament is essential to a postmodern agenda, in which all things are possible but nothing is probable. The only certainty of postmodernism is uncertainty itself. Concomitant with this is an intellectual pride—pride that one 'knows' enough to be skeptical about all positions" (J. Ed Komoszewski, M. James Sawyer, and Daniel B. Wallace, *Reinventing Jesus: How Contemporary Skeptics Miss the Real Jesus and Mislead Popular Culture* [Grand Rapids: Kregel Publications, 2006], 66).

[39] Ben Witherington writes, "There is a reason that both Ehrman's mentor in text criticism and mine, Bruce Metzger, has said that there is nothing in these variants that really challenges any Christian belief: they don't. I would like to add that other experts in text criticism, such as Gordon Fee, have been

equally emphatic about the flawed nature of Ehrman's analysis of the significance of such textual variants" (*What Have They Done With Jesus?* 7).

40 Wallace explains this in a succinct way in *Dethroning Jesus*, 52–71. For a more detail discussion in how the science of textual criticism (i.e., the investigation involved at how to arrive at the original text) works see Eldon Jay Epp and Gordon D. Fee, *Studies in the Theory and Method of New Testament Textual Criticism*, Studies and Documents, ed. Irvin Alan Sparks, vol. 45 (Grand Rapids: Wm. B. Eerdmans Publishing, 1993); Bruce M. Metzger and Bart D. Ehrman, *The Text of the New Testament: Its Transmission, Corruption, and Restoration*, 4th ed. (New York and Oxford: Oxford University Press, 2005).

41 With some modifications this chart is based on the following two sources: Komoszewski, Sawyer, and Wallace, *Reinventing Jesus*, 71; and Josh McDowell, *Evidence That Demands a Verdict: Historical Evidences for the Christian Faith*, vol. 1 (San Bernardino, CA: Here's Life Publishers, 1972), 42–43.

42 Metzger and Ehrman, *Text of the New Testament*, 126.

43 Komoszewski, Sawyer, and Wallace, *Reinventing Jesus*, 50–51 (italics his).

44 Wright, *Resurrection of God*, 15. See the discussions in Christopher F. Evans, *Resurrection and the New Testament* 2nd ed., Studies in Biblical theology, no. 12. (London: SCM Press, 1970); Marxsen, *Resurrection of Jesus of Nazareth*; C. F. D. Moule and Willi Marxen, *The Significance of the Message of the Resurrection for the Faith in Jesus Christ*, trans. Dorothea M. Barton and R. A. Wilson, 2nd ed., Studies in Biblical theology, no. 8 (Naperville, IL: A. R. Allenson, 1968).

45 Craig and Ehrman, *Historical Evidence for the Resurrection of Jesus* (accessed), 12.

46 As Wright correctly explains, this view says "both too little and too much." "Too little: in standard positivism fashion it appears to suggest that we can only regard as 'historical' that to which we have direct access (in the sense of 'first-hand witness accounts' or near equivalent). But, as all real historians know, that is not in fact how history works. Positivism is, if anything, even less appropriate in historiography than in other areas. Again and again the historian has to conclude, even if only to avoid total silence, that certain events took place to which we have no direct access but which are the necessary postulates of that to which we do have access. Scientists, not least physicists, make this sort of move all the time; indeed, this is precisely how scientific advances happen. Ruling out as historical that to which we do not have direct access is actually a way of not doing history at all.

"As a result, this view also says too much. On its own epistemology, it ought not even to claim access to the disciples' faith. Even the texts themselves do not give us direct access to this faith in the way that Marxsen and others seem to regard as necessary. All we have in this case are texts; and though Marxsen did not address this question, the same relentless suspicion, applied in regular postmodern fashion, might lead some to question whether we even have those. If, in other words, you want to be a no-hold-barred historical positivist, only accepting as historical that to which you have (in this sense) direct access, you have a long and stony road ahead of you. Few if any actual practicing historians travel by this route" (*Resurrection of God*, 15–16).

[47] Ibid., 12–13.

[48] To say that history must be a provable event "is somewhat more controversial." For example, "To say 'x may have happened, but we can't prove it, so it isn't really *historical*' may not be self-contradictory, but is clearly operating with a more restricted sense of 'history' than some of the others" (ibid., 13).

[49] Except for the arrowhead pointers everything else comes from Wright (ibid., 12–13 [italics his]). The historical Jesus argument attempted at locating the person of Jesus in light of first-century culture and strips away all supernatural attributes. Conversely, the Christ of faith does little to anything in locating the Jesus of history but only attributes the theological and supernatural elements attributed to Him. The correct view is to hold to both a historical first-century understanding of Jesus' culture and an unbiased acceptance of supernatural elements attributed to Him that were recorded and witnessed by many of that day. Not keeping these distinct resulted in the confusion that appears in John D. Crossan, *The Historical Jesus: The Life of a Mediterranean Jewish Peasant* (San Francisco: Harper SanFrancisco, 1991), xxvii.

[50] Wright, *Resurrection of God*, 12. For further discussion how theologians have used these five views of history see pages 14–31.

[51] Ibid., 32–47. For example, in *Iliad* 24.549–51, the last sentence literally translates this concept emphatically: "you will not resurrect him [*oude min ansteseis*] before you suffer as further evil." See also *Iliad* 24.756; Aeschylus *Eumenides* 647ff.; Sophocles *Electra* 137–39; Aeschylus *Agamemnon* 565–69, 1019–24, 1360ff.; Euripides *Helena* 1285–87; Aristotle *De Anima* 1.406b.3–5; Aristophanes *Ecclesiazusae* 1073–74; Herodotus 3.62.3ff. (ibid., 32–33 n. 1– 4, see also n. 5–9).

[52] Edwin M. Yamauchi's research suggests that the Christian concept of resurrection is absent in the fertility cults of Tammuz, Adonis, Attis, Osiris, and Baal. "Furthermore, P. Lambrechts has shown recently that the belief in the resurrection of Adonis and in the resurrection of Attis was a late development.

In the case of Adonis, the beautiful youth beloved of Aphrodite, who was slain by a boar, Lambrechts points out that there is no trace of a resurrection in the pictorial representations of Adonis or in the early texts — Sappho, Aristophanes, Plutarch, Pausanias, Theocritus" ("Tammuz and the Bible," *Journal of Biblical Literature* 84 [September 1965]: 290). Therefore the typical accusation that Christians derive the resurrection concept from these cults is false.

[53] For his view see Jon Davies, *Death, Burial, and Rebirth in the Religions of Antiquity* (New York: Routledge, 1999), 28–39.

[54] Wright, *Resurrection of God*, 47 (italics his). He quotes this from Davies, *Death, Burial, and Rebirth in the Religions of Antiquity*, 34. For further discussion to understand what Egypt, Canaan, Mesopotamia, and Persia believed about the resurrection, Davies's book is pivotal.

[55] Wright, *Resurrection of God*, 47–48.

[56] Ibid., 49.

[57] Along with Wright, who documents this, numerous scholars note this, including these: James Barr, *The Garden of Eden and the Hope of Immortality* (London: SCM Press, 1992); John J. Collins, *Daniel: A Commentary on the Book of Daniel* Hermeneia: A Critical and Historical Commentary on the Bible, ed. Frank Moore Cross (Minneapolis: Fortress Press, 1993); Christian Grappe, "Naissance de l'idée de résurrection dans le Judaïsme," in *Résurrection: L'aprè-mort dans le monde ancien at el Nouveau Testament*, ed. Odette Mainville and Daniel Marguerat (Geneva and Montreal: Labor et Fides and Médiaspaul, 2001); Leonard Greenspoon, "The Origin of the Idea of Resurrection," in *Traditions in Transformation: Turning Points in Biblical Faith*, ed. Baruch Halpern and Jon D. Levenson (Winona Lake, IN: Eisenbrauns, 1981), Philip S. Johnston, *Shades of Sheol: Death and Afterlife in the Old Testament* (Downers Grove, IL: InterVarsity Press, 2002); Matthias Krieg, *Todesbilder im Alten Testament, oder, "Wie die Alten den Tod gebildet,"* Abhandlungen zur Theologie des Alten und Neuen Testaments, vol. 73 (Zürich: Theologischer Verlag, 1988); Tryggve N. D. Mettinger, *The Riddle of Resurrection: "Dying and Rising Gods" in the Ancient Near East*, Coniectanea biblica. Old Testament series vol. 50 (Stockholm: Almqvist & Wiksell International, 2001); Ben C. Ollenburger, "If Mortals Die, Will They Live Again? The Old Testament and Resurrection.," *Ex Auditu* 9 (1993); Emile Puech, *La croyance des Esséniens en la vie future: immortalité, résurrection, vie éternelle? Histoire d'une croyance dans le judaïsme ancien*, 2 vols., Etudes bibliques, 21–22 (Paris: J. Gabalda, 1993); Alan F. Segal, "Life After Death: the Social Sources," in *The Resurrection: An Interdisciplinary Symposium on the Resurrection of Jesus*, ed. Stephen T. Davis, Daniel Kendall, and Gerald

O'Collins (Oxford: Oxford University Press, 1997); Klaas Spronk, *Beatific Afterlife in Ancient Israel and in the Ancient Near East*, Alter Orient und Altes Testament 219. (Kevelaer: Butzon & Bercker, 1986; reprint, Neukirchen-Vluyn: Neukircherner Verlag); Nicholas J. Tromp, *Primitive Conceptions of Death and the Nether World in the Old Testament*, Biblica et orientalia 21 (Rome: Pontifical Biblical Institute, 1969); Wright, *Resurrection of God*, 85 n. 4.

[58] Wright, *Resurrection of God*, 86.

[59] Bock and Wallace, *Dethroning Jesus*, 209. For an interpretation of Romans 8:18–30 see René A. Lopez, *Romans Unlocked: Power to Deliver* (Springfield, MO: 21st Century Press, 2005), 175–82.

[60] Ben Witherington III, *Jesus, Paul and the End of the World* (Downers Grove, IL: InterVarsity Press, 1992), 185.

[61] Wright says, "It is of course true that the third position, explicit belief in resurrection, is only one of several strands in the range of biblical belief about death and what happens afterwards, and that this belief developed markedly in the post-biblical period. In particular, the third, though clearly cutting across the first in certain ways, joins the first in affirming the goodness and vital importance of the present created order, which is to be renewed by YHWH, not abandoned. For both, the substance of hope lies within creation, not beyond it" (*Resurrection of God*, 86).

[62] Ibid., 87.

[63] See Psalms 30:9; 88:3–7, 10–12; Isaiah 38:10–18; Job 3:13–19; 7:7–10; 14:1–14; 16:22; Jeremiah 51:39, 57. Even using poetic license, like that of Isaiah 14:9–11, descriptive of a scene of a king arriving in the depths of *sheol*, the point made is that such a tyrant's power is now ineffective. For further discussion on how most of the OT emphasizes the point that "to die is to be forgotten for good" see Wright, *Resurrection of God*, 92–99.

[64] Ibid., 91. See Ecclesiastes 2:24; 3:12–22; 5:18–20; 6:3–6; 8:15; 9:7–10; 11:9; 12:1–8.

[65] See Ecclesiastes 1:3, 9, 14; 2:11, 17–20, 22; 3:16; 4:1, 3, 7, 15; 5:13, 18; 6:1, 12; 8:9; 9:3, 6, 9, 11, 13; 10:5.

[66] Once the LXX translations came to the fore many ambiguous passages were made clearer (Margaret Williams, "The Contribution of Jewish Inscriptions to the Study of Judaism," in *The Cambridge History of Judaism*, ed. William Horbury, W. D. Davies, and John Sturdy, vol. 3 [Cambridge: Cambridge University Press, 1999], 60). Wright suggest, "That possibility (of an early Christian reading in support of a christological belief) may cautiously be explored in a relation to a few prophecies of a coming king... any early Christian reading 2 Samuel 7.12, *kai anasteso to sperma sou*, would have

had no difficulty identifying who the *sperma* was. So too the various messianic promises in Jeremiah and Ezekiel could easily have been taken, and were perhaps intended by their LXX translator(s) to be taken, as indicating the resurrection through which God's leader(s) would 'arise' in the age to come. God will 'raise up' shepherds, and especially a righteous Branch, to rule over Israel and the world. 'I will raise up one shepherd over them, my servant David,' declares YHWH: *kai anasteso ep' autous pimena hena, ton doulon mou Dauid*. We should be wary of reading too much into these verses like this; equally, we should be just as wary of reading too little" (*Resurrection of God*, 149).

67 These promise passages were well known to OT Jews. Hence Wright suggests "they must be recalled here in case any impression be given that the absence, for most ancient Israelites, of any statement of human life beyond the grave meant that they were without a living and vibrant hope" (*Resurrection of God*, 102).

68 Derek Kidner says, "The assurance that Isaac as well as Abraham would *come again* from the sacrifice was no empty phrase: it was Abraham's full conviction, on the ground that 'in Isaac shall thy seed be called' (21:12). Hebrews 11:17–19 reveals that he was expecting Isaac to be resurrected; henceforth he would regard him as given back from the dead" (*Genesis: An Introduction and Commentary*, Tyndale Old Testament Commentaries, ed. D. J. Wiseman, vol. 1 [Downers Grove, IL: InterVarsity Press, 1967], 143).

69 Numerous passages seem have a temporal earthly emphasis instead of eternal bodily resurrection in mind (Ps. 116; Prov. 12:28; 14:32; 15:24; 23:14).

70 Collins, *Daniel*, 391–92.

71 Wright, *Resurrection of God*, 129. That the Pharisees believed in the bodily resurrection and the Sadducees did not is well known (Matt. 22:23; Mark 12:18; Luke 20:27; Acts 23:7–9). But according to Wright because Sadducees followed such a strict interpretation of the OT they saw life simply existing no further than earth. Thus life and blessings for them were seen as enjoyed by their relationship to God here on earth. In fact, "the contemporary instinct to see the Sadducees as radicals, because they denied the resurrection, is 180 degrees wide of the mark. They denied it because they were conservatives" (ibid., 131).

72 Ibid., 130.

73 See Sirach 11:26–28; 14:16–19; 17:27–32; 38:21–23; 41:4.

74 Why would such a wealthy group not want to believe in any form of existence after death since many wealthy advocates of the past desired to take their present riches with them to the after life? It seems that this would benefit them in another way. For example, "Powerful groups have sometimes advocated a

strong post-mortem hope as a way of stopping the poor and powerless grumbling about their lot in the present life. And, where 'resurrection' has become an official dogma within a powerful system, it has had the capacity to become simply another instrument to keep ordinary people in line. It goes against such sociological assumptions to see first-century Jewish aristocrats staunchly denying any future life." The Sadducees denied this for several reasons. They did not find any such passages supporting resurrection in the Torah (Law), their primary source of interpretation, or the Former Prophets (the historical books from Joshua to Kings). Also an unduly interest in the dead, like pagan cults, came close to violating the Law (Lev. 11:31–32; 19:28; 21:1, 11; Num. 6:6; 19:11, 18; Deut. 18:11) (Wright, *Resurrection of God*, 137). Since the teaching of Daniel 12:2–3, Isaiah 26:19, and Ezekiel 37:1–14 were not part of the Pentateuch, they simple discounted it. Wright points out other passages that seem to argue for the absence of any future life (1 Macc. 2:49–70; Tob. 4:10; 12:9; 13:2, 5; 14:10; 1 Baruch 2:27). However, the same can be said about these texts that were said of the OT perspective on life. That Sadducees and other groups may have misinterpreted and used them wrongly to defend their belief, and others used them to show how this belief arose, does not make this interpretation correct, since nothing in these texts argues definitively that resurrection was impossible. In fact other passages argue just the opposite in a clear and forceful way. Wright does not believe the silence of any direct resurrection statement "is not as weak as is sometimes supposed" (ibid., 139).

[75] Ibid., 142-43.

[76] Ibid., 144.

[77] Wright notes a number of scholars who agree on this point (ibid., 144 n. 57). Two of these are Peder Borgen, "Philo of Alexandria," in *Compendia Rerum Iudaicarum as Novum Testamentum, Section Two: The Literature of Jewish People in the Period of the Second Temple and the Talmud*, ed. Michael E. Stone, Jewish Writings of Second Temple Period: Apocrypha, Pseudepigrapha, Qumran Sectarian Writings, Philo, Josephus. 2 vols. (Philadelphia: Fortress Press, 1984), 233–82; John M. Dillon, *The Middle Platonists, 80 B.C. to A.D. 220* rev. 2nd ed. (Ithaca, NY: Cornell University Press, 1996), 139–83. For example Philo says in the following statements: "The death of the good is the beginning of another life; for life is a twofold thing, one life being in the body, corruptible; the other without the body, incorruptible" (*Quaestiones* Gen 1.16). "What does it mean of, 'But thou shalt go to thy fathers in peace, being nourished in a fair old age?'" (*Quaestiones* Gen. 3.11). He here clearly indicates the incorruptibility of the soul. "Whatever else you may choose to call this concrete animal; but rather

the purest and most unalloyed mind, which, while contained in the city of the body and of the mortal life is cramped and confined, and like a man who is bound in a prison confesses plainly that he is unable to relish the free air" (*De Ebrietate* 26, 101). "For it is not possible for one who dwells in the body and belongs to the race of mortals to be united with God, but he alone can be so whom God delivers from that prison house of the body" (*Legum* 3.14, 42). See also *De Migratione* 2 (9); *Quod Deterius* 22 (80). This, by no means is an exhaustive list.

[78] All passages from the Apocrypha are from *New Revised Standard Version* (New York: American Bible Society, 1989).

[79] Bock makes a similar observation in *Dethroning Jesus*, 209.

[80] Whether we agree with Judas's theological conclusion is not the point here but whether belief in a bodily resurrection was part of the culture. A reading of 2 Maccabees makes this clear. "Resurrection belief, throughout 2 Maccabees, means new bodily life, a life which comes after the 'life after death' that dead people currently experience. And the whole book is introduced with the reported prayer, from the time of Nehemiah, that God would gather the scattered people of Israel, punish the Gentiles for their arrogance and oppression, and plant his people in the holy place [2 Macc. 1:24–9]. Resurrection, in other words, is both the personal hope of the righteous individual and the national hope for faithful Israel" (Wright, *Resurrection of God*, 153). For a contrary view of 2 Maccabees see Stanley E. Porter, "Resurrection, the Greeks and the New Testament," in *Resurrection*, ed. Stanley E. Porter, Michael A. Hayes, and David Tombs, Journal for the Study of the New Testament. Supplement series, vol. 186 (Sheffield: Sheffield Academic Press, 1999), 59. See 4 Macc. 8–17.

[81] *1 Enoch* 1:8; 25–27; 37 71 does not make it clear, although in various places it mentions a future world to come where the righteous will dwell. This would imply physical resurrection since the future world is analogous in form, without the sin element, with the present world.

[82] The translation is accessed from OakTree Software: Accordance 7.4, electronic book R. H. Charles, "Old Testament Pseudepigrapha," (Oxford: The Clarendon Press, 1913).

[83] Wright points this out but did not include Dan. 7:13 (*Resurrection of God*, 155).

[84] For the highly debatable Wisdom of Solomon passages that may or may not refer to physical resurrection see Ibid., 162–74.

[85] On another occasion the question asked how a person can live again since in death he turns to dust. In *bSanh* 90b–91a it is answered, "*Queen Cleopatra asked R. Meir, saying, 'I know that the dead will live, for it is written, 'And [the*

righteous] shall blossom forth out of your city like the grass of the earth' [Psa. 72:16]. 'But when they rise, will they rise naked or in their clothing?' He said to her, 'It is an argument a fortiori based on the grain of wheat.' 'Now if a grain of wheat, which is buried naked, comes forth in many garments, the righteous, who are buried in their garments, all the more so [will rise in many garments]!' *Caesar said to Rabban Gamaliel, 'You maintain that the dead will live. But they are dust, and can the dust live?' His daughter said to him, "Allow me to answer him:* 'There are two potters in our town, one who works with water, the other who works with clay. Which is the more impressive?' He said to her, 'The one who works with water.' She said to him, 'If he works with water, will he not create even more out of clay?' *A Tannaite authority of the house of R. Ishmael [taught],* '[Resurrection] is a matter of an argument a fortiori based on the case of a glass utensil.' 'Now if glassware, which is the work of the breath of a mortal man, when broken, can be repaired, 'A mortal man, who is made by the breath of the Holy One, blessed be he, how much the more so [that he can be repaired, in the resurrection of the dead]'" (italics original).

[86] In these quotations the word Sadducees appears in some manuscript. See Efraim E. Urbach, *The Sages, Their Concepts and Beliefs*, trans. Israel Abrahams, World and Wisdom of the Rabbis of the Talmud (Cambridge, MA: Harvard University Press, 1987), 652; Wright, *Resurrection of God*, 135 n. 17–19. Perhaps these texts should be understood as a rabbinic polemic against the Sadducee notion that any form of resurrection was impossible.

[87] Wright mentions *mBerakhot* 4:1–5:5 and records the translation of the prayer from S. Singer, *The Authorized Daily Prayer Book of the Hebrew Congregations of the British Commonwealth of Nations* (London: Eyre and Spottiswood, 1962), 46–47 (*Resurrection of God*, 146).

[88] Wright, *Resurrection of God*, 177, see also 178–81. See also N. T. Wright, *The New Testament and the People of God*, vol. 1 (Minneapolis: Fortress Press, 1992), 324–27. Wright points out in numerous places the common Pharisaic belief in the resurrection that was obviously also Paul's since he was a Pharisee (Josephus, *The Jewish War* 2.163; Josephus, *The Antiquities of the Jews* 18:14).

[89] Wright reaches this conclusion after investigating the following passages: Josephus, *The Jewish War* 2.151; 153 [compare with 2 Macc. 7:11, 29]; 154–8; Josephus, *The Antiquities of the Jews* 18.18 (*Resurrection of God*, 185-86).

[90] Puech, *La croyance des Esséniens en la vie future*. This was noted by Wright (*Resurrection of God*, 186).

[91] Paragraphs two and three are translated by Geza Vermes and appear in Wright, *Resurrection of God*, 186. Where brackets and ellipsis appear, the text

is missing and the probable words that fit the context are added.

92 The translation of paragraphs four and five are from the electronic version of Accordance 7.4 Michael O. Wise, Jr. Martin G. Abegg, and Edward M. Cook, "The Dead Sea Scrolls: A New English Translation," (New York: HarperCollins Publishers, 1996).

93 Philip Jenkins, *Hidden Gospels: How the Search for Jesus Lost Its Way* (Oxford: Oxford University Press, 2001), 80. See Scrolls 1QSa, 1Q28a, and the complete 4Q521 in Wise, Martin G. Abegg, and Cook, "The Dead Sea Scrolls: A New English Translation."

94 Wright, *Resurrection of God*, 189. See also Puech, *La croyance des Esséniens en la vie future*, 791–92; Wright, *New Testament and the People of God*, 203–9.

95 Levy Yitzhak Rahmani, *A Catalogue of Jewish Ossuaries in the Collections of the State of Israel*, ed. Ayala Sussmann and Peter Schertz (Jerusalem: Israel Antiquities Authority, 1994), 53. Rachael Hachlili also says, "One of the main Jewish burial rites characterizing the Second Temple period is the *Ossilegium*, a deliberate procedure of gathering the skeletal remains of an individual after the decay of flesh and placing them in a special container, an ossuary, while retaining this individual burial within the family tomb to await the individual's physical resurrection" (*Jewish Funerary Customs Practices and Rites in the Second Temple Period*, Supplements to the Journal for the Study of Judaism, ed. John J. Collins, vol. 94 [Leiden: E. J. Brill, 2005], 483).

96 Wright, *Resurrection of God*, 147.

97 I am indebted to Wright for this observation. See the *Gospel of Thomas* sayings 11; 21; 29; 37; 51; 71; 87; 112; The *Book of Thomas the Contender* 138:39–139:30; 141:16–19; 142:10–144:19; 145:8–16; The *Epistle to Rheginos* [also known as *Treatise on Resurrection*] 44:13–38; 45:32–46:2; 46:16–47:27; 48:6–16, 34-8; The *Gospel of Philip* 68:31–7 ["true flesh"?]; 56:15–57:8; 59:9–22; 73:1–8. In agreement with Wright, we cannot be sure exactly what the *Gospel of Philip* wanted to say since it is too obscure, but an attempt to harmonize the Jewish concept of bodily resurrection with the Hellenistic belief of a returning soul may be intended, as argued by J. E. Menard, "La notion de résurrection dans l'épître à Rheginos," in *Essays on the Nag Hammadi Texts in Honor of Pahor Labib*, ed. M. Krause (Leiden: E. J. Brill, 1975). See also the *Apocalypse of Peter* 83:6–84:6; the *Apocryphon of James* 7:35–8:84; 14:32–6; *1 Apocalypse of James* 29:16–19; the *Letter of Peter to Philip* 133:15–17; the *Letter of Philip* 134:9–19; 137:6–9; the *Exegesis of the Soul* 134:6–29; the *Gospel of the Savior* 100:7.1–6.

98 *Epistle to Rheginos* 47:2–27; 49:14–24. This is a different rising that occurs to believers as Paul mentions in Romans 6:1–23 and 8:10–13 See Wright, *Resurrection of God*, 540.

[99] See chapter 3 for a discussion of Gnostic literature.

[100] Wright, *Resurrection of God*, 548.

[101] This has been the argument of various scholars today. They seek to smuggle Gnostic books back into the first century by dating them earlier than they actually are and push the NT books into the second century by dating them later than they actually are. This creates an illusion as if orthodoxy and Gnosticism are competing views that coequally existed in the same period. Philip Jenkins says, "As in the case of the 'other gospels,' assertions about the independent authority of the Gnostic tradition rely on misleading claims about the dates of key documents. Basically, the orthodox position is thoroughly spelled out in texts from the first century onward, while the documents which Pagels, King, and others cite to illustrate rival Gnostic concepts are far later, and in many cases assume a knowledge of one or more of the four canonical gospels" (*Hidden Gospels*, 116). See Karen L. King, *The Gospel of Mary Magdala: Jesus and the First Woman Apostle* (Santa Rosa, CA: Polebridge Press, 2003); Elaine Pagels, *The Gnostic Gospels* (New York: Random House, 1979). Gregory Riley argues from the *Gospel of Thomas* that early Christianity denied the bodily resurrection (*Resurrection Reconsidered: Thomas and John in Controversy* [Minneapolis: Fortress Press, 1995], 133–56).

[102] Jenkins, *Hidden Gospels*, 116.

[103] Ibid., 118.

[104] This translation is from the electronic version of Accordance 7.4, Michael William Holmes, ed., *The Apostolic Fathers: Greek Texts and English Translations*, trans. J. B. Lightfoot and J. R. Harmer, 2nd ed. (Grand Rapids: Baker Books, 1992).

[105] Wright, *Resurrection of God*, 481–3.

[106] See how the phrase "enter His kingdom" also appears in *2 Clement* 11:7.

[107] Holmes, ed., *Apostolic Fathers*, 293. This is just one of the suggested dates, but no one knows for sure.

[108] Wright says, "This [passage] could, at a stretch, be understood to be compatible with, say, 2 Corinthians 4 and 5; but it seems more natural to take it as a moderate Platonic statement, not seeing an incorruptible body as a gift from heaven but seeing the immortal soul awaiting a complete immortality, away from the corruptible material world, as a gift which will be enjoyed in heaven itself. Diognetus thus probably articulates the view of personal eschatology which many western Christians still assume to be that of the New Testament." He also acknowledges in a footnote that Hill "suggests, more positively, that though the work does not clearly refer to the resurrection, there is no evidence that the author doubted it" (*Resurrection of God*, 494 n.

78). See Charles E. Hill, *Regnum Caelorum: Patterns of Millennial Thought in Early Christianity*, 2 ed. (Grand Rapids: Wm. B. Erdmans Publishing, 2001), 103.

[109] See the Koran, *Surah* 56:60–61.

[110] Caroline Walker Bynum, *The Resurrection of the Body in Western Christianity, 200–1336* (1995), 54, 57–58.

[111] Wright, *Resurrection of God*, 147. See also Williams, "Contribution of Jewish Inscriptions to the Study of Judaism," 91, as quoted by Wright.

Chapter Eleven

[1] Williams Milligan, *The Resurrection of Our Lord* (New York: Macmillian Company, 1927), 71.

[2] Electronic, "Dictionary," (Apple Computer, 2005).

[3] Accordance 7.4 version electronic sources: Walter Bauer et al., *A Greek English Lexicon of the New Testament and Other Early Christian Literature*, rev. and ed. Frederick William Danker, 3rd ed. (Chicago: University of Chicago Press, 2000); Ludwig Koëhler and Walter Baumgartner, *The Hebrew and Aramaic Lexicon of the Old Testament*, trans. M. E. J. Richardson, rev. Walter Baumgartner and Johann Jakob Stamm ed., ed. M. E. J. Richardson, vol. 2 (Leiden: E. J. Brill, 2001).

[4] Craig R. Koester acknowledged that even if the stories in Kings refer to resuscitation since those in the stories would die again, those involved (like Isaac's deliverance from being sacrificed in Gen. 22) foreshadow the future final resurrection (*Hebrews: A New Translation with Introduction and Commentary*, Anchor Bible, ed. Williams F. Albright and David N. Freedman, vol. 36 [New York: Doubleday, 2001], 514). This was also noted by N. T. Wright, *The Resurrection of God*, Christian Origins and the Question of God, vol. 3 (London: SPCK, 2003), 458 n. 18.

[5] D. J. Wiseman, *1 & 2 Kings: An Introduction and Commentary*, Tyndale Old Testament Commentaries, ed. D. J. Wiseman, vol. 9 (Downers Grove, IL: InterVarsity Press, 1993), 205.

[6] Wright, *Resurrection of God*, 96.

[7] Marvin H. Pope says, "This verse is notoriously difficult. The ancient versions all differ and no reliance can be placed in any of them. Various emendations have been proposed, but are scarcely worth discussing. Many Christian interpreters since Origen have tried to read here an affirmation of immortality or resurrection, but without success: Chrysostom quite correctly refuted this interpretation with the citation of xiv 12ff. If one sticks to the text as received, the given translation appears to fit the context as well as any,

though many problems persist" (*Job*, Anchor Bible, ed. William Foxwell Albright and David Noel Freedman, vol. 15 [Garden City, NY: Doubleday & Company, 1965], 135). For a good bibliography and various view points on this passage see Wright, *Resurrection of God*, 98 n. 63.

[8] Bold type is added for emphasis.

[9] T. J. Meek, "Job 19:25–27," *Vetus Testamentum* 6 (January 1956): 100–3.

[10] Roy B. Zuck, "Job," in *The Bible Knowledge Commentary, Old Testament*, ed. John F. Walvoord and Roy B. Zuck, vol. 1 (Wheaton, IL: Victor Books, 1985; reprint, Colorado Springs: Cook Communications, 1996), 742.

[11] F. Delitzsch said, "The hope of a resurrection as a settled principle in a creed of Israel is certainly more recent than the Solomonic period. Therefore by far the majority of modern expositors have decided that Job does not indeed here avow the hope of the resurrection, but the hope of a future spiritual beholding of God, and therefore of a future life; and thus the popular idea of Hades, which elsewhere has sway over him, breaks out…. This rendering … does not exhaust the meaning of Job's confession" (*The Book of Job*, trans. Francis Bolton, Commentary on the Old Testament in Ten Volumes, ed. C. F. Keil and F. Delitzsch, vol. 4 [reprint, Grand Rapids: Wm. B. Eerdmans Publishing, 1980], 360).

[12] Wright, *Resurrection of God*, 98 n. 63. In another place Wright says regarding Job 19:25–26. "Finally, one of the most blatant denials of the resurrection to be found in the Old Testament, that in Job 14.12, has been altered in the Targum, as in the LXX, so that it only denies the future life of the wicked, leaving the way clear for a resurrection of the righteous—which may indeed be mentioned in the Targum on Job 19.25–26, though this passage, like its Masoretic original, is obscure. As with the main rabbinic writings themselves, so with the Targumim; there is no question but that they insist, again and again, on interpreting scripture in the direction of bodily resurrection" (ibid., 199).

[13] For this view see Isaiah 26:19 in Edward J. Kissane, *The Book of Isaiah*, trans. Edward J. Kissane (Dublin: Richview Press, 1941–43).

[14] Wright says, "But those who seek YHWH in distress find themselves in pangs like a woman giving birth; and when birth comes it turns to be a new birth of the dead themselves (26:16–19)" (*Resurrection of God*, 117).

[15] J. Alec Motyer, *Isaiah: An Introduction and Commentary*, Tyndale Old Testament Commentaries, ed. D. J. Wiseman, vol. 18 (Downers Grove, IL: InterVarsity Press, 1999), 178 (italics his). Others who interpret this as referring to literal bodily resurrection are Arthur S. Herbert, *The Book of the Prophet Isaiah, Chapters 1–39* (Cambridge: University Press, 1973); Kissane, *Isaiah*; John A. Martin, "Isaiah," in *The Bible Knowledge Commentary, Old*

Testament, ed. John F. Walvoord and Roy B. Zuck, vol. 1 (Wheaton, IL: Victor Books, 1985; reprint, Colorado Springs: Cook Communications, 1996), 1075; Harold H. Rowley, *The Faith of Israel: Aspects of Old Testament Thought* (London: SCM Press, 1956), 1160; John Skinner, *The Book of the Prophet Isaiah: Revised Version, with Introduction and Notes*, rev. ed. (Cambridge: University Press, 1915–17).

[16] Wright, *Resurrection of God*, 117; see n. 140 for the names of other scholars. Motyer makes an interesting observation. "The evolutionary supposition that OT thought progressed from poor beginnings to brilliant endings has led to the conclusion that this doctrine of death and resurrection must be late. How insubstantial is all this! The Egyptians had an intricate theology of life after death centuries before Isaiah. Even Canaanite religion, for all its brutishness, depended on the annual triumph of Baal over death. In the name of all logic, how could Israel, with its foundational belief in the living God lack, within revealed religion, what others arrived at by wishful thinking and natural religion?" (*Isaiah*, 178 n. 2). While Motyer is correct in some sense, one must be careful in fully attributing to Israel the "life after death" beliefs of their pagan neighbors since Israel's belief in bodily resurrection was not the same. See Edwin M. Yamauchi, "Tammuz and the Bible," *Journal of Biblical Literature* 84 (September 1965): 283–90.

[17] Some have tried using this passage to prove Ezekiel teaches literal bodily resurrection, and others that it teaches spiritual regeneration. The symbolic two sticks have also been incorrectly interpreted as British Israelites and have also been used to refute them. See John B. Taylor, *Ezekiel: An Introduction and Commentary*, Tyndale Old Testament Commentaries, ed. D. J. Wiseman, vol. 20 (Downers Grove, IL: InterVarsity Press, 1969), 234.

[18] The Qumran community interpreted Ezekiel 37 as metaphor and literal resurrection: "[And I said, 'O LORD,] I have seen many from Israel who have loved Your name and have walked in the ways[of Your heart. So,] when will [th]ese things come to pass? And how will their faithfulness be rewarded?' And the LORD said to me, 'I see the Children of Israel, and they shall know that I am the LORD.' (vacat) [And He said,] 'Son of man, prophecy over these bones, and say, "Come together, bone to its bone and joint [to its joint."' And it wa]s s[o.] And He said a second time, 'Prophecy, and let sinews come upon them and let skin cover [them.' And it was so.] And He s[ai]d, 'Again prophecy to the four winds of the heavens, and a let them blow a wind [upon the slain.' And it was so.] And a great many people [revi]ved (Ezekiel 37:4–10). And they blessed the LORD of hosts wh[o] [had revived them. (vacat) And] I said, 'O LORD, when will [th]ese things come to pass?' And the LORD said to [me, 'Until']" (4Q385 f2:2–9; see also 4Q386

f1:1–10; 4Q388 f8:4–7). This translation comes from the electronic version of Accordance 7.4 Michael O. Wise, Jr. Martin G. Abegg, and Edward M. Cook, "The Dead Sea Scrolls: A New English Translation" (New York: HarperCollins Publishers, 1996). Wright also notes this (*Resurrection of God*, 188–89).

[19] In the following OT passages "sleep" refers to "death": 2 Kgs. 4:31; 13:21; Job 13:13; 14:12; Ps. 13:3; Jer. 51:39, 57; Nah. 3:18. The word "dust" also refers to where the dead will end: Gen. 3:19; Job 19:9; 34:15; Ps. 104:29; Eccl. 3:20; 12:7; Isa. 26:19.

[20] J. Dwight Pentecost makes this point. ("Daniel," in *The Bible Knowledge Commentary, Old Testament*, ed. John F. Walvoord and Roy B. Zuck, vol. 1 [Wheaton, IL: Victor Books, 1985; reprint, Colorado Springs: Cook Communications, 1996], 1372).

[21] Gleason L. Archer, Jr., "Daniel," in *The Expositor's Bible Commentary with the New International Version: Daniel and the Minor Prophets*, ed. F. E. Gaebelein, vol. 7 (Grand Rapids: Zondervan Publishing House, 1985), 152.

[22] Wright, *Resurrection of God*, 110.

[23] Ibid.

[24] The NET Bible recorded in a note on Daniel 12:2, "This verse is the only undisputed reference to a literal resurrection found in the Hebrew Bible" (*The NET Bible: New English Translation*, [Dallas], TX: Biblical Studies Press, 2001], 1608 n.10).

[25] Wright, *Resurrection of God*, 109.

[26] John J. Collins, *Daniel, with an Introduction to Apocalyptic Literature* (Grand Rapids: Wm. B. Eerdmans Publishing, 1984), 391.

[27] Describing one of the parallel accounts (Mark 5:21–43; Luke 8:40–56) will be enough to illustrate the point.

[28] *mKetubot* 4:4 mentions, "R. Judah says, 'Even the poorest man in Israel should not hire fewer than two flutes and one professional wailing woman.'"

[29] David F. Strauss notes that Paulus, Schleiermacher, and Olshausen believe the girl was not dead but asleep (*The Life of Jesus Critically Examined*, trans. Geroge Eliot, Life of Jesus Series, ed. Peter C. Hodgson [Philadelphia: Fortress Press, 1972], 478–79 n. 10).

[30] *BDAG*, 490.

[31] Louis A. Jr. Barbieri, "Matthew," in *The Bible Knowledge Commentary, New Testament*, ed. John F. Walvoord and Roy B. Zuck, vol. 2 (Wheaton, IL: Victor Books, 1985; reprint, Colorado Springs: Cook Communications, 1996), 40.

[32] D. A. Carson, "Matthew," in *The Expositor's Bible Commentary: with The New International Version of the Holy Bible*, ed. Frank E. Gaebelein, vol. 8

(Grand Rapids: Zondervan Publishing House, 1984), 581–82.

33 It appears that Jesus ascended after forty days according to Acts 1:3 instead of fifty days, as Glasscock suggests. Kenneth Barker argues, however, "The number 'forty' in Scripture means a full period of time, a rounded-out period; it does not necessarily mean literally forty calendar days. In this context, then, it means that Jesus appeared to his disciples regularly for a period and then left them permanently" ("Jesus Ascended Into Heaven," in *Fundamentals of Catholicism*, vol. 1 [San Francisco: Ignatius Press, 1995], 78). Without any markers telling us otherwise, it is bets to interpret forty days literally as the actual time when Jesus ascended after rising bodily.

34 Ed Glasscock, *Matthew*, Moody Gospel Commentary (Chicago: Moody Press, 1997), 541.

35 Darrell L. Bock, *Acts*, Baker Exegetical Commentary on the New Testament, ed. Robert W. Yarbrough and Robert H. Stein (Grand Rapids: Baker Academics, 2007), 68.

36 Ibid., 378.

37 Robert L. Thomas, *Revelation 8–22: An Exegetical Commentary* (Chicago: Moody Press, 1995), 96.

Chapter Twelve

1 Quote by Josh McDowell, *Evidence That Demands a Verdict: Historical Evidences for the Christian Faith*, vol. 1 (San Bernardino, CA: Here's Life Publishers, 1972), 167.

2 Josh D. McDowell, *The New Evidence that Demands a Verdict* (Nashville: Thomas Nelson, 1999), 168.

3 Ibid., 144, 167.

4 Ibid., 167.

5 Numerous views exist in how to interpret Ps. 16:8–11: the ancient views, hermeneutical error view, *sensus plenior* view, canonical approach view, typological view, single message view, direct prophecy view. For a thorough description of all these views see Gregory Vance Trull, "Peter's Use of Psalm 16:8–11 in Acts 2:25–32" (Ph.D. diss., Dallas Theological Seminary, 2002), 13–59.

6 Ibid., 133.

7 For a complete analysis of Psalm 16:10 see Gregory Vance Trull, "An Exegesis of Psalm 16:10," *Bibliotheca sacra* 161 (July–September 2004): 304–21.

8 Gregory Vance Trull, "Peter's Interpretation of Psalm 16:8–11 in Acts 2:25–32," *Bibliotheca sacra* 161 (October–December 2004): 447. Peter, how-

ever, acknowledges David's meaning of the shift from the first person pronoun of himself to refer to the third person pronoun as a referent of Messiah, Jesus, by himself inserting the third person pronoun instead of the Hebrew second person pronoun. Δαυὶδ γὰρ λέγει εἰς αὐτόν ("For David says of Him," Acts 2:25). See also Gregory Vance Trull, "Views on Peter's Use of Psalm 16:8–11 in Acts 2:25–32," *Bibliotheca sacra* 161 (April–June 2004) 194–214.

[9] Darrell L. Bock, *Proclamation from Prophecy and Pattern*, Journal for the Study of the New Testament Supplement Series (Sheffield: Sheffield Academic, 1987), 175–76; idem, *Acts*, Baker Exegetical Commentary on the New Testament, ed. Robert W. Yarbrough and Robert H. Stein (Grand Rapids: Baker Academics, 2007), 124–25; Trull, "Peter's Interpretation of Psalm 16:8–11 in Acts 2:25–32," 435; Trull, "Psalm 16:8–11 in Acts 2:25–32," 179 n 13.

[10] Trull said, "The likelihood of ancient Near Eastern religious serving as the source of the Old Testament belief in resurrection seems questionable.... However, the above evidence demonstrates the rich afterlife views of cultures surrounding Israel. Therefore, expressions of physical immortality, perhaps even resurrection ought not be surprising in the Old Testament" ("Psalm 16:8–11 in Acts 2:25–32," 148).

[11] Bock, *Acts*, 125.

[12] Bock says, "Peter's reading presses all the language here in a very literal direction. The text is not about premature death but about not being left in hades. The status of the flesh is part of the text's promise as well. It is Jesus' σὰρξ (*sarx*) that does not see corruption; this stresses the bodily nature of his resurrection" (ibid., 126).

[13] The Babylonian Talmud *Baba Bathra* 1.11 mentions David's tomb being in Jerusalem that was moved there because an underground brook was constantly removing the uncleanness. Herod tried raiding the tomb for money at the time of Antiochus VII (135–34 B.C.), which actions were stopped by fire that killed two guards. "This also led Herod to build a marble memorial to the tomb, and so it was an impressive site in Peter's day. The location was 'probably on the south side of the southeast hill of Jerusalem near the pool of Siloam" (ibid., 126–27). See also I. Howard Marshall, *The Book of Acts: An Introduction and Commentary*, Tyndale New Testament Commentaries, ed. Leon Morris (Grand Rapids: Wm. B. Eerdmans Publishing, 1980; reprint, 2002), 76.

[14] Trull, "Psalm 16:8–11 in Acts 2:25–32," 246–52. I. Howard Marshall also says "it seems likely that *thy Holy One* was understood as a reference to the Messiah (*cf.* 13:35 where the same Psalm is quoted)" (*Acts*, 76). Derek Kidner

further notes, "Admittedly some commentators see here [Ps. 16:9–10] no more than recovery from an illness (*cf.* Is. 38:9–22); but the contrast in Psalms 49 and 73 between the end of the wicked and that of the righteous supports a bolder view. And at its full value, as both Peter and Paul insisted (Acts 2:29ff.; 13:34–37), this language is too strong even for David's hope of his own resurrection. Only 'he whom God raised up saw no corruption'" (*Psalms 1–72: An Introduction and Commentary*, Tyndale Old Testament Commentaries, ed. D. J. Wiseman, vol. 14*a* [Downers Grove, IL: InterVarsity Press, 1973], 86).

[15] Trull, "An Exegesis of Psalm 16:10," 307.

[16] Trull, "Peter's Interpretation of Psalm 16:8–11 in Acts 2:25–32," 448.

[17] Enemies of Jesus' resurrection were not denying that He rose bodily but that He rose then instead of in the anticipated future resurrection when everyone would rise.

[18] John N. Oswalt, *The Book of Isaiah Chapters 40–66*, New International Commentary on the Old Testament, ed. Jr. Robert L. Hubbard (Grand Rapids: Wm. B. Eerdmans Publishing, 1998), 403.

[19] N. T. Wright, *The Resurrection of God*, Christian Origins and the Question of God, vol. 3 (London: SPCK, 2003), 164. A similar argument can be made in Psalm 22 but it seems to be a bit more ambiguous than Isaiah 53:1–12, which refers to the suffering servant that fits the person of Jesus of Nazareth.

[20] William Lane Craig, *Assessing the New Testament Evidence for the Historicity of the Resurrection of Jesus*, Studies in the Bible and Early Christianity, vol. 16 (Lewiston, NY: Edwin Mellen Press, 1989), 9–13.

[21] Though some may say this servant is Cyrus (cf. Isa 44:28), Israel, or a prophet, Oswalt explains it best. "It means exactly what has been talked about throughout the book, but particularly from ch. 49. This man, *my Servant*, is the Anointed of God to restore sinful Israel to himself, just as Cyrus was to the anointed to restore exiled Israel to her land. In contrast to Cyrus, this man's servanthood is redemptive. It finds it [*sic*] true fulfillment in th realization of what the whole sacrificial system prefigured. When an offerer accepted and carried out the provision of God for his guilt as stated in the manual of sacrifice (Lev. 1–11), he could be clean in the sight of God. But that cleansing was only symbolic, because an animal life is no substitute for a human one. Now a human life, yet obviously more than just a human life (he will make 'many' righteous), has been freely given, and the symbol is a reality. Fellowship with God is possible. As the body can come home to the land, so the heart can come home to its God. No prophet could do this for Israel, much less the world, and neither Israel as a whole nor any segment of Israel could do it either. Whoever he is, the Servant stands in the place of

God pronouncing a pardon that the Sinless One alone can offer (51:4–6)" (*The Book of Isaiah Chapters 40-66*, 404–5 [italics his]).
22 Romans 4:24–25 says, "but also for us. It shall be imputed to us who believe in Him who raised up Jesus our Lord from the dead, who was delivered up because of our offenses, and was raised because of our justification." J. Alec Motyer says that because the "Servant's work is successful" (i.e., the sacrificial atonement), the Lord's prolongation of the Servant's life mentioned in Isaiah 53:10 reflects the "resurrection" in Romans 4:25 (*Isaiah: An Introduction and Commentary*, Tyndale Old Testament Commentaries, ed. D. J. Wiseman, vol. 18 [Downers Grove, IL: InterVarsity Press, 1999], 338).
23 Merrill C. Tenney, *The Reality of the Resurrection* (Chicago: Moody Press, 1963), 39.
24 John A. Martin, "Isaiah," in *The Bible Knowledge Commentary, Old Testament*, ed. John F. Walvoord and Roy B. Zuck, vol. 1 (Wheaton, IL: Victor Books, 1985; reprint, Colorado Springs: Cook Communications, 1996), 1109.
25 G. W. Grogan, "Isaiah," in *The Expositor's Bible Commentary with the New International Version: Isaiah, Jeremiah, Lamentation, Ezekiel*, ed. F. E. Gaebelein, vol. 6. (Grand Rapids: Zondervan Publishing House, 1986), 304.
26 Norman L. Geisler and Ronald M. Brooks, *When Skeptics Ask* (Grand Rapids: Baker Books, 1990), 119.
27 See chapters 10–11.
28 See Genesis 5:21–24; Genesis 22:5; Deuteronomy 32:39; 1 Samuel 2:6; Job 19:25–27; Psalms 17; 22; 49; 73. Trull views these as either having an implicit or explicit view of physical resurrection. ("Psalm 16:8–11 in Acts 2:25–32," 148–65).

Chapter Thirteen

1 Hugh J. Schonfield, *The Passover Plot: New Light on the History of Jesus* (New York: Random House, 1965), 163–65.
2 John 1:29, 32; see also Genesis 3:15; Psalm 22; and Isaiah 53:1–12.
3 Hugh J. Schonfield is a British Bible scholar with a doctorate from the University of Glasgow. He has written over forty books. See also Hugh J. Schonfield, *After the Cross* (London: Tantivity Press, 1981).
4 Gary G. Cohen, "The Passover Plot: Verdict, Not Guilty," *Grace Theological Journal* 13 (winter 1972): 33–45; Gary R. Habermas, *The Historical Jesus: Ancient Evidence for the Life of Christ* (Joplin, MO: College Press Publishing, 1996), 69–99.
5 Elmar R. Gruber, *The Jesus Conspiracy: The Turin Shroud and the Truth*

about the Resurrection, trans. Holger Kersten and Elmar R. Gruber (Munich: Langen and Verlag, 1992; reprint, Rockport, MA: Element, 1994), 249–50.

[6] Michael Baigent, *The Jesus Papers: Exposing the Greatest Cover-Up in History* (San Francisco: HarperSanFrancisco, 2006), 126. In summary the more popular views today are wide ranging: "Jesus never died on the cross; he was connected with the Qumran community; someone else changed his message to fit their own desires; he traveled to various parts of the world during the so-called 'silent years' or even after the crucifixion" Habermas, *Historical Jesus*, 69. See also the Appendixes in this book for further analysis.

[7] The Greek word for "beat," κολαφίζω, means "to strike with a fist" and/or "to cause physical impairment." This is much more severe than to "slap," which is a different Greek word ῥάπισμα, meaning "a blow on the face with someone's hand" (Walter Bauer et al., *A Greek English Lexicon of the New Testament and Other Early Christian Literature*, rev. and ed. Frederick William Danker, 3rd ed. [Chicago: University of Chicago Press, 2000], 555, 904).

[8] R. Bucklin, "The Legal and Medical Aspects of the Trial and Death of Christ," *Science Law* 10 (1970): 14–26, quoted in John Ankerberg and Dillon Burroughs, *What's the Big Deal about Jesus?* (Eugene, OR: Harvest House Publishers, 2007), 135. Roman soldier deserters were also flogged.

[9] John P. Mattingly, "Crucifixion: Its Origin and Application to Christ" (Th.M. thesis, Dallas Theological Seminary, 1961), 21. Mayo Foundation holds the copyright for the pictures in this chapter. All rights to these pictures appear in the following article, which belong solely to Mayo Foundations and are used by permission of Mayo Foundation for Medical Education and Research: William D. Edwards, Wesley J. Gabel, and Floyd E. Hosmer, "On the Physical Death of Jesus Christ," *Journal of the American Medical Association* 255 (March 21, 1986): 1455–63.

[10] See http://the-crucifixion.org/scourging.htm#2. Interested researchers are encouraged to visit the site in order to see other documentations regarding the quote.

[11] Mattingly, "Crucifixion: Its Origin and Application to Christ," 36.

[12] Norman L. Geisler and Ronald M. Brooks, *When Skeptics Ask* (Grand Rapids: Baker Books, 1990), 120–30.

[13] Nails of this size driven into the wrist "would crush or server the rather large sensorimotor median nerve. The stimulated nerve would produce excruciating bolts of fiery pain in both arms" (Edwards, Gabel, and Hosmer, "On the Physical Death of Jesus Christ," 1460).

[14] Gary R. Habermas and Michael R. Licona, *The Case for the Resurrection of Jesus* (Grand Rapids: Kregel Publications, 2004), 102. He notes, "The many physicians who have studied crucifixion over the years have invariably con-

cluded that the major problem faced by victims of crucifixion was breathing, or more precisely—asphyxiation. Once on the cross, the victim would want to take the pressure off his nailed feet. To do this, he would allow the weight of his body to be held up by his nailed hands. However, in this 'down' position, certain muscles would be in the inhalation position, making it difficult to exhale. Thus, the victim would have to push up on his pierced feet in order to exhale. However, the first several times he did this would cause intense pain, since it would cause the nail to tear through the flesh in the feet until it enlodged itself against one of the bones. Thus, the crucifixion victim would be seen pushing up quite often and retuning to the down position. Sever muscle cramps and spasms would also make breathing all the more difficult and painful" (ibid., 101) See also Edwards, Gabel, and Hosmer, "On the Physical Death of Jesus Christ," 1461.

[15] Gruber, *Jesus Conspiracy*, 249.

[16] *BDAG*, 682–3.

[17] Edwards, Gabel, and Hosmer, "On the Physical Death of Jesus Christ," 1463.

[18] Josh McDowell, *Evidence That Demands a Verdict: Historical Evidences for the Christian Faith*, vol. 1 (San Bernardino, CA: Here's Life Publishers, 1972), 198–99.

[19] Habermas, *Historical Jesus*, 73. See David F. Strauss, *A New Life of Jesus*, vol. 2 (London: Williams and Norgate, 1865), 408–12.

[20] Wilbur M. Smith, *Therefore Stand: Christian Apologetics* (Grand Rapids: Baker Book House, 1965), 370–71.

[21] John Ankerberg and John Weldon, *The Passion and the Empty Tomb* (Eugene, OR: Harvest House Publishers, 2005), 42–43.

[22] Josephus, *The Jewish Wars* 4:51; Cicero *Against Verres* 2.5.64 cited by Gerard S. Sloyan, *The Crucifixion of Jesus: History, Myth, Faith* (Minneapolis: Fortress Press, 1977), 13. See also Martin Hengel, *Crucifixion* (Philadelphia: Fortress Press, 1977), 8.

[23] See Hengel, *Crucifixion*, 8–9.

[24] Josephus, *The Antiquities of the Jews* 18:64 (18.3.3.64) taken from Accordance 7.4 of the electronic volume, Flavius Josephus, *The Works of Josephus: Complete and Unabridged*, trans. William Whiston, New Updated ed. (Peabody, MA: Hendrickson Publishers, 1987).

[25] Tacitus, *Annals* 15.44 (A.D. 115), cited in Habermas and Licona, *Case for the Resurrection of Jesus*, 59.

[26] Lucian of Samosata, *The Death of Peregrine*, 11–13 (A.D. 150–175) cited in ibid.

[27] This translation is in Alexander Roberts, James Donaldson, and A.C.

Coxe, eds., *The Ante-Nicene Christian Library: Translations of the Writings of the Fathers Down to A.D. 325*, trans. A. Roberts, J. Donaldson, and A.C. Coxe (Oak Harbor, OR: Logos Research Systems, 1997), cited in Habermas and Licona, *Case for the Resurrection of Jesus*, 59.

28 *bSanhedrin* 43a (6.2.1e) translation from Accordance 7.4 electronic volume Jacob Neusner, *The Babylonian Talmud: A Translation and Commentary* (Peabody, MA: Hendrickson Publishers, 2005).

29 John D. Crossan, *Jesus: A Revolutionary Biography* (San Francisco: Harper SanFrancisco, 1994), 145, see also 154–55, 196, 201.

30 Gerd Lüdemann, *The Resurrection of Christ: A Historical Inquiry* (Amherst, NY: Prometheus Books, 2004), 50.

31 James D. Tabor, *The Jesus Dynasty: The Hidden History of Jesus, His Royal Family and the Birth of Christianity* (New York: Simon & Schuster, 2006), 230 (italics his). Hence Habermas concludes, "Such strange 'twists' to the swoon theory have been virtually ignored by scholars with good reason, for serious problems invalidate each of these theses" (*Historical Jesus*, 93).

32 Smith, *Therefore Stand*, 373–74.

33 These eight points are taken from William Lane Craig, *The Son Rises: The Historical Evidence for the Resurrection of Jesus* (Chicago: Moody Press, 1981), 45–90; and *idem*, *Reasonable Faith: Christian Truth and Apologetics*, rev. ed. (Chicago: Moody Press, 1984; reprint, Wheaton, IL: Crossway Books, 1994), 272–78.

34 Craig, *Reasonable Faith*, 272.

35 N. T. Wright, *The Resurrection of God*, Christian Origins and the Question of God, vol. 3 (London: SPCK, 2003), 321, see also n. 21. Craig says, "Second, the expression 'on the third day' implies the empty tomb. Since no one actually saw Jesus rise from the dead, why did the early disciples proclaim that he had been raised 'on the third day'? The most likely answer is that it was on the third day that the women discovered the tomb of Jesus empty; and so naturally, the resurrection itself came to be dated on that day. In this case, the expression 'on the third day' is a time-indicator pointing to the discovery of the empty tomb" (*Reasonable Faith*, 274).

36 The date one picks depends on how one dates Jesus' death. See Harold W. Hohner, *Chronological Aspects of the Life of Christ* (Grand Rapids: Zondervan Publishing House, 1977), 37.

37 Habermas and Licona, *Case for the Resurrection of Jesus*, 52–53, see also n. 25. See also Craig, *The Son Rises*, 47–51; Habermas, *Historical Jesus*, 29–30, 143–44.

38 Habermas and Licona, *Case for the Resurrection of Jesus*, 53.

39 Craig, *Reasonable Faith*, 274.

40 Craig, *The Son Rises*, 51–52; Craig, *Reasonable Faith*, 274–75.
41 Craig, *Reasonable Faith*, 275.
42 *The Gospel of Peter* 8:28; 9:34–35; 10:38. Christian Maurer, "The Gospel of Peter," in *New Testament Apocrypha*, ed. Wilhelm Schneemelcher, trans. E. McL. Wilson, vol. 1 (Tübingen: J. C. B. Mohr (Paul Siebeck), 1990; reprint, Louisville: John Knox Press, 1991), 224–25.
43 Craig, *Reasonable Faith*, 275–76.
44 Matthew 28:1–8; Mark 16:1–8; Luke 24:1–10; John 20:1–8.
45 Accordance 7.4 electronic volume Josephus.
46 Accordance 7.4 electronic volume Neusner, "The Babylonian Talmud: A Translation and Commentary."
47 Gary R. Habermas, *The Secret of the Talpiot Tomb: Unravelling the Mystery of the Jesus Family Tomb* (Nashville: Broadman & Holman Publishing, 2007), 72.
48 Gaius Suetonius, *The Twelve Caesars*, trans. Robert Graves, Augustus 44 (New York: Penguin, 1989), 80, cited in Habermas and Licona, *Case for the Resurrection of Jesus*, 73.
49 Habermas and Licona, *Case for the Resurrection of Jesus*, 73 (italics his). See also Craig, *The Son Rises*, 77–78.
50 Craig, *Reasonable Faith*, 277.
51 Mark 14:30, 47 [John 18:10], 50–51, 66–72.
52 Louis A. Jr. Barbieri, "Matthew," in *The Bible Knowledge Commentary, New Testament*, ed. John F. Walvoord and Roy B. Zuck, vol. 2 (Wheaton, IL: Victor Books, 1983; reprint, Colorado Springs: Cook Communications, 1996), 93.
53 Craig, *Reasonable Faith*, 277–78.

Chapter Fourteen

1 Clark Pinnock, "A Dialogue on Christ's Resurrection," *Christianity Today*, April 12, 1968, 11.
2 Simcha Jacobovici and Charles Pellegrino, *The Jesus Family Tomb: The Discovery, the Investigation, and the Evidence That Could Change History* (San Francisco, CA: HarperSanFrancisco, 2007), 70–71.
3 For a chronological chart pinpointing these appearances see Louis A. Barbieri, Jr., "Matthew," in *The Bible Knowledge Commentary, New Testament*, ed. John F. Walvoord and Roy B. Zuck (Wheaton, IL: Victor Books, 1983; reprint, Colorado Springs: Cook Communications, 1996), 91. Twelve appearances rather than 10 may be counted if one includes Paul's vision of Jesus on the road to Damascus in Acts 9:1–9 and the witness of the

500 believers (1 Cor. 15:6). See John Ankerberg and John Weldon, *The Passion and the Empty Tomb* (Eugene, OR: Harvest House Publishers, 2005), 64–65.

[4] For an orderly account of how these events progressed see J. Dwight Pentecost, *The Words and Works of Jesus Christ: A Study of the Life of Christ* (Grand Rapids: Zondervan Publishing House, 1981), 496–97.

[5] See the discussion in chapter 13.

[6] Pentecost, *Words and Works of Jesus Christ*, 496.

[7] J. Carl Laney, *John*, Moody Gospel Commentary, ed. Paul Enns (Chicago: Moody Press, 1992), 360–61.

[8] Raymond E. Brown, *The Gospel According to John (XII–XXI)*, Anchor Bible, ed. W. F. Albright and D. N. Freedman (New York, NY: Doubleday, 1969), 987.

[9] Pentecost, *Words and Works of Jesus Christ*, 496.

[10] Scholars debate whether Mark 16:9–20 was originally part of the Gospel or whether it was added later. Even if one accepts that it was added later, that does not mean it was not part of the original Gospel at one point. Since all Bibles carry the longer ending and that is what people continue to read, I assume its inclusion since it serves (whether or not it belongs here) to show the common first-century belief in Jesus' physical resurrection. However for further studies see William R. Farmer, *The Last Twelve Verses of Mark* (Cambridge: Cambridge University Press, 1974); Kelly R. Iverson, "A Further Word on Final Γάρ," *Catholic Biblical Quarterly* 68 (January 2006): 79–94; J. Carl Laney, *Answers to Tough Questions From Every Book of the Bible: A Survey of Problem Passages* (Grand Rapids: Kregel Publications, 1997), 217; Bruce M. Metzger, *A Textual Commentary on the Greek New Testament*, 2d ed. (Stuttgart: Biblia Druck, 1994), 102–7.

[11] See chapter 13.

[12] Walter Bauer et al., *A Greek English Lexicon of the New Testament and Other Early Christian Literature*, rev. and ed. Frederick William Danker, 3rd ed. (Chicago: University of Chicago Press, 2000), 272–73.

[13] Joel B. Green sees a similar contrast between Jesus and Philip's disappearance (*The Gospel of Luke*, New International Commentary on the New Testament, ed. Gordon D. Fee [Grand Rapids: Wm. B. Eerdmans Publishing, 1997], 850).

[14] See my explanation of Romans 1:4 of Jesus' glorified state in René A. Lopez, *Romans Unlocked: Power to Deliver* (Springfield, MO: 21st Century Press, 2005), 32-33. Of course, this in itself does not disprove He was not spiritually resurrected, since angels are spirits that can materialize and dematerialize; but it does not prove that Jesus was spiritually resurrected either, especially when

considering all of the evidence in the Gospel accounts and background research which points to bodily resurrection as the best option. See Appendix B.

[15] Darrell L. Bock, *Luke 9:51—24:53*, Baker Exegetical Commentary on the New Testament (Grand Rapids: Baker Books, 1996), 1933. See Appendix B.

[16] Ibid., 1934.

[17] Ibid.

[18] Ibid., 1935.

[19] C. K. Barrett, *The Gospel According to John: An Introduction with Commentary and Notes on the Greek Text*, 2 ed. (Philadelphia, PA: Westminster Press, 1955; reprint, 1978), 572. Tabor, however, argues that Jesus' body can be viewed like that of angels materializing. See Appendix B.

[20] Frederick L. Godet correctly interprets the point of the section. "That Jesus intended, however, to teach some lesson of dependence on His wisdom and guidance as related to the future work of the apostles, and as, in some sense, preparatory for what was to be said to Peter, is to be regarded as probable" (*Commentary on the Gospel of John: Vol. 2 John 6 to End*, trans. Timothy Dwight, Classic Commentary Library [n.p.: Funk & Wagnalls, 1893; reprint, Grand Rapids: Zondervan Publishing House, n.d.], 538).

[21] Ed Glasscock, *Matthew*, Moody Gospel Commentary (Chicago: Moody Press, 1997), 552.

[22] *BDAG*, 252.

[23] Craig L. Blomberg, *Matthew*, The New American Commentary: An Exegetical and Theological Exposition of Holy Scripture, ed. David S. Dockery (Nashville: Broadman Press, 1992), 430; I. P. Ellis, "But Some Doubted," *New Testament Studies* 14 (July 1968): 574–80. Ankerberg sees Jesus appearing to the 500 witnesses as a separate event (*Passion and the Empty Tomb*, 65).

[24] N. T. Wright, *The Resurrection of God*, Christian Origins and the Question of God, vol. 3 (London: SPCK, 2003), 560 n. 22.

[25] Because of time, space and limited scope of this book, I have chosen to deal only with the crucial and most used passage to defend the spiritual resurrection view. For a comprehensive treatment covering other passages (e.g., 2 Cor. 4–5:10), which do not contradict the exegesis and conclusions arrived here, see ibid., 209–309, 361–72.

[26] See Otto Pfleiderer, *Paulinism: A Contribution to the History of Primitive Christian theology*, trans. Edward Peters, vol. 1 (London: Williams and Norgate, 1877), 201; Johannes Weiss, *Earliest Christianity: A History of the Period A.D. 30-150*, trans. Frederick C. Grant, vol. 2 (New York: Harper Collins, 1959), 535. "Startling, since all exegetical, theological, and lexicographical evidence is against it, Louw and Nida astonish us by placing 15:44 almost alone in a

short sub-category under the heading 'pertaining to not being physical'" (Anthony C. Thiselton, *The First Epistle to the Corinthians: A Commentary on the Greek Text*, New International Greek Testament Commentary, ed. I. Howard Marshall and Donald A. Hagner [Grand Rapids: Wm. B. Eerdmans Publishing, 2000], 1277). See J. P. Louw and E. A. Nida, *Lexical Semantics of the Greek New Testament: A Supplement to the Greek-English Lexicon of the New Testament Based on Semantic Domains*, vol. 1 (Atlanta: Scholars Press, 1992), 694, sect. 79–3.

[27] Darrell L. Bock and Daniel B. Wallace, *Dethroning Jesus: Exposing Popular Culture's Quest to Unseat the Biblical Christ* (Nashville: Thomas Nelson, 2007), 211 (italics theirs).

[28] See chapter 10. Wright makes this point that creation was redeemed by the new bodily resurrection (*Resurrection of God*, 313–14). See also Ben Witherington III, *Jesus, Paul and the End of the World* (Downers Grove, IL: InterVarsity Press, 1992), 185.

[29] "Philosophers made distinctions between different kinds of substance, but they did not draw the line in the same place that modern western thought has done, between 'physical' and 'non-physical'" (Wright, *Resurrection of God*, 348–49).

[30] Thiselton, *1 Corinthians*, 1276. He notes, "This is confirmed by… the generally accepted modal use of ἐάν in the sets of contrasts."

[31] Wright, *Resurrection of God*, 347.

[32] In fact, Thiselton observes, "On rare (always non-Pauline) occasions in the New Testament, πνεῦμα may denote a ghost or spirit being (almost exclusively Mark 14:26; Luke 24:37; Acts 23:8), but such a use is generally avoided because of its association with evil spirits (Mark 9:25; cf. Mark 1:34, δαίμων)" (*1 Corinthians*, 1276).

[33] Charles L. Quarles also notes, "In other contexts it is clear that they do not refer to persons or objects as either made of matter or spirit. In 1 Corinthians 2:14–15, for example, the terms refer respectively to people influenced by human drives versus people under the control of the Spirit. It is likely that Paul's use in 1 Corinthians 15:44 is related to this earlier use" (*Buried Hopes or Risen Savior: Is the Talpiot Tomb the Burial Place of Jesus of Nazareth?* (online:https://www.lacollege.edu/ifl/jesus_tomb.pdf, March 4, 2007, accessed October 18, 2007), 12.

[34] Paul used *pneumatikos* ten times in 1 Corinthians (2:13, 15; 3:1; 9:11; 10:3; 12:1; 14:1, 37; 15:44, 46).

[35] Elsewhere in the letter Paul contrasted believers to unbelievers as they are controlled by carnal desires and thus act like unbelievers. See René A. López, "Does the Vice List in 1 Corinthians 6:9-10 Describe Believers

or Unbelievers?," *Bibliotheca sacra* 164 (January-March 2007): 59–73. "The overall structure and logic of the chapter thus confirms what we would have guessed from the direction in which the rest of the letter points: that this is intended by Paul as a long argument in favour of a future *bodily* resurrection.... Paul repeatedly indicates earlier in the letter that Christian behaviour in the present life is predicated upon continuity between this life and the future one. It would be surprising if now, addressing the issue head on at last, he were to undermine what he said all along. There was, in any case, no indication in Judaism either before or after Paul that 'resurrection' could mean anything other than 'bodily'; if Paul was going to argue for something so oxymoronic as a '*non*-bodily resurrection' he would have done better not to structure his argument in such a way as to give the appearance of articulating a Pharisaic, indeed biblical, worldview in which the goodness of the present creation is reaffirmed in the age to come. Since that is the kind of argument he has composed, at the conclusion of a letter which constantly points this way, no question should remain. When Paul said 'resurrection,' he meant 'bodily resurrection'" (Wright, *Resurrection of God*, 314).

[36] A similar observation is made by Quarles, *Buried Hopes or Risen Savior: Is the Talpiot Tomb the Burial Place of Jesus of Nazareth?* (accessed), 12; and Thiselton, *1 Corinthians*, 1276.

[37] Thiselton clarifies the difference between both of these adjectives. "The widely accepted (although not decisive) lexicographical distinction between –ινος endings, which often, perhaps regularly, denote composition, in distinction from –ικος endings, which regularly denote modes of being or characteristics" (*1 Corinthians*, 1276). See also Quarles, *Buried Hopes or Risen Savior: Is the Talpiot Tomb the Burial Place of Jesus of Nazareth?* (accessed), 12.

[38] Thiselton, *1 Corinthians*, 1277. See also Eduard Schweizer, "πνευματικός," in *Theological Dictionary of the New Testament*, ed. Gerhard Friedrich and Geoffrey W. Bromiley, trans. Geoffrey W. Bromiley, vol. 6 (Grand Rapids: Wm. B. Eerdmans Publishing, 1968; reprint, 1999), 389–455.

[39] Thiselton, *1 Corinthians*, 1276 (iltalics his).

[40] F. F. Bruce, *1 & 2 Corinthians*, Life Application Bible Commentary, ed. Grant R. Osborne (Wheaton, IL: Tyndale House, 1999), 152.

[41] C. K. Barrett, *A Commentary on the First Epistle to the Corinthians*, Harper's New Testament commentaries. (New York: Harper & Row, 1968), 372.

[42] See David E. Garland, *1 Corinthians*, Baker Exegetical Commentary on the New Testament, ed. Robert W. Yarbrough and Robert H. Stein (Grand

Rapids: Baker Academic, 2003), 734.

[43] For an explanation of the "new man" in all regenerate Christians see Lopez, *Romans Unlocked*, 129–31.

[44] "Body, therefore, affirms the biblical tradition of a positive attitude toward physicality as a condition for experiencing life in its fullness, but also assimilates, subsumes, and transcends the role of the physical in the public domain of the earthly life. Hence it would be appropriate to conceive of the raised body as a form or mode of existence of the whole person including every level of intersubjective communicative experience that guarantees both the continuity of personal identity and enhanced experience of community which facilitates intimate union with God in Christ and with differentiated 'others' who also share this union" (Thiselton, *1 Corinthians*, 1278).

[45] Schweizer also makes a similar observation based on the context. "The idea that σῶμα as a form represents the continuum which simply exchanges the carnal substance for the spiritual substance is also quite untenable. The true concern of Paul may be seen in the fact that ψυχικός (v. 44) on the one side is interpreted by φθορά (v.[sic] 42, 50), ἀσθένεια and ἀτιμία (v. 43; cf. Phil. 3:21 ταπείνωσις), and πνευματικός on the other side is interpreted by ἀφθαρσία (v. [sic] 42, 50), δύναμις and δόξα (v. 43; Phil. 3:21). Behind the form of thinking in terms of substance there thus lies the OT distinction between weakness and power. Man is referred to the creative power of his Lord, who will raise him up. Continuity between the earthly and the heavenly body rests on a miracle. The same is to be seen in v. 47, where the first clause with γῆ denotes that stuff from which the first man is made, while the second clause characterises [sic] the second man, not by the substance of which he consists but by his origin. Thus the σῶμα πνευματικόν of either Redeemer or believer is to be understood, not as one which consists of πνεῦμα, but as one which is controlled by the πνεῦμα" ("πνευματικός," 6:421).

[46] Thiselton, *1 Corinthians*, 1277.

[47] Hence Bock concludes, "In experiential form, this is what Paul discusses conceptually in 1 Cor. 15:35–49, especially 15:41–44.... Paul's point is that another force is the key to the resurrection body; it is a 'spiritual' body as opposed to a 'soulish' body. This is why it is more than flesh and bone and can be immortal." Then he points out that the resurrection bodies of believers will be similar in that of Jesus' body. "The resurrection body is flesh and bone transformed into a form that is able to move through material matter.... There is no way to distinguish the person of Jesus from the risen Christ except that his existence now takes place at an additional dimension of reality. They are basically one and the same. A spirit has not taken his place, nor is he just a spirit. The

person buried in the tomb is raised and transformed, but Jesus is sufficiently distinct in appearance that he is not always immediately recognizable. In his resurrected state, he clearly is transformed, though in a way that still leaves traces of his former existence (e.g., the nail prints in his hands and feet)" (Darrell L. Bock, *Luke 9:51—24:53*, Baker Exegetical Commentary on the New Testament [Grand Rapids: Baker Books, 1996], 1933–34). Paul Lampe also said, "For him, the term 'spiritual' emphasizes that God's Spirit is the *only* force that creates the new body. The creation of this new body is totally *beyond* all the possibilities of the present nature and creation. That is all that Paul wants to convey with this term. Therefore I do not see how the natural sciences could help us to understand the totally different 'nature' of this future body—unless natural science were able to transcend the nature of this universe. Paul asserts that our spiritual body will be very similar, even 'conformed' (*symmorphon*), to that of the resurrected Christ (Phil. 3:21). But he refrains from giving further details, which later evangelicals pretend to 'know' by describing the resurrected Christ. The apostle only affirms that our spiritual body 'in heaven' will be a 'body of glory' as opposed to the 'body of lowliness' in which we now live (Phil. 3:20–21)" ("Paul's Concept of a Spiritual Body," in *Resurrection: Theological and Scientific Assessments:*, ed. Ted Peters, Robert John Russel, and Michael Welker [Grand Rapids: Wm. B. Eerdmans Publishing, 2002], 109 [italics his]). See Appendix B.

Chapter Fifteen

[1] Josh McDowell, *A Ready Defense* (San Bernardino, CA: Here's Life Publishers, 1990), 231.
[2] Ibid.
[3] James B. Conant, *Science and Common Sense* (New Haven, CT: Yale University Press, 1951), 25.
[4] Josh McDowell, *The Resurrection Factor: Does the Historical Evidence Support the Resurrection of Jesus Christ?* (San Bernardino, CA: Here's Life Publishers, 1981), 21 (italics added).
[5] Josh McDowell, *More Than a Carpenter* (Wheaton, IL: Tyndale House Publishers, 1977), 38–39. See also John Ankerberg and John Weldon, *The Passion and the Empty Tomb* (Eugene, OR: Harvest House Publishers, 2005), 97–113.
[6] N. T. Wright, "The Resurrection: Historical Event or Theological Explanation? A Dialogue," in *The Resurrection of Jesus: John Dominic Crossan and N. T. Wright in Dialogue*, ed. Robert B. Stewart (Minneapolis: Fortress Press, 2006), 23.

[7] For an excellent scholarly discussion on numerous scientific-based arguments and the resurrection see Ted Peters et al., eds., *Resurrection: Theological and Scientific Assessments* (Grand Rapids: Wm. B. Eerdmans Publishing, 2002).

[8] McDowell, *A Ready Defense*, 231.

[9] Norman L. Geisler and Ronald M. Brooks, *When Skeptics Ask* (Grand Rapids: Baker Books, 1990), 124.

[10] John R. W. Stott, *Basic Christianity* (Downers Grove, IL: InterVarsity Press, 1971), 51.

[11] A. T. Robertson, *The Gospel According to Matthew*, Word Pictures in the New Testament, vol. 4 (Grand Rapids: Baker Book House, 1931), 239.

[12] McDowell, *A Ready Defense*, 230.

[13] Robertson, *Matthew*, 239.

[14] McDowell, *A Ready Defense*, 233.

[15] The information in this section is from John Foxe, *The New Foxe's Book of Martyrs*, rewritten and updated by Harold J. Chadwick ed. (Gainesville, FL: Bridge-Logos Publishers, 2001), 3–10. Of this list we only possess reliable evidence of martyrs 1. Stephen, 2. James the son of Zebedee, 4. James the less (who was killed in A.D. 62 not in A.D. 66), 8. Peter, and 9. Paul. All of the rest of the accounts are based on legendary hagiography. Foxe's list is used because of its popularity. For a better list of authentic martyr accounts see Herbert A. Musurillo, *The Acts of the Christian Martyrs* (Oxford: Clarendon Press, 1972). I am indebted to Edwin M. Yamauchi who pointed this out.

[16] Gary R. Habermas and Michael R. Licona, *The Case for the Resurrection of Jesus* (Grand Rapids: Kregel Publications, 2004), 59. "A skeptic may reply, 'How do you know they *willingly* died for their beliefs? What if they were arrested and executed against their will and perhaps even recanted under torture before they died?' This is a fair question. From the early martyrdoms of Stephen and James the brother of John as well as the imprisonments and sufferings of Peter, Paul, and others, the disciples became well aware that publicly proclaiming Jesus as risen Lord in certain times and places made sufferings and, perhaps, martyrdom inevitable. Therefore, to continue on this path, fully aware of the probable outcome, was to demonstrate a *willingness* to endure suffering and martyrdom, regardless of whether these were actually experienced. Furthermore, the primary purpose of getting someone to recant under torture is to gain evidence by which to discourage others publicly. Recantation under torture would not necessarily indicate a change in the victim's mind. Nevertheless, there is no evidence of a recantation being announced. Instead, all the reports testify to steadfast courage during suffering. If the news spread that several of the original disciples had recanted, we could expect that

Christianity would have been dealt a severe blow. If those in management of a publicly traded company are bailing out, the workers are not going to dump their life savings into the company stock. And yet we find early Christians willingly suffering and dying for their beliefs" (ibid., 59–60 [italics theirs]).

[17] Romans; 1 Corinthians; 2 Corinthians; Galatians; Ephesians; Philippians; Colossians; 1 Thessalonians; 2 Thessalonians; 1 Timothy; 2 Timothy; Titus; Philemon. Though many regard Hebrews as Pauline, I prefer not to include it. And though others believe the pastoral letters (1 and 2 Tim. and Titus, and perhaps others) are not Pauline I have chosen to include these traditionally accepted Pauline Epistles.

[18] Habermas and Licona, *Case for the Resurrection of Jesus*, 65.

[19] Elias Andrews, in *The Encyclopaedia Britannica*, vol. 17 (Chicago: William Benton Publisher, 1970), 469; Archibald MacBride, *Chamber's Encyclopedia*, vol. 10 (London: Pergamon Press, 1966), 516, quoted in McDowell, *More Than a Carpenter*, 86.

[20] Norval Geldenhuys, *Commentary on the Gospel of Luke*, The New International Commentary on the New Testament, ed. F. F. Bruce (Grand Rapids: Wm. B. Eerdmans Publishing, 1951), 628.

[21] For a good discussion of the early martyrs see http://www.letusreason.org/Doct13.htm.

[22] This testimony in a revised form appeared in René A. López, "Change: Not Mission Impossible," *Kindred Spirit*, Summer 2005, 1–2. It also appears online in http://scriptureunlocked.com/pdfs/Change-Its-Not-A-Mission-Impossible.pdf.

Chapter Sixteen

[1] Darrell L. Bock and Daniel B. Wallace, *Dethroning Jesus: Exposing Popular Culture's Quest to Unseat the Biblical Christ* (Nashville: Thomas Nelson, 2007), 212.

[2] David Horowitz, *Editor's Notes: Giving 'Jesus' the Silent Treatment* (online: http://www.jpost.com/servlet/Satellite?cid=1171894551868&pagename=JPost%2FJPArticle%2FShowFull, March 3, 2007, accessed June 21, 2007). See also Tim McGirk, *Jesus 'Tomb' Controversy Reopened* (online: http://www.time.com/time/world/article/0,8599,1704299,00.html, January 16, 2008, accessed February 14, 2008).

[3] Horowitz, *Giving 'Jesus' the Silent Treatment* (accessed).

[4] McGirk, *Jesus 'Tomb' Controversy Reopened* (accessed).

[5] Ibid. (accessed).

6 Eric M. Meyers and Jodi Magness, *The Talpiot Tomb Controversy Revisited* (online:http://ntgateway.com/weblog/2008/01/talpiot-tomb-controversy-revisited.html, January 21, 2008, accessed February 24, 2008). See also the following article titled "Back to Talpiot" that Jodi Magness alerted me to: http://www.heardworld. com/higgaion /?p=943

7 McGirk, *Jesus 'Tomb' Controversy Reopened* (accessed).

8 David Horowitz, *Editor's Notes: It Should Have Elicited a 'WoW'!* (online: http://www.jpost.com/servlet/Satellite?apage=1&cid=120 1070788587&pagename=JPost%2FJPArticle%2FShowFull, January 25, 2008, accessed February 14, 2008).

9 See http://www.bib-arch.org/Tomb/bswbTombFuchs.asp; http://www.bible review.org/Tomb/bswbTombPrinceton.asp; http://www.biblicalarchaeology. org/tomb/bswbTombCharlesworth2.asp; http://www.archaeologyodyssey. org/tomb/bswbTombCohen2.asp; http://www.bib-arch.org/tomb/bswbTomb Dubious.asp; http://www.biblereview.org/Tomb/bswbTombJacobovici2.asp; h ttp://www.biblicalarchaeology.org/tomb/bswbTomb Claim.asp. There are many more issues discussed that date earlier than the discussions that appear in these sites.

10 Dillon Burroughs, *The Jesus Family Tomb Controversy: How the Evidence Falls Short* (Ann Arbor, MI: Nimble Books LCC, 2007), 93.

Appendix A

1 F. David Farnell succinctly notes this very thing through the anti-supernatural philosophical bias that has always existed: "Philosophical opposition to the supernatural is not new. Paul encountered such in Athens (Acts 17:16-34), for his biblical world-view included the resurrection of the material body, but that his philosophical listeners had no room for the supernatural. Philosophy's clash with Christianity in the New Testament appears in Colossians, 1 John, 2 Peter, Jude, and Revelation 2–3. It emerged early in the post-Apostolic church and continued through the Middle Ages. It was not until the Reformation corrected hermeneutical abuses of philosophy that a resolution of the problem surfaced. But just after a hundred years after the Reformers, philosophy reasserted itself to haunt the church" ("Philosophical and Theological Bent of Historical Criticism," in *The Jesus Crisis: The Inroads of Historical Criticism into Evangelical Scholarship*, ed. Robert L. Thomas and F. David Farnell [Grand Rapids: Kregel Publications, 1998], 85). See also Norman L. Geisler, "Inductivism, Materialism, and the Rationalism: Bacon, Hobbes, and Spinoza," in *Biblical Errancy: An Analysis of Its Philosophical Roots*, ed. Norman L. Geisler (Grand Rapids: Zondervan Publishing House,

1981), 11-19. By noting the helpfulness of Farnell's essay in this section it does not mean I completely endorse all the chapters in the *Jesus Crisis*.

[2] These are not exhaustive but are the ten major philosophical systems foundational to Thomas Hobbes, "Leviathan," in *Great Books of the Western World*, ed. Robert M. Hutchins et al., vol. 23 (Chicago: William Benton, 1952). Usually historical criticism is opposed to an orthodox view of the Bible. These views are thoroughly explained by Farnell, "Philosophical and Theological Bent," 85-131.

[3] See Francis Bacon, "Novum Organum," in *Great Books of the Western World*, 30:133-34.

[4] Farnell, "Philosophical and Theological Bent," 121.

[5] Hobbes, "Leviathan," 41-49.

[6] Farnell, "Philosophical and Theological Bent," 89.

[7] Benedict de Spinoza, "Biographical Note, Benedict de Spinoza," in *Great Books of the Western World*, 31:354.

[8] Colin Brown, *Christianity and Western Thought* (Downers Grove, IL: InterVarsity Press, 1990), 185-86. These terms are noted by Farnell, "Philosophical and Theological Bent," 89.

[9] Farnell, "Philosophical and Theological Bent," 89.

[10] Ibid., 94. Men like Matthew Tindal (1655-1733), John Toland (1670-1722), Anthony Collins (1676-1729), and others also followed this system of thought.

[11] Ernest C. Mossner, *The Life of David Hume*, 2nd ed. (Oxford: Clarendon Press, 1980), 612. David Hume states, "The idea of substance as well as that of a mode, is nothing but a collection of simple ideas, that are united by the imagination, and have a particular name assigned them, by which we are able to recall, either to ourselves or others, that collection," (*A Treatise of Human Nature*, ed. Ernest C. Mossner [New York: Penguin, 1969], 63).

[12] Farnell, "Philosophical and Theological Bent," 97, 99. John Locke (1632-1704), George Berkeley (1685-1753), and others also followed the same system.

[13] Ibid., 100; cf. Immanuel Kant, *Critique of Pure Reason*, ed. Vasilis Politis (New York: Everyman, 1993), 30-68; Colin Brown, *Philosophy and the Christian Faith* (Downers Grove, IL: InterVarsity Press, 1968), 96.

[14] Other promoters of this view include Jean Jacques Rousseau (1712-1778), Johann Wolfgang Goethe (1749-1832), Friedrich Schiller (1759-1805) and Friedrich Hölderlin (1770-1843).

[15] Farnell, "Philosophical and Theological Bent," 103, 106.

[16] Proponents of this philosophy also include Johann Gottlieb Fichte (1762-1814) and Friedrich W. J. von Schelling (1775-1854).

[17] Farnell, "Philosophical and Theological Bent," 107.

[18] Charles Darwin, *The Origin of Species by Means of Natural Selection; or, the Preservation of Favored Races in the Struggle for Life* (n.p.: n.p., 1859; reprint, New York: J. A. Hill, 1904); Charles Darwin, *The Descent of Man and Selection in Relation to Sex* (London: J. Murray, 1871).

[19] Farnell correctly acknowledges the origins of Darwinian thought. "To a large extent, the hypothesis of evolution resulted from a presupposition exclusion of God and religion from science and stemmed from the philosophies prevalent immediately before and during the Enlightenment (for example deism, agnostocism, uniformitarianism—'the present is the key to the past and'—and atheism" ("Philosophical and Theological Bent," 110), For a more detail discussion see John C. Hutchinson, "Darwin's Evolutionary Theory and 19th-Century Natural Theology," *Bibliotheca Sacra* 152 (July-September 1995): 334-54.

[20] This is known as the Documentary Hypothesis theory in which scholars seek to determine how the Scriptures were formulated by determining how different terms and phrases are employed and who wrote them. Evolutionary theology, however, ultimately led to the well-known form-critical analysis of the New Testament popularized by Karl L. Schmidt (1891-1956), Martin Dibelius (1883-1947), and Rudolph Bultmann (1884-1976). Form-critical analysis espouses that the Christian community gradually developed the four Gospel accounts from the simplest form—including oral accounts—to a more complex written account.

[21] See Wilhelm Bousset, *Kyrios Christos*, trans. John E. Steely (Nashville: Abingdon Press, 1970). Conceptual parallels appear in a number of pagan religions with that of Christianity. However, many of these parallels are not identical; neither is Christianity dependent on their religious neighbors for their theology. In fact in many cases (e.g., the mystery religions) it can be shown that the opposite is true. For a thorough and excellent treatment showing similarities and distinctions between pagan and Christian religion and thereby demonstrating Christianity's uniqueness see Gregory A. Boyd, *Jesus Under Siege* (Wheaton, IL: Victor Books, 1995), 43-62, and J. Ed Komoszewski, M. James Sawyer, and Daniel B. Wallace, *Reinventing Jesus: How Contemporary Skeptics Miss the Real Jesus and Mislead Popular Culture* (Grand Rapids: Kregel Publications, 2006), 219-62.

[22] For a thorough discussion of these views see Frederick Copleston, *Contemporary Philosophy, Studies of Logical Positivism and Existentialism* (New York: Barnes and Noble, 1972), 148-200, cited in Farnell, "Philosophical and Theological Bent," 113-14.

[23] Søren Kierkegaard, *The Journals of Søren Kierkegaard*, trans. and ed.

Alexander Dru (New York: Harper & Brothers, 1959), 185.

[24] Farnell, "Philosophical and Theological Bent," 115. For more on these issues see Kierkegaard, *Journals of Søren Kierkegaard*, 109; Paul R. Sponheim, *Kierkegaard on Christ and Christian Coherence* (New York: Harper & Row, 1968), 173-264.

[25] Bart D. Ehrman, *Misquoting Jesus: The Story Behind Who Changed the Bible and Why* (San Francisco: HarperSanFrancisco, 2005); James D. Tabor, *The Jesus Dynasty: The Hidden History of Jesus, His Royal Family and the Birth of Christianity* (New York: Simon & Schuster, 2006); Michael Baigent, *The Jesus Papers: Exposing the Greatest Cover-up in History* (San Francisco: HarperSanFrancisco, 2006). Though not as recent as these other contemporary works intent on redefining the historical and biblical Jesus, there are numerous others including Earl Doherty, *Challenging the Verdict* (Ottawa: Age of Reason, 2001); John D. Crossan, *Jesus: A Revolutionary Biography* (San Francisco: Harper SanFrancisco, 1994); Bart D. Ehrman, *The Orthodox Corruption of Scripture: The Effect of Early Christological Controversies on the Text of the New Testament* (Oxford: Oxford University Press, 1993); Burton L. Mack, *The Lost Gospel: The Book of Q and Christian Origins* (San Francisco: Harper SanFrancisco, 1993); M. Baigent and R. Leigh, *The Dead Sea Scrolls Deception* (New York: Summit, 1992); John D. Crossan, *The Historical Jesus: The Life of a Mediterranean Jewish Peasant* (San Francisco: HarperSanFrancisco, 1991); H. Koester, *Ancient Christian Gospels* (Philadelphia: Trinity Press, 1990); Burton L. Mack, *A Myth of Innocence* (Philadelphia: Fortress Press, 1988); Marcus J. Borg, *Jesus: A New Vision* (San Francisco: Harper & Row, 1987); M. Baigent, R. Leigh, and Henry Lincoln, *Holy Blood, Holy Grail* (New York: Dell, 1983); Ron Cameron, *The Other Gospels: Non-Canonical Texts* (Philadelphia: Westminster Press, 1982); H. Koester, *Introduction to the New Testament II: History and Literature of Early Christianity* (Philadelphia: Fortress Press, 1982); J. M. Robinson and H. Koster, *Trajectories through Early Christianity* (Philadelphia: Fortress Press, 1971).

[26] See note 31 for a better idea of how many scholars are involved. The *Jesus Seminar* gives the misguided impression that the majority of scholars agree with them. Actually it is just the opposite.

[27] Robert W. Funk, Roy W. Hoover, and the Jesus Seminar, *The Five Gospels: The Search for the Authentic Words of Jesus*, ed. R. Funk and J. V. Hills (New York: MacMillian Publishing, 1993), 37.

[28] Boyd, *Jesus Under Siege*, 88.

[29] See Ibid., 24; Funk, Hoover, and Seminar, *The Five Gospels*, 1-36, acknowledge this same conclusion.

[30] Komoszewski, Sawyer, and Wallace, *Reinventing Jesus*, 39-50; Craig A. Evans, *Fabricating Jesus: How Modern Scholars Distort the Gospels* (Downers Grove: InterVarsity Press, 2006), 46-51; Craig L. Blomberg, "Where Do We Start Studying Jesus?" in *Jesus Under Fire: Modern Scholarship Reinvents the Historical Jesus*, ed. Michael J. Wilkins and J. P. Moreland (Grand Rapids: Zondervan Publishing House, 1995), 19-22.

[31] Clearly the *Jesus Seminar* gives the impression by the constant use of the word "scholar" that anyone disagreeing with their conclusion is unscholarly. But the opposite is true. "As a matter of fact, a great many scholars, from a wide variety of persuasions, disagree with elements of this highly controversial list of 'pillars.'" Furthermore the *Seminar* also gives the impression that they represent the majority of scholars but they do not. "Indeed, the conclusions of the Jesus Seminar participants are usually representative only of the left-most fringe of the New Testament scholarship" (Boyd, *Jesus Under Siege*, 89-91). Hence, "Sometimes, for example, the phrase 'some two hundred scholars' has occurred. To someone unacquainted with the immensity and complexity of higher education in America, two hundred scholars may seem an impressively large number. In fact, however, it is a very small number when placed against the number of New Testament scholars alone who are involved in the work of SBL (at least half of the 6, 900 members of the organization), let alone the thousands more with substantial scholarly training in the New Testament who for personal or ideological reasons do not take part in the society's activities. And even the number *two hundred* is somewhat misleading, since it includes all of those who were part of the Seminar's proceedings in any fashion—by receiving its mailings, for example, or reading its reports" (Luke Timothy Johnson, *The Real Jesus: The Misguided Quest for the Historical Jesus and the Truth of the Traditional Gospels* [San Francisco, CA: HarperSanFrancisco, 1996], 2). See also pages 1-27 for another thorough analysis of the *Jesus Seminar* movement and its founders.

[32] Boyd, *Jesus Under Siege*, 24-25, 91 (italics his).

[33] Evans, *Fabricating Jesus*, 242, acknowledges this as well.

[34] See Ben Witherington III, *What Have They Done with Jesus? Beyond Strange Theories and Bad History—Why We Can Trust the Bible* (San Francisco: HarperSanFrancisco, 2006), 7, also sees this dichotomy of flesh and spirit played out. Evans explains the details involving the discovery: "At the best investigators can determine, a leather-bound codex (or ancient book), whose pages consist of pyparus, was discovered in the late 1970s perhaps in 1978, in Egypt, perhaps in a cave. For the next five years the codex, written in the Coptic language [Egyptian language written in Greek letters], was passed around the Egyptian antiquities market. In 1983 Stephen Emmel,

a Coptic scholar, ... concluded that the codex was genuine (that is, not a forgery) and that it probably dated to the fourth century. Subsequent scientific test confirmed Emmel's educated guest" (*Fabricating Jesus*, 240). The *Gospel of Judas* actually appears in pages 33-58 in the book (Codex Tchacos) that contains three other tractates.

35 Irenaeus wrote, "They [the Gnostics] declare that Judas the traitor was thoroughly acquainted with these things [i.e., that Cain and others derived their being from above and did not suffer injury], that he alone, knowing the truth as no others did, accomplished the mystery of the betrayal; by him all things, both earthly and heavenly, were thus thrown into confusion. They produce a fictitious history of this kind, which they style the *Gospel of Judas*" (*Against Heresies* 1.31.1).

36 Witherington, *What Have They Done with Jesus?* 8.

37 Komoszewski, Sawyer, and Wallace also note, "These criticisms were made of his earlier major work, *Orthodox Corruption of Scripture*, from which *Misquoting Jesus* has drawn extensively. Yet, the conclusions that he put forth there are still stated here without recognition of some of the severe criticisms of his work the first go-around" (*Reinventing Jesus*, 112). For a complete bibliography of both of Ehrman's books see note 25. See also chapter 10 where Bart D. Ehrman's *Misquoting Jesus* is examined.

38 Ehrman, *Misquoting Jesus*, 11.

39 This topic was discussed in chapter 10. For answers to a similar argument see Komoszewski, Sawyer, and Wallace, *Reinventing Jesus*, 65-73, 275.

40 Ehrman, *Misquoting Jesus*, 208.

41 See Komoszewski, Sawyer, and Wallace, *Reinventing Jesus*, 113-14.

42 Witherington, *What Have They Done with Jesus?* 7. Since Ehrman studied in two locations—which teach the approach explained here—Evans is baffled by Ehrman's position and concludes: "I must admit that I am puzzled by all this. If not at Moody Bible Institute, then surely at Wheaton College, Ehrman must have become acquainted with a great number of textual variants in the biblical manuscripts. No student can earn a degree in Bible and not know this. Yet Bible students are not defecting in droves. I am also puzzled by Ehrman's line of reasoning. For the sake of argument, let's suppose that the scribal errors in the Bible manuscripts really do disprove verbal inspiration and inerrancy, so that the Bible really should be viewed as a *human book* and not as *God's words*. Would we lose everything as a result? No. Moderate and liberal Christians have held essentially this view for a century or more. The real issue centers on what God accomplished in Jesus of Nazareth" (Evans, *Fabricating Jesus*, 27-28). For more on Ehrman's position see ibid., 28-33, and Komoszewski, Sawyer, and Wallace, *Reinventing Jesus*,

110-17. See also chapter 10 that discusses Ehrman's position further.

[43] Tabor, *Jesus Dynasty*, 273-74.

[44] Others have also noticed Tabor's dubious approach (Witherington, *What Have They Done with Jesus?* 299-300; Evans, *Fabricating Jesus*, 217-20).

[45] Witherington, *What Have They Done with Jesus?* 293.

[46] Evans, *Fabricating Jesus*, 217.

[47] Contrary to Baigent and Brown, Tabor admits that Jesus could not have faked His death. He believes this event has biblical and historical support. Citing Mark 16:6; Matthew 28:1-7; and Luke 24:2-5, he concludes, "None of these theories appear to have any basis whatsoever in reliable historical sources. I think we need have no doubt that given Jesus' execution by Roman crucifixion he was truly *dead* and that his temporary place of burial was discovered to be empty shortly thereafter" (Tabor, *Jesus Dynasty*, 229-30, italics his). Of course, Tabor's citing the biblical account of the Resurrection does not mean he interprets it as Jesus rising physically. Instead he believes Jesus' body was moved to the city Tsfat outside of Galilee (ibid., 233-38). He also believes Jesus rose spiritually. See Appendix B.

[48] Witherington also makes the same observation (*What Have They Done with Jesus?* 293-295).

[49] Tabor, *Jesus Dynasty*, 59.

[50] See note 19.

[51] Tabor, *Jesus Dynasty*, 137, 243.

[52] Tabor, *Jesus Dynasty*, 43, 135, 140.

[53] Ibid., 56-57.

[54] Ibid., 64-72, 76-77.

[55] Irenaeus, *Against Heresies* 78.7.5; Epiphanius (A.D. 315-403).

[56] Evans, *Fabricating Jesus*, 218.

[57] Tabor, *Jesus Dynasty*, 230-37.

[58] Ibid., 232. Interestingly, Tabor seems to admit this. "In Judaism to claim that someone has been 'raised from the dead' is not the same as to claim that one has died and exists as a spirit or soul in the heavenly world. What the gospels claim about Jesus is that the tomb was empty, and that his dead body was revived.... He was not a phantom or a ghost, though he does seem to 'materialize' abruptly, and at times is first unrecognized, then suddenly recognized by those who saw him. But Paul seems to be willing to use the term 'resurrection' to refer to something akin to an apparition or vision" (ibid.). Tabor actually believes Jesus rose spiritually. See Appendix B.

[59] He says about the *Gospel of Thomas*: "It is clearly the most precious lost Christian document discovered in the last two thousand years" (ibid., 63).

[60] Ibid. (italics his).

61 Ben Witherington III, *The Gospel Code: Novel Claims about Jesus, Mary Magdalene and Da Vinci* (Downers Grove, IL: InterVarsity Press, 2004), 96-109.
62 Tabor, *Jesus Dynasty*, 86. Yet he contradicts himself since he accepts the above quotation from the *Gospel of Thomas* as a valid historical reference that he thinks illuminates Jesus' illegitimate birth. He also accepts late traditions in other places as well (ibid., 64-72, 233-38). A similar observation was made by Witherington, *What Have They Done with Jesus?* 230.
63 Baigent, *Jesus Papers*, 269-70.
64 Ibid., 269, 271.
65 Evans, *Fabricating Jesus*, 216.
66 Baigent, *Jesus Papers*, 126-32.
67 Witherington, *What Have They Done with Jesus?* 7

Appendix B

1 Simcha Jacobovici and Charles Pellegrino, *The Jesus Family Tomb: The Evidence Behind the Discovery No One Wanted to Find* (San Francisco, CA: HarperOne, 2007), 213–34.
2 Ibid., 220.
3 See chapter 10 for a discussion on this point.
4 Jacobovici and Pellegrino, *Jesus Family Tomb Revised and Updated*, 221–22.
5 See chapters 1 and 9 for further discussion of this point.
6 Jacobovici and Pellegrino, *Jesus Family Tomb Revised and Updated*, 222.
7 See chapter 3.
8 Jacobovici and Pellegrino, *Jesus Family Tomb Revised and Updated*, 222–23.
9 Ibid., 223.
10 Levy Yitzhak Rahmani, *A Catalogue of Jewish Ossuaries in the Collections of the State of Israel*, ed. Ayala Sussmann and Peter Schertz (Jerusalem: Israel Antiquities Authority, 1994), 17. See chapter 9 for further discussion.
11 Jacobovici and Pellegrino, *Jesus Family Tomb Revised and Updated*, 223.
12 Ibid., 224–25, see also pages 232–33.
13 James D. Tabor, *The Jesus Dynasty: The Hidden History of Jesus, His Royal Family and the Birth of Christianity* (New York: Simon & Schuster, 2006), 4.
14 Jacobovici and Pellegrino, *Jesus Family Tomb Revised and Updated*, 226.
15 Ibid.
16 See chapter 4 for further discussion of this point.

[17] Jacobovici and Pellegrino, *Jesus Family Tomb Revised and Updated*, 226.
[18] See his technical article online: http://www.ingermanson.com/jesus/art/tomb/IngermansonTombComments.pdf.
[19] See chapter 7.
[20] For a summary of these points see http://www.ingermanson.com/jesus/art/stats3.php.

SCRIPTURE INDEX

Genesis
  1:22, 26–28, 83
  3:1–22, 227
  3:15, 236
  3:19, 161, 335
  12:3, 221
  22, 163, 185, 270, 332
  22:5, 163, 185, 270
  25:24, 303
  47:29–30, 116
  49:9, 72

Exodus
  6:4, 168
  15:20–21, 301
  20:12, 88

Leviticus
  11:31–32, 327
  19:26, 34

Numbers
  6:6, 327
  12:1, 301
  23:19, 256

Deuteronomy
  18:11, 327
  18:11–14, 34
  21:22–23, 204
  21:23, 33, 137, 208
  24:9, 301
  25:3, 201
  31:16, 168, 169

1 Samuel
  15:29, 256
  28:11–20, 181

2 Samuel
  7:12–16, 193, 221
  7:12–21, 162
  14:14, 162

1 Kings
  17, 183
  17:17–22, 182, 183

2 Kings
  4:25–32, 183
  4:31, 335
  4:32–36, 182, 183
  4:35, 190
  13:20–21, 183, 190, 283
  19:7, 181

1 Chronicles
  4:17, 301

Job
  3:13–19, 325
  7:7–10, 185, 325
  13:13, 325
  14:22, 283
  19:9, 335
  19:25–27, 163, 184, 333, 339
  33:15–30, 185
  42, 185

Psalms
  2:7, 219
  6:5, 161
  13:3, 335
  16, 192-195, 336-339
  16:10–11, 163, 194, 336, 338
  16:10b, 193, 195
  16:8–11, 192-195, 221, 336-339
  72:1–12, 71, 163, 171, 221, 288, 299, 310, 329, 353
  72:16, 329
  104:29, 335
  115:17, 161
  116, 326

Proverbs
  12:28, 326

Ecclesiastes
  1:3, 325
  2:24, 325
  3:20, 335
  9:5–10, 162

Song of Solomon
  4:5, 303

Isaiah
  8:19, 283
  9:6, 197
  14:9–11, 325
  25:6–10a, 186
  26:16–20, 186
  26:19, 163, 169, 182, 185-187, 327, 333, 335
  38:10–18, 325
  52:10, 219
  52–53, 219
  53, 35, 195-197, 221, 222, 244, 338, 339
  53:1–12, 221, 244
  53:9, 35
  53:10–12, 195, 196
  55:8-9, 256
  61:1–11, 163
  66:24, 283

Jeremiah
  51:39, 57, 325, 335

Ezekial
  36, 187
  37, 163, 182, 283
  37:1–14, 163
  37:11, 187

Daniel
  2:44, 197
  6:17, 235
  7:13, 167, 328
  12:2, 168, 172, 182, 335
  12:2–3, 163, 187, 327

Micah
  6:4, 301

Nahum
  3:18, 335

Zechariah
  13:1, 197
  14:4, 226

Matthew
  1:1–17, 115
  1:16, 49
  1:18, 76
  2:23, 132, 138
  3:17, 320
  4:1–11, 320
  4:18, 72
  4:21, 89
  5:1, 153
  5:9, 89
  5:17, 151
  8:6–9, 153
  9:23–25, 182, 188
  12:38–40, 237
  19:12, 273, 302
  21:11, 315
  22:23, 326
  26:69–75, 153
  27:26, 200
  27:29, 204
  27:52, 220
  27:55–56, 77
  27:56, 49, 76-77, 90
  27:57–59, 35
  27:57–60, 137
  27:57–28:8, 211
  27:62–66, 235
  28:1, 77
  28:1–8, 343
  28:1–20, 138
  28:2, 236
  28:2–4, 218
  28:9, 220
  28:11–15, 213
  28:16–20, 225
  28:17, 225
  28:19–20, 225

Mark
  1:9, 315

1:11, 320
1:24, 132
1:34, 346
3:14–19, 84
3:17, 72
3:18, 84
4:17, 241
5:41–42, 183
6:3, 48, 49, 81
6:24–29, 89
6:49, 181
7:24, 264
8:31, 219
9:25, 346
12:18, 326
14:3, 78
14:17, 90
14:26, 346
14:30, 47, 343
14:50, 235, 237
14:65, 201
14:66–72, 153
15:15, 200
15:25, 33, 204
15:40, 49, 77
15:40–41, 77
15:42, 204
15:42–16:8, 211
15:44, 205, 235
15:47, 77
16:1, 77, 219
16:1–8, 138, 343
16:1, 9, 77
16:2, 211
16:3–4, 236
16:4, 218
16:5, 218
16:5–7, 219
16:9–11, 220
16:12–13, 220
16:15–18, 225
16:9–20, 301, 344
31, 84
65–72, 237

Luke
1:27, 30, 34, 38, 49
1:30-31, 76, 301
1:63, 223
2:39, 315
2:52, 302
3:23–34, 115
3:34–26,132, 320
3:29, 49, 288
4:1–13, 320
6:17, 153
6:14, 300
6:15, 84
6:17, 153
7:3–8, 153
7:36–50, 78
7:15, 189, 190
7:11–15, 182, 188
8:2, 76-77
8:1–3, 77, 78, 271
8:42, 188
8:53, 188
8:54, 189
20:27, 326
22:55–62, 154
22:37, 197
22:46, 188
23:25, 200
23:55–56, 138
23:50–24:10, 211
24:1–10, 343
24:2, 218, 236
24:3, 219
24:4, 218
24:10, 77
24:11, 212
24:13, 15–16, 220
24:17–24, 221
24:13–32, 220
24:13–20, 229
24:29–32, 221
24:25–27, 221
24:31, 229
24:33–37, 222
24:34, 220
24:37, 346
24:38–43, 223
24:39, 181, 223
24:41, 166, 223
24:44–49, 225

John
- 1:1–18, 291
- 1:6, 15, 19, 26, 29, 89
- 1:12, 37, 244
- 1:20, 264
- 1:30–34, 320
- 1:42, 89
- 2:1–10, 90
- 2:18–22, 236
- 3:16, 37, 244, 2904:20–22, 96
- 5:2, 90
- 7:5, 84, 225, 237
- 10:18, 237
- 11:1, 61, 76
- 11:4, 40, 190
- 11:12, 220
- 11:16, 72, 83-8411:43, 189
- 11:39, 189
- 11:43–44, 182, 188, 189
- 12:3, 78
- 12:24, 175
- 12:27–32, 219
- 12:36, 89
- 12:40, 90
- 13:23, 89, 90, 237
- 17:5, 222
- 18:10, 50–51. 66–72, 343
- 18:15–18, 25–27, 154
- 18:33–39, 87
- 19:16, 200
- 19:25, 76, 77
- 19:25, 76-77, 88
- 19:26, 34, 82, 89-91, 185
- 19:26, 82, 89, 90
- 19:26–27, 88
- 19:32–33, 204
- 19:34, 205
- 19:38–20:8, 211
- 20:1, 77, 218, 236
- 20:1–8, 343
- 20:1–9, 219
- 20:1–10, 138
- 20:2, 49, 55, 89
- 20:11–18, 77, 220
- 20:14, 229
- 20:16, 20, 27–28, 229
- 20:18, 77
- 20:19–20, 222
- 20:19–25, 223
- 20:24, 222
- 20:25, 224
- 20:26, 224
- 20:27–28, 224
- 21:1–14, 224
- 21:19, 238
- 26:1, 175

Acts
- 1:9–11, 226
- 1:13, 84
- 1:15–26, 238
- 2–4, 237
- 2:22, 315
- 2:23–31, 163
- 2:24, 237
- 2:27, 194
- 2:29, 194
- 2:30, 193
- 4:5–6, 89
- 7:59, 237
- 8:5, 183
- 8:27, 237
- 8:30–34, 82
- 8:39, 222
- 8:40 and 21:8, 222
- 9:1–9, 218, 226, 344
- 9:1–22, 240
- 9:36–40, 182, 188, 190
- 9:40, 183
- 11:19, 241
- 12:1–2, 237
- 12:12, 89
- 12:14, 223
- 12:17, 237
- 12:19, 220
- 13, 194
- 15, 82, 271, 295
- 22:9–11, 240
- 23:7–9, 326
- 23:8, 346

Romans
- 1:4, 222
- 1:16, 240
- 3:21–4:25, 37, 236, 244, 290
- 4:24–25, 244

4:25, 196, 339
6:1–23, 200
6:1–23 and 8:10–13, 330
6:6, 229
8:11, 237
16:16, 77
16:20, 236

1 Corinthians
2:13-15, 228, 346
2:14, 228, 307
5:7, 225
6:9-10, 347
9:5, 82
15:1–8, 226
15:1–9, 148
15:1–50, 226
15:1–58, 229
15:3, 196, 211
15:3a, 210
15:3–4, 244
15:3–5, 210
15:4, 159, 210
15:5, 220
15:6, 225, 344
15:12–23, 200, 227
15:12–26, 236
15:15, 29, 32, 35, 52, 220
15:16–17, 247, 251
15:35, 227
15:35–49, especially 15:41–44, 33, 348
15:36–38, 227
15:39–41, 22715:44, 22, 226, 228, 270, 346
15:42–43, 227

2 Corinthians
4 and 5, 331
4–5:10, 345
12:2, 226

Galatians
1:4, 196
1:18–19, 210
1:22–23, 240
5–6, 229
5:11, 241, 291

5:23, 248
6:16, 151

Ephesians
2:2, 89
2:8–9, 37, 244
2:20, 151, 242

Philippians
3:1–10, 240
3:21, 348, 349

Colossians
1:15–20, 226
4:16, 151

1 Thessalonians
5:21, 249

1 Timothy
1:2, 89
1:3–7, 55
5:18, 151

2 Timothy
2:1, 89
2:17–18, 55
3:12, 241
3:16–17, 151

Titus
1:4, 89
3:5, 37

Philemon
10, 89

Hebrews
1:1–2, 151
1:7, 14, 181
11:17–19, 163, 221

1 Peter
1:10-11, 194
2:24, 202

2 Peter
1:19–21, 151, 194
16, 151, 352

1 John
1:1–4, 291

3:2, 37
4:1, 249
16, 37, 55, 89, 249, 262, 291, 352

Jude
9, 218

Revelation
1:3, 151
11:8, 11, 182, 188
20:6, 182
22, 37
22:13, 140

Apocrypha
295, 327, 328, 343

Ecclesiasticus
15, 163

Wisdom of Jesus ben Sirach
163

Sirach
11:26–28, 326
15, 163, 326

I Maccabees
2–10, 47
2:49–70, 163, 327
13:27–29, 135-136
13:27–30, 135-136

II Maccabees
7 and 14:46, 173
7:9, 164
7:10–11, 165
7:11, 29, 329
7:14, 165
7:20–23, 165
7:28–29, 165
12:40–42, 166
12:43–44, 166
14:37, 166
14:43–46, 166

Tob.
4:10, 327

1 Baruch
2:27, 327

Pseudepigrapha
15, 327, 328

IV Maccabees
3:18, 163

Jubilee
23:27–29, 164
23:30–31, 164

1 Enoch
1:8, 328
51:1–5, 167
62:13–15, 167
91:10, 167
96:1–3, 167

Pseudp–Phocylides
102–105, 167

Testament of Moses
10:8–10, 167

Life of Adam and Eve
13:3–6, 167

Sibylline Oracles
4:179–92, 167-68

Testament of Levi
18:3, 168

Testament of Judah
25:4, 168

Testament of Zebulon
10:1–3, 168

Testament of Benjamin
10:6–9, 168

4 Ezra
7:28–44, 168

2 Baruch
30:1–5, 168

Scripture Index

Josephus
15, 65, 115, 139, 170, 207, 212, 214, 237, 266, 284, 310, 327, 329, 341, 343

Jewish Antiquities
15.11.2, 284

Antiquities of the Jews
18:14, 329
18.18, 329
18:64, 341

Antiquities
4.219 [4.8.15.219], 212

Ant.
13, 211, 135

Jewish War
2.151, 294, 328, 329
2.163, 329
3.374, 170
4:51, 341
7.2.2, 284

Apion
2.218, 170

Philo
15, 164, 327

Quaestiones Gen 1
3.11, 327
16, 327

De Ebrietate
26, 101, 328

Legum
3.14, 42, 328

De Migratione
2 (9), 328

Quod Deterius
22 (80), 328

Babylonian Talmud
15, 72, 207, 208, 282, 337, 342, 343

Mo'ed Katan
80c, 282

Rosh Hashshanah
17a, 282

Pesahim
113b–114a, 72

Gittin
34b, 72

bSanh
90, 169
90b–91a, 328

bPesahim
65a [5.10.10.1], 212

Rosh Hashanah
22a [1:8], 212

bSanhedrin
43a, 342

Jerusalem Talmud
15, 282, 284

Semahot
12–13, 284

Mishnah
15, 168, 180, 282

'Eduyyot
2:10F, 282

Sanhedrin
6:6, 284

mSamh.
10:1, 169

mBer.
9:5, 169

– 367 –

mBerakhot
    4:1–5:5, 329
Gnostic Writings
    292

Acts of Philip
    48, 53-55, 59-61, 64-67, 70,
        79, 294-297, 299
    8:94, 66

Gospel of Judas
    259, 261, 262, 291, 357

Gospel of Mary
    55, 57, 58, 61, 63, 65, 67-70,
        79, 293, 294, 297-299, 331

Gospel of Philip
    8:94–95, 60
    8:97, 60
    55-59, 63, 70, 79, 293-296, 330
    58–59, 57
    63:32–33, 57
    63:32–64:10, 56
    68:31–7, 330
    81:34–82:19, 294
    81:34–82:19, 58, 294

Gospel of Thomas
    60, 68, 83, 85, 260, 265, 291-
        293, 303, 330, 331, 358, 359

Gospel of Thomas saying
    4, 16, 23, 30, and 76, 85
    11, 77, 83, 301, 303, 330, 357
    16, 85
    49, 49, 61, 72, 85, 116, 159,
        163, 177, 181, 213, 263,
        288, 296, 323, 324, 330,
        338, 339, 343, 358
    59, 85
    72, 85
    103, 46, 74, 85, 167, 174, 300,
        331, 332, 353
    114, 85

Book of Thomas the Contender
    138:39–139:30, 330

Epistle to Rheginos [also known as
Treatise on Resurrection]
    44:13–38, 330
    47:2–27, 330

Infancy Gospel
    265

Pistis Sophia
    1:17–18, 62
    61-63, 65, 68, 296, 297

PiSo
    26:17–20, 297-98
    218:10–219:2, 298

The Gospel of the Egyptians
    68

Apocalypse of Peter
    83:6–84:6, 330

Apocryphon of James
    7:35–8:84, 330

1 Apocalypse of James
    29:16–19, 330

Letter of Peter to Philip
    133:15–17, 330
Letter of Philip
    134:9–19, 330

Exegesis of the Soul
    134:6–29, 330

Gospel of the Savior
    100:7.1–6, 330

Dead Sea Scrolls
    172, 265, 330, 335, 355
4Q521
    171, 330

4Q385
    335

4Q386
    335

4Q388
    335

1QHa
    19:15, 171
    4:32–40, 172

Church Fathers
    55, 151, 155, 156, 173, 174, 177, 180, 260-262, 264, 292

1 Clement
    5:4, 176
    24:1, 175
    24:5, 175
    50:3–4, 175

II Clement
    9:1–6, 175
    11:7, 331
    151, 175

Letters of Ignatius to the Trallians
    9:2, 176

Letters of Ignatius to the Philadelphia
    8:2, 176

Letters to the Smyrnaeans
    2:1, 176
    3:1–3, 176

Letter of Polycarp to the Philippians
    2:21, 176

The Martyrdom of Polycarp
    14:2, 176

Didache
    9:4, 177
    16:6–8, 177

Letter of Barnabas
    5:6, 177
    15:8–9, 177

Shepherd of Hermas
    177

Shepherd
    60:1–4, 177

Parables or Similitudes
    5.7.1–4, 177

Epistles to Diognetus
    6:6–8, 178

Fragments of Papias
    3:12, 178
    7:3, 178
    16:1, 179

Contra Celsum
    5.62.14–17, 61
    I2, 1, 61, 133

Pan.
    26.7.5, 62
    30, 17, 133

Origen, De princ.
    4, 22, 132

Greco–Roman
    33, 160, 284, 292

Tacitus, Annals
    15.44, 341

Lucian of Samosata, The Death of Peregrine
    11–13, 341

Koran
    203, 332

Surah
    4:157, 203
    56:60–61, 332

AUTHORS INDEX

Anderson, Robert, 320
Ankerberg, John, 8, 276, 340, 341, 344, 345, 349
Archer, Gleason L., 320, 335
Bacon, Francis, 254, 255, 352, 353
Bagatti, P. B., 49, 114, 288, 300, 301, 308, 310
Baigent, Michael, 142, 200, 259, 263, 265, 266, 340, 355, 358, 359
Barbieri, Louis A., Jr., 335, 343
Barker, Kenneth, 336
Barnard, L.W., 315
Barr, James, 324
Barrett, C. K., 224, 228, 345, 347
Bauckham, Richard, 115, 276, 285, 287, 306, 308-310
Blomberg, Craig L., 276, 303, 345, 356
Bock, Darrell L., 12, 14, 50, 51, 55-59, 63, 69, 83, 85, 115, 121, 126, 144, 152, 161, 223, 248, 276, 283, 286, 288-295, 298-303, 306, 307, 309-312, 315, 316, 319-321, 325, 328, 336, 337, 345, 346, 348, 349, 351
Borg, Marcus J., 355
Bousset, Wilhelm, 258, 354
Bovon, François, 44, 53, 54, 60, 62, 64-66, 72, 87, 287, 294, 296-300, 304
Boyd, Gregory A., 261, 276, 354-356
Brock, Ann Graham, 247, 297
Brown, Colin, 353
Brown, Dan, 31, 54, 82, 142, 150, 249, 291, 319
Brown, Raymond E., 344
Bruce, F. F., 151, 228, 262, 320-322, 344, 347, 351
Bruyne, L. de., 315
Burge, Gary M., 90, 304, 305
Burke, David G., 315
Burroughs, Dillon, 8, 97, 99, 276, 288, 306, 340, 352
Bynum, Caroline Walker, 179, 277, 332
Cameron, James, 20, 28, 59, 246, 281, 295, 310
Cameron, Ron, 355
Carson, D. A., 335
Charles, R. H., 328
Cohen, Gary G., 339
Collins, John J., 188, 278, 287, 300, 305, 307, 309, 314, 324-326, 330, 335, 345, 353
Conant, James B., 232, 349
Copleston, Frederick, 354
Cox, Steven, 128, 313
Craig, William Lane, 317, 318, 338, 342
Crossan, John Dominic, 27, 34, 83, 208, 277, 280, 282, 284, 302, 303, 317, 323, 342, 349, 355
Darwin, Charles, 258, 354
Davies, Jon, 160, 324, 325
Dean, Cornelia, 210, 243, 281
Delitzsch, F., 333
Dembski, William A., 309
Desmond, Peter H., 295
Dillon, John M., 8, 97, 276, 288, 306, 327, 340, 352
Dinkler, Erich, 316
Doherty, Earl, 149, 319, 355
Donaldson, James, 296, 342
Ehrman, Bart D., 149, 154-157, 259, 262, 263, 291, 317-319, 321, 322, 355, 357, 358
Ellis, I. P., 345
Epp, Eldon Jay, 322
Eusebius, 90, 132, 133, 238, 303, 305, 316
Evans, Christopher F., 322
Evans, Craig A., 7, 14, 58, 282, 286, 290, 294, 321, 356
Farnell, F. David, 255-257, 277, 352-355
Fee, Gordon D., 263, 322, 344
Ferguson, Everett, 141, 142, 315
Feuerverger, Andrey, 110, 111, 115, 274, 309, 311
Fishwick, Duncan, 316
Fitzmyer, Joseph A., 132, 134, 313

Authors Index

Funk, Robert W. , 260, 319, 345, 355
Gafni, I., 282
Garlow, James L., 302, 320
Gat, Joseph, 23, 25, 27, 120, 121, 246, 280, 311
Geisler, Norman L., 197, 320, 339, 340, 350, 352, 353
Geldenhuys, Norval, 241, 351
Genna, Robert, 127, 128, 312
Gewertz, Ken, 295
Gibson, J. C. L., 25, 26, 30, 201, 247, 311, 321
Goodacre, Mark, 301, 307, 308
Goodenough, Erwin Ramsdell, 284
Gordon, A. E., 263, 282, 322, 344
Grappe, Christian, 324
Green, Joel B., 344
Green, Michael P., 320
Greenspoon, Leonard, 324
Gruber, Elmar R., 200, 205, 206, 340, 341
Guthrie, Donald, 304
Habermas, Gary R., 6, 14, 21, 82, 103, 111, 117, 148, 150, 204, 206, 210, 213, 277, 279, 302, 306-310, 317, 319, 339-343, 350, 351
Hachlili, Rachael, 94, 135, 247, 277, 278, 287, 300, 305, 307-310, 313-315, 330
Heard, Christopher , 67, 183, 211, 221, 240, 249, 281, 286, 295
Herbert, Arthur S., 256, 333, 350
Hill, Charles E., 332
Horowitz, David, 286, 351, 352
Hume, David, 256, 353
Hutchinson, John C., 354
Ilan, Tal, 46, 48, 70, 74, 115, 287, 288, 299, 301, 308, 310
Isenberg, Wesley W., 58, 293, 295
Jacobovici, Simcha, 7, 8, 20, 28, 29, 48, 49, 59, 64, 71, 120, 121, 127, 132, 134, 143, 145, 245, 246, 269, 274, 275, 279-281, 284-289, 293, 295-299, 302-306, 308, 311-316, 343, 359, 360
James, Montague Rhodes, 299
Jenkins, Philip, 172-174, 278, 290, 330, 331
Jerphanion, P. de., 315

Johnson, Luke Timothy, 27, 356
Johnston, Philip S., 324
Jones, Peter, 302, 320
Josephus, 15, 65, 115, 139, 170, 207, 212, 214, 237, 266, 284, 310, 327, 329, 341, 343
Kane, J. P, 316
Kant, Immanuel, 256, 353
Karen, King, 57, 63, 68, 291, 293, 298, 331
Keener, Craig S., 5, 14, 294
Keil, C. F., 333
Keppie, L. J., 282
Kidner, Derek, 326, 338
Kierkegaard, Søren, 258, 259, 355
King, Karen L., 293, 298, 331
Kissane, Edward J., 333
Klauck, Hans-Josef, 292
Kloner, Amos, 25-27, 31, 42, 45, 47, 51, 71, 72, 75, 99, 115, 121, 122, 125, 126, 247, 250, 279, 280, 285-289, 299, 301, 303, 306, 307, 311, 312, 314
Koester, Craig R., 332
Koester, Helmut, 291, 303, 355
Komoszewski, J. Ed., 290, 302, 321, 322, 354, 356-358
Koppel, Ted, 12, 20, 127, 309
Krieg, Matthias, 324
Lampe, Peter, 349
Laney, J. Carl, 88, 219, 304, 305, 320, 344
Leigh, R., 55, 355
Lemaire, André, 123, 125, 126, 312
Lincoln, Andrew T., 304
López, René A., 1, 2, 9, 12, 325, 344, 351
Lüdemann, Gerd, 208, 317, 342
Lutzer, Edwin W. , 4, 302
MacBride, Archibald, 241, 351
Mack, Burton L., 355
MacRae, George W., 298
Magness, Jodi., 35, 246, 247, 272, 283, 314, 352
Marjanen, Antti, 296
Martin, John A., 196, 334, 339
Marxsen, Willi., 148, 317
Mattingly, John P., 203, 340
Maurer, Christian, 343
McDowell, Josh, 191, 231, 322,

336, 341, 349
McGirk, Tim, 351
McHenry, Robert, 316
Mead, G. R. S., 297
Meek, T. J., 333
Meier, Samuel A., 321
Menard, J. E., 330
Mettinger, Tryggve N. D. , 324
Metzger, Bruce M., 322, 344
Meyers, Eric M., 247, 284, 352
Milik, J. T., 49, 114, 288, 300, 308
Milligan, Williams, 332
Mims, Christopher, 117, 310
Mommsen, Theodor, 282
Mossner, Ernest C., 186, 333, 339
Motyer, J. Alec, 322
Moule, C. F. D., 350
Musurillo, Herbert A., 342
Ollenburger, Ben C., 324
Oswalt, John N., 196, 338
Ozen, Alf, 317
Pagels, Elaine, 291, 331
Pellegrino, Charles R., 29, 281
Pentecost, J. Dwight, 243, 335, 344
Peters, Ted, 349, 350
Pfann, Stephen J., 42, 73, 102, 111, 283, 286, 289, 298, 306-309
Pfleiderer, Otto, 345
Philo, 15, 164, 327
Pinnock, Clark, 343
Poole, Gary, 302
Pope, Marvin H., 332
Porter, Stanley E., 294, 328
Puech, Émil, 171
Rahmani, L. Y., 41, 53, 112, 119, 139, 172, 272, 282, 284
Levy Yitzhak Rahmani,, 27, 280, 285, 289, 305, 307, 309, 314, 330, 359
Rahmani, Levy Yitzhak, 27, 277, 280
Riley, Gregory, 331
Roberts, Alexander, 296, 342
Robertson, A. T., 235, 350
Robinson, J. M., 355
Robinson, James M. , 291
Rowley, Harold H. , 334
Rudolph, Kurt, 290
Sausa, Don, 280, 284
Schonfield, Hugh J., 200, 339
Schweizer, Eduard, 347

Segal, Alan F., 247, 324
Shanks, Hershel, 123, 281, 287, 312
Shannon, Jeff, 281
Shore, P., 282
Silberman, N. A., 282
Singer, S., 329
Skinner, John, 334
Sloyan, Gerard S., 341
Smith, Robert H., 316
Smith, Wilbur M., 207, 341
Sponheim, Paul R., 355
Stott, John R. W., 350
Strauss, David F., 206, 255, 256, 335, 341
Strobel, Lee, 302
Suetonius, Gaius, 343
Tabor, James D., 27, 29, 87, 120, 208, 259, 263, 269, 289, 297, 304, 307, 311, 342, 355, 359
Taylor, John B., 334
Tcherikover, Victor A., 288
Tenney, Merrill C., 196, 339
Thiselton, Anthony C., 346
Thomas, Robert L., 190, 277, 336, 352
Tromp, Nicholas J., 325
Trull, Gregory Vance, 336, 337
Urbach, Efraim E., 329
Wallace, Daniel B., 47, 154, 276, 288, 290, 301, 302, 310, 315, 321, 346, 351, 354
Weiss, Johannes, 345
Weldon, John, 276, 341, 344, 349
Wessel, W. W., 313
White, James R., 21, 111, 279, 289, 308, 312, 316
Williams, Margaret, 325
Witherington, Ben, 4, 14, 95, 104, 122, 262, 287, 290, 302, 306, 307, 311, 312, 321, 325, 346, 356, 359
Witherington III, Ben, 4, 14, 95, 104, 122, 262, 287, 290, 302, 306, 307, 312, 321, 325, 346, 356, 359
Wright, N. T. , 157, 183, 196, 209, 225, 234, 317, 319, 329, 332, 338, 342, 345, 349
Yamauchi, Edwin M., 9, 14, 323, 334, 350
Zias, Joe , 103, 122, 139, 247, 272, 307, 312, 314

SUBJECT INDEX

Acts of Philip, 48, 53-55, 59-61, 64-67, 70, 79, 294-297, 299
afterlife, 324, 325, 337
agnosticism, 254, 256, 267
Alexander, 151, 241, 296, 342, 355
Alexandria, 36, 90, 238, 327
Alexandrian, 164
Apocrypha, 295, 327, 328, 343
Apocryphal, 15, 48, 101, 294, 299
Aramaic, 40, 42, 45, 46, 70-72, 74, 83, 84, 93-95, 97, 123, 140, 266, 273, 285, 286, 332
archaeological, 6, 7, 20, 24, 28, 36, 43, 97, 116, 121, 123, 124, 263-265, 282, 287, 312
archaeology, 29, 123, 248, 249, 263, 281, 282, 284, 312, 316

beloved disciple, 31, 81, 86, 88-91, 304
biblical names, 28, 30, 142, 254
bodily resurrection, 6, 7, 116, 150, 160, 161, 163, 166-168, 170, 172, 173, 179, 180, 184-188, 190, 194, 197, 217, 226, 234, 240, 241, 247, 250, 290, 317, 326, 328, 330, 331, 333, 334, 345-347

body
22, 27, 33-35, 37, 69, 77, 137, 138, 142, 147, 149, 160, 162, 164, 169, 171, 173, 175, 176, 178, 179, 182, 184-187, 190, 193-195, 199, 206, 209, 214, 218-224, 226-229, 235, 236, 244, 247, 253, 261, 270, 272, 277, 280, 282, 314, 318, 327, 328, 331, 332, 338, 341, 345, 348, 349, 352, 358
spiritual, 19, 22, 35, 37, 38, 57-59, 79, 88, 98, 147, 149, 159, 163, 173, 188, 218-220, 226, 228, 229, 247, 249, 251, 255, 257, 265, 270, 271, 290, 291, 294, 298, 333, 334, 345, 348, 349
natural, 22, 29, 147, 148, 157, 181, 223, 226, 228, 255, 256, 258, 263, 318, 331, 334, 349, 354
immaterial, 226-228, 270
brother, 19, 48, 49, 51, 67, 68, 76, 81-86, 97, 117, 119, 120, 123-127, 130, 132, 137, 164, 165, 237-239, 250, 263, 287, 289, 304, 311, 312, 350
James, 2, 6, 12, 16, 19-21, 27-29, 31, 50, 51, 59, 60, 72, 76, 82, 87, 90, 95, 97, 111, 114, 119-130, 132, 137, 142, 151, 208, 210, 218, 225, 232, 237-239, 246, 259, 263, 269, 271, 279, 281, 283, 289-291, 295-297, 299, 302, 304, 307, 308, 310-312, 316, 320, 321, 324, 330, 342, 349, 350, 354, 355, 359
Judas , 9, 17, 30, 31, 39, 46, 47, 51, 81, 83-89, 91, 94, 98, 114, 115, 118, 166, 238, 259, 261, 262, 291, 310, 328, 357
of Jesus, 3, 5-9, 17, 19-22, 27, 28, 30-33, 35, 37, 39, 41, 43-47, 50, 51, 53, 54, 62, 64, 66, 76, 78, 81-89, 91, 93, 94, 96-98, 110-112, 116, 117, 119, 120, 123-127, 129-132, 134, 138, 139, 141, 142, 146, 147, 149-151, 153, 155, 157-159, 161, 163, 164, 172, 174, 177, 179, 180, 182, 190-192, 194, 197, 199-202, 207, 209, 210, 213, 214, 218, 220-222, 224-226, 230-234, 236-238, 240-244, 246, 248-250, 254, 260, 261,

263-265, 267, 269, 271, 272, 274, 277, 279, 283-289, 291, 296-298, 301, 303, 304, 306-312, 314, 315, 317-320, 322, 323, 325, 335, 338-344, 346-351, 355, 359
  of John, 27, 30, 66, 81, 89, 90, 139, 178, 263, 299, 304, 305, 345, 350
burial, 6, 8, 22-24, 33-38, 44, 75, 93, 95, 97-99, 116, 126, 131, 132, 135, 137, 146, 189, 207, 209, 211, 220, 232, 235, 271, 280, 282, 283, 285, 286, 309, 310, 312, 313, 324, 330, 346, 347, 358
  box, 6, 22, 76, 126, 147, 282, 312
  cave, 23, 30, 55, 99, 121, 131, 289, 356

chamber
  25, 26, 34, 141, 143, 189, 207, 283, 295, 351
  kind, 64, 65, 97, 102, 127, 144, 157, 158, 160, 161, 183-185, 188, 227, 229, 232, 281, 314, 347, 357
  practice, 22, 33-38, 44, 46, 98, 103, 116, 134, 136, 152, 169, 207, 262, 283
  place, 24, 34, 37, 44, 46, 65, 66, 88, 98, 116, 123, 132, 135, 137-141, 143, 145, 151, 152, 155, 158, 159, 163, 170, 175, 186, 203, 208, 209, 219, 221, 238, 239, 241, 242, 246, 271, 272, 280, 285, 286, 288, 302, 309, 310, 321, 322, 328, 333, 339, 346-349, 358
  site, 23, 51, 75, 99, 116, 120, 121, 123, 125, 137, 274, 286, 310, 337, 340

burials
  12, 34, 97, 103, 137, 283, 284
  Palestine, 204, 284, 287, 299, 305, 308, 316

Caiaphas
  43, 210, 272, 287
  ossuary, 5, 17, 19, 22, 26, 28, 30, 31, 33-36, 39-47, 49-51, 53-55, 57, 59, 61, 63, 65, 67, 69-71, 73-77, 79, 81, 84, 86, 94-98, 103, 104, 110, 112, 115, 119-131, 140, 142, 143, 145-147, 149, 172, 199, 217, 224, 250, 273, 280, 282-289, 299-301, 306, 307, 311, 312, 315, 316, 330
carnal, 346, 348
carnally, 228
Celsus, 61, 264
cemeteries, 306
chevron, 31, 131, 132, 134-136, 145
Christian symbols, 142
Clement
  90, 145, 151, 174, 175, 331
  of Alexandria, 90, 238, 327
  of Rome, 90, 208, 244
Clopas, 76
cluster of names, 19, 30, 31, 39, 109-111, 117, 118, 121, 249, 250, 308
Combination, 17, 36, 39, 73, 102, 109, 111, 113, 115, 117, 158, 223, 250, 300
common names, 39, 46, 48, 51, 74, 99, 114, 117, 274, 310
conspiracy, 5, 17, 28, 31, 38, 55, 119-123, 125, 127, 129, 142, 200, 253, 340, 341
conservative, 59, 83, 110, 129, 197, 248, 274, 308
Contra Celsum, 61, 264, 296
contradiction, 149, 153, 259
Coptic, 57, 58, 261, 293, 356, 357
creed, 210, 292, 320, 333

creedal
  210, 211
  statement, 62, 85, 90, 115, 129, 161, 178, 196, 209-212, 257,

273, 326, 327, 331
information, 4, 22, 30, 31, 38, 66, 83, 99, 110, 117, 121, 129, 149, 210, 220, 263, 265, 275, 288, 295, 301, 350
cremation, 33, 282
crucified, 204, 205, 208, 238, 319
crucifixion, 77, 78, 138, 140, 199-201, 203-205, 207-209, 223, 224, 235, 238, 241, 265, 266, 315, 340, 341, 358

Da Vinci Code, 5, 31, 47, 54, 67, 82, 142, 144, 150, 249, 276, 289, 291-295, 298, 299, 301, 302, 316, 319, 320
deism, 254, 256, 267, 354
Didymos Judas, 83
Discovery Channel, 12, 20, 28, 122, 127, 248, 261, 280, 309
disciple, 31, 72, 81, 83, 85-91, 151, 223, 242, 261, 304
DNA, 6, 17, 19, 31, 76, 98, 101-105, 107, 127, 128, 250, 281
Dominus Flevit, 49, 73-75, 114, 288, 300, 301, 308, 310

East Talpiot, 23, 112
Ebionites, 131-134, 145, 313
empty tomb, 32, 200, 209-215, 219, 220, 231, 236, 244, 276, 279, 289, 295-298, 300, 308, 312, 316, 341, 342, 344, 345, 349
enemies, 33, 138, 234-236, 238, 244, 338
entombment, 235
Epiphanius, 55, 62, 132, 133, 264, 358
eternal life, 176, 195, 200, 243, 244, 251
evolution, 29, 84, 149, 254, 258, 267, 281, 354
excavation, 23, 24, 49, 121
excavated, 125, 246
existentialism, 254, 258, 267, 354

Family Names, 110, 116, 117, 277,
287, 305, 307, 308
family tomb, 1-3, 5-9, 16-20, 22, 24, 26-28, 30-36, 38-40, 42, 44-46, 48, 50, 52, 54, 56, 58, 60, 62, 64, 66, 68, 70, 72, 74, 76, 78-80, 82, 84-86, 88, 90, 92-94, 96, 98-100, 102, 104, 106-108, 110, 112, 114, 116-118, 120-122, 124-126, 128, 130, 132, 134, 136-140, 142-144, 146, 148, 150, 152, 154, 156, 158, 160, 162, 164, 166, 168, 170, 172, 174, 176, 178, 180, 182, 184, 186, 188, 190, 192, 194, 196, 198, 200, 202, 204, 206, 208, 210, 212, 214, 216-218, 220, 222, 224, 226, 228, 230, 232, 234, 236, 238, 240, 242, 244-246, 248-250, 252, 254, 256, 258, 260, 262, 264-272, 274, 276-282, 284-290, 292-296, 298-316, 318, 320, 322, 324, 326, 328, 330, 332, 334, 336, 338, 340, 342-344, 346, 348, 350, 352, 354, 356, 358-360
fellowship, 9, 57, 58, 223, 338
fingerprints, 126-128
flesh, 33, 34, 54, 69, 175-179, 184, 192, 193, 201, 202, 222, 223, 227, 229, 247, 261, 269, 290, 319, 330, 337, 341, 348, 356
fleshly, 58, 228, 294
flesh and blood, 176
flesh and bones, 222, 223, 269
forgeries, 97
forgery, 39, 97, 124, 261, 357

genealogy, 50, 115, 264
Gnostic, 5, 22, 54-56, 60-64, 66-71, 78, 79, 83-85, 88, 132, 173, 174, 211, 263, 265, 290-293, 296-298, 304, 320, 331
Gnostics, 54, 56, 59, 62, 63, 68, 85, 173, 174, 291, 294, 296, 357
Gnosticism, 54, 55, 63, 68, 69, 173, 262, 290-292, 298, 331
Golden Legend, 78, 79

Gospel of John, 66, 81, 89, 90, 263, 299, 304, 305, 345
Gospel of Judas, 259, 261, 262, 291, 357
Gospel of Luke, 239, 344, 351
Gospel of Mary, 55, 57, 58, 61, 63, 65, 67-70, 79, 293, 294, 297-299, 331
Gospel of Mary Magdalene*****
Gospel of Mary Magdala, 293, 294, 297, 298, 331
Gospel of Matthew, 133, 238
Gospel of Peter, 211, 291, 292, 343
Gospel of Philip, 55-59, 63, 70, 79, 293-296, 330
Gospel of the Savior, 292, 330
Gospel of Thomas, 60, 68, 83, 85, 260, 265, 291-293, 303, 330, 331, 358, 359
graffiti-like, 43
grave, 3, 4, 44, 117, 135-138, 150, 161, 162, 181, 194, 197, 200, 214, 218, 219, 221, 235, 314, 326
grave trenches, 35, 138
Greek, 45, 48, 49, 54, 57, 60, 61, 65, 70-74, 83, 84, 93-97, 99, 113, 140, 155, 156, 159, 161, 163, 179, 182, 200, 202, 205, 208, 219, 220, 225, 261, 282, 293, 296, 301, 303, 314, 315, 331, 332, 340, 344-346, 356
Greek names, 45, 94
Greco–Roman, 33, 160

Hebrew, 15, 27, 29, 32, 40, 45, 47-50, 71, 83, 84, 93-97, 132, 140, 159-161, 168, 179, 181, 184, 187, 194, 201, 208, 277, 279, 285, 287, 299, 301, 305, 307, 308, 310, 329, 332, 335, 337
Hebrew names, 71, 277, 287, 305, 307, 308, 310
heirs, 81, 86
Hippolytus, 55, 78, 301
historians, 150, 154, 157, 158, 210, 311, 318, 322, 323

Historical Ecclesiastical, 303, 305

historical
3, 6, 12, 17, 32, 56, 61-67, 69, 70, 79, 82, 83, 95, 105, 110, 111, 115, 116, 134, 138, 139, 144-147, 149-153, 155, 157-159, 161, 163, 165, 167, 169, 171, 173-175, 177, 179, 189, 205, 207-209, 217, 232, 233, 235, 241, 247, 249, 250, 254, 257, 259-263, 266, 276, 277, 293, 294, 297, 303, 305, 316-318, 322-324, 327, 336, 339-342, 349, 352, 353, 355, 356, 358, 359
blunder, 134, 150, 152
document, 31, 32, 51, 56, 57, 67, 149, 150, 153, 179, 235, 250, 260-262, 293, 298, 359
event, 25, 109, 152, 153, 158, 159, 174, 181, 183, 189, 190, 210-212, 233-235, 270, 280, 288, 318, 323, 345, 349, 358
events, 66, 152, 153, 158, 177, 182, 187, 221, 223, 231-233, 269, 304, 322, 344
evidence, 4, 6, 12, 17, 19, 20, 22, 25, 28, 31, 32, 35-37, 44, 46, 47, 49, 54, 55, 58, 59, 62, 67, 71, 72, 74, 77, 81-83, 87-91, 95, 99, 102, 104, 105, 107, 109, 112, 116, 121, 125, 129, 134, 136, 138, 141, 142, 145, 146, 150, 156, 159, 161, 170, 172-174, 179-182, 190, 201, 203, 205, 212, 215, 217, 228-235, 237, 239, 241, 243-247, 250, 258-260, 262, 264-267, 270-273, 276, 277, 279, 281, 283, 284, 288, 289, 302, 303, 305, 306, 308, 311-314, 316, 318, 320, 322, 332, 336-339, 341-343, 345, 349, 350, 352, 359
Jesus, 1-9, 11, 12, 16-54, 56-70, 72, 74, 76-94, 96-98, 100-106, 108, 110-112, 114-134,

Subject Index

136-144, 146-164, 166, 168, 170, 172, 174-184, 186, 188-226, 228-274, 276-326, 328, 330-332, 334-360
Mary Magdalene , 9, 17, 19, 30, 45, 46, 48, 49, 53-57, 59-71, 73, 75-79, 81, 86-88, 95, 101-103, 111, 117, 218, 219, 250, 273, 278, 289, 290, 294-302, 304, 359
NT Mary Magdalene, 61, 71, 79, 297
proof, 4, 9, 32, 139, 157, 217, 232-235, 261, 288, 318
sources, 5, 30, 32, 59, 66, 110, 129, 135, 139, 150, 156, 163, 173, 174, 179, 207, 209, 214, 263, 266, 298, 322, 324, 332, 358

history
7, 9, 12, 20, 29, 30, 33, 37, 38, 56, 86, 126, 134, 142-144, 152, 155, 157-159, 174, 181, 207, 212, 234, 245, 249, 257, 259, 266, 278, 279, 282, 284, 289, 290, 297, 298, 302, 304-308, 311, 313, 316-318, 321-323, 325, 339-343, 345, 355-357, 359
of Gnosticism, 55, 63, 290, 292, 298
of Jesus, 3, 5-9, 17, 19-22, 27, 28, 30-33, 35, 37, 39, 41, 43-47, 50, 51, 53, 54, 62, 64, 66, 76, 78, 81-89, 91, 93, 94, 96-98, 110-112, 116, 117, 119, 120, 123-127, 129-132, 134, 138, 139, 141, 142, 146, 147, 149-151, 153, 155, 157-159, 161, 163, 164, 172, 174, 177, 179, 180, 182, 190-192, 194, 197, 199-202, 207, 209, 210, 213, 214, 218, 220-222, 224-226, 230-234, 236-238, 240-244, 246, 248-250, 254, 260, 261, 263-265, 267, 269, 271, 272, 274, 277, 279, 283-289, 291, 296-298, 301, 303, 304, 306-

312, 314, 315, 317-320, 322, 323, 325, 335, 338-344, 346-351, 355, 359

IAA, 24, 25, 27, 37, 41, 48, 51, 64, 70, 103, 120, 122, 124, 125, 139, 280, 286, 287, 299
IDAM, 24, 250
idealism, 254, 257, 267
inductivism, 254, 267, 352
Irenaeus, 55, 90, 132, 134, 178, 179, 262, 290, 291, 313, 357, 358
Israel Antiquities Authority, 24, 125, 280, 284, 285, 289, 306, 307, 309, 314, 330, 359
Israel Department of Antiquities and Museums, 24

James, 2, 6, 12, 16, 19-21, 27-29, 31, 50, 51, 59, 60, 72, 76, 82, 87, 90, 95, 97, 111, 114, 119-130, 132, 137, 142, 151, 208, 210, 218, 225, 232, 237-239, 246, 259, 263, 269, 271, 279, 281, 283, 289-291, 295-297, 299, 302, 304, 307, 308, 310-312, 316, 320, 321, 324, 330, 342, 349, 350, 354, 355, 359
James ossuary, 31, 97, 119, 120, 122-130, 283, 311, 312
James, son of Joseph, brother of Jesus, 19, 97, 119, 120, 123, 125-127, 130, 289, 311
James, the son of Zebedee, 237, 350
James, the less, 237, 350
Jesus, 1-9, 11, 12, 16-54, 56-70, 72, 74, 76-94, 96-98, 100-106, 108, 110-112, 114-134, 136-144, 146-164, 166, 168, 170, 172, 174-184, 186, 188-226, 228-274, 276-326, 328, 330-332, 334-360
Jesus Family Tomb, 1-3, 5-9, 16-20, 22, 24, 26-28, 30-34, 36, 38, 40, 42, 44, 46, 48, 50, 52, 54, 56, 58, 60, 62, 64, 66, 68, 70, 72, 74, 76, 78, 80, 82, 84, 86,

88, 90, 92-94, 96, 98, 100, 102, 104, 106, 108, 110, 112, 114, 116-118, 120-122, 124-126, 128, 130, 132, 134, 136-138, 140, 142-144, 146, 148, 150, 152, 154, 156, 158, 160, 162, 164, 166, 168, 170, 172, 174, 176, 178, 180, 182, 184, 186, 188, 190, 192, 194, 196, 198, 200, 202, 204, 206, 208, 210, 212, 214, 216, 218, 220, 222, 224, 226, 228, 230, 232, 234, 236, 238, 240, 242, 244-246, 248-250, 252, 254, 256, 258, 260, 262, 264-270, 272, 274, 276-282, 284-290, 292-296, 298-316, 318, 320, 322, 324, 326, 328, 330, 332, 334, 336, 338, 340, 342-344, 346, 348, 350, 352, 354, 356, 358-360
Jesus Seminar, 259-261, 265, 319, 355, 356
Jesus, son of Joseph, 19, 30, 31, 39-44, 48, 51, 64, 94, 98, 102, 105, 110, 112, 116, 119, 127, 131, 139, 250, 272, 274, 285, 308
Jewish names, 70, 112, 113, 117, 287, 288, 299, 301, 308, 310
Jose, 30, 39, 47-49, 51, 97, 105, 110, 117, 250, 308
Joseph, 19, 25, 27, 30, 31, 35, 39-44, 48, 49, 51, 64, 76, 94, 97, 98, 102, 103, 105, 110-112, 114-116, 119, 120, 123-127, 130, 131, 137-139, 200, 209, 213, 246, 250, 271, 272, 274, 280, 285, 286, 289, 308, 310, 311, 313-315
Joseph son of Caiaphas, 43
Joseph, the father of Jesus, 110

Judah
30, 45, 46, 64, 72, 81, 84, 85, 105, 110, 139, 168, 250, 287, 335
Son of Jesus, 17, 30, 31, 39, 45, 46, 51, 81-87, 89, 91, 94, 98, 110
son of Jesus, 17, 30, 31, 39, 45, 46, 51, 81-87, 89, 91, 94, 98, 110
Judas, 9, 17, 30, 31, 39, 46, 47, 51, 81, 83-89, 91, 94, 98, 114, 115, 118, 166, 238, 259, 261, 262, 291, 310, 328, 357
brother, 19, 48, 49, 51, 67, 68, 76, 81-86, 97, 117, 119, 120, 123-127, 130, 132, 137, 164, 165, 237-239, 250, 263, 287, 289, 304, 311, 312, 350
Iscariot, 47, 238, 261
Maccabeus, 47, 166
the brother of Jesus, 81, 84, 287, 312
the son of Jesus, 46, 87, 91
the Son, 43, 46, 87, 89, 91, 133, 167, 237, 242, 265, 285, 294, 342, 343, 350
the traitor, 357

kiss, 56-59, 77, 293
kissed, 57-59, 293, 294
kokhim, 26, 283
kokh, 26, 280

Latin, 49, 76, 93, 97, 99, 113, 141, 156, 262, 282
Latinize, 94, 97
Lazarus, 61, 78, 79, 182, 189, 299
Liberal, 47, 59, 83, 129, 148, 206, 260, 357
loculi, 280
logical errors, 128

Maccabean brothers, 138
Maccabees, 15, 164, 166, 328
Mara, 30, 31, 39, 44, 45, 51, 53, 54, 70-74, 76, 96, 102-104, 106, 111, 207, 208, 214, 273, 285, 299, 300, 310
Maria, 30, 39, 48-51, 53, 61, 65, 72, 74-76, 79, 94, 97, 110, 115, 118, 274, 288, 296-298, 301, 308, 309

Subject Index

Mariam, 45, 65, 70-73, 76, 79, 273, 295, 296, 300, 301
Mariame, 45, 51, 72-76, 94, 102, 104-107, 310
Mariammes, 61
Mariamne, 19, 30, 31, 53, 54, 59-62, 64-67, 70-73, 76, 79, 96, 110, 117, 250, 273, 289, 295, 296, 298, 301, 308
Mariamene, 30, 39, 44, 45, 53, 54, 60, 71, 72, 76, 285, 289
Mariamenou, 70-72, 74, 76, 111
married, 9, 19, 44, 46, 47, 56, 57, 59, 62, 64, 76, 81-83, 87, 102, 103, 105, 106, 250, 273, 288, 297, 301-303
marriage, 47, 57-59, 62, 64, 82, 86, 87, 101, 105, 274, 294, 295
marry, 50, 303
Martha, 45, 61, 67, 71-76, 78, 79, 94, 96, 97, 105, 115, 139, 189, 273, 294, 297, 299, 300, 310

Mary
9, 17, 19, 30, 39, 45-51, 53-73, 75-79, 81, 85-88, 91, 95-97, 101-104, 111, 114, 115, 117, 137, 139, 218-220, 250, 264, 273, 278, 288-290, 293-302, 304, 310, 319, 331, 359
of Bethany, 61, 66, 67, 78, 294, 297, 304
of Magdala, 57, 65, 66, 70, 139
of Nazareth, 19, 20, 30-33, 37, 39, 41, 43, 44, 46, 48, 54, 59, 79, 81, 85, 94, 96, 97, 101, 102, 104, 110-112, 114, 115, 117, 119, 138, 139, 142, 149, 172, 179, 181, 191, 192, 195, 197, 214, 221, 224, 233, 234, 249, 250, 272, 274, 281, 284-286, 309, 310, 317, 322, 338, 346, 347, 357
of the first century, 47, 50, 54, 174, 250, 300, 309
Marya, 48, 49, 285
Mary Magdalene, 9, 17, 19, 30, 45, 46, 48, 49, 53-57, 59-71, 73, 75-79, 81, 86-88, 95, 101-103, 111, 117, 218, 219, 250, 273, 278, 289, 290, 294-302, 304, 359
Mary, mother of Jesus, 88, 288
Mary, the mother of Jesus, 66, 304
Master, 8, 29, 45, 70, 71, 95, 96, 175, 312
materialism, 254, 255, 257, 267, 352
Matia, 30, 39, 50, 110
Matthew, 16, 39, 50, 51, 55, 82, 89, 90, 94, 97, 110, 115-118, 133, 153, 188, 189, 213, 218, 225, 237, 238, 253, 264, 273, 302, 310, 315, 335, 336, 343, 345, 350, 353, 358
Matya, 30, 50, 105, 110, 285
Miriam, 45, 48, 49, 72, 76, 299
mouth, 56-59, 167, 293, 294

Nag Hammadi, 55, 291, 293, 298, 303, 330

names
17, 19, 28, 30, 31, 39, 40, 45, 46, 48, 50, 51, 61, 70-76, 86, 89, 93-95, 99, 105, 109-118, 121, 132, 139, 142, 152, 178, 215, 245, 246, 249, 250, 254, 272-274, 277, 280, 284, 287, 288, 299-301, 305, 307-310, 334
in first century, 50
in Jerusalem, 12, 19, 34-36, 39, 40, 42, 43, 45, 46, 48, 82, 96, 97, 110, 111, 116, 117, 123, 126, 132, 137-139, 141, 143, 144, 150, 209, 213, 235, 238, 249, 253, 265, 266, 271, 272, 274, 282, 287, 337
of the Talpiot, 4, 6, 25, 27, 37, 50, 70, 94, 97, 99, 109, 110, 112, 117, 121, 122, 124, 127-130, 135, 246, 277, 279, 289, 302, 306-311, 343
associated with Jesus, 30
associated with the family of

Jesus, 30
Nazarenes, 131-134, 145
nefesh, 135-137, 146, 314
New York Times best-seller*****
noninscribed, 51, 98, 111, 250
nonornamented, 35, 40, 51

one, 6, 8, 12, 17, 19-22, 24, 25, 28, 30-37, 39, 40, 42-48, 50, 51, 54, 56-64, 66, 67, 69-79, 83-86, 88-91, 93-99, 101-105, 107, 110-112, 116, 117, 119-122, 125-127, 129, 131, 133, 136, 138, 141, 143, 145, 147-150, 152-160, 162-170, 172-178, 182, 184, 186, 188, 189, 192-194, 196, 199-202, 204, 208-214, 218-222, 224, 227-229, 231-237, 239-245, 248, 250, 254-256, 258-265, 267, 269, 271, 273, 274, 279, 280, 282, 283, 285, 288, 290-298, 300, 308, 311, 314, 317-319, 321, 325-335, 337-339, 341-344, 347-349, 358, 359
Origen, 61, 62, 65, 90, 132, 133, 200, 264, 296, 297, 332
ornamented, 27, 35, 44, 46, 51, 122, 280, 285
ossilegium, 33-37, 172, 282, 283, 330
Ossilegium, 33-37, 172, 282, 283, 330
ossuary inscriptions, 5, 17, 39, 41, 43, 45, 47, 49-51, 94-96, 288

Pantera, 264, 265
Papias, 90, 139, 178, 179, 304, 305
Patina, 17, 119-121, 123, 125-130, 281
patina, 17, 119-121, 123, 125-130, 281
peer review, 129
Pharisee, 78, 240, 241, 329
Pompeii, 141, 142
Pontius Pilate, 266, 319
power
61, 69, 137, 143, 145, 166, 177, 188, 203, 229, 235, 237, 241, 242, 251, 325, 344, 348
of the Lord, 171, 179, 195, 207, 222
of the Spirit, 135, 229, 248, 258, 346
over death, 188, 334

physical
3, 5, 17, 19, 22, 30, 32-35, 37-39, 88, 98, 102, 147, 149, 151, 153, 155, 157-161, 163, 165, 167, 169, 171-173, 175-179, 181-183, 185-190, 194-197, 199, 201, 206, 207, 209, 213, 218, 220, 223, 225-227, 229, 235-237, 244, 249, 261, 265, 270, 271, 291, 328, 330, 337, 339-341, 344, 346, 348
resurrection, 3-9, 17, 19, 21-23, 30, 32-35, 37, 38, 77, 84, 116, 134, 138, 147-151, 153, 155, 157-161, 163-197, 199, 201, 203, 205, 207, 209-211, 213-215, 217-237, 239-244, 247, 250, 251, 253, 254, 265, 269-271, 277-279, 283, 290, 297, 298, 313, 317-319, 322-335, 337-352, 358
Personal Name, 45
Personal names, 113, 277, 287, 300, 305, 307, 308
probabilities, 119, 191, 250, 289
plain, 35, 47, 49-51, 84, 121, 122, 125, 126, 140, 153, 250, 283, 284
plain ossuaries, 35, 51, 122, 140, 250, 284
plain ossuary, 47, 49, 50, 283
population, 36, 40, 46, 48, 132, 287, 288
Questions of Mary, 62
Qumran, 134, 170-172, 187, 313, 327, 334, 340

rationalism, 254-256, 267, 352
Resurrection, 3-9, 17, 19, 21-23, 30, 32-35, 37, 38, 77, 84, 116,

Subject Index

134, 138, 147-151, 153, 155, 157-161, 163-197, 199, 201, 203, 205, 207, 209-211, 213-215, 217-237, 239-244, 247, 250, 251, 253, 254, 265, 269-271, 277-279, 283, 290, 297, 298, 313, 317-319, 322-335, 337-352, 358

resurrection
   3-9, 17, 19, 21-23, 30, 32-35, 37, 38, 77, 84, 116, 134, 138, 147-151, 153, 155, 157-161, 163-197, 199, 201, 203, 205, 207, 209-211, 213-215, 217-237, 239-244, 247, 250, 251, 253, 254, 265, 269-271, 277-279, 283, 290, 297, 298, 313, 317-319, 322-335, 337-352, 358
   appearance, 4, 36, 50, 74, 124, 125, 176, 219, 220, 222-225, 241, 317, 347, 349
   belief, 9, 32, 34, 35, 37, 54, 55, 63, 64, 145, 151, 161, 163, 164, 166, 170, 173, 174, 177, 180, 181, 184, 207, 247, 259, 263, 283, 290, 292, 293, 321, 323, 325, 327-330, 334, 337, 344
   body, 22, 27, 33-35, 37, 69, 77, 137, 138, 142, 147, 149, 160, 162, 164, 169, 171, 173, 175, 176, 178, 179, 182, 184-187, 190, 193-195, 199, 206, 209, 214, 218-224, 226-229, 235, 236, 244, 247, 253, 261, 270, 272, 277, 280, 282, 314, 318, 327, 328, 331, 332, 338, 341, 345, 348, 349, 352, 358
   claim, 22, 32, 33, 47, 48, 59, 62, 63, 69, 83, 84, 86, 88, 91, 93, 116, 120, 121, 125, 134, 137-139, 157, 164, 166, 170, 185, 199, 203, 214, 217, 221, 226, 231, 245, 246, 263, 265, 272, 280, 281, 286, 291, 308, 318, 323, 352, 358
   from the dead, 3, 7, 19, 23, 32, 138, 148, 149, 157, 163, 175-177, 179, 180, 182, 183, 188-190, 192, 194, 197, 215, 218, 219, 226, 229, 233-237, 241, 242, 244, 250, 263, 270, 271, 290, 326, 339, 342, 358
   of Christ, 4, 5, 133, 175, 178, 189, 190, 194, 209, 229, 235, 241, 271, 277, 297, 298, 315, 339, 340, 342, 344
   of God, 9, 21, 82, 133, 151, 152, 170, 172, 175, 190, 200, 207, 208, 228, 234, 242, 255, 278, 283, 291, 319, 322-335, 338, 339, 342, 345-347, 354
   of Israelite, 162, 168, 169, 185
   of Jesus, 3, 5-9, 17, 19-22, 27, 28, 30-33, 35, 37, 39, 41, 43-47, 50, 51, 53, 54, 62, 64, 66, 76, 78, 81-89, 91, 93, 94, 96-98, 110-112, 116, 117, 119, 120, 123-127, 129-132, 134, 138, 139, 141, 142, 146, 147, 149-151, 153, 155, 157-159, 161, 163, 164, 172, 174, 177, 179, 180, 182, 190-192, 194, 197, 199-202, 207, 209, 210, 213, 214, 218, 220-222, 224-226, 230-234, 236-238, 240-244, 246, 248-250, 254, 260, 261, 263-265, 267, 269, 271, 272, 274, 277, 279, 283-289, 291, 296-298, 301, 303, 304, 306-312, 314, 315, 317-320, 322, 323, 325, 335, 338-344, 346-351, 355, 359
   of the dead, 24, 34, 134, 137, 146, 162, 163, 168, 169, 171, 172, 177, 178, 180, 181, 185, 187, 319, 329, 333
   of the Messiah, 172, 192, 194, 195
   physical, 3, 5, 17, 19, 22, 30, 32-35, 37-39, 88, 98, 102, 147, 149, 151, 153, 155, 157-161, 163, 165, 167, 169, 171-173, 175-179, 181-183, 185-190, 194-197, 199, 201, 206, 207, 209, 213, 218, 220, 223, 225-227,

229, 235-237, 244, 249, 261, 265, 270, 271, 291, 328, 330, 337, 339-341, 344, 346, 348
physically, 1, 2, 6, 17, 19, 33, 98, 181-185, 189, 190, 192, 200, 215, 217-227, 229, 230, 263, 270, 271, 290, 358
power, 61, 69, 137, 143, 145, 166, 177, 188, 203, 229, 235, 237, 241, 242, 251, 325, 344, 348
spiritually, 3, 19, 33, 58, 67, 172, 176, 181, 183, 189, 199, 214, 217-219, 222, 270, 271, 344, 345, 358

resurrected
9, 173, 177, 183-185, 187-190, 195, 199, 200, 203, 207, 218, 222, 223, 225, 226, 229, 270, 326, 344, 345, 349
body, 22, 27, 33-35, 37, 69, 77, 137, 138, 142, 147, 149, 160, 162, 164, 169, 171, 173, 175, 176, 178, 179, 182, 184-187, 190, 193-195, 199, 206, 209, 214, 218-224, 226-229, 235, 236, 244, 247, 253, 261, 270, 272, 277, 280, 282, 314, 318, 327, 328, 331, 332, 338, 341, 345, 348, 349, 352, 358
physical, 3, 5, 17, 19, 22, 30, 32-35, 37-39, 88, 98, 102, 147, 149, 151, 153, 155, 157-161, 163, 165, 167, 169, 171-173, 175-179, 181-183, 185-190, 194-197, 199, 201, 206, 207, 209, 213, 218, 220, 223, 225-227, 229, 235-237, 244, 249, 261, 265, 270, 271, 291, 328, 330, 337, 339-341, 344, 346, 348
physically, 1, 2, 6, 17, 19, 33, 98, 181-185, 189, 190, 192, 200, 215, 217-227, 229, 230, 263, 270, 271, 290, 358
righteous, 167, 171, 188, 195, 197, 326, 328, 329, 333, 338

spiritually, 3, 19, 33, 58, 67, 172, 176, 181, 183, 189, 199, 214, 217-219, 222, 270, 271, 344, 345, 358
rich, 35, 78, 137, 271, 337
rock, 33, 166, 214, 218, 314
rock–cut tomb, 137-139

Roman
22, 81, 84, 86, 96, 150, 151, 201, 202, 204, 207, 209, 214, 220, 235, 236, 242, 264-266, 282, 284, 340, 358
Catholics, 22
culture, 33, 39, 76, 153, 276, 288, 290, 301, 302, 310, 315, 321, 323, 328, 346, 351, 354
crucifixion, 77, 78, 138, 140, 199-201, 203-205, 207-209, 223, 224, 235, 238, 241, 265, 266, 315, 340, 341, 358
execution, 138, 201, 203, 207-209, 214, 235, 274, 358
guards, 201, 205, 214, 220, 236, 337
seal, 33, 143, 145, 235, 236, 244
scourging, 201-204
soldiers, 166, 201-205, 211, 213, 220, 253
tombstone, 35, 137, 264, 265
romanticism, 254, 257, 267

Sadducees, 34, 163, 170, 326, 327, 329
Salome, 61, 115, 218, 310
salvage, 23
science, 33, 64, 87, 145, 146, 157, 191, 232, 234, 247, 249, 255, 322, 340, 349, 354
seal, 33, 143, 145, 235, 236, 244
sealing, 235
Second Clement, 151, 175
sex, 60, 212, 264, 354
sexual, 57-59, 67-69, 293, 295
silence, 86, 161, 235, 244, 262, 274, 302, 322, 327
Simon, 72, 75, 114, 115, 138, 139, 220, 285, 289, 297, 304, 307,

Subject Index

310, 311, 342, 355, 359
skepticism, 254, 256, 257, 267, 279, 289, 308, 312, 316
soul, 135, 137, 146, 160, 162-164, 171, 176, 178, 179, 183, 184, 187, 190, 192-196, 212, 243, 314, 328, 330, 331, 358
Spirit, 5, 54, 69, 135, 165, 166, 170, 171, 175-177, 184, 185, 220-223, 225, 226, 228, 229, 237, 248, 257, 258, 261, 290, 319, 346, 349, 351, 356, 358
spirit, 5, 54, 69, 135, 165, 166, 170, 171, 175-177, 184, 185, 220-223, 225, 226, 228, 229, 237, 248, 257, 258, 261, 290, 319, 346, 349, 351, 356, 358
spiritual resurrection, 22, 35, 37, 173, 218, 220, 251, 345
spiritually resurrected, 222, 344, 345
spouse, 54, 56-59, 63, 77
statistical, 17, 109-113, 115-118, 250, 269, 274, 288, 307-310
analysis, 17, 20, 39, 75, 95, 101-103, 105, 107, 111, 112, 116-118, 161, 192, 200, 250, 263, 273, 274, 281, 288, 289, 317, 318, 322, 336, 340, 352, 354, 356
fallacies, 275, 309
stone, 33, 36, 128, 135, 189, 211, 218, 235, 236, 244, 327

Talpiot
3, 4, 6, 8, 23, 25, 27, 28, 30-33, 35, 37, 41, 44, 49-51, 70, 71, 75, 79, 84, 87, 93, 94, 96-99, 103, 104, 109-112, 115, 117, 119-122, 124-131, 134-140, 144-146, 246, 254, 269, 272, 274, 277, 279, 280, 285, 286, 288, 289, 298, 301-303, 306-312, 315, 343, 346, 347, 352
cave, 23, 30, 55, 99, 121, 131, 289, 356
Discovery, 6, 7, 12, 19, 20, 22, 23, 27, 28, 30, 31, 37, 38, 42, 103, 115, 120-123, 125, 127, 141, 143, 144, 147, 172, 210, 245, 247, 248, 254, 261, 279, 280, 284, 285, 288, 289, 301-303, 305-309, 311-313, 316, 342, 343, 356, 359
friend, 9, 14, 87, 90, 200, 240, 285, 295
in 1980, 19, 51, 103, 120, 125, 144, 217, 246, 249, 254, 285, 295
inscribed, 9, 27, 30, 41, 42, 45, 48, 71, 73-75, 84, 94, 104, 106, 111-114, 119, 122-124, 127, 272, 279, 280, 285-289, 299, 301, 306, 307, 310, 312, 314
inscriptions, 5, 17, 30, 35, 39-41, 43-47, 49-51, 64, 72, 74, 93-97, 111, 112, 116, 117, 121, 135, 139, 140, 146, 272, 281-283, 285-288, 298-301, 305-307, 309, 310, 315, 325, 332
inscription, 30, 31, 39-51, 54, 59, 60, 64-66, 70-76, 79, 81, 86, 93-97, 104, 110, 112, 115, 116, 119, 121, 123-125, 250, 264, 272, 273, 283, 285, 286, 288, 289, 299, 300, 309, 312, 314, 316
Ossuary, 5, 17, 19, 22, 26, 28, 30, 31, 33-36, 39-47, 49-51, 53-55, 57, 59, 61, 63, 65, 67, 69-71, 73-77, 79, 81, 84, 86, 94-98, 103, 104, 110, 112, 115, 119-131, 140, 142, 143, 145-147, 149, 172, 199, 217, 224, 250, 273, 280, 282-289, 299-301, 306, 307, 311, 312, 315, 316, 330
ossuary, 5, 17, 19, 22, 26, 28, 30, 31, 33-36, 39-47, 49-51, 53-55, 57, 59, 61, 63, 65, 67, 69-71, 73-77, 79, 81, 84, 86, 94-98, 103, 104, 110, 112, 115, 119-131, 140, 142, 143, 145-147, 149, 172, 199, 217, 224, 250, 273, 280, 282-289, 299-301, 306, 307, 311, 312, 315, 316, 330

ossuaries, 9, 19, 24, 26, 27, 30, 33-36, 39, 40, 42, 47-51, 54, 71-75, 93-95, 98, 99, 101-106, 111-117, 119, 121, 122, 125-132, 136-143, 146, 172, 249, 250, 272, 273, 277, 279, 280, 282-289, 299-301, 305-310, 312, 314-316, 330, 359
tomb burial, 137-139
tomb discovery, 6, 19, 23, 37, 38, 115, 144, 248, 280
tomb DNA, 104
tomb, 1-9, 12, 16-20, 22-28, 30-42, 44-48, 50-52, 54, 56, 58, 60, 62, 64-66, 68, 70-72, 74-80, 82, 84-86, 88, 90, 92-112, 114-122, 124-132, 134-140, 142-146, 148-150, 152, 154, 156, 158, 160, 162, 164, 166, 168, 170, 172, 174, 176, 178, 180, 182-184, 186, 188, 190, 192-196, 198, 200, 202, 204, 206, 208-220, 222, 224, 226, 228, 230-232, 234-236, 238, 240, 242, 244-246, 248-250, 252, 254, 256, 258, 260-262, 264-272, 274, 276-290, 292-316, 318, 320, 322, 324, 326, 328, 330, 332, 334, 336-338, 340-352, 354, 356, 358-360
Talpiyot, 12, 139, 279, 280, 285-289, 299, 301, 306, 307, 312, 314
Tao, 140

Templars, 31, 131-132, 142
Templar Knights, 143, 144
tenth ossuary, 17, 19, 31, 51, 119-125, 127, 129, 130, 250, 280, 289
Tertullian, 55, 90, 142, 316, 321
tombstone, 35, 137, 264, 265
Twin Judas, 83

undercover, 17, 81, 83, 85, 87, 89, 91

wife, 11, 19, 44-46, 57, 59, 76, 79, 81, 104, 105, 162, 250, 294, 303
Wisdom, 56, 58, 59, 79, 141, 162, 163, 167, 185, 192, 294, 328, 329, 345

X wife of Y, 46

year, 4-6, 17, 27, 34, 124, 238, 261, 266, 269, 280, 282, 318
Yeshua, 40-43, 45, 46, 48, 86, 102, 104-107, 112, 272, 285, 286
    son of Yehosef, 40, 42, 102, 104-106, 285
    bar Yehosef, 41, 112
Yose, 47, 49, 285
Yosef, 23, 25, 43, 121, 311

Zebedee, 89, 91, 237, 350